HITLER'S
WAR

HITLER'S WAR

Germany's Key Strategic Decisions
- 1940–1945 -

HEINZ MAGENHEIMER

BARNES
&NOBLE
BOOKS
NEW YORK

CONTENTS

CONTENTS

III

The Turn of the War 1942–1943:
The Final Loss of the Strategic Initiative
by the Axis Powers, 125

IV

The Failure of the Offensively Conducted
Defence of 'Fortress Europe' in 1943, 177

V

The Law of Gravity 1944, 221

VI

Final Considerations, 275

PREFACE

The present substantially revised and extended edition of my book *Turns of the War in Europe 1939–1945* is based on new source material and detailed research on the history of the German–Soviet war in 1941, as well as on the heated controversy being conducted in Russia about Stalin's co-responsibility for unleashing the war and the Soviet preparations for an attack in 1940–1. The debate in Russia in particular, augmented by noteworthy contributions from Germany, France and the United States, demonstrates that historical theses must continually be re-examined, re-evaluated and corrected in favour of the current state of knowledge resulting from new sources and documents, even if the newly gained insights contradict conventional majority opinion to a substantial degree. It is highly illogical to appeal to 'the science of history' as the ultimate authority, simply in order to stifle criticism of outdated theses; moreover, it would be unprofessional to uphold a declining majority opinion as conclusive, simply in order to brand a minority opinion as questionable.

In the final analysis, historical research must serve the discovery of the truth. Insight into the processes of disseminating and manipulating information should always be governed by doubts concerning allegedly 'conclusive' knowledge. It was with good reason that Max Weber called doubt the 'father of all insight'.

H.M.
Vienna, Easter 1997

INTRODUCTION

Ducunt fata volentem, nolentem trahunt

Was Germany doomed from the very beginning to lose the European war of 1939? Was there no realistic opportunity for her to decide the issue in her favour during the early stages? Are we really justified, from the vantage point of the present, in accusing the German higher military command of having contributed to the outbreak of, or even of having unleashed, a war it could not, under any circumstances, expect to win? Did the escalation of the European war into a world war at the end of 1941 already signify the final portent for the Axis powers; or was there still a chance, even then, for a strategic turn-about, or at least a strategic 'draw'?

Would it be correct to describe the German defeat before Moscow in December 1941 and the simultaneous entry into the war by the United States as the *ultimate turn*? This at least was the opinion of Colonel General Jodl, who dictated on 15 May 1945, shortly after the end of the war: 'All of us, and in particular every soldier, went into this war against Russia with a feeling of depression when considering its outcome. When the catastrophe in the winter of 1941–2 broke over us, it became particularly clear to me, that from this culmination point at the beginning of the year 1942 on, victory was no longer possible.'[1]

These, and similar questions, still confront the observer more than 50 years after the end of the most violent and bloody struggle in the history of war, and still await an answer. Since the political and military course of the war has been so abundantly researched and discussed that even the experts find it difficult to keep abreast, it might seem somewhat audacious to add yet another book to this wealth of literature. Yet, in the author's opinion, there is one aspect that has not as yet been given due attention: the attempt to determine which decisions, within the framework of the current political-strategic situation, contributed primarily to a turn in the course of the war, and to consider the consequences of such decisions.

There is also a need to examine the criteria which at the time appeared of paramount importance in assessing such turns in the war.

The author therefore intends to offer not just a new interpretation of the decisive battles of World War Two, but rather a new evaluation of strategies, their success or failure. Strategy is defined as conceptual planning tied to options and directed towards success, normally embracing the fields of politics, military activities, economics and technology. Strategic planning, in essence, offers various possibilities of action based on the concrete evaluation of a given situation, combines calculation with prognosis, and, finally, covers the execution of the plan with a view to achieving the objective. In this context, the author has endeavoured to present the reader with a summary of new information and research material that has come to light since 1990, primarily from Soviet/Russian sources.[2]

It would be unhistorical, even mistaken, to approach German military-strategic decision-making during World War Two from the viewpoint of present-day moral-ethical values. To maintain, therefore, that the German political leadership and, to a lesser extent, the military command was already stained with an indelible legal and moral guilt by reason of the very unleashing of the war, would be to preclude from the start any valid consideration of the decisions to be discussed, as well as their alternatives. These decisions were simply intended to achieve the objective of victory, or at least to avoid defeat, quite regardless of the question of the war's legitimacy. Had the key individuals of the time been confronted with the modern moral-ethical evaluation of World War Two as the guiding principle for their actions, then every one of them would have been bound to choose surrender at the first opportunity. In this light it would not have been legitimate for the generals in command to plan and execute any operation that promised victory; rather they would have been duty bound to bring about the defeat of the Wehrmacht as quickly as possible. But no army, of course, goes to war with the intention of losing. In this context it is worth recalling a statement made at the symposium to commemorate the year 1938: 'The historian should be neither a judge nor an upholder of moral standards.'[3]

The use of the term 'turning-point' has been deliberately avoided, because decisive events, particularly in the military sphere, cannot be reduced to a single point in time. As will be demonstrated, the decisive 'turn-about' of an operation or a military-strategic event is only the perceptible consequence of acts of will, which themselves have a history and therefore cover a certain span of time. Our concern, therefore, is to search for the more or less hidden 'roots', to seek the reason as to why, in a specific situation, this and not that decision was taken, why this option was chosen and another option rejected. Such an approach must necessarily focus on the possible alternatives, and an evaluation and comparison of these alternatives with the actual events.

The historian or political scientist should obviously be very wary in posing the question 'What would have happened if...?' In retrospect, however, as in a game of chess, the only way one can correctly evaluate, with hindsight, the expediency and likely consequences, the advantages and disadvantages, of a particular decision is to take into account those alternatives that were available to the decision maker at the time, including those that were rejected or ignored. One cannot avoid, therefore, keeping an eye fixed on the *historia eventualis*.[4] Even though this may run the risk of straying into the realm of speculation, it recognizes that many decisions are not merely based on information, knowledge, rational calculation or personal experience, but simply on intuition and speculative conjecture: '*Gouverner, c'est prévoir!*'

In the case of fateful decisions such as occurred in the course of World War Two, there is ample reason to consider what might have happened if a particular decision had been taken differently. The issue, therefore, as Max Weber stated in a fundamental study, is the discovery of 'the causal importance that can actually be attributed to this singular decision within the totality of the infinitely numerous "moments"... and therefore, what position it can assume in the historical portrayal. If history desires to be more than just a chronicle of strange events and personalities, then it has no other means than to raise such questions.'[5] With this approach, the observer assumes a position that begins by regarding history as a 'development'. After a discussion of the process by which the decision was reached, he then ascertains, based on what actually transpired, whether, and to what degree, the concrete decision taken was justified by the existing circumstances; and the success or failure of the historic action may at least serve him as a point of reference.

The measuring yardstick of success, however, is at best only an imperfect instrument, a means of proving, in a sense, that the historic decision was 'correct'. In the military sphere in particular, there are examples which, although crowned by success, reveal specifically inauspicious or problematical decisions which considerably reduced the extent of that success. And whereas, on the one hand, in the case of a failed operation, one can identify the causal connection with a decision that proved to be disadvantageous, there is no concrete proof, on the other hand, that an 'alternative operation' based on a potentially more advantageous, in other words 'better', decision would have been successful. The most sensible procedure, therefore, is to apply the theory of 'objective possibility', according to which the observer, when analysing an historic sequence of events, disregards certain causal components and mentally alters them, thereby automatically raising the question as to whether, under these different circumstances, 'the same or some other success could have been expected'.[6]

This fundamental method has been applied throughout the present study, which is restricted to the discussion of the military 'turn-about' phases of the war in Europe and the Mediterranean theatre arising from the decisions of the German leadership, i.e. Führer Headquarters, the Foreign Ministry, the Supreme Commands of the three branches of the Wehrmacht and, in specific instances, the armament directors. Also included, in certain cases, are the viewpoints of senior individuals in the different theatres of war, such as commanders of army groups or Luftflotten (air fleets)*. The study is not intended to be a military history of World War Two and certainly not a comprehensive overview. The reader looking for such an appraisal is referred to the summary by Andreas Hillgruber [7] which is still highly useful in many respects.

The present author is not concerned to determine how certain operations might have led to victory for the Wehrmacht, nor whether a strategic formula for the Endsieg (final victory) ever existed. It is surely far more intriguing and meaningful to analyse the motives and objectives behind the individual leadership decisions and to evaluate, in the sense of 'objective possibility', the alternatives that were available. Consequently, the attempt at accurate historical reconstruction is designed not so much to identify the faultiness of a given decision, as 'to explain with understanding'[8] the point of view taken by the decision maker in a specific situation.

---

* These consisted of bombers, fighters and reconnaissance aircraft under a single command and acting as a unit. A given Luftflotte could contain as many as 1000–2000 aircraft.

The central issue, in other words, is not justification or the attribution of guilt, but rather the search for the truth, insofar as this truth can be brought to light by the methods of the science of history. As we know, this key word 'truth' is indigenous both to the realm of fact as well as to the realm of values.[9] The historian is required to take both spheres into account, yet is obliged to keep them neatly separated. In this sense, two great historians are in complete agreement with the statement that history is a report on 'what one age found worthy of recording about another age'.[10]

In the interpretation of World War Two, this has led to some rather strange evaluations of the turns of the war, according to the specific 'politics of history' of the nations concerned. Over-estimation of the importance of a single decisive battle, no matter how momentous the consequences, in the context of the outcome of the war, must inevitably lead to a mental dead end. The notion that the entire conduct of the war on land, at sea and in the air was directed more or less towards a single military operation which finally culminated in a battle, the result of which reversed the previous course of the war and sealed Germany's defeat, must be strongly contradicted. One author even attributes 'a turning point in European history' to a single campaign,[11] which, though well reasoned, is, to say the least, highly questionable.

Consideration has to be given, too, to the historical-political dimensions of certain turns in the war, in the light of open or hidden demands subsequently made by a victorious power based on its alleged contribution to events. Thus representatives of the Soviet Union, and later Russia, have continually emphasized that in their opinion the three most important turns of the war – before Moscow in 1941–2, at Stalingrad in 1942–3, and in the Kursk area in July 1943 – were brought about solely by the Red Army. Did not the Red Army, after all, bear the major burden of the war, sustaining terrible losses up to June 1944?[12] Indeed, controversy over the wisdom of such conduct of a war, which accepted such catastrophic losses and sacrifices in order to bring about these turns, still affect political life in Russia to this day. Where now are the fruits of victory more than 50 years after the events?

In this context, a prominent Russian writer has recently accused the former wartime allies, Britain and the United States, of not having given sufficient support to the Soviet Union in the battle against Germany, thus being equally responsible for its terrible losses, and of having worked treacherously to bring about the subsequent Cold War even before the end of hostilities in 1945.[13] Subliminally, his book also echoes the deep bitterness felt by many about the collapse of the USSR in 1991. This is perhaps a strange variation of the now-current theory of a nation 'bled dry'.

The present author differentiates between real turns of the war which actually occurred – in other words, episodes which set the course of the war in a new direction – and those which may best be described as 'virtual' turning points, i.e. such combinations of events or military situations which offered the participants an obvious, concrete opportunity to reverse developments and redistribute the military 'balance'. That certain of these opportunities were not exploited by one side or the other says nothing about their historic importance. These 'virtual', i.e. available or potential, turns of the war, while not having the same historical effect as the genuine turns, must nonetheless be placed on the same level if only because they offered the protagonists concerned an irretrievable and unique opportunity.

A useful example of this point of view may be seen in the Allied invasion of Normandy on 6 June 1944. The factors that determined the final loss of this decisive battle by the German western army are of less interest here than the following considerations: 1. Did the German Supreme Command recognize the fundamental option that occurred and was invited as a result of the invasion by the Western allies? 2. Did Germany take the necessary measures in time, in order to exploit this option to the full, so as to turn the war in her favour?

The invasion of Normandy in 1944 offers a particularly good demonstration of the difference that exists between the appreciation of the situation by the protagonists of the time, including the consequences they drew or omitted to draw on that basis, and the state of contemporary knowledge. Only if one manages to determine whether German command decisions and measures were taken 'in accordance with the situation', in other words, in line or not with the knowledge available at the time, is one entitled to make well-founded statements about the relative importance of these 'virtual turns'. A leadership measure not based on contemporary knowledge, but arising, say, as a result of being deceived by the enemy, belongs to the category of intellectual mistakes, but does not fundamentally reduce the option of the turn inherent in the concrete situation.

In this sense, the author rejects those opinions which claim the German war effort to have been hopeless from the very beginning, and which even describe the concept of a Blitzkrieg as an 'anachronism'. Can the claim be upheld that the Wehrmacht operationally 'killed itself by victories'?[14] It would be far too simple, even downright naïve, to attribute Germany's defeat in World War Two *a priori* to the preponderance of all of the eventual opposing powers, their superiority in manpower and *matériel*, or their superior weapons technology. That would signal an acceptance of historical determinism and the denial of any attempt to have events 'explained with understanding'.

FROM THE BATTLE OF BRITAIN
TO THE BEGINNING OF
THE CONFRONTATION WITH
THE SOVIET UNION:
JULY TO DECEMBER 1940

The Political-Strategic Situation in the Summer of 1940: Considerations, Options, Alternatives

The surrender of the French armed forces on 22 June 1940 was for the Wehrmacht the culminating point of its successes to date. Hitler regarded himself as undisputed master of continental Europe from the Atlantic to the River Bug. The Wehrmacht now possessed bases from the North Cape of Norway southward to the French Atlantic coast, and had achieved victory over western Europe with surprisingly small losses. The realization of having won a Blitzkrieg against France – the enemy who had been assessed to be militarily the strongest – and of having driven the might of the British Army off the continent with heavy losses, opened unimagined perspectives of further victory. Public opinion (not only within the German Reich) assumed that this triumph of arms would be followed by a peace agreement with Great Britain. With this expectation in mind, the neutral nations of Europe were reassessing their previous policies. Most of them were inclined to seek close ties with the Berlin. The power of the German Reich had indeed reached its apogee.[15]

The extent of German predominance in western, central, northern and southern Europe in July 1940, fuelling the expectation of Great Britain shortly extending peace feelers and at least of an Anglo-German peace compromise, tallied completely with official German political logic and reasoning. Leading figures such as State Secretary Ernst von Weizsäcker, General Jodl and Colonel General Keitel, were thus firmly convinced, in terms of such political realism, that the war had been won and only needed to be brought to an end.[16] It is therefore quite understandable, judged by the situation as it was then and as it appears today, that Germany momentarily held back and left the initiation of peace feelers to the British government. Why should the government of the Reich rush ahead? A public announcement by Hitler of a detailed peace plan would surely have flown in the face of all diplomatic tradition. Would such a blunt approach not have offended a London that was prepared to negotiate and throttled any existing readiness to compromise? Would not the official rejection of such a peace offer by Britain have condemned any further German initiative to failure?

An extensive and detailed study[17] reveals, that in the weeks preceding and following the signature of the Franco-German

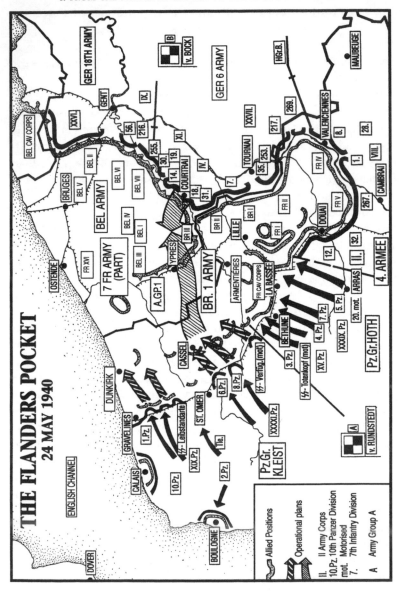

THE FLANDERS POCKET
24 MAY 1940

Allied Positions

Operational plans

II.   II Army Corps
10.Pz. 10th Panzer Division
mot.   Motorised
7.   7th Infantry Division

A   Army Group A

armistice, several peace feelers were put out between Berlin and London, via Carl Jakob Burckhardt, for example, which nevertheless did not lead to any tangible results. These noteworthy attempts mainly reflected the desire of the German authorities to ascertain the conditions under which Great Britain would be prepared to accept the victory of German arms on the continent and her consequent hegemony. But since the very few steps undertaken on the British side to bring these feelers to the level of concrete negotiations were immediately blocked by the Churchill government, Germany was forced to recognize that official Britain was not prepared to entertain thoughts of peace. Moreover, if it was clear that even in her darkest hour, when she was at her weakest, in June–July 1940, Britain was not prepared to negotiate a peace or reach some form of compromise with Germany, how could Hitler and Ribbentrop assume that London would show a greater inclination towards peace at any subsequent time?

The claim by one author that Hitler did not make a 'clear offer' to London in time, that he regarded negotiations with the enemy as out of the question, and that the failure of his peace-making concept subsequently became apparent,[18] does not accord with the situation as it existed in the summer of 1940. Churchill's unshakable will to continue the fight – on 4 July he had the French fleet sunk off Mers el-Kebir without the slightest regard for his former ally France – underlines the fact that the British government rejected any sort of peace compromise. Is it therefore justifiable to state that Germany 'erected insurmountable obstacles to a settlement'[19], when at that very time in the summer of 1940 it became apparent to the world, that Churchill's Britain rejected any form of compromise? Hence the understandable perception in Germany that Britain could only be compelled to agree to peace by force of arms, that only military means could spell success. To summarize: shortly after the rejection of Hitler's 'appeal to reason' on 19 July 1940, the German command had no other recourse than to let the guns speak.

The frequently voiced objection that after the failure of this 'appeal', the German government should have accepted the British demands, despatched on 11 September in the course of secret negotiations in Stockholm, which challenged the legality and morality of Germany's conduct of the war, is historically unrealistic. It implied that state policy and strategy should be judged absolutely by moral standards. Any political and military leadership, which at the summit of its success in the field, agreed to bow to the demands of the side that had lost – let alone permit that enemy to impose its yardstick for the legitimacy of the war – would not only have lost face, but also the very basis for its further actions. Such a step by a victorious power would have been tantamount to surrender. It would have been understood neither in most of the world's capitals, nor by its allies, and certainly not at home. In such a situation, the German political and military leadership was surely entitled to seek ways and means to compel an opponent, equally prepared to go to the final extreme, to give in.[20]

Nor can the claim be upheld that after the rejection of his 'appeal to reason', Hitler's concept had failed and that his strategy had proved to be a 'grandiose miscalculation at the decisive moment'.[21] The allegation that within the framework of its attack in the West on 10 May 1940, the leadership of the Wehrmacht – with the exception of the Kriegsmarine (German navy) – had no concrete objectives against England and had made no preparations to bring about her downfall, merely demonstrates that Britain was not regarded as the main enemy and that, initially, the prime objective had been victory on land in western Europe. Even in hindsight, German policy in the summer of 1940 cannot be said to have been a failure. Nor was the political initiative renounced. Indeed, it was the British politicians who were now called upon to propose reasonable, realistic conditions for a peace treaty.

A further criticism claims that the German Supreme Command had no 'war plan for the course of the war as a whole', in which context Great Britain would have had to be regarded as the main enemy.[22] Of the three branches of the Wehrmacht, only the Kriegsmarine had considered Britain as the main opponent from the very beginning, but because of its own material weakness, had seen no possibility of an early, decisive success. As for the Luftwaffe (German air force), a study presented by General Hellmuth Felmy on 22 September 1938 had already shown that the air force would not be capable of waging a decisive 'strategic' air war against Britain. The results of a planning exercise conducted by *Luftflotte 2* in May 1939 confirmed this estimation. An air war at sea also offered only limited prospects of success. The professional opinion that the Luftwaffe was primarily organized and prepared for cooperation with the Army

(German army) appears, therefore, to be correct.[23] During the campaigns in Poland, the Netherlands, Belgium and France, support of the ground forces had consequently been the air force's primary activity.

In the spring of 1940 the concentration of all human and material resources upon the defeat of the Allied forces on the western front appeared to be the order of the day. Any further considerations, and more far-reaching plans in case of a victory, depended on the manner in which such a victory was achieved. Firm guidelines in this respect were not predictable before 10 May 1940, because it was impossible to foresee that the campaign in the west would end in an overwhelming victory after only six weeks. It is therefore an exaggeration to accuse the German command of a 'lack of direction' for having not only omitted to destroy the BEF in the pocket at Dunkirk, but also neglected to prepare the invasion of the British Isles and plan for it immediately after the first phase of the campaign in France.[24]

Apart from the fact that an invasion of the British homeland represented a considerable risk in any case, such an operation at that time would have overtaxed the strength of the Wehrmacht, given its deployment against France, the forces required and the insufficient naval preparations. However, the fact the BEF and substantial French forces were allowed to escape became a weighty factor in the assessment of British defensive strength during the subsequent planning of the invasion of Britain. Today the so-called 'miracle of Dunkirk', as British historians like to term it, is more or less explained, even if the complexity of the problem does not permit a simple answer. It is clear in any case that the ominous 'order to halt' of 24 May did not so much originate with Hitler, but can be traced back to a fundamental operational disagreement between the various levels of command about how the battle in Flanders could best and most rapidly be brought to an end.[25]

The Commander-in-Chief of the Fourth Army gave the 'order to close up' on 23 May because he was concerned about the continuous state of combat-readiness of the armoured forces under his command before Dunkirk, and wished to give them a breather for closing ranks and technical overhaul. This in itself was an initial mistake, albeit not irretrievable. The intervention by the OKH (*Oberkommando des Heeres* or Army Supreme Command) during the night of 24 May, which put all of the forces along the encircling front under the command of Army Group B, thus relieving Army Group A from any further responsibility for the attack, was intended to correct this order and bring the battle of encirclement to a rapid conclusion.

Even Hitler's personal intervention at the headquarters of Army Group A on the morning of 24 May, when he rescinded the order by the OKH and gave the Commander-in-Chief of Army Group A, Colonel General von Rundstedt, a free hand to continue the operation, would not have been fatal. It was only von Rundstedt's insistence that the armoured forces close up and the attack be temporarily halted that culminated in the notorious 'order to halt'. This order was issued by the Supreme Command of this army group at noon on 24 May and remained in force until the afternoon of 26 May, despite violent protests by officers of senior and top rank. When the attack was finally renewed on the morning of 27 May, the unique opportunity to capture the bulk of the BEF had already passed, particularly since the over-taxed forces of the Luftwaffe over Dunkirk had not been able, also due to weather conditions, to prevent the evacuation.[26]

It may be true that Hitler was acting primarily with the intention of imposing his operational control on the commanders-in-chief of the two army groups advancing on the encircled enemy. It would be wrong, however, to attribute the sole blame for the 'miracle of Dunkirk' to him personally. For one thing, it cannot be assumed that Hitler drove to Army Group A headquarters at Charleville with the firm intention of stopping the movement of the armoured forces and motorized units. What proved to be decisive, on the other hand, was the assessment within the Supreme Command of Army Group A that operational success had already been achieved by the advance of the neighbouring Army Group B, so that all the armoured forces needed to do was to 'bag' the retreating enemy formations.[27] The roots of this mistaken decision lie, if anywhere, in conflicting notions of leadership and the personal touchiness of the commanders involved, as well as in opposing schools of thought at the operational and tactical level. In the final analysis, all that was accomplished by the measures taken by Hitler and von Rundstedt on 24 May was to negate the corrective intervention by the OKH, which had aimed at unifying and concentrating the operation in order to avoid friction.[28]

In any case, it is reasonable to believe that Hitler, regardless of which of the two army groups was to give the enemy the *coup de grâce*, had no intention of building 'golden bridges'[29] for the enemy, as former Lieutenant Colonel i.G. (*im Generalstab* = member of the General Staff) Heusinger alleged, but rather that he was seeking a complete and overwhelmingly decisive victory in the Dunkirk area.[30] Even if the experts agree that the omission at Dunkirk was a major operational, even strategic, blunder, such a blunder cannot be attributed to the lack of an overall concept of the war on the German side. Whereas it is probably incorrect to call the 'miracle of Dunkirk' the fundamentally decisive turn of the war, it still proved to be a fatal blow for German strategy. It cannot be denied that had Dunkirk resulted in complete victory, the German military command would have gone into the Battle of Britain under much more favourable circumstances, and the option of a subsequent invasion of southern England would have appeared far more encouraging. Furthermore, after the loss of the BEF, the British cabinet would have been under serious pressure. To speak of a 'virtual turn' of the war, however, would only be justified if there were sufficient proof that after the loss of the BEF, the British government might have been ready to negotiate a peace settlement. It is true, nonetheless, that until the early summer of 1940 Hitler had not developed any basic plans for the continuation of the war against Britain.[31]

As for British strategy, the unwavering decision to pursue the war after the collapse of her major ally France and the heavy losses already suffered on the continent, appeared to many observers to be incomprehensible, foolish and, in the final analysis, even self-destructive. At first glance, the stance of the British was in complete contradiction to the traditions of foreign policy, whereby a defeated nation seizes the first opportunity to initiate peace talks with the victorious power, before the fortunes of war result in even heavier reversals.

Assessment of the situation, however, by Churchill, Eden and Lord Beaverbrook led to the conclusion that the issue was no longer the search for some acceptable compromise with the enemy. In fact, the prospect of a strengthened, victorious Germany posed a threat, in the forseeable future, to the British Empire itself. Furthermore, the quest for a compromise peace would entail a renunciation of the fundamental values of the Western democracies. It was to uphold such values that the Allies had declared war against Germany in the first place. In any event, a negotiated peace would leave the larger part of Poland and the subsequently occupied nations of western and northern Europe under German rule. This was the fundamental argument whereby Churchill fanned the spirit of resistance, and he was quite serious in his statement that his government would have continued the war from overseas, even without the rescue of the BEF from Dunkirk, and even if 'England had been devastated by a catastrophe'.[32]

This determination to continue the war under any circumstances until victory over Germany was won is substantiated by remarkable documents. In order to brief the British representative on the secret negotiations being conducted with the Germans in Stockholm – which the British were only attending for form's sake – Sir Robert Vansittart, chief adviser to the Foreign Secretary, felt compelled to make the following very explicit statement to his minister on 6 September 1940:

> ... but the German Reich and the Reich concept have been the curse of the world for 75 years, and if we do not destroy it this time, we will never do it, and it will destroy us. *The enemy is the German Reich and not only Nazism,* and those who have not yet understood this, have not understood anything, and would let us stumble into a sixth war, even if we were to survive the fifth...[33]

In the telegram sent to the British representative in Stockholm on 11 September for transmission to the German representative, the basic precepts of British policy were again underlined:

> His Majesty's Government did not enter this war for selfish reasons, but with the noble objective of protecting the freedom and independence of many European nations... It is therefore up to the German Government to make proposals how the injustices Germany committed against other nations can be rectified. It is even more important, before such proposals may be taken into consideration, that Germany give effective guarantees, not only verbally but in actual fact...[34]

From these few sentences it is already evident that the conditions set by the British, as compared to German expectations, belonged to a completely different world of thought. To comply with them would not only have meant abandoning all conquests made since the beginning of the war, but also acceptance of the British legal and moral viewpoint as a criterion of German political practice. In Berlin these demands appeared to be so rigorous and unreasonable as to cast fundamental doubt on Great Britain's willingness to make peace.

It is therefore safe to assume that the will of the British government to pursue the war relentlessly and unwaveringly triggered all further strategic considerations on the German side. The ensuing phase of the conflict, described by one author as 'war in suspension',[35] provided the opportunity for an assessment of the situation and an analysis of the various opposing combinations, which had to take into account not only the actions of the British, but also the possible options open to the United States and the Soviet Union. The subsequent strategic decisions by the German command, therefore, were based upon the assessment of the probable reactions of the USA and the USSR to the central issue, namely the Anglo-German war.

It is important to note that in expectation of an imminent defeat of France and in the immediate aftermath, Hitler, together with the chiefs of the Wehrmacht, had not wholly excluded the eventuality of continuing the war against Great Britain. Directive No. 13 of 24 May 1940, for example, opened the way for the Luftwaffe to wage air war against England 'in full measure' once the necessary forces became available, and decreed that the battle against the British homeland was to continue even after the resumption of operations against the remaining French forces.[36] Among numerous testimonies to the debate about continuation of the war against Britain, there is the conversation between Hitler and Colonel General von Brauchitsch in the first half of June, in which the latter stated that if London were not prepared to make peace, Germany should invade the island as quickly as possible. Furthermore, State Secretary von Weizsäcker remarked, immediately after the French surrender, that if necessary, bombs would be required to persuade England to become 'peace-loving', and voiced a thought that would increasingly influence all considerations, namely that there would most likely be an 'accounting' with the Soviet Union.[37]

That German Foreign Minister von Ribbentrop, too, was not necessarily counting on a peace compromise was underlined by the statement he issued to his ministry on 30 June, to the effect that Germany would pursue the war until victory over England was achieved. On the same day, Major General Jodl, chief of the Wehrmacht Operations Office – and from August on the Wehrmacht Operations Staff – presented a memorandum on future strategic options, in which he recommended an invasion of Britain as *ultima ratio* once command of the air had been won.[38] But it was the Supreme Command of the Kriegsmarine which had been most vociferous in urging that direct war should be waged against England. Großadmiral Raeder had presented his ideas on this to Hitler on 21 May and again on 20 June in his *Wolfsschlucht* headquarters near Bruly de Pêche. It can be deduced from what he said that the navy had been reflecting on the problems of an invasion since November 1939.[39]

As final evidence that the German leadership had not spent the time following the defeat of France without ideas or plans, there is Directive No. 16 of 16 July on 'the preparations of an invasion of England', which were to be completed by mid-August. The intensification of the air war, which began in early August, was intended to create the necessary conditions under which an invasion, 'Operation Sea Lion', could be carried out with some chance of success. For this it was essential above all to gain a temporary and limited air superiority, if not actual command of the air, so as to protect the invasion from the air and to counteract the expected intervention by the superior British navy.

Granted that the central importance of the Battle of Britain for all further fundamental decisions by the German authorities can hardly be over-estimated, due consideration must also be given to the other influential changes and decision-making processes that were taking place simultaneously, which will be discussed later. What, then, were the options and means available to the Wehrmacht, during the summer of 1940, whereby Britain could be persuaded to make peace?

Option No. 1

An invasion of the British Isles, which was the most effective, but also the most risky. A failure of this operation would have had unimaginable consequences for Germany, not the least of them the destruction of the myth of invincibility. The army command was particularly eager to pursue preparations for the invasion, which was under extreme time pressure due to the lack of suitable shipping capacity. The deadline was finally set for 20 September. The Army provided 39 divisions, including reserves, a relatively large force given the extent of the landing area, but bound to take into consideration the fact that the enemy could depend on the professional soldiers rescued from Dunkirk. Actually, the British army was able to deploy 15 infantry and 3 armoured divisions, as well as numerous detached brigades and Home Guard units in the threatened sectors of southern and south-western England.[40] The reservations of the Kriegsmarine, at whose insistence the OKH had reduced the planned landing area to a 120 km-wide front, were certainly well founded and probably exerted considerable influence on Hitler's notion to use the intended invasion primarily as a means of political-psychological intimidation. Because of the risks inherent in 'Sea Lion', it appeared to make sense first to await the results of the Battle of Britain and to look upon the invasion as the *coup de grâce*.[41]

Option No. 2

An operational or, in modern terminology, 'strategic' air war, with the objective of decisively damaging Britain's economy, particularly the armaments and food industries, threatening the nation's supplies, and thus inducing eventual surrender. Even at the time, this strategy offered modest prospects of success, although Göring, as Commander-in-Chief, and General Jeschonnek, as Chief of Staff of the Luftwaffe, over-estimating its power and previous achievements,[42] were more optimistically going their own way. In itself, therefore, this was not a realistic option. Nevertheless, an operational air war, in close cooperation with a naval strategy, would have been a valuable addition to the next option.

Option No. 3

A concentrated and intensified attack on supply routes, i.e. a 'siege' of the British Isles by sea and air, entailing very close cooperation between U-boats, long-range reconnaissance aircraft and bombers. It was Admiral Dönitz, commander of the U-boat arm, who, more than anyone and from the beginning of the war, had been an advocate of concentrating every effort on submarine warfare. With the gaining of the French Atlantic coastline, the chances of this strategic option being successful were greatly enhanced.[43] However, the decision makers recognized that a war against supplies, however energetically waged, could not guarantee immediate results. Dönitz was aware that the successful outcome of a siege of Britain would depend upon an extreme concentration of all available means of war, including a big increase in the number of front-line submarines and the repudiation of any secondary theatres of war. He reckoned that this would not be possible before the autumn of 1941 or even during 1942.[44] In fact, by February 1941 the number of available front-line boats had only increased to 22, and of these only 12-14 (excluding some Italian submarines deployed from time to time) were on patrol in the areas of operations in the autumn of 1940. In August the U-boats sank 56 ships totalling 267,618 tonnes, followed by record sinkings in October of 63 ships with 352,407 tonnes, including the singularly successful destruction of convoy SC-7 during the night of 20 October.[45]

Nevertheless, any chance of a siege reaching a successful conclusion would seem to require the sinking of a far greater tonnage – as much as one million tonnes of shipping per month, in the opinion of Großadmiral Raeder. The critical factors in the waging of such a sea war were a) whether the rate of German sinkings would manage to outpace new British naval construction, and b) whether Germany could prevent the United States from entering the war for as long as possible, or at least restrict the volume of American aid to Britain. The question of United States intervention, however, could only be considered in the light of an overall political-strategic decision as to how Germany intended to bring the war to a victorious conclusion. As will appear later, the American factor represented a very serious problem in the calculations of the decision makers, notably that of Hitler personally. Should Britain not be forced to submit, it was probable that Roosevelt would react to any increased threat to Britain, to any subsequent British defeat, by redoubling the American effort to strengthen Britain's power of resistance. Any medium-term German strategy, such as siege warfare, would have to reckon with the danger of United States entering the war.[46]

Option No 4

Transfer of the war to the Mediterranean in order to topple, in conjunction with the Italian ally, British positions in North Africa, Malta and the Middle East. It was self-evident that control of the exits to the Mediterranean (the Suez Canal and Gibraltar) would force England to reroute its shipping to the Middle East and southern Asia via the arduous detour around the Cape of Good Hope. Furthermore, the Axis powers would thereby protect their southern flank, the 'soft underbelly of Europe' and render impossible any attempt by the British to establish bases in the Balkans or elsewhere, or even to open a second front. In addition, this option offered the possibility of acquiring the Vichy French positions in Morocco (Dakar and Casablanca) as bases for the war in the Atlantic. Finally, it could open the way to the seizure of the greatly desired oilfields of Iraq. The advantages offered by such an 'indirect' strategy were plausible, and were urged upon Hitler by representatives of the Kriegsmarine, whose key objective was doubtless the destruction of British predominance at sea.[47]

Differing perceptions of this strategic option soon became apparent. Leaders of the Kriegsmarine, such as Raeder (albeit in disagreement with the concepts of the Commander of U-boats), saw a Mediterranean war, with the inclusion of Italy, and possibly even Vichy France, as an independent, potentially decisive operation, whereas the OKW (*Oberkommando der Wehrmacht* or Supreme Command of the armed forces), notably Major General Jodl, only regarded joint German-Italian strategy in the Mediterranean as an 'interim solution'. Such an action could result in the gaining of jumping-off points for further land operations against the British in the Middle East. It could also create optimum conditions for other, not yet clearly defined, strategic alternatives. In the summer of 1940 this meant the still vague considerations and plans stemming from the incipient confrontation between the German Reich and the Soviet Union.[48] The probable majority conclusion, however, was that while a Mediterranean strategy by the Axis powers could make a substantial contribution to victory, it could not be decisive for the outcome of the war.

Option No. 5

Establishment of a Euro-Asian 'continental bloc', including the Soviet Union and Japan, in order to confront the United States and Great Britain. This concept of a geo-political concentration of power into areas ranging from the European Atlantic coast to the Japanese Pacific coast gained some credibility among the German command in the early autumn of 1940, not least after the unsatisfactory outcome of the Battle of Britain, and found its first expression in the conclusion of Germany's tripartite agreement with Italy and Japan

31

dated 27 September 1940. However, since the presence of the Soviet Union within this concept was based, as will be seen later, on very shaky and doubtful assumptions, the idea of a 'continental bloc' was looked upon at best as a temporary, substitute expedient. A political alliance without the Soviet Union would, in any event, have proved a blunt instrument, quite apart from the fact that, even with the cooperation of the USSR, such a power combination could clearly remain useful only for a limited time, and could only play an indirect part in forcing Britain to agree to peace negotiations.[49]

Much can be said for assuming that in the summer of 1940 the potential and feared intervention by the United States had become a major problem in Hitler's overall strategy; yet it is questionable whether all of the military and political options briefly summarized above were designed primarily with a view to subsequent conflict with the United States, as an indirect method of 'eliminating' that power.[50] After all, in the summer of 1940 the results of the Battle of Britain and a possible invasion of the British Isles were not yet known. It was still far from certain that the direct strategy against Britain would fail. Nor was it yet a foregone conclusion that the German command would be faced by the need increasingly to turn its attention to the problem of the Soviet Union.

The best way, of course, to prevent a possible intervention by the United States in western Europe was to destroy British resistance at home, entailing invasion and occupation. Control of the British homeland would be bound to have decisive consequences for the continuation of the war, even if Churchill were to decide to carry on the fight from Canada. German occupation of Britain, the 'unsinkable aircraft carrier', would have ended any likelihood of American involvement in western Europe. Such an eventuality, if possible linked with the build-up of a strong submarine fleet in the Atlantic, would have helped to make Germany virtually impregnable against the USA. The rapid 'elimination' of the main enemy, Britain, would have been the strongest barrier to American intervention, simply by denying Washington, from the start, its obvious intention of gaining an advance foothold in Europe.

Against the background of these considerations, the Battle of Britain has to be seen as the key element in the first major turn, with all its consequences for the further course of the war. Even though the German command was becoming increasingly concerned with the problem of the Soviet Union at the time of the initial air attacks against England, it was only the result of this aerial battle that provided the decisive impulse for German's ensuing overall strategy. It is therefore appropriate to turn to the air battle over Britain before discussing the Soviet-German confrontation.

The Battle of Britain and its
Contribution to the First Turn of the War

Since this study does not aim to provide a comprehensive analysis of the German air offensive against England and its repulse[51], the issue here is to trace the major reasons why the Luftwaffe broke off the air battle, and to illuminate the historical setting of the operation in general. Based on OKW directive No. 17 of 1 August and verbal instructions by Göring, the major phase of the air battle began on 13 August ('Eagle Day'). Based upon experience to date and the demonstrated conduct of the British fighter forces, the assault against the air defence forces and their ground organizations was to have priority for as long as it took to weaken British resistance decisively. Only after the British fighter defence had been destroyed and sufficient command of the air over southern England achieved, were the attacks against industrial targets (notably the aircraft industry), ports and food depots to be initiated. With hindsight it is generally agreed that the primary objective, i.e. the destruction of the British air defence – or what today would be termed the 'counter air offensive' – was correct and appropriate, but that it suffered, among other things, from a decisive omission: failure to attack and destroy the British air warning system, particularly the radar stations on the English south coast.[52]

The Luftwaffe Supreme Command had nevertheless marshalled an impressive force, which was extended over bases from Holland, Belgium and northern France all the way to Brittany, and which occasionally included units from *Luftflotte 5* in southern Norway and Denmark. On 10 August *Luftflotten 2* and *3* reported the following aircraft ready for combat: 875 bombers, 316 dive-bombers, 702 single-engine fighters, 227 twin-engine fighters and 45 long-range reconnaissance aircraft. At *Luftflotte 5* (Norway) the relative numbers were 123 bombers, 34 twin-engine fighters and 33 long-range recon-

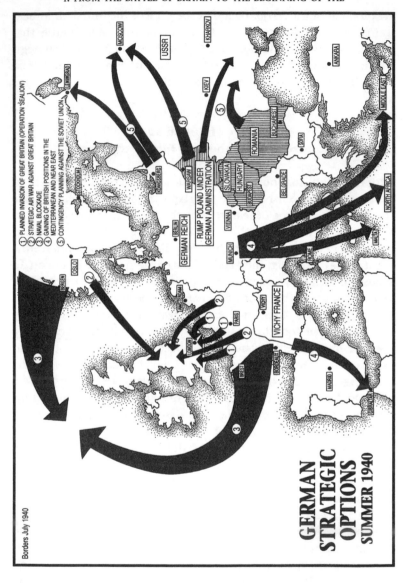

Borders July 1940

① PLANNED INVASION OF GREAT BRITAIN (OPERATION 'SEALION')
② STRATEGIC AIR WAR AGAINST GREAT BRITAIN
③ NAVAL BLOCKADE
④ GAINING OF BRITISH POSITIONS IN THE MEDITERRANEAN AND NEAR EAST
⑤ CONTINGENCY PLANNING AGAINST THE SOVIET UNION

GERMAN STRATEGIC OPTIONS SUMMER 1940

naissance aircraft, in other words a total of 2350 combat-ready front-line aircraft.[53] The Luftwaffe was thus able to deploy a force in a single theatre of war that it was never to attain again, even during the campaign against the Soviet Union: eleven bomber, four dive-bomber, one training (bomber), eight single-engine and three twin-engine fighter wings. On the British side, on 10 August, Fighter Command disposed of 711 fighters, and on 17 August 631 fighters, organized into 56 squadrons. Numerically, therefore, the German and British fighter forces were about equal; but what weighed heavily was that the average monthly British fighter production during the second half of 1940 was double that of Germany.[54]

Whereas in the beginning, by the application of clever tactics, Fighter Command had been able to avoid a battle of attrition, fighter against fighter, the massive and systematic German attacks against the fighter bases in southern England had pushed British fighter defence to the brink of collapse by early September. The condition of 11 Fighter Group, which was deployed in the centre of the defence, was near-catastrophic. All key statements agree that the German discontinuation of these attacks in their former intensity and the shift of target to the London area on 7 September was the biggest blunder of the entire air war. With the prospect of achieving complete air superiority in sight, an enemy hardly able to resist any longer was given an invaluable breather.[55]

This point of view, however, which stems from Göring's directive to deal the decisive blow in the air war by destroying the last British fighter reserves over London, requires some corrections. British Fighter Command still had the option of evacuating southern and south-eastern England and moving its decimated squadrons north in order to make it impossible for the standard German fighter, the Me 109, with its extremely short range, to accompany and protect the bombers should they attempt to extend their attacks northward against the British planes. An additional factor was that the Luftwaffe General Staff, partly due to an over-estimation of the limited successes achieved to date, partly due to contradictory and erroneous calculations provided by its Intelligence Service (Ic) at the very height of the battle, persistently under-estimated the capacities of British fighter defence to replace men and *matériel*. Immediately following the big attack against London on 15 September (Battle of Britain Day), which resulted in such heavy German losses, Göring himself informed his generals that, according to the reports he had received, British fighter defence now comprised in all only 177 fighter aircraft. According to a later admission by the Chief of Operations of the Luftwaffe General Staff, during those decisive months Germany had under-estimated the strength of the British fighter arm by 100 per cent.[56]

It is possible that Germany, by means of a cleverly conducted operation, could have achieved command of the air; but such superiority would only have prevailed within a restricted area for a limited time, so that it would have been vital to capitalize immediately on this advantage by launching the invasion. Until 15 September, however, the German air offensive had been aimed almost exclusively at gaining aerial superiority and not towards direct preparation of the invasion, which would have entailed attacks against British warships and coastal batteries. That the Luftwaffe command paid so little attention to this latter endeavour – so important for defeating Britain – may be explained by the fact that its forces, and the time schedule it had been set, were barely sufficient for the destruction of British fighter defence.[57]

Even if Germany had managed to achieve clear and incontestable air superiority over large areas of England by mid-September, the invasion would still have remained a risky operation. First, given the advanced time of year, the weather must have played an important role. Second, a mass air assault would have been launched against the invasion fleet not only by the remaining British fighters, but also by bombers. Third, Britain held a trump card in the superior strength of her fleet, which would have been despatched immediately, regardless of risk, against the German invasion forces.[58] To continue this scenario, the success of the invasion would have depended on a superior Luftwaffe being able to compensate for Germany's naval inferiority.

All this, however, is pure speculation. That Hitler decided on 17 September to delay the invasion 'until further notice', and on 12 October even postponed it until the spring of 1941, was obviously due to the failure of the air offensive, but in no small part also to the existence of the untouched British Home Fleet. At the time, and also in the light of subsequent assessments, the navy had some right to claim that the German abandonment of the invasion had constituted its own 'silent victory'.[59]

The historical importance of the Battle of Britain (the ensuing phases of which will not be pursued here) lies in the fact that on the one hand, after breaking off the daytime air battle and giving up her plans for invasion, Germany's direct strategy against Great Britain had to be seen as a temporary failure; moreover, Britain's position in the international balance of power had been greatly strengthened. From the tactical and operational viewpoint, the air battle may be accounted a 'draw', but in terms of politics and strategy, it was a victory for Britain and can therefore claim to have been a major contribution to the first turn of the war. Britain's enhanced position led to a reassessment of the international combinations, not only by the German Reich, but also by Japan, the United States and, above all, the Soviet Union.

Even if one subscribes to the view that during the summer and autumn of 1940 Hitler's strategy had been to 'force Great Britain to make peace by substance-sparing blows and political manœuvres',[60] it is clear, from what has been said so far, that the operational air war alone would not have been sufficient to make Britain give in 'substance-sparingly', even allowing for continuous German technical and tactical improvements. The only decisive means was the invasion of the British homeland.

It has been claimed, too, that Hitler was not really interested in a rapid military solution to the British problem, by virtue of being preoccupied, as early as July 1940, with the Soviet threat, which, by implication, took precedence over the conflict with Britain. This appears to be an exaggeration. Only the insight gained by mid-September that Britain could not be forced to make peace save by an invasion, and that based on experience to date, such an operation could not be risked before the spring of 1941, brought other unsolved political problems more urgently to the fore.

This is not to suggest, however, that the German leadership was now faced only with the alternatives of admitting the failure of its policy or of attacking the Soviet Union as a 'diversion' to compel London to give in.[61] The gist of such an argument is that Hitler would have attacked the Soviet Union in any case, regardless of Moscow's stance and policies towards Germany and Britain: in other words, that he would have initiated his eastern strategy in single-minded pursuit of the key element of his 'programme', namely the destruction of 'Bolshevist Russia', even if Britain had 'eaten humble pie' in the summer of 1940.[62] This would imply a degree of logic or, conversely, of involuntary provocation – a hypothesis that is untenable in the context of a thorough analysis of the situation. It demands nothing less than the firm belief that Hitler had a rigid 'time-table', which could be affected little, if at all, by changes in the overall political situation.

It is far from certain, all other things being equal, that there would have been a German-Soviet war at all if Britain had been brought down or occupied by German troops. A German Reich that had defeated Britain, or at least forced her surrender, would have been in a far stronger position than a Germany with a resurgent Britain off the coast of western Europe. As an aside, it is worth noting that in the spring of 1941 the occupation of France alone tied down 38 German infantry divisions as well as several other formations. The Soviet Union would have seen a victorious Germany as a potential enemy against whom it would have been futile to devise the type of war plans (which will be discussed later) that were being forged, from the summer of 1940 onward, by Stalin, Molotov, Timoshenko and Zhukov. It is conceivable that under such conditions Stalin would have preferred a policy of tolerance and conciliation. On the other hand, it is equally possible that in 1940, after having disposed of Britain, Hitler, even if allegedly motivated by ideological considerations, would have hesitated to unleash a war against the Soviet Union regardless of circumstances. In this instance, very much would have depended on Soviet policy towards Germany.[63]

It was only the unsatisfactory outcome of the Battle of Britain and the cancellation of the invasion, in recognition of the fact that direct strategy could not compel London to make peace, which forced the German command to search for alternative solutions. The air battle was decisive, therefore, in that it had closed the door on direct action against Britain and forced Germany to divert her energies into an indirect, time-consuming strategy, with all its imponderables. As a result of Great Britain's 'silent victory', Hitler had to be satisfied with his positions in the occupied parts of continental Europe and risked facing, in the medium and long term, a situation in which Stalin would exercise his increasing power to become the 'arbiter of Europe'.[64] The British defensive victory in September 1940 was therefore both a real and a tacit turn – real in the sense that Germany, while not having been openly defeated, had to acknowledge failure in the achievement of its strategic objectives, and tacit in that for the first time the belief in the invincibility of German arms was shaken.

The fact that many observers envisaged Hitler as the 'referee', as, for example, at the second arbitration conference in Vienna on 30 August, when unsettled territorial disputes in south-eastern Europe were decided, should not cloud our eyes to the broader picture. Britain had not only gained impetus through her defensive victory in the air, but she was now assured of Roosevelt's support because her strategic value was now enhanced.

Since the summer of 1940 Roosevelt had been pursuing an increasingly open policy of support and cooperation with Britain that can rightly be termed 'short of war'. As early as 17 June the American President had proposed a bill in Congress concerning the build-up of a fleet on two oceans. This was followed on 2 September by the signing of the treaty in which Britain was given 50 American destroyers in return for use of British bases in the West Indies and the Atlantic. This helped the British navy to strengthen its protection of convoys.[65]

On 10 January 1941, in continuation of his policy against the Axis powers, Roosevelt presented Congress with the draft of his Lend-Lease bill which promised England a comprehensive supply of war material. Congress passed the bill on 11 March. Offensive support by the American Atlantic fleet under Admiral King, whose zone of operations was greatly extended eastward to 30° West, and the increasing production of new cargo vessels in America, were shots in the arm for Britain. Indeed, in the spring of 1941, London was fully justified in believing that the threat at sea had, for the present, been banished.

The 'anti-Axis' policy of the United States, in fact, dated back to the pre-war period. It was evident, for example, immediately before and after the German-Soviet treaty of 23 August 1939, when Roosevelt initially urged Stalin to take sides with Britain and France;[66] even after the treaty was signed, he did nothing to isolate the Soviet Union. The President's mild and lenient policies towards the Soviet Union, stemming from his conviction, even prior to the outbreak of war, that Russia could be a potential ally against Germany and Japan, have been the subject of many studies and will not be pursued here.[67] In the present context the question is: what importance did the German leaders assign to the so-called American factor?

As already explained, Hitler reckoned with the probability of the United States entering the war if it were to be prolonged, and this was to play an important role in his considerations how best to deal with the Soviet Union. That he clearly recognized the growing weight of the United States was revealed, in early July, by the Z-plan – the temporary resumption of the Kriegsmarine's ship-building programme – and the discussions of basic principles with leaders of the OKW and the branches of the Wehrmacht in summer and early autumn. The objective was to delay American open intervention or even entry into the war for as long as possible. As will be shown in due course, the plan under consideration to eliminate the threat from the east by a quick campaign against the Soviet Union during 1941 was likewise designed to anticipate intervention by the United States on Britain's side. On the one hand, the issue was to establish an impregnable empire in continental Europe, on the other, to ensure that Japan kept its back free for a confrontation with Britain and the United States in eastern Asia and the Pacific. And since Japan's attitude remained ambiguous despite the conclusion of the tripartite treaty on 27 September 1940, consensus with that nation was of great importance.

Although Hitler was not unduly impressed by the scale of American arms production, reckoning that this potential would not make itself felt in the war before 1944–6,[68] he still placed great emphasis on not provoking the USA and giving her an excuse for intervention. Logically, this principle was all the more important in relation to Hitler's increasingly concrete plans for a confrontation with the Soviet Union. In other words, during the time required for the planning and execution of the campaign in the east, entry into the war by the United States had to be prevented at all costs. Since, according to Hitler's calculations, America might be expected to declare war at any time after 1942, it was mandatory that the campaign against the Soviet Union be victoriously concluded in 1941. Therefore, as Hitler told General Jodl on 17 December 1940, the objective must be to solve all 'continental political problems' in the course of 1941.[69]

The Kriegsmarine had to bear the brunt of the effects of this declared policy of restraint towards the United States. It was forbidden to attack American warships, even if they acted in breach of international law or appeared within the designated zone of blockade. An incident of this nature occurred on 20 June 1941, two days before the German attack on the USSR, when a German submarine brought the battleship *USS Texas* to bay within the blockade zone and attacked it unsuccessfully. From the spring of 1941 the burden of the war against supply routes fell ever more heavily on the submarine force, after the deployment of battleships and cruisers had led to losses that could hardly be made up. One such decisive action was 'Operation Rheinland', which ended with the destruction on 27 May 1941 of the *Bismarck* by superior British forces.[70]

A further important consideration in the assessment of British resistance policy by the German command was that of a possible Anglo-Soviet *rapprochement*. Even if, as is evident today, the appointment of Sir Stafford Cripps as the new British Ambassador in Moscow in June 1940 did not lead to any tangible results in the sense of wooing the Soviet Union into some form of alliance, Hitler still remained highly suspicious. The spectre of an Anglo-Soviet alliance was subsequently to exert a weighty influence on German strategic planning. And there were other actions by Churchill, too, that underline his intention to establish a 'big alliance' with the United States and the Soviet Union, an intention that appeared to be quite logical within the framework of existing national combinations.

The Sphinx in the East:
The Confrontation with the Soviet Union

Having discussed the contribution made by the Battle of Britain to the first turn of the war, and the increasing influence of the United States in the assessment of Britain's power to resist, we must now ask what share the Soviet Union had in this turn and which strategic options offered themselves to the German leadership after the failure of direct action against Britain. How realistic was the prospect of defeating England by means of indirect strategy? Would a transfer of the strategic focus to the Mediterranean sphere and a concentrated effort by the Axis powers against British positions there not have brought about a more rapid decision than the 'détour via Moscow'? This is a controversial question which cannot be answered with a simple 'yes' or 'no'. The decisive factor in German assessments was to become Stalin's policy following the German victory in the west in June 1940, and the development of German-Soviet relations in the ensuing months.[71]

We must now discuss to what degree the failure of the direct strategy against Britain and Germany's growing dependency on the Soviet Union, seen against the background of Stalin's policy of expansion – which Germany regarded as a threat – were decisive for the command decisions in Berlin. In the light of German-Soviet relations and the extent to which they influenced the leading statesmen on either side, culminating in mutual war preparations, can one really call the campaign against the Soviet Union 'a racial-ideological war of extermination',[72] as one prominent historian has emphatically repeated, or even describe it as a 'monstrous war of conquest, enslavement and destruction'?[73] Is it true to claim that the complicated strategic situation in the summer of 1941 was only 'a minor explanatory factor'?[74] Finally, can the decision to attack the Soviet Union be termed 'the ultimate and most grievous of those suicidal decisions'[75] which were allegedly characteristic of Hitler? As will be shown, the German attack against the Soviet Union was, militarily, far from being a hopeless endeavour doomed to failure. Incontrovertible statements of this nature are best avoided.

Scientific discussion is not really advanced by using Hitler's 'step by step programme' and his *Ostprogramm* (literally eastern programme, whereby 'living room' could be gained and resources acquired for Germany in the east at the expense of the Slav countries of the Soviet Union) as the key argument. The author is strongly opposed to this form of 'closed circle argument', which endeavours to explain a causal chain of incidents that extend over a long period and culminate in a multiple, complex combination of events, simply by pointing to statements made by one of the protagonists in the distant past. An example of this is the attempt to explain World War Two and the attack on the Soviet Union in terms of declarations Hitler made in the 1920s, to wit: the war he had started in 1939 had only been 'the prelude to the great war against the Soviet Union' which he had intended to wage with all the forces at his command.[76]

This study does not intend to discuss in detail the history leading up to the attack on the Soviet Union.[77] Nor is it concerned to assess and compare the strategic and ideological motives contributing to the decision to launch that attack. The primary intention is to illustrate the importance of Soviet policy and potential in the summer of 1940 as it affected the German assessment of the situation at the time. It makes more sense, in any case, and it is less disputable, to focus on the political-strategic facts that led to the decision to attack, than to trace and analyse the ideological motives which – though undeniable – are open to a far greater measure of uncertainty and hence controversy.

The Hitler-Stalin Pact was signed during the night of 23 August 1939. Today there are numerous studies, some of them very profound, on the background and motives of this pact. For decades Soviet authors have vigorously denied that the main points and the subsequent political steps had already been fixed at a secret session of the Politburo and the Comintern on 19 August 1939, even that such a meeting took place at all. The existence of the 'secret rider' was also denied until 1989. The first to admit that such a meeting was an historic fact was Dmitri Volkogonov in 1993. The transcript of the speech Stalin gave at this conference was recently discovered in a former secret archive of the Soviet Union by a Russian historian and published. Even though the circumstances under which this document found its way into the archives have not yet been fully resolved, a conference of Russian historians held at Novosibirsk in April 1995 left no doubts as to its authenticity.[79]

The message contained in Stalin's speech of 19 August is that the war between Germany and the Western powers, England and France, was imminent, that the Soviet Union should support Germany, which was seen as being the weaker nation, and do everything possible to make the war drag on and lead to the total exhaustion of both sides. Stalin discussed the possibility of a victory by the Western powers, but then outlined the following option in case of an unexpected German victory:

> In a defeated France the PCF (French Communist Party) will always be very strong. The communist revolution will inevitably come, and we can use this opportunity to support France and make her our ally. Later on all the nations which have fallen under the 'protection' of a victorious Germany will also become our allies. We will then have a broad field of activity for furthering the world revolution.[80]

A critical appraisal of Soviet policy during 1939–41 and a parallel assessment of German actions over the same period neither increases nor diminishes the responsibility of Hitler and his henchmen for plunging Europe into war. In this context, therefore, it is surely important to examine Stalin's long-term strategy and to consider, for example, the allegation that 'in the pursuit of his objectives, the "red" dictator was possibly just as unscrupulous as the "brown" dictator'.[81] Based on the sources available today, a growing number of authors assert that the Soviet leaders must bear a far greater share than was previously thought in the unleashing of World War Two, and that, from the very beginning, they were pursuing far-reaching objectives. Among the more important are Werner Maser, Lothar Rühl, Ernst Topitsch and Richard R. Raack.[82] It is the French historian François Furet, however, who is most explicit about the ruthless Soviet expansion policy. Concerning the aggressive policy against Finland, this author is of the opinion that Stalin's invasion in late autumn 1939 shows the determination 'to secure his booty right at the beginning of the world war he had already seen coming for so long and had begun under such favourable auspices'.[83] Furet summarizes the process that led to the outbreak of war by stating: 'Stalin and Hitler jointly share the responsibility for the war.'[84]

Initial steps by Germany for dealing with the strategic problem of the Soviet Union were taken during July 1940, but these were still in the nature of a contingency plan, and had been provoked mainly by the question as to whether the rigid response in London was based not only on hopes of the United States but also the Soviet Union, and even whether secret contacts between London and Moscow were in the offing. Hitler's question on 13 July to the Chief of the General Staff, General Halder, can be understood in this context, when he asked who would benefit from the dissolution of the British Empire. In his opinion, British resolution to resist was based on a hope of support by the Soviet Union.[85] An even more far-reaching argument was expressed during the conferences with senior officers of the Wehrmacht on 21 and 30 July, at which Hitler drew the causal link between the destruction of the Soviet Union and a strong enhancement of Japan's position in eastern Asia, and hence a containment of the United States.

While the repeatedly quoted statement by Hitler, that in the course of this conflict Russia had to be 'eliminated' in the spring of 1941, does indicate the beginning of a confrontation with the Soviet Union, it would be highly audacious to portray this as an 'unalterable' decision.[86] The relatively long time-span until 18 December

1940, when the basic Directive No. 21 on the preparation of the attack was issued, and diplomatic steps that were still taken in the interim, in particular the visit to Berlin by Soviet Foreign Minister Molotov in November, both support the theory that Hitler's final decision must have been reached at a much later stage. Even that vital directive on 'Barbarossa' does not convey an irrevocable decision. On the contrary, the summary in paragraph IV notes that the measures to be taken by the commanders-in-chief must clearly be designed to be 'measures of precaution in case Russia changes its present stance towards us',[87] which again argues for the theory that Soviet actions and Stalin's conduct since the summer of 1940 markedly influenced German calculations. It would be too naïve to deduce an immutable German 'about-turn' towards the Soviet Union merely from the failure of an Anglo-German agreement in the summer of 1940! So it is both simplistic and misleading to regard Hitler's decision for war against the Soviet Union as being completely independent of Stalin's political and military actions during the period in question.[88]

It must be pointed out, nonetheless, that on its own initiative the Wehrmacht Operations Staff began to initiate preliminary plans against the Soviet Union as early as the end of June/beginning of July 1940 and that General Halder received initial assignments to prepare operational plans addressed to this problem on 3 July, which led very rapidly to preliminary considerations. In other words, the OKW and the OKH were already considering how best to deal militarily with a likely confrontation in the east.[89] So the point of departure in the operational planning of 'Barbarossa' was not necessarily Jodl's order to selected staff officers, dated 29 July (for which he could refer to Hitler's directive), to embark on systematic preparations for the 'eastern build-up' in Poland.

It needs to be emphasized, however, that staff studies and contingency planning form parts of a military routine in western and central Europe, and do not traditionally require political impetus. All of the subsequent planning exercises (the 'Marcks Plan', the 'Loßberg Study', the 'Sodenstern-Plan', and the plans prepared by General Paulus), were dictated by contingency. Since the steps taken during the summer and autumn of 1940 to control armaments production (which will be discussed later) were also taken *ad hoc* and without any long-term perspectives, one cannot define German strategy towards the Soviet Union as irrevocable, at least not until 18 December 1940. During the summer and autumn of that year everything was still in a state of flux.[90]

Given this situation, Soviet policy during the period in question assumed great importance. Was it all that ridiculous for Germany to suspect that Stalin was keenly interested in the continuation of British resistance? Would an effective military shackling of Germany by Britain, and possibly the United States, not have been in Moscow's interest? Would not the position of the Soviet Union continue to be strengthened the longer the war between Germany and Britain dragged on? After all, official Moscow noted with satisfaction that Germany 'had not yet solved its main problem'.[91] From the viewpoint of the senior German leadership, assessment of future Soviet conduct were the war to escalate very much depended on how Moscow reacted to the German victory in the west and the continuing resistance of Britain.

Yet in this context Moscow had already taken unequivocal action. In mid-June, shortly before the victorious conclusion of the German campaign in the west, Stalin had annexed the three Baltic states as 'Soviet Republics' and imposed the cession of Bessarabia and northern Bukovina at the end of June/beginning of July. The cession of the latter region, moreover, had not been covered by the Hitler-Stalin Pact of 23 August 1939. The haste with which these actions were carried out was bound to arouse German suspicions, especially since Germany only disposed of extremely weak security forces along the borders between the mutual spheres of interest. The Soviet Union had thus stolen a march on Germany. In July 1940 there was no longer any vestige of a buffer zone between the two powers.[92]

Soviet obstinacy was further demonstrated in relatively minor disagreements, such as the refusal to cede the border strip of Mariampol which, according to the exchange of territories agreed in the 'Border and Friendship Treaty' of 28 September 1939, was to fall to Germany in compensation for the 'strip of Vilna'. The stubborn doggedness with which Soviet diplomacy clung to set objectives on the most spurious pretexts was a very unpleasant indicator for future German-Soviet relations. The Germans subsequently learned through secret channels that not only was the British government urgently interested in an arrangement with Stalin, but that Yugoslavia, too, through its ambassador in Moscow, had requested the Soviet Union to take a stance against Germany. Finally it was discovered that the Soviet leadership was disgruntled by the Vienna arbitration decision of 30 August and the German guarantees to Romania, and was increasingly considering a confrontation with Germany.[93]

The close ties of the Soviet Union to Yugoslavia became clearly apparent immediately after the military putsch in Belgrade on 27 March 1941, with the attempt of the new rulers to obtain Moscow's backing. On 6 April 1941, for example, Stalin told Gavrilovic, Belgrade's ambassador to Moscow, that he hoped the Yugoslav army would hold up the German troops as long as possible. According to Soviet files that were only published in 1989, the government that had come to power had immediately sent Stalin and Molotov a request for Soviet troops and proposed the conclusion of a military alliance. The Soviet *chargé d'affaires* in Belgrade reported to Molotov on 30 March 1941 that the Yugoslav government desired full military and political cooperation with the Soviet Union.[94] The development of Soviet-Yugoslav relations up to the beginning of the German campaign in the Balkans, and the indirect support Stalin gave Belgrade, suggest the theory that Hitler's decision to attack the Soviet Union only finally became firm at the beginning of April 1941.

It was the visit – highly unsatisfactory from the German point of view – by Foreign Minister Molotov to Berlin in mid-November 1940, which decisively influenced the assessment of the situation and the option to attack the Soviet Union in 1941. Molotov's demands, which were precisely in line with Stalin's objectives, were not only unacceptable to Germany if she wished to survive as a major power, but were bound strongly to reinforce the impression that Moscow posed a long-term threat. This signified the failure of the final German attempt to bring the Soviet Union into a 'continental bloc' against Great Britain.[95] Soviet ambitions to large parts of the Balkans, the Turkish straits, Hungary, the western part of Poland and the exits from the Baltic went far beyond anything that could have been expected from Germany as the price for Stalin's continued good behaviour.

In this context, the Soviets obviously intended to sound out the limits of Germany's will to make concessions. Viewed objectively, Molotov's tactics were nothing more than attempted blackmail. But it would be sheer speculation to claim that Molotov was acting on the assumption of a situation in which Britain and the United States might be on the verge of gaining a foothold in western Europe.[96] It would hardly make sense for an experienced, pragmatic politician such as Molotov to make demands of his partner in negotiations, which tacitly counted upon that partner's *defeat.*

There is much to be said, however, for the hypothesis that the Soviet government believed that a German success over Great Britain still lay far in the future, that the war would continue for a long time, and that as a result it could step up considerably its demands on Berlin. The issue was to gain a superior starting position for further, even more stringent demands, which, if granted, would have made Stalin the arbiter, even the permanent ruler, of Europe. Given the possibility of an unlimited duration of the war in the west, the Germans therefore faced two alternatives following Molotov's visit to Berlin: either increased dependence on the Soviet Union and acceptance of the danger of being blackmailed in the forseeable future, or a turn-about against the Soviet Union by means of a decisive attack. In the ensuing period both Hitler and Stalin became convinced, if only from their political assessment of the situation in terms of strategic security, that a war against each other was inevitable.[97]

To be explicit: it was not the offensive preparations for war by the Soviets that decisively influenced Hitler's calculations, because Germany only gained sufficient information about these in the final weeks before 22 June 1941; rather it was the consideration of the existing and opposing political attitudes associated with concepts of power and security, as well as the ideological contradictions, that sooner or later made military conflict between these two nations inevitable. And taking into account corresponding statements by Stalin, for example his speech to the graduates of the Frunse Military Academy on 5 May 1941, which is based mainly on reconstructed transcripts of interrogations of captured Soviet officers, there can be no doubt that Stalin and Molotov were also thinking in terms of as quick a military solution as possible.[98] According to a recently published report by Valery Danilov on the subject of this much-interpreted speech, Stalin announced:

And now, after we have reconstructed our army, equipped it with technology for modern war, have become strong – now we must shift from the defensive to the attack. If we are to defend our country, we are obliged to do so offensively.[99]

From the German viewpoint, then and now, Stalin was in the far more favourable position. Because of the German-Soviet pact of 23 August 1939 he had a firm foothold in eastern-central Europe, was not entangled in any armed conflicts, could develop his military and armaments potential without interference, was being courted openly and indirectly by important powers, and enjoyed something which gave him a far-reaching advantage over Germany: he had time. He could capitalize on the fact that in the spring of 1941 the Wehrmacht (49⅔ divisions in all) continued to be tied down by land, sea and air in France, in Norway and in the Mediterranean, and thus had a free hand politically, forcing Germany either to surrender peacefully or risk military collapse.

In addition, Stalin could assume, based on the experiences of World War One, that Germany would not run the high risk of a war on two fronts. Only the feared Anglo-German accord or peace compromise could rid Germany of this risk. As long as such an accord was not in sight, as long as Germany and Britain continued to weaken each other, Stalin could continue to play his role as arbiter. His plans of attack, which have come to light recently, reveal his intention, even if in 1940 the German leadership was only aware of them in broad outline: the objective was to defeat Germany unaided and to create a *fait accompli* in Europe, before the Western powers in their turn were able to win and pocket the top political prize.[100]

Such considerations by Stalin and Molotov were much applauded by the Soviet military leaders who, according to traditional doctrine, wanted to conduct a predictable military conflict offensively, in other words on enemy territory.[101] This is why the actual deployment orders, to be discussed, clearly display an offensive character. They drew on offensive plans which had already been made in 1938 and were mainly based on the considerations which Marshal Tukhachevsky, who had been executed in June 1937, had given to offensive procedures.[102] What is apparent is the intention, dating back into the 1930s, to wage aggressive war, which can hardly be explained, therefore, in terms of the incipient deterioration of Soviet-German relations in the summer of 1940. It would be a mistake to believe that the operational planning by the Soviet General Staff was merely a contingency, without a basic order from Stalin. Soviet state and party practice would never have condoned military strategic-operational planning without the knowledge of the senior leadership, because any war plan could only be the expression of an over-riding political will. Furthermore, based on the well-publicized experiences of 1936–8, soldiers of 'independent' mind would have faced dismissal and exemplary punishment at the hands of Beria.[103]

A deployment against central Europe of 258 divisions, some 23,000 tanks, and roughly 9000 front-line aircraft in European Russia – with a total availability of 303 divisions – which was largely complete by June 1941, represented an overpowering attacking potential, even if this potential was only recognized in broad terms by the German General Staff shortly before its own attack. On 22 June 1941 Germany – without allies – disposed of roughly 149 divisions and 3580 tanks, including all reserves not yet available in the east, of which only 120 divisions made up the initial attack force.

In addition, there were weighty factors which underlined the aggressive nature of the Soviet deployment, most of which, however, were only recognized after 22 June 1941. Only the most recent publications tell the full tale: deployment of most of the armoured forces in exposed front-line positions so that they were hardly suitable for defence; improvement of the road network only in areas close to the front; deliberate omission of lines of defence in depth; creation of five airborne corps from the summer of 1940 onward; advanced deployment of numerous fighter squadrons for offensive air defence; and distribution to the troops of military maps on which the territory shown reaches far into Poland and Germany. In one case, such a captured map shows arrows of attack to the west over the Vistula.[104]

Soviet intentions to attack are clearly underlined by the deployment of eighteen armies in the western parts of the Soviet Union, and in particular the concentration of the strongest attack groupings in salients jutting far into enemy territory, where, in the event of a German attack, they would have been threatened by rapid encirclement. The actually completed deployment includes the 1st Strategic Line with sixteen armies, the 2nd Strategic Line with seven armies whose deployment was not yet completed, and the 3rd Strategic Line with three armies, which were deployed in the greater Moscow area as a central reserve.

It can be claimed as a counter-argument that the Soviets would have run a high risk in launching such an attack against the battle-proven Wehrmacht, then at the height of its success and confident of victory. It would therefore have made sense only to attack the

Wehrmacht after it had suffered a resounding defeat in some other theatre of war. This can be answered by pointing out that Stalin and his military advisers were reckoning on a German attack in the foreseeable future, which for reasons of principle, and based on Soviet military doctrine, they did not wish to await. After all, defence is that form of battle in which no decision can be gained. Furthermore, Soviet military intelligence was already counting upon a threatening German deployment in the autumn of 1940, which did not correspond to the actual situation. The reasons underlying this – deliberate – misassessment will not be discussed here. For all of these reasons, Stalin had to be very concerned to be the first to complete his deployment and to launch a surprise attack. His conduct during the critical days in June 1941, therefore, does not reflect the defensive attitude of the Red Army, but rather his desire to play for time.[105]

'Preventive War' or the War of Two Aggressors?

Even though the debate as to whether the German attack on 22 June 1941 can be called 'preventive war' is only of marginal interest to the topic at hand, it will be briefly treated in order to prevent misunderstandings and false interpretations. It should first be pointed out that the recently published document, *Considerations on the Strategic Deployment Plan of the Soviet Armed Forces*, of May 1941,[106] explicitly mentions an intended preventive war by the Soviet Union against Germany and its allies. The Soviet intention was to counter the danger of an attack by the German army in the east, the strength of which had been greatly over-estimated – deliberately or otherwise – by launching a massive pre-emptive blow, as likely to offer a far greater chance of success. Here, then, were two antagonists, both convinced, for political-strategic reasons, of the 'inevitability' of a conflict, and both seeking the advantage by simultaneously preparing for an attack, with one side probably anticipating the other only by a small margin of time.[107]

As is proved beyond any doubt by a number of facts and circumstances,[108] and as many Russian authors now also admit, on 22 June 1941 the Wehrmacht launched its attack into the centre of an offensive deployment that was largely completed. There is much evidence to suggest that the second half of June was the latest date for a poten-

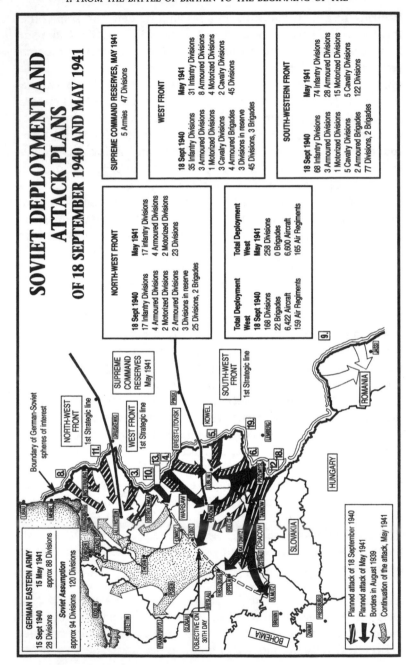

SOVIET DEPLOYMENT AND ATTACK PLANS
OF 18 SEPTEMBER 1940 AND MAY 1941

SUPREME COMMAND RESERVES, MAY 1941
5 Armies   47 Divisions

WEST FRONT

18 Sept 1940	May 1941
35 Infantry Divisions	31 Infantry Divisions
3 Armoured Divisions	8 Armoured Divisions
1 Motorized Division	4 Motorized Divisions
3 Cavalry Divisions	2 Cavalry Divisions
4 Armoured Brigades	45 Divisions
3 Divisions in reserve	
45 Divisions, 3 Brigades	

SOUTH-WESTERN FRONT

18 Sept 1940	May 1941
68 Infantry Divisions	74 Infantry Divisions
3 Armoured Divisions	28 Armoured Divisions
1 Motorized Division	15 Motorized Divisions
5 Cavalry Divisions	5 Cavalry Divisions
2 Armoured Brigades	122 Divisions
77 Divisions, 2 Brigades	

NORTH-WEST FRONT

18 Sept 1940	May 1941
17 Infantry Divisions	17 Infantry Divisions
4 Armoured Divisions	4 Armoured Divisions
2 Motorized Divisions	2 Motorized Divisions
2 Armoured Divisions	23 Divisions
3 Divisions in reserve	
25 Divisions, 2 Brigades	

Total Deployment West

18 Sept 1940	May 1941
168 Divisions	258 Divisions
22 Brigades	0 Brigades
6,422 Aircraft	6,600 Aircraft
159 Air Regiments	165 Air Regiments

GERMAN EASTERN ARMY

15 Sept 1940	15 May 1941
28 Divisions	approx 88 Divisions

Soviet Assumption
approx 94 Divisions   120 Divisions

Boundary of German-Soviet spheres of interest

NORTH-WEST FRONT
1st Strategic line

SUPREME COMMAND RESERVES
May 1941

WEST FRONT
1st Strategic line

SOUTH-WEST FRONT
1st Strategic line

ROMANIA
HUNGARY
SLOVAKIA
BOHEMIA

OBJECTIVE ON 30TH DAY

Planned attack of 18 September 1940
Planned attack of May 1941
Borders in August 1939
Continuation of the attack, May 1941

tially successful attack. Even if there is no documentary proof for the exact date of a Soviet attack, the circumstances of the deployment itself, and the pressures of time on deployment, logistics and mobilization, all indicate a deadline in the latter half of the year, no later than the beginning of autumn.[109] For reasons that will be discussed later, the possibility of an attack by the Red Army as late as 1942, as was long maintained by historical opinion, can very probably be excluded.

It is only recently that research has begun in Russia on this question of 'preventive war'. Back in 1952 Theodor Plievier published theses which dismissed the Soviet claim of an 'insidious German attack on the unsuspecting Soviet Union' as pure myth.[110] But since then, in the latest statements by Russian experts, one can detect a substantial change of position. In some cases, the claim that the Wehrmacht launched a 'surprise attack' on the Soviet Union is still being upheld.[111] However, a surprise attack requires an unsuspecting, unprepared opponent, which was not the case here, as is evident from the following documents and facts. The publication by Colonel Vladimir Karpov, Dimitri Volkogonov and Yuri Kirshin[112] of the Soviet assault plans of May 1941, was followed in 1991–2 by the revelation of four important documents from Russian archives, of which the first three were published in a Russian specialist journal of note. The documents referred to are the deployment and attack plans of July 1940, 18 September 1940, 11 March 1941 and May 1941.[113]

The publication of these documents, and also other previously unknown archive material, reveals much about the German-Soviet war that was not known prior to 1991. What is especially important here is the light thrown on early offensive intentions, which can be traced back in their basic concept to the autumn of 1939. This led to a whole series of documents up to May 1941, including one dated 18 September 1940 which discloses the same attack plan as does the 'final document' of May 1941. The basic operational intention was to launch the decisive assault from the western Ukraine and the area north of Brest-Litovsk in the direction of southern Poland and Upper Silesia in the form of a double pincer movement, in order thereby to annihilate the bulk of the opposing German forces. The Soviet Supreme Command, which had provided 168 divisions and 22 mechanized brigades, was not faced by any serious opposition in mid-September 1940. Whereas the document identifies Germany as 'the most likely enemy', it also attributes to her a greatly exaggerated 243 divisions. At the time, the Luftwaffe was still valiantly engaged in the Battle of Britain, and the actual forces deployed in East Prussia and the occupied part of Poland by the Army consisted of only 28 divisions.[114]

It is therefore impossible to agree with the claim, as for example, does Manfred Messerschmidt,[115] that the Soviet offensive preparations were merely a reaction to German offensive plans, and to suggest that Stalin had acquired knowledge of Directive No. 21, 'Barbarossa', by treason as early as December 1940. Since Soviet deployment and attack preparations had been in full swing since the summer of 1940, the most one can deduce from the Soviet leadership's learning of Directive No. 21, is their decision to speed up the offensive preparations already under way.

The original document of May 1940 revealed by Valery Danilov in 1992–3, however, differs in one significant aspect from that of its predecessors. The author of this detailed plan of attack, Deputy Chief of Operations Staff Major General A. M. Vassilevsky, who was acting under Zhukov's orders, demanded a pre-emptive attack before the Wehrmacht took the offensive and gave as his reason that German deployment was almost completed. Altough this was a gross exaggeration, his demand may also be interpreted as reflecting the desire of the military command to get Stalin to agree to a rapid completion of Soviet offensive deployment. This plan of deployment and attack, which was presented to Stalin on 15 May 1941 by Zhukov and Defence Minister Timoshenko, carries Stalin's monogram. Contrary to the opinion that this is merely a formal sign by Stalin that he had taken cognisance and is thus of no importance, it would appear to be more logical, in the light of Soviet practice, to regard it as his approval, particularly as the document itself explicitly requests the approval of the intentions expressed therein. This interpretation is supported by an interview given by Marshal Vassilevsky in 1967.[117]

Within the context of publications on this topic during recent years, harsh criticism has been voiced against Stalin's policies of expansion, the pact of 23 August 1939, and Stalin's misguided behaviour in the spring of 1941. It is admitted, however, that there is no conclusive evidence that 'Stalin would have launched a surprise attack against Germany at the first opportunity to offer itself'.[118] Thanks are due to a number of Russian experts for additional research on Soviet political and military offensive preparations. Additionally, Valery Danilov, Boris Sokolov, B. N. Petrov, Vladimir Neveshin, L. N. Neshinsky and Mikhail Meltyukov have all devoted themselves to this subject. According to this research, the Soviet General Staff was working, with Stalin's approval, on plans for an offensive against Germany from the autumn of 1939 onward, as can be learned, for example, from a collection of documents published in 1995. One of the authors of this work even stated that the directives of the Central Committee of the Communist Party of the Soviet Union, issued in agreement with the military preparations, 'clearly testify to the intention of the Soviet leadership to launch an attack against Germany in the summer of 1941'.[119]

In another publication, historian Mikhail Meltyukov states that the General Staff of the Red Army had already begun to draw up a plan for a war against Germany in October 1939. This plan, after being revised to include offensive objectives, was approved by the Soviet government, and therefore naturally also by Stalin, on 14 October 1940. Simultaneously with the operational provisions, a plan for mobilization was also developed, which was likewise approved by the Soviet government on 12 February 1941. Among other things, this called for the provision of nine million men, 37,800 tanks and 22,200 aircraft. That this plan was indeed realistic was to be confirmed by the subsequent course of the war. Astonishingly, at the end of his study the author even expresses regret that the government omitted to carry out this plan, claiming that had it been executed, the Red Army would have been in Berlin no later than 1942! This, he continues, 'would have brought a much larger territory in Europe under the control of Moscow than was to be the case in 1945'.[120] Is this not an open plea for a decisive offensive launched in time? In any event, the counter-theory that there were certainly 'no plans for a Soviet preventive attack during the phases of the German deployment'[121] can safely be consigned to legend.

Others, too, have admitted that a Soviet 'preventive attack' was quite possible in 1941, and documentation supports the opinion that 'a Soviet preventive attack would have spared both nations much and probably forced Hitler to capitulate much sooner'.[122] But since such an attack takes a relatively long time to prepare, particularly if success is to be guaranteed, it may be deduced that the plan must have been to prepare an attack for its own sake. Such preparations must have begun a considerable time before the German offensive deployment became known in detail. It is hardly conceivable that the Soviets could have managed to deploy 23 armies on the first and second Strategic Lines, together with the enormous arms production this required – as was to be revealed immediately after 22 June 1941 – within the short time-span that remained *after* they had taken note of Germany's deployment, in other words from March–April 1941 onward.

It can also be deduced that the Soviet General Staff did not develop such important offensive plans on its own initiative, but that this could only have been done with Stalin's knowledge and approval. As with most other nations, politics governed military decisions. Thus the underlying basic political interests and intentions can be inferred from the concrete military plans. The theory of a routine contingency planning by the military, who were allegedly acting without Stalin's approval, as well as the claim that Stalin was only reacting to the German offensive planning that had just come to his knowledge, can both be rejected. Furthermore, after January 1941, Soviet propaganda, bolstered by prominent writers, began to adopt a decidedly anti-Fascist and anti-German mood, and received additional impetus following the above-mentioned speech by Stalin on 5 May.[123]

A final piece of evidence for a comprehensive military and political offensive plan is that the Politburo took the decision on 4 June 1941 to create a 'Polish Red Army of Liberation'. This army was to consist of all Soviet citizens of Polish descent and was to be recruited from the Polish eastern territories occupied since September 1939. Its direction of advance was to be the Cracow–Kattowitz area, in other words within the bounds of the main attack by the South-west Front (in Russian military terminology a 'front' was the equivalent of a Western-style army group), and its assignment was primarily to be indoctrination and propaganda.[124]

The claim that Germany, for her part, had been forced to fight a preventive war was made by Goebbels after the German attack had begun. Without attempting to justify German motives, it has to be emphasized that a decisive criterion for 'preventive' action is that the side which attacks first does so in order to anticipate an enemy attack which it has concluded, from serious evidence, is imminent. In other words, it is conducting a 'forward defence'.[125] If, therefore, we define preventive war in the narrow, military sense and compare this with the political-strategic decisions by the German leadership, one fact becomes evident: since the German General Staff was only able to draw a relatively accurate picture of Soviet deployment a few weeks before 22 June 1941, the claim of a German preventive war in the classical sense – as a reaction to an impending attack by the enemy – cannot be upheld. During the summer and autumn of 1941, neither Hitler, nor the OKW or the OKH, were considering a war against the Soviet Union on the grounds of anticipating an imminent Soviet attack.[126]

If, however, one defines pre-emptive action as the consequence of an analysis of the situation in terms of geopolitics, strategy and security, then the German attack against the Soviet Union can certainly be considered, in the medium term, to have had a preventive function.[127] Soviet foreign policy since the summer of 1940, the unacceptable demands made by Molotov and, finally, the burgeoning Soviet-Yugoslav alliance, had created contradictions that could hardly be endured any longer. Even though this meant the temporary acceptance of a war on two fronts, the German attack was thus intended to prevent a threatening scenario which either entailed blackmail by Stalin, or even a war on two fronts in which the Soviet Union would have dictated the course of events. The alternatives, therefore, were: attack or submit.

To be precise: our present knowledge that the Wehrmacht most probably only anticipated the Red Army by a few weeks is based on a reconstruction of the actual events. The eastern campaign of 1941, therefore, can be described as a 'war of two aggressors', both of whom had simultaneously prepared themselves for an offensive, but not a preventive war in the traditional sense. This assessment does not in any way condone the offences committed against international law during the German-Soviet war, nor does it justify the ideology which was responsible for many war crimes. Any attempt to use the strategic motives and the subjective 'inevitability' of 'Operation Barbarossa' as a justification of war crimes would be reprehensible.

The claim that many proponents of a strategic and security-political assessment of the German-Soviet war in 1941 are merely playing down the National Socialist war aims, or attempting to exonerate or even vindicate the Third Reich, misses the point entirely.[128] These authors are accused of using the hypothesis of 'preventive war' to mitigate or relativize the war crimes committed by, or in the name of,

Germany. Such an accusation would only be valid, however, if the said author were attempting to offset the crimes committed by one side against those committed by the other – for example, the murder of prisoners of war – and to use the resulting numerical ratio as an exoneration of his own side.[129] Such a procedure would not only be an insult to the victims who suffered on both sides, it would also lead to a quantification of guilt – something that is completely at variance with the Western concept of legality. No serious author who is dealing with the political and strategic aspects of the 1941 campaign in the east would dare to make such a comparison. If, for example, it were proved that Stalin planned many conquests in pursuit of the world revolution, this would in no way mitigate Hitler's criminal actions.[130]

Further questions requiring examination are the role ideology played in the planning of the campaign and the extent to which it was a 'war of extermination'. It is hardly possible to weigh with accuracy the ideological motives behind the decision to attack,[131] but there is clear evidence that from the start of the confrontation with the Soviet Union in the summer of 1940, Hitler was motivated by the need to resolve the problem in the east in order to clear the way for the struggle against Great Britain and the United States. At key meetings with military leaders on 5 December 1940, on 9 January 1941 and again in his speech to the commanders of the future eastern armies on 30 March 1941, he stressed that the central issue was to eliminate the Soviet Union as Britain's 'continental sword'. In regard to this speech, Field Marshal von Bock, for example, noted in his diary: 'Constant threat to our back, constant Communist danger, possibility for England and America to build a new front against us in Russia...'[132] Even in his fundamental speech to the leaders of the Wehrmacht on 14 June 1941, in other words one week before the attack, Hitler was still pursuing the theme of the 'continental sword'. Only after removal of the threat to Germany's rear would she have a free hand militarily, and Britain would no longer have any hope of an ally on the continent.[133]

In contrast to this, the earliest statement by Hitler which reveals an ideological objective to the campaign in the east was made at the end of February 1941.[134] Attention must be directed to the notorious 'criminal orders',[135] consisting of the 'directive on jurisdiction' of 13 May and the 'commissar order' of 6 June 1941, as well as the racially motivated assignments of the so-called *Einsatzgruppen* of the SS, the Security Service and the police – task forces with the principal purpose of rounding up and killing Jews.[136] A further consideration is the involvement of members of the Wehrmacht in war crimes during the German-Soviet war. The reluctant collaboration by members of the army command in the drafting of the above-mentioned orders can be partly explained by their consideration that, given the minimal forces available to maintain military security within the vast territories to be occupied behind the front, and opposed, in all likelihood, by irregular enemy units, they would have to accept the support of SS and police formations, despite the crimes and acts of violence that these might be expected to commit.[137] But are such objectives, even if entailing breaches of international law, in themselves sufficient to be described in terms of a 'war of extermination'? It might be possible to crush divisions and armies, demolish homes and property, wipe out certain segments of the population, but there was no way of destroying a nation's *Weltanschauung*.

What, if anything, is the distinction between a so-called 'war of extermination' and any 'ordinary' war in which uncounted human beings, soldiers as well as civilians, are similarly killed and material possessions destroyed? Advocates of the theory of a 'racial-ideological war of extermination', even described on one occasion as an 'unique war of extermination',[138] summarize their arguments as follows: from his earliest days in politics, Hitler had consistently regarded the Soviet Union as the main ideological, racial and cultural enemy. The fight against this principal enemy, the conquest and exploitation of *Lebensraum* ('room to live') in the east, had been one of the key points in his 'step-by-step' racial-ideological programme, which had culminated, in 1941, in the ruthless execution of 'Operation Barbarossa', without the existence of any compelling political or strategic need. Furthermore, in an attempt at justification after the fact, Hitler and his henchmen had then invented the spurious argument of 'preventive war'.[139]

Whereas the above-mentioned 'criminal orders', and the commitment of other breaches of international law, did darken the scene of the war in the east and did lead to extremely vicious fighting on both sides, the campaign of 1941 primarily pursued the strategic objective of a rapid decision of the war in Europe. Nor did Hitler and his closest associates use the term 'war of extermination', as some authors would have us believe.[140] Regardless of any ideological motives, the German political leadership would hardly have decided to risk 'Operation Barbarossa' – the likely political success of which seemed very doubtful to many a senior commander and diplomat – if the issue had only been the pursuit of racial-ideological objectives, or the fight against Bolshevism as a *Weltanschauung*. The campaign in the east was therefore primarily fought in order to achieve victory against the Red Army and to free Germany's rear strategically, and not primarily to practise extermination in the conquered territories.

With regard to war aims, at the beginning of June, Field Marshal von Bock questioned whether 'this war can be won by force of arms alone?';[141] nothing short of an invasion of the island could deal Britain a vital blow. At the end of May, even Goebbels, normally brimming with confidence, had expressed his worries about the risks of war on two fronts that the planned campaign entailed, although he then quickly accepted Hitler's arguments as his own.[142] And finally, individuals like the future minister Rosenberg, State Secretary von Weizsäcker, leading military figures such as Raeder, Jodl and Warlimont, and even Göring, who was worried lest his Luftwaffe be over-taxed in the forthcoming war on two fronts, all expressed their concerns. Either they doubted the realistic possibility of a lasting political restructure of the Soviet Union or did not believe that military defeat of the Soviet Union would affect the outlook of Great Britain and the United States.[143]

What is open to criticism, in any case, is the assumption by many of the leaders that a victory for German arms would automatically be followed by a victory for German *Weltanschauung*. As already stated, before the campaign began, very few voices were raised in warning against the assumption that all that was required to being about the collapse of the enemy's political system was a series of few heavy defeats.[144] And if in statements made during the course of the war, the term '*Weltanschauungs* war' appears, this only discloses a major weakness, if not a fundamental mistake, by those politically responsible: on the one hand they were trying to justify mass acts of brutality that showed an utter contempt for humanity; on the other hand they were avoiding the admission that they had pinned their hopes on a military victory and had not given any thought to a political solution for the peoples of the Soviet Union, indeed that they were aiming at the exploitation of the conquered territories. Given such an objective, the fact that Germany made no attempt to convert the 'defeated' populace into 'liberated' subjects – and possibly even future allies – as quickly as possible has been the subject of many studies, but is only of marginal interest to our present discussion.[145]

Certain authors, in their attempts to disprove the validity of the political-strategic viewpoint, have advanced a variety of arguments, in particular the Soviet leadership's exaggerated need for security, and the relative weakness of the Red Army following the 'great purges' of 1937 and 1938. Furthermore, they have been accused either of ignoring the most recent research results, or of not giving them merited attention.[146] Quite apart from the political dimensions this controversy has assumed against the backdrop of the 'historians' controversy' of 1986, the issue here is to focus primarily upon Soviet documents and research results, which have come to light since the end of Gorbachev's term of office. We have no desire to renew a political argument which has been used since the 1950s to justify the German attack in 1941, and thereby to reject post-war Soviet demands against Germany, but to take recognition of the new facts and material presented since 1989–90.

Current historical research agrees that the General Staffs of major Western armies were of the opinion that, because of the drain in personnel Stalin had caused among the officer corps of the Red Army – the execution of approximately 60–70 per cent of the senior and top ranks – and among the leadership of the armaments industry, the Soviet armed forces had been 'decapitated',[147] and were thus incapable of waging a serious offensive war. The deficiencies and weaknesses that had become apparent during the Soviet-Finnish winter war of 1939–40 appeared to confirm this assessment. The historians, moreover, are unanimous in their opinion that this obvious underestimation of the Soviet armed forces was an important factor in the attack plans of the German military command.

In retrospect, however, this weakened condition of the Red Army does not imply that Stalin, Merezkov, Timoshenko and Zhukov were not envisaging an offensive war against Germany and had not made the appropriate preparations. Stalin evidently believed that he could even accept the liquidation of a large part of his officer corps, provided he could then rely upon the blind obedience of the survivors and the junior ranks. With hindsight, this appears a quite incredible, highly cynical calculation, which follows a cruel logic for the preservation of absolute power and rule. Yet even today the question of the guilt or innocence of leading officers has not been conclusively answered. We have, for example, the recent, albeit unsubstantiated, claim that Marshal Tukhachevsky was a member of the secret order of the 'Northern Light'.[148] In any case, the negative effects of liquidating or dismissing at least 27,000 officers by the autumn of 1938 on the morale and fighting power of the Red Army are attested, and were to play a major role during the initial phase of the German-Soviet war.[149]

The conduct of the Soviet political leadership after June 1940 leads to the conclusion that Stalin intended to use any weakness of the German Reich to extend the borders of the Soviet Union westward, and to exploit the unstable situation in the Balkans to build up a strong anti-German position there. A Soviet dictator who had an untroubled relationship with Germany, at least in his mind, would certainly have acted quite differently during this critical phase. From this viewpoint it appears naïve to claim that 'in the spring of 1941 the Soviet Union was still begging for permission to ally itself with Hitler'.[150] Even if the Soviet war effort was at first only partially and vaguely recognized by Germany, from the spring of 1941 the overall conduct of Soviet foreign and military policy was considered to be increasingly threatening. As early as March, Field Marshal von Bock was in possession of reports by agents according to which major Soviet manoeuvres that were being conducted in the Baltic were to be regarded as a secret deployment for an attack against Germany.[151] At the end of March 1941, Supreme Command of Army Group B, later Army Group Centre, even requested orders in case of a Soviet attack – although this was not judged to be highly probable – and the need to defend the frontier. In early April, Chief of Staff General Halder was not far wrong in his assessment of Soviet preparations for war when he wrote that 'the Russian deployment actually does permit a rapid shift to the attack, which could become very uncomfortable for us'.[152]

Even Moscow's exaggerated need for security could well have been served by preparing for a strictly strategic defence, for example along the Dvina–Beresina river sector. However, this was not happening. The decisive factors were the operational and organizational preparations in terms of personnel, logistics and armaments undertaken by the Soviet Union since July 1940, which culminated in a gigantic offensive-preventive deployment and which the Germans only recognized to their great surprise after the invasion of 22 June. The gigantic numbers of prisoners and weapons captured during the initial days and weeks of the offensive – the Soviet air force alone lost about 4600 aircraft by the end of June[153] – do not permit any other conclusion than that the Wehrmacht thrust right into the centre of an overpowering offensive deployment with armoured and motorized troops massed on the borders.[154]

Several remarks by Hitler in July and August 1941 express his consternation at the extent of Soviet military power that was now revealed. He is alleged to have emphasized several times that he would hardly have decided in favour of the campaign in the east had he been aware of the real strength and armament of the Red Army before the attack began. That the issue for Hitler and his closest advisers had not been an attack at any price may also be inferred from a conversation he had with Goebbels in mid-August. As Goebbels noted, had the Soviet military strength been known, Germany might 'actually have recoiled from attacking the now pressing question of the East and Bolshevism'.[155]

Because the full facts only became known to the German leaders after the invasion began, it is hard to explain the confrontation with the Soviet Union which began in the late summer and autumn of 1940, or to substantiate the theory of a preventive war in the classical sense. Based on current knowledge, however, it cannot be denied that the leadership in Moscow did nothing to alleviate the Germans' increasing suspicion that the Soviet Union would sooner or later pose a threat. The growing differences and the recognition that Germany would inevitably become dependent on Moscow for very survival if the war were to drag on interminably, brought about the maturation of plans to eliminate 'the sphinx in the East'. Simply to conclude from the subsequent failure of the campaign against the Soviet Union that this had been a 'decisive mistake of the war'[156] contributes little to explaining the roots and motives of the decision, because it implies that the validity of such a decision is to be measured solely by the yardstick of eventual success or failure.

To summarize: amid the 'tangle' of motives involved in German decision-making, the primary one was to eliminate a growing Soviet political and strategic threat. Removal of the British 'continental sword' in her rear would give Germany the freedom to create *Lebensraum* by conquest,[157] and to construct an impregnable continental empire, the all-important consideration of which was economic self-sufficiency. This fully concurs with Hitler's statement made several months after the highly successful beginning of the campaign: 'The struggle for the hegemony in the world will be decided for Europe by the possession of the Russian space. It makes Europe the one place in the world that is most impregnable to blockade.'[158]

In this sense, the campaign in the east was also a war of aggression and conquest, designed to destroy the enemy state and exploit the conquered territory. At the same time it would pave the way ideologically for a 'final accounting' with Bolshevism. The complexity of motives in the decision-making process reveals little of a 'step-by-step programme' or 'plan'. In any event, it was clear at the time that 'Operation Barbarossa' was not an end in itself, but only intended as a preliminary to a future showdown with the Western powers.

German Armaments Production
as the Outcome of Strategic Improvisation

The German victory in the west in June 1940, and the diplomatic and military attempts to induce Britain to give in, were accompanied by several endeavours to redirect the German armaments industry. This reveals the full extent to which further planning of the war was based on improvisation. As early as mid-June, when total victory over France was in sight, the basic decision was taken at Führer headquarters to reduce the Army to 120 divisions, while simultaneously doubling the number of armoured divisions. The logical consequence of an evaluation which regarded Great Britain as the only remaining enemy was the strengthening of the Luftwaffe and the Kriegsmarine. On 19 June Göring managed to seize the lion's share of armament resources for his branch of the Wehrmacht. On 20 June the first step to demobilization was initiated by the commander of the reserve army, while the basic directives by the chief of the OKW were issued on 25 June.[159]

The state of uncertainty which prevailed in armaments planning shortly after the French capitulation was sharply accentuated by the Führer directive of 16 July, because priorities in aerial and naval weaponry had to be adjusted as quickly as possible to the requirements of an amphibious landing in England. It must be stressed that in August and September, when officers of the OKW and OKH were already occupied with preparations for a campaign against the Soviet Union, 'Operation Sea Lion' still enjoyed the highest priority in armaments. The directive of 9 July, for example, set the figure for tank production at 380 per month, in accordance with the planned reduction of the Army. By this reckoning, the calculated total requirement of 26,700 tanks would only have been reached by 1946. And looking merely at the number of tanks required to double the existing armoured divisions to twenty, given the rate of production during the summer of 1940,[160] the objective would not have been reached before 1947.

It was the armaments directive by the OKW of 28 September which finally drew the conclusions from the cancellation of 'Operation Sea Lion' and the requirements facing the Army in a future war in the east. Production of tanks was realistically adjusted to only 1490 for the period up to 1 April 1941, which equated to a monthly figure of 213 and signalled the abandonment of the previous completely unrealistic planning objectives. In practical terms, this meant that most of the armoured divisions now disposed of only one tank regiment of two companies, a reduction to about 60 per cent of the previous number of tanks in a division; and even that could only be achieved in part by falling back on captured vehicles.[161] Despite this, on 21 November, Hitler agreed that the arms plans for the Luftwaffe and the Kriegsmarine must retain their high level of priority and should under no circumstances be reduced in favour of the impending armaments programme of the Army. As is obvious today, this led to rivalry between the priorities of the Army on the one hand and, on the other, those of the Luftwaffe and Kriegsmarine.

The leadership was clearly not prepared to assign top priority to the Army, despite its enormous requirements in arms and equipment for 'Operation Barbarossa'. The acceptance of such a high risk – in the short time-span until May 1941 it was already impossible to equip the Army to the desired extent – may be explained both by the confidence inspired by the results achieved so far, and by an under-estimation of the enemy. This again underlines the fact that the war against the Western powers was the real issue and the campaign against the Soviet Union only intended to bring about a preliminary decision. It shows, too, that from the beginning of hostilities in 1939, the Supreme Command did not have an all-encompassing war plan which could have served as the basis for a well-conceived and well-founded armaments programme.[162]

Germany's greatly restricted material and manpower potential also explains why the often misunderstood term 'Blitzkrieg' – which even Hitler rejected – can be envisaged merely as a temporary stopgap in the absence of an overall war policy. Many experts agree, that as far as arms production was concerned at the outbreak of war in 1939, the German Reich was neither prepared for the conflict against the Western powers, nor for a war of longer duration.[163] The term 'Blitzkrieg' was primarily used by Western journalists in order to gloss over the real reasons for the defeat of the French and British forces in the spring of 1940. As later understood, the concept of 'Blitzkrieg' applied to an amalgamation of elements of foreign policy, strategy, operations, war economy and social politics: it describes the leadership principle of deploying one's own strengths against the weaknesses of the enemy and concentrating the maximum military and arms capacity against a single enemy in the shortest possible time, in order thereby to achieve the preconditions for the defeat of the next enemy. The German generals, however, were to understand 'Blitzkrieg' primarily as being an operational war of mobility aimed at achieving a rapid decision in the field by means of deep penetrations, in particular through the cooperation of armoured and air forces, capitalizing on the element of surprise.[164]

In the early autumn of 1940, however, the German Supreme Command was faced with the dilemma of becoming involved in a war on two fronts resulting from the continuation of the war against Great Britain and the looming confrontation in the east, even if the latter was seen as an 'intermediate step', in other words as a quick victory. During the autumn and winter of 1940–1 several people at senior levels became increasingly aware of the risks entailed in the sectors of manpower, organization and armaments by preparing for the campaign in the east. The original plan, to demobilize as many army divisions as possible and immediately to transfer the manpower thus made available to the armaments industry, had to be given up at an early stage. Although during July and August 1940 at least seventeen divisions had been demobilized and another eighteen sent on leave, Hitler's precise demands at the end of September for a Army of 200 divisions – 140 infantry, 10 mountain troops, 20 armoured, 10 motorized, and 20 occupation divisions – plunged arms production into a dilemma. The release by the field army of a vital work force to the armaments industry at the very time when the expansion of the army was under way, illustrates the bottleneck in manpower: there was already a lack of 300,000 skilled workers, of which the armaments industry could only make up 150,000 during the autumn of 1940 because of the continuing establishment of new army formations.[165]

The consideration of temporarily releasing a large number of soldiers to the armaments industry from the field and reserve armies in order to produce the weapons they would need at the front in the spring of 1941 after the men had been called back into service, underlines the narrow confines within which such a 'Blitzkrieg' economy was operating. The policy could only succeed if the still not fully equipped army formations were able to achieve decisive victories as quickly as possible, and if the campaign did not involve any untoward losses in men and *matériel*. As regards manpower, the reserve army disposed of a total of 475,000 men as replacements for the field army and the Luftwaffe, which were only sufficient, however, to make up the losses expected up to September 1941.[166]

The raw materials situation, particularly the supply of fuel – the 'Achilles heel' of the war economy, so to speak – also caused considerable headaches. Once the campaign started, only oil from Romania and from domestic synthetic production would still be available. With a reserve of about 1.4 million tonnes at the end of 1940, the requirements of all three branches of the Wehrmacht could be met for approximately three months. This factor was to have a major influence on later operations.[167] Despite various improvisations, arms and munitions supply of the Army did not reach the originally planned figures. On 1 April 1941, the day set as the deadline, there were supply gaps of up to 35 per cent in the most important categories of weapons. In artillery alone, the paradoxical situation arose that in June 1941 the eastern army could only deploy 7184 guns of all calibres, whereas during the campaign in the west in 1940 there had been 7378 guns available on a considerably narrower front.[168]

Even if in certain sectors the Army was expanded and improved in quality, mainly by utilising weapons captured so far, it is still true to say that the eastern army in June 1941 was only slightly stronger and larger than the western army had been in the spring of 1940. The equipment of the eastern army verged on a condition that has been described as a 'patchwork quilt'.[169] This unsatisfactory situation can be explained by the fact that the Luftwaffe was not required to accept any reduction in its arms programme in favour of the Army, and only trailed the Army by ten per cent in its assignment of labour. The Führer directive of 20 December 1940 reaffirmed once again that the war against Britain was not to be restricted in any way by the arms programme of the Army. The extreme level of arming that was considered necessary for a victorious conclusion of the war against Britain can be gauged from a statement by General von Waldau to the Chief of Staff of the Army, when in early October 1940 he demanded a fourfold increase in the equipment of the Luftwaffe.[170]

It is clear that during the summer and autumn of 1940 armaments control did not follow an overall long-term plan, but was more a short-term improvisation designed to serve several strategic objectives. Furthermore, the confrontation with the Soviet Union did not lead to any clear concentration of arms on the Army in order to provide it with the power that might have brought about a rapid victory. This leads to the conclusion that the campaign against the Soviet Union did not occupy the central position – neither in overall planning, nor in armaments production – that it merited, given the requirements it demanded of the Wehrmacht. The campaign in the east was seen merely as an intermediate, albeit important, step designed to create the conditions for the 'final battle' in the west. The fluctuations in the strategic assessment of the situation, the rivalries between the three branches of the Wehrmacht, the over-estimation of German strength and the under-estimation of the capabilities of the future enemy, reveal the shaky ground on which the first major turn of the war was to appear.

The first 'fall from grace' in Germany's overall conduct of the war was most probably her omission to initiate a general mobilization of the armaments industry and of the entire economy no later than in the autumn of 1940. This decision would have required a stringent utilisation of all available female labour and all those measures to convert production and increase productivity that were only taken in the spring of 1943 under the impact of the catastrophe at Stalingrad.[171] The enormous challenges that would be posed for the Wehrmacht in a campaign against the Soviet Union which had been conceived as a Blitzkrieg should have induced the German leadership, as early as the autumn of 1940, to reject a system that was characterized by improvisation and compromise.

Results and Conclusions

Let us briefly turn at this point to an alternative concept already mentioned, which was primarily recommended by the command of the Kriegsmarine in 'competition', so to speak, to the campaign against the Soviet Union. It envisaged shifting the war from the direct conflict against Britain to an indirect conflict on the perimeter, namely the Mediterranean area. After the Chief of the Wehrmacht Operations Staff had already recommended on 30 June 1940 'to extend the war on the perimeter', shortly thereafter representatives of the Army, including Commander-in-Chief Field Marshal von Brauchitsch and Chief of Staff General Halder, also gave consideration to this promising alternative. Even General Guderian, the subsequent commander of Panzer Group 2, envisaged sending an armoured force to North Africa.[172]

It was Großadmiral Raeder, however, more than anyone else, who several times (on 26 September, for example) impressed upon Hitler the 'decisive importance' of an offensive against British positions in the Mediterranean. In his opinion, this would not be an 'intermediate action', but an encompassing alternative strategy against Britain. The military failure of the Italians in their attack upon Greece at the end of October 1940, and the heavy losses suffered by the Italian fleet as an outcome of the British attacks on the port of Taranto on 11–12 November, caused the idea of an effective support of Italy in North Africa and the eastern Mediterranean to resurface. General Halder, for example, envisaged the inclusion of Turkish territory in a pincer movement, which would be directed against Egypt and Syria, and for which two motorized corps would be deployed. But it was only further setbacks of the Italians in Albania, and the disastrous defeat of the Italian Tenth Army in Cyrenaica from 9 December on, that led to the decision of a limited support on land and in the air. The transfer of X *Fliegerkorps* (air corps) to Sicily and southern Italy, the preparation of an attack against Greece from Bulgaria ('Operation Marita'), and the decision of 9 January 1941 to send an 'interdictory armoured formation' to Tripoli, illustrate a 'secondary strategy' which was primarily designed as a peripheral defensive operation.[173]

The critical omission on the German side, however, was not to have shifted the temporary strategic focus to the Mediterranean in the summer of 1940, despite political opposition in Rome. Sending an expeditionary force of only a few armoured divisions and the appropriate air forces to North Africa and Sicily might not only have prevented the collapse of the Italian army in December 1940, but also offered an excellent chance of striking at British positions in North Africa and the Middle East. A rapid conquest of Malta would have been the key condition for command of the central Mediterranean. Promising options offered themselves – above all the capture of the Suez Canal and the gaining of the valuable oilwells in Iraq – which would have given the German war economy a decisive boost. The support given to the anti-British uprising in Iraq in May 1941, insufficiently prepared and conducted with minimal forces, can best be described as an improvisation.[174]

As already stressed, while such a strategy could not envisage a British defeat to decide the war, nevertheless the advantages of such an intermediate solution were self-evident: timely securement of the Axis's southern flank, prevention of a British military intervention in the Balkans, avoidance of a subsequent division of forces, access to valuable sources of oil, and the gaining of a geopolitical position that could have been important not only for a continuing war against Britain, but also for a possible attack on the Soviet Union in respect of the Caucasus. The strategy would have been conditional, however, on operations against British forces being successfully completed by the spring of 1941 in order to free the engaged forces for the campaign in the east – or for other assignments. With hindsight it appears that political-military developments in the Balkans from the spring of 1941 onward would have been far more favourable for Germany under such auspices, giving, for example, the decided advantage of an earlier date of attack than 22 June for the campaign against the Soviet Union.

While the Afrika Korps under Lieutenant General Rommel was subsequently able to deliver the British serious defeats after its deployment in mid-February 1941, the German leadership was not prepared to give substantial reinforcement to the Afrika Korps because of the priority and requirements of the campaign in the east. Germany was even unable to capitalize upon the outstanding position gained in early June 1941 after the victorious campaign in the Balkans and the capture of Crete, because of the imminent attack on the Soviet Union. The objective was rather to postpone the plans for the destruction of British positions in the Mediterranean and the Middle East until after 'Barbarossa'.[175]

The fact that the period from the summer of 1940 to the spring of 1941 was not used for a limited offensive in the Mediterranean, constitutes a 'virtual turn' of the war to the detriment of the Axis powers. This is not to suggest that they had missed the opportunity to decide the war against Britain, but that Germany embarked upon the decisive struggle with the Soviet Union under the burden of an uncleared southern flank and *a very late starting date*. If 'Operation Barbarossa' could not be quickly concluded, and if Great Britain shifted to the offensive in the Mediterranean, then a costly secondary theatre of war, with unforeseeable consequences, would develop. An attack by the Axis powers in the Mediterranean was not an alternative in the sense of deciding the war against Britain. Nor would it have contributed towards resolving the German-Soviet confrontation. But the failure to take any timely initiative in the Mediterranean during the period up to the spring of 1941 did mean an 'interim victory thrown away'.[176]

A summary of the key components of the first turn of the war points to the inextricable link between the German failure in the Battle of Britain and the confrontation with the Soviet Union. However, on the basis of Stalin's war aims, the military threat posed by the Soviet Union, even if not fully recognized by Germany, was in itself significant. So it is justifiable to conclude that the failure of the direct strategy against Great Britain and the potential threat by the Soviet Union each contributed in equal measure to the first turn in the war. Renunciation of a strategic 'intermediate step' in the Mediterranean, utilising the time interval up to the spring of 1941, proved an irrevocable handicap to Germany's subsequent conduct of the war.

II

PRELIMINARY DECISION:
THE TURN OF THE WAR
IN THE AUTUMN OF 1941

Relative Strengths, Initial Positions and Victory
in the First Phase of the Attack

When German artillery opened preparatory fire at dawn on 22 June, the door to uncertainty was thrown wide open. Based on numerous new insights, statements by prisoners, captured documents, radio surveillance and the tactical and operational reactions of the enemy, during the coming days and weeks the intelligence sections in the German staffs were to have their hands full correcting the previous perceptions of the Red Army. It was soon to become apparent that while the distribution and concentration of forces belonging to the 1st Strategic Line, up to a depth of about 300 km, had been more or less realistically assessed, the number of tanks, artillery, aircraft and other heavy equipment had been greatly under-estimated. According to current knowledge, the actual deployment on either side was as follows:[1]

Wehrmacht
Army
Army Group North: 26 divisions, 3 security divisions
Army Group Centre: 47 divisions, 1 reinforced regiment,
                       3 security divisions
Army Group South: 38 divisions, 1 brigade, 3 security divisions
OKH reserve: 24 infantry divisions, 2 armoured divisions,
                       1 mountain division, 1 motorized division,
                       1 motorized brigade
Total: 148 divisions, 2 brigades, 1 regiment
(including the security divisions and formations of the Waffen-SS)
Note: An additional 3 divisions and 1 SS brigade were deployed on the Finnish front.

Luftwaffe
Reconnaissance aircraft, single-engine fighters, twin-engine fighters, dive-bombers, bombers, including seven replacement groups in the reserve areas. (The first figure shows the number of aircraft listed, the second figure the number of operational aircraft.)

	Official strength	Operational
Luftflotte 5:	98	82
Luftflotte 1	540	431
(attached to Army Group North)		

	Official strength	Operational
Luftflotte 2	1,252	927
(attached to Army Group Centre)		
Luftflotte 4	772	610
(attached to Army Group South)		
C-inC Luftwaffe	51	32
TOTAL:	2713	2082
Transport aircraft	292	175
Less the seven replacement groups		
in the reserve areas	2510	1945

Red Army
Army

	Assigned	Deployed
Northern Front	21	21
(Leningrad Military District)		
North-western Front	23	25
(Baltic Military District)		(19 infantry, 4 armoured, 2 motorized)
Western Front	45	44
(Special Western Military District)		(24 infantry, 12 armoured, 6 motorized, 2 cavalry)
South-Western Front	122	80
(Special Kiev Military District)		
— in Special Kiev Military District		58
		(32 infantry, 16 armoured, 8 motorized, 2 cavalry)
— in Military District Odessa		
(later South Front)		22
		(13 infantry, 4 armoured, 3 motorized, 2 cavalry)
Total:	211	170

Assigned to General Headquarters Reserves: 47 divisions
Total assigned after completion of deployment: 303 divisions

Air Force
(In regiments of fighters, short-range bombers, fighter-bombers, long-range bombers, heavy bombers, long-range fighters, whereby

the strength of the regiments varied between 36 and 48 aircraft per regiment, split into 3 to 4 squadrons of 9 to 12 aircraft each):

Northern Front:	18 air regiments
North-western Front:	13 air regiments
Western Front:	21 air regiments
South-western Front:	91 air regiments
TOTAL:	143 (or 144) air regiments

General Headquarters reserves:	21 air regiments
Other air forces (including home defence):	53 air regiments
Grand Total:	217 (or 218) air regiments, equating to 9,100 front-line aircraft
In process of formation:	115 air regiments with approximately 4,800 front-line aircraft

On the front between the Baltic and the Black Sea, the Wehrmacht deployed 148 and ⅔ divisions, including the security divisions and the General Headquarters reserves deployed later on, 3580 tanks including 250 self-propelled guns, 7146 guns excluding infantry field pieces and mortars, and barely 2100 operational front-line aircraft of the Luftwaffe. Not counting the replacement formations in the reserve areas, the Luftwaffe disposed of only 1945 operational aircraft. It is noteworthy that compared to the size of the territory in question, the OKH only disposed of a modest reserve of 28 divisions, including two armoured divisions and one brigade, and that these formations were only thrown into the battle many weeks after the beginning of the war. Therefore at the outset the German eastern army went to war with no more than 120 and ⅔ divisions, a force that by no means provided the superiority in material and manpower that might be expected from an attacker. The total force deployed meant that on the eastern front including Finland, the Wehrmacht had committed – actively or in reserve – 73 per cent of the Army and 64 per cent of the Luftwaffe.

Based on contemporary knowledge, the picture on the Soviet side was as follows: the four, later five, western military districts disposed

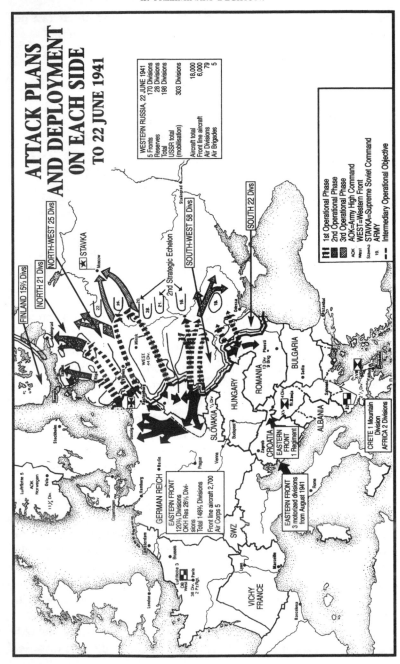

ATTACK PLANS AND DEPLOYMENT ON EACH SIDE TO 22 JUNE 1941

WESTERN RUSSIA, 22 JUNE 1941
5 Fronts   170 Divisions
Reserves   28 Divisions
Total   198 Divisions
USSR total
(mobilisation)   303 Divisions

Aircraft total   18,000
Front line aircraft   6,000
Air Divisions   79
Air Brigades   5

1st Operational Phase
2nd Operational Phase
3rd Operational Phase
AOK=Army High Command
WEST=Western Front
STAVKA=Supreme Soviet Command
ARMY
Intermediary Operational Objective

of 170 divisions plus two brigades of all categories, whereas a further 80 divisions were in the process of deployment or mobilization along the 2nd Strategic Line. The total number of tanks was 23,200, of which 15,000 were combat-ready. There were almost 116,000 guns and mortars of all types and calibres, of which 34,700 were deployed in the western military districts. Finally there were over 20,000 aircraft, including 9000 front-line aircraft available in European Russia, of which 13,300 were operational.[2]

According to the plans of Zhukov and his closest associate in the operational department of Supreme Headquarters, Major General A. M. Vassilevsky, the original intent had been to deploy 258 divisions for the offensive operations within the four, later five, western military districts. The total number of divisions available or to be mobilized at the start of the war was 303.[3] Support of ground operations was initially to be provided by 143 air regiments comprising 6000 front-line aircraft. From former Soviet statements it appears that at the time of the German attack the Red Army allegedly disposed of 198 infantry, 61 armoured and 31 motorized divisions, a total of 290, of which about 25 per cent were still in a state of replenishment and mobilization.[4] This number of 290 major formations is quite close to the claim of 303, thereby making the latter figure quite believable.

In fact, the commanders of the western military districts were able to count on a relatively rapid reinforcement by 28 divisions in addition to the 170 divisions deployed, because these forces were already in transshipment over the Dnieper and the Dvina. Part of them were destined as reinforcements for the 1st Strategic Line which according to the plan discussed above was to conduct the first massive offensive westward, but had to fight an unwilling defensive battle after the German attack. The 1st Strategic Line was to have comprised 186 divisions and to be reinforced by a further 51 divisions from General Headquarters' reserves, so that the total number of divisions deployed against the west would have come to 237. The remaining divisions making up the previously mentioned total of 303 were to be employed in securing the southern and eastern frontiers and several sectors of the coastline.[5]

The difference between the claim of 258 divisions, as compared to 237, that would have been available against Germany in European Russia, according to the plan of operations, can probably be explained as follows: the first number appears in the afore-mentioned *Considerations for the Strategic Deployment of the Armed Forces of the Soviet Union* of May 1941, the author or final editor of which was Major General Vassilevsky. The second number, however, probably stems from corrections to this document that were most likely made by Lieutenant General N. F. Vatutin, former First Deputy Chief of the General Staff, after 15 May 1941, when he revised the document in his capacity as the superior of the author. There are hand-written notes and corrections in the copy and on the margins which were made, for example, to correct mistakes in calculations in the original. Since 14 June 1941 has been mentioned as the deadline for the last deployment option,[6] it may be assumed that the General Staff incorporated the delays in deployment which had meanwhile occurred into the document. The numerous difficulties that arose as a result of the deployment of enormous masses of troops in the final weeks before the war began is evident from the fact that in June 77 divisions were still in transit to the western Soviet territories.[7]

In any event, in the four Soviet military districts there were at least 198 divisions actually present or available at short notice, against which the assault of the initial 120 German divisions was directed. Even taking into account the normally greater number of men in a German division and their greater combat power as compared to a Soviet division,[8] the fact remains that – calculated on the basis of the total extent of the front – there was a numerical equality, whereas in weapons and equipment there was a decided superiority on the Soviet side. These calculations do not take into consideration the armies of Germany's allies because of their greatly varying equipment and combat power.

Comparison of the actual deployment of forces with the calculations of the Intelligence Department of the German General Staff shows that whereas at the beginning of 1941 its assumption had still been 100 infantry and 25 cavalry divisions as well as 30 motorized or mechanized brigades,[9] immediately prior to the offensive it was estimating 226½ major formations in European Russia, which was quite close to actual fact. The force deployed in the four western military districts was assumed by the German General Staff to total 181 divisions and brigades,[10] which is also fairly near the 198 divisions mentioned above. A further document, entitled the *Operational Organization of the Red Army*, from the files of Colonel General Hoth, former commander of Panzer Group 3, lists Soviet forces on 1 June

1941. According to this the Soviets disposed of 189 major formations, including 36 motorized brigades, in the areas bordering on Germany, Hungary and Romania.[11] If one compares the Soviet deployment as it was entered on contemporary German maps with the currently available Soviet documents, this was more or less accurate for a depth of about 300 km. Despite much subsequent criticism, as far as Soviet forces of the 1st Strategic Line close to the border were concerned, the General Staff of the Army had performed quite well despite many inadequacies in the gathering and evaluation of intelligence.

Nevertheless, serious deficiencies in the assessment of the enemy situation lay in the fact, for example, that the forces beyond the depth of 300 km had hardly been reconnoitred at all, that there was hardly any information on the restructuring into armoured divisions and corps (mechanized corps),[12] that not all of the armoured corps deployed close to the front, eleven in all, had been identified, and that strategic reserves and armaments capacity had generally been under-estimated. These deficiencies were mainly due to the highly inadequate and unreliable gathering of information within the Soviet Union, which protected itself against attempts at espionage by an extremely elaborate and hardly penetrable security network. This under-estimation of the enemy also explains the widely held belief that the campaign would be victoriously concluded within a few short months and no later than by mid-October. It was only in August that General Halder admitted to himself that the Red Army had been greatly under-estimated, having already had to note down 360 (!) identified major formations instead of the 200 originally assumed.[13]

Without wishing to anticipate, it should be added that by 1 December 1941, and despite the immense losses of territory and population incurred by then, the Red Army was able to mobilize anew 177 infantry and 54 armoured divisions as well as nine armoured brigades. The enormous efforts made, especially after the beginning of secret mobilization in February 1941 which envisaged the provision of nine million men and 37,800 tanks, can only be explained if one realizes that the mobilization of 303 divisions approved in May 1941 was merely an intermediate objective which could, if necessary, be exceeded. Only one week after the beginning of hostilities, the Soviet High Command was even able to set in march seven armies from its strategic reserve in the 2nd Strategic Line and despatch them to the most threatened sectors of the central front.[14] Considering the results achieved later in the area of replacement, one can safely assume that in the summer of 1941 the Red Army had the potential to set up about 350 infantry and 65 armoured divisions.[15]

We must now examine the consequences that the relatively late start of the campaign had on its course and on the turn of the war before Moscow in December 1941. As Hitler said later in a statement to Martin Bormann in February 1945, the postponement of 'Operation Barbarossa', due to the effects of the campaign in the Balkans, had robbed him of the fruits of success in 1941: 'Without the Italians and the problems they caused with their idiotic campaign in Greece, I would in fact have attacked the Russians several weeks earlier.'[16] However, the facts hardly warrant this analysis of cause and effect. It was not 'Operation Marita', i.e. the German supporting offensive against Greece from Bulgaria, which caused the delay, but the extension of the operation against Yugoslavia and Crete, which led to an improvised reallocation of German forces in southern Europe, with many logistic disadvantages.

The delays caused by bringing back the formations employed in the Balkans and Crete were, in fact, not serious enough to prevent the deployment of the eastern armies being more or less completed by 10 June 1941. Furthermore, the option existed to assign the few units still in transshipment to the strategic reserve and to begin the campaign in the east no later than mid-June without waiting for these units to reach the areas to which they had been allocated. Nevertheless, the fact that not all of the forces consigned for deployment in Romania were able to arrive in time created an awkward handicap for the 'Barbarossa' plan. In the end, with only seven divisions available there for the Eleventh Army, Army Group South had to forgo an encirclement from Romania of the Soviet forces in the western Ukraine and make do with a 'one-armed' attack from southern Poland. Because of the changed situation the OKH also had to cancel the deployment of an armoured corps in Romania, but although the attack in the sector of Army Group South was thereby 'diluted',[17] this was not in any way decisive for the outcome of the campaign.

After Hitler had agreed to the projected continuation of the preparations on 6 June and simultaneously confirmed 22 June as the date for the attack, deployment was completed according to plan. There were no perceptible indications that the OKH was urging an earlier start of the campaign in order to achieve a victorious conclusion before the onset of the period of autumn mud in early October. Nor were any warning voices raised in the General Staff against the conquest of Crete on the grounds of time pressure, even though this was only completed on 1 June. What mitigated against a theoretical invasion date at the end of May or in early June was the fact that many rivers in the western Soviet Union which would have to be crossed in the course of the attack, including the Bug and the Narev, were still in flood until well into June and would therefore have presented a very disagreeable obstruction.[18] For this reason alone, an attack after 10 June appeared to be the only realistic possibility.

On the other hand, such a time advantage of about ten to twelve days could have been of decisive importance for the war, because this was roughly the time that would have been needed for a victorious completion of the general offensive against Moscow the following autumn. As will appear later, when the German offensive began on 2 October, there were only ten to twelve days available before the attack 'drowned' hopelessly in the mud and rain-drenched ground. At this stage, Moscow lay only two days' march ahead of the spearheads. One can only speculate as to what might have happened if the final German attack had been launched no later than 22 September rather than 2 October.

Shortly after 3 a.m. the German attack of 22 June struck at an enemy who, tactically and to some extent operationally, was taken by surprise. However, this was true only of the Soviet armies in a very limited sense and not to the fronts. Through informers, Stalin had known about the German attack plan 'Barbarossa' – Directive No. 21 – since the end of 1941. In Moscow, Chief of the General Staff, Zhukov, and Chief of Military Intelligence, Lieutenant General Golikov, had attempted several times during the preceding months to convince Stalin of the dangers of a German attack, grossly exaggerating the threat posed by the Wehrmacht – as many well-known authors have done ever since.[19] A total of 84 warnings from at home and abroad had allegedly come to Stalin's ears since June 1940. By decoding German signals, the British had uncovered 'Operation Barbarossa' at least two months before the date of the attack.[20] Stalin's only reaction had been a strict order to the General Staff to avoid any provocation of the Germans at all cost. One consequence of this was that in the end only 'rosy red' reports about the presumed enemy were passed on to Stalin.[21]

All of this was in line with the logic of the Soviet offensive planning described above. A force of 13 armies and roughly 3.1 million men in the western areas – North-west, West and South-west Fronts – could only stage an effective defence if it were to evacuate salients in the front line, pull back the valuable armoured corps, deploy them in depth for counter-attacks, and station the bulk of the troops behind natural barriers in such a way as to prevent, if possible, a breakthrough by the German spearheads. The 'Stalin Line', behind the former Soviet-Polish border, or a line along the Beresina and lower Dniester, would both have served as important defences. The former, well camouflaged, had thirteen 'fortified' sectors to depths of 30–50 km.[22] A change-over to such a system of defence would still have been possible in the spring of 1941. But since Stalin did not want to take up defensive positions, which would have meant renouncing any strategic offensive action, all he could do now was to leave the troops in their present areas, speed up offensive deployment and play for time.

Papers from Zhukov's estate confirm that the attack by the Wehrmacht itself was not a surprise for the Soviet Chief of Staff, because he had more or less accurate information about its preparations. The claim that he had been surprised by the Wehrmacht's 'power of attack' must therefore be seen as a belated excuse. What may be conceded is that his information about the extent of the forces concentrated in the breakthrough areas was not up-to-date at the time immediately preceding the attack. However, if 22 June came as a shock for Stalin – as reliable witnesses attest – then this was not due to his having lost all the sense of reality, as is often claimed, but because he had miscalculated his timing. It meant admitting that his game of playing for time against Berlin had failed. Shortly before the fighting began, his perplexity culminated in the question: 'Why are we always late?'[23]

In the ensuing days and weeks, the German operational war of movement achieved its greatest and most impressive successes to date. By mid-July the three army groups had gained positions that brought a victorious continuation of the campaign within their grasp. In the north Panzer Group 4 had won several bridgeheads over the River Luga and thereby gained the 'gateway to Leningrad'. In the centre, after the capture of Smolensk on 16 July, Army Group Centre held a deeply extended salient, the tip of which was only 310 km from Moscow. By early August it was able to encircle and capture a large part of the enemy forces in the battle of Smolensk. In the south the spearheads had reached the approaches to Kiev by mid-July, while Army Group South was on the verge of encircling the mass of the opposing forces on the lower Bug.

The fact that in the centre there had been three Soviet mechanized corps deployed in exposed positions in a salient had proved an advantage for the attacker, because already in the initial phase these forces had been encircled and almost completely annihilated. The double battle of Minsk–Bialystok alone had cost the defenders 320,000 prisoners and 3300 tanks. In the subsequent battle of Smolensk the Red Army had lost a further 310,000 captured, 3200 tanks and vast quantities of other material by 5 August. The higher German staffs were frequently nonplussed by the huge amounts of weapons destroyed and captured. It was only in the final phase of the war in 1944–5 that they were able realistically to assess the number of Soviet tanks available at the beginning of the offensive – just under 22,000 – but by that time this information was only of statistical value.[24] As for losses in killed and wounded, at the beginning these were numerically much higher than those captured, but were more or less on a par by the end of the year. The Soviet air force also suffered such heavy losses during the initial weeks of the war that it was no longer a serious opponent for quite some time to come. By 12 July the Soviet Union had lost over 6800 aircraft, as compared to only 550 totally destroyed and 336 damaged aircraft on the German side.[25]

The fact that Army Group Centre took a breather after the battle of Smolensk was not so much due to increasing resistance by the Soviet forces as to the need to spend several weeks replenishing, resupplying and reorganizing the formations and bringing them back up to strength. After all, the supply depots had to be moved east over the Dnieper and the Dvina. It is therefore a gross distortion of the facts to claim that the energetic Soviet defence east of Smolensk had dealt the Germans a defeat and thereby prevented their immediate further advance on Moscow.[26] Even if resistance by the Red Army had diminished after the battle of Smolensk, the German troops would have required a break of about three weeks for replenishment and supply, particularly in order to increase the offensive power of the weakened armoured formations. Such a break had already been foreseen in the basic plan of operations and would have occurred in any case in order to prepare the manpower and logistic requirements for the 'final attack' on Moscow.

In its unparalleled drive to victory up to the end of July, the Wehrmacht had, in any event, achieved the preconditions for a successful continuation of the campaign. In detail this meant: in the north the capture of Leningrad and union with the Finnish army; in the centre the destruction of the armies deployed for the defence of Moscow and the capture of the capital; in the south the rapid crossing of the Dnieper below Kiev with a subsequent advance into the eastern Ukraine and the Donetz basin. There was still enough time to attain these objectives.

The Question of the 'Major Blunders' in July and August 1941

With all due respect for Soviet resistance and defence efforts, which reached an extreme on 10 July with the measures taken to create partisan forces, greater importance must be attached to the deceptive belief in Germany that the battle had already been won. From the early weeks of the campaign, this feeling of euphoria contributed to the continued under-estimation of enemy strength. Even more serious was the failure of the German leadership to take timely decisions. The opportunity was therefore missed to convert the extraordinary initial successes into factors that could have been decisive for the outcome of the war.

Without examining in detail all the operational problems, it is appropriate to draw attention to the following negative decisions. In the north, by stopping Panzer Group 4 in the bridgeheads on the River Luga, the OKH missed the chance of the early capture of Leningrad which was well within the realm of possibility up to the beginning of August.[27] In early August, Army Group Centre failed to clear its northern and southern flanks rapidly enough to disperse the strong Soviet forces which threatened to become a serious disruptive factor for the continuation of the advance on Moscow. In the south a quick attack on Kiev in mid-July was not undertaken; even more seriously, Army Group South, after its victory in the battle of Uman in early August, lost precious time in the pursuit of the defeated enemy without gaining the important crossings over the Dnieper.[28] The three army groups had thus let slip critically important operational advantages, partly for lack of sufficient forces, partly from fear of the risks, but also because of operational concepts that differed from those of the OKH.

Had the OKH shown courage and vision, German armies could have taken full advantage of their opportunities, capturing Leningrad and Kiev, and establishing deep bridgeheads on the lower Dnieper by no later than mid-August. It would have been quite impossible for the Soviets to make Leningrad the centre of a bitter resistance in the north, to tie down the inner flanks of Army Groups Centre and South on the eastern edge of the Pripet marshes, or to prepare an extensive defence on the Dnieper. With the fall of Leningrad and the link-up with the Finns, Army Group North would have gained operational freedom south-eastward, in other words for a massive support of the main attack against Moscow. Under these circumstances, Army Group Centre would have found it far easier to prepare the conditions for the attack on Moscow in time, and Army Group South would – with or without the subsequent battle of Kiev – have been in the position to support the attack on Moscow from the south far sooner.

Even if Field Marshal von Bock, Commander-in-Chief of Army Group Centre, had clearly recognized by early August that the precondition for any further advance towards Moscow was the elimination of the enemy on the rear flanks of his army group,[29] this task could only have been completed with the utmost effort and with no secondary diversions, particularly any actions in support of Army Group South. Even much later, von Bock still believed himself capable of achieving the conditions for the decisive attack on Moscow with his own forces, and only began to clear the northern flank of his army group very late in the day. With hindsight it is clear that until well into August all three army groups were primarily concerned with the pursuit of their own operational objectives and that the OKH did very little to achieve the original basic strategic objective, namely to solve the 'northern problem' *before* launching the attack on Moscow. Obviously the Chief of Staff believed that it was not yet necessary to set priorities, to initiate an overall coordination of the three army groups in pursuit of an overriding strategic objective. Army Groups North and South were therefore not in a position to cover the flanks of the advance on Moscow, or at least to attempt to support it.[30]

The frequently criticized Führer Directives Nos 33, 33a and 34, including amendments, that were issued from 19 July 1941, are not merely examples of Hitler's interference in the operational leadership, and accepted by the General Staff only with great reluctance, but also reactions by the Supreme Command to the unsolved strategic-operational problems as they appeared at the end of the first phase of the campaign. Hitler's insistence on a rapid capture or at least investment of Leningrad, and an active cooperation of the inner flanks of Army Groups Centre and South, cannot merely be attributed to his pursuit of military-economic objectives such as the Ukraine and the Donetz basin. An equally strong motive was his desire to adhere to the original plan which had put the capture of Leningrad and the clearing of the northern flank ahead of other objectives, such as the destruction of the final enemy reserves in front of Moscow.[31]

Hitler's decision of 21 August to invest Leningrad and to destroy the bulk of the Soviet armies in the south between the inner flanks of Army Groups Centre and South by means of concentric attacks[32] – which was only accepted by the OKH after much controversy – has generally been attributed to his one-sided preoccupation with ideological and economic objectives. In fact, as will be assessed in due course, it was primarily the logical consequence of the unsatisfactory overall situation on the eastern front, considering the advanced time of year. Superficially there was a contradiction between the objectives, on the one hand, of destroying the enemy's living power and, on the other, of capturing his base of raw materials and food supply. More important, however, is the question as to whether the situation in mid-August was conducive to an immediate offensive against Moscow, or more precisely, whether there was still time to create the conditions for such a decisive attack.

As German and Soviet experts mostly agree, the tying down of the German forces on the inner flanks of Army Groups Centre and South reached such a pitch that neither of the two army groups could pursue their more far-reaching aims without first jointly removing this threat to their flanks. The subsequent highly successful battle of Kiev, lasting until 26 September 1941, was therefore the result of an operational need to lay the foundations for further offensive actions. Furthermore, the controversy between Hitler and the OKH in August 1941 not only uncovered errors in the evaluation of the enemy, but also mistakes in operational planning.[33] In the light of the subsequent course of the campaign, it is highly questionable whether there was any chance of success for Colonel General Halder's plan to advance on Moscow in mid-August against a still unbroken enemy, knowing that the northern and southern flanks of Army Group Centre were unprotected, and without any strategic reserves.[34] The controversial directives of July and August 1941 cannot, therefore, actually be described as blunders. More to the point was the belated admission of the fact that mistaken assessments of the enemy's potential strength had remained uncorrected, and that controversies about the operational deployment of forces, which had already become evident in the planning phase, had not been resolved in time.

Of far graver consequence on the strategic level than the tug-of-war between Hitler and the leaders of the OKH as to which of the alternatives for the continuation of the campaign in the east promised the greater chance of success, was Hitler's directive of 14 July.[35] Dealing with the reorganization of the Wehrmacht in manpower and equipment, it was issued in expectation of a rapid victory over the Soviet Union. After a reduction of the size of the Army, the Kriegsmarine was to increase its armament according to the needs of a war against Britain and the USA, while priority was clearly given to the Luftwaffe, which was to quadruple its strength. The Army, on the other hand, was to reduce its supply of arms and ammunition to a six-months requirement – an indication that victory on the eastern front was considered imminent.

This general intention to redirect armaments was a sequel to the basic intent of Directive No. 32 of 11 June 1941, which – on the assumption of a speedy destruction of the Soviet forces – had planned a shift of arms production to the Luftwaffe and the Kriegsmarine and the intensification of the war against British positions in the Mediterranean and the Middle East. Führer Directive of 20 June 1941, a mere two days before 'Barbarossa' began, had also decreed a reduction of weaponry to the Army in favour of the so-called 'Göring

Programme'. In view of the superior Anglo-American armament in the air, Field Marshal Milch, at the end of June, had demanded as a first objective 'the doubling of bombers by 1200 machines', with one-third of the production to be moved to the as yet unconquered Russian territories.[36]

Even though the command of the Army, particularly the Chief of Armaments, warned about a permanent loss of production capacity to the disadvantage of the Army in case such a shift were to take place, recommendations for the reduction of weapons and ammunition for the Army were soon drawn up. It was tacitly assumed that the war in the east would soon be concluded victoriously. However, another reason for the redirection of arms production also lay in the realization that the German war economy would be hopelessly over-taxed if the Army and the Luftwaffe continued to be treated on equal terms. In a discussion on 16 August between the chief of the OKW and leading representatives of the three branches of the Wehrmacht concerning the execution of the armaments directives, the point was again made that in the concluding battles the Wehrmacht need no longer reckon with 'any serious opponent'.[37] That in mid-July the OKH also considered the war in the east to be more or less won can be seen from the plan of 15 July to restructure the Army after the 'conclusion of Barbarossa', whereby the intention was to end up with six armies comprising 56 divisions, including twelve armoured divisions, as an occupation force in the captured eastern territories. Furthermore, on the same day, the General Staff planned a reduction of the Army from 209 major formations to 175, including security divisions. On the other hand, the number of armoured divisions was to be increased from 21 to 36 and that of motorized divisions from 14 to 18,[38] a measure that would equally have over-taxed armament capacities.

A revealing incidental detail is that Hitler did not agree to a substantial reinforcement of the armoured forces on the eastern front despite the high losses in tanks and self-propelled guns which – depending on the burdens that had been placed on the division in question – had reached 40–50 per cent of original complement by mid-July. Apart from a modest resupply, most of the newly produced tanks were used to set up the 22nd, 23rd and 24th Panzer Divisions which were earmarked for use in North Africa and the Middle East after the conclusion of 'Barbarossa'. Furthermore, Hitler would not, for the time being, release the 2nd and 5th Panzer Divisions belonging to the OKH reserve for combat, because they were to serve as the nucleus for the creation of a new Panzer army.

These measures, as well as Hitler's policy statement of 16 July on the exploitation and securing of the occupied eastern territories, and also his decree of 17 July in connection with the 'General Plan East',[39] all lead to the conclusion that at this juncture the German leadership already regarded the war in the east as having been won. Thus the time appeared to have arrived to initiate the policies relating to economic and racial objectives. But the basic consideration was to prepare as quickly as possible for the war against the USA and Great Britain. The fact that American troops occupied Iceland on 7 July may have influenced Hitler's offer to the Japanese Ambassador on 14 July of a comprehensive offensive alliance that was directed firstly against the USA and secondly against the Soviet Union. The fact that Hitler was no longer urging Japan to make a rapid entry into the war against the Soviet Union, as Ribbentrop had done shortly before, leads to the conclusion that Hitler considered the need of the immediate future to be the possible confrontation with the United States and Great Britain, and was no longer prepared to await the outcome of the campaign in the east.

In retrospect, the secret decision of the Imperial Conference in Tokyo on 2 July to renounce – against the advice of the Foreign Ministry – any military activities against the Soviet Union, and instead pursue Japanese interests in south-east Asia as war objectives, may be regarded as a major blunder, even as a 'virtual turn' of the war. But the German leadership judged the military situation to be so encouraging that it believed it could carry the day without an intervention by Japan against the Soviet Union in the Far East. This seems to be the sole reason why Hitler, Ribbentrop and the OKH did not urge as rapid and as massive an intervention as possible by the Japanese army in eastern Asia at the very outset of the war in the east.[40] In any event, in the decisions taken in mid-July 1941 relating to strategy, occupation policy and armaments production were of far greater import and consequence than the controversy over the continuation of the campaign on the eastern front.

During that same period, when victory for the Wehrmacht in the east appeared still to hold out the possibility of a triumphant German conclusion to the campaign in 1941, the United States and Great

Britain gave notice of their intentions, on 14 August, by signing the Atlantic Charter.[41] This declaration of principles, which had previously been agreed between Roosevelt and Churchill on board the battleship *Prince of Wales*, cemented, to all intents and purposes, the 'Anti-Hitler Coalition', even if a formal alliance between the Western powers and the Soviet Union had not yet been concluded and Stalin still regarded the conduct of his allies-to-be with some mistrust. While the Anglo-Soviet aid agreement of 12 July restricted London's contribution to the delivery of war materials, effective support – for example by the opening of a second front which was soon to be demanded – still lay far in the future. By the end of 1941 only eight British convoys with 55 cargo ships reached the north Russian ports through which virtually all of the supplies to the Soviet Union were channelled.[42]

Ever since the conclusion of the German-Soviet Pact of 28 August 1939, Roosevelt's policies – the importance of which for the formation of the war coalition has been mostly underrated – had been guided by a cautious response to those who called for drastic measures against both Germany and the Soviet Union, regardless of their different positions. Via the American Embassy in Moscow, which had made use of a German informer, Roosevelt received information about the salient points of the pact immediately after it had been signed.[43] He was convinced that the pact would fall apart because of its inner tensions and that if this happened the Soviet Union would have to be offered an alternative option. After the war began, Roosevelt's policy was designed to make the Soviet leadership understand, in a low-key but clear manner, that the door for an arrangement was being kept open. In addition, important members of the State Department were in favour of encouraging the outbreak of a German-Soviet war in order to draw the Wehrmacht away from western Europe to the east.[44]

After 1 September 1939 Roosevelt took great pains to promote the Soviet Union, in the eyes of the Western world, as a 'peace-loving' nation and not an 'imperialistic' power. He tacitly accepted the annexation of the Baltic States and parts of Poland and Romania by the Soviet Union, did nothing to halt the Soviet attack on Finland at the end of November 1939, and in late winter of 1941 even warned the Soviet dictator about a likely German attack after the contents of Directive No. 21 ('Barbarossa') of 18 December 1940 had been conveyed to him by a member of the American Embassy in Berlin immediately after it had been issued.[45] Furthermore, the clauses of the Lend-Lease Act of 11 March 1941 had been worded in such a way that the president could also extend the bill to include the Soviet Union should the need arise. By the end of the war in 1945, the Soviet Union had received from the United States 18,700 aircraft, 10,800 tanks, 9600 guns and a total of over ten million tonnes of supplies.

Roosevelt was sufficiently well informed about the German preparations for the attack as well as the German General Staff's assessment of Soviet strength. Furthermore, from the autumn of 1940 on, an improvement in diplomatic relations between Washington and Moscow can be noted. It is safe to assume that Roosevelt proceeded on the assumption of a German-Soviet war in the foreseeable future, that he strongly furthered this development and that he based his decisions on the advent of such a war.[46]

After the start of the German offensive against the Soviet Union, Roosevelt received valuable support from Joseph E. Davies, the former American ambassador in Moscow, who was considered to be a great admirer of Stalin and who had attempted to justify the actions by the courts and the state security service during the mass purges and show trials of 1936–8.[47] In contrast to the General Staffs of other nations, Davies did not believe that the combat power of the Red Army had been weakened by the purges and had come out in favour of political cooperation between the Western powers and the Soviet Union even before the war began. In early July 1941 he presented Roosevelt with a memorandum which stated that the resistance displayed by the Red Army rendered the likelihood of a rapid German victory improbable, so that Hitler would possibly be content with the occupation of large and economically valuable territories. German possession of vital sources of raw materials would then enable them to resist a Western sea blockade and to continue the war indefinitely.

On the other hand, much would depend on Stalin's ability to retain power and avoid a possible attempt at revolution. He might also seize the opportunity to make peace with the Germans, after which the Soviet Union would quit the war and Germany would be relieved of its highly dangerous pressure from two fronts. Under no circumstances should Stalin be made to believe that he would be burdened with the major weight of the fight against the Axis powers.

The memorandum ended with the recommendation to give quick and massive support to the Soviet Union before Stalin was overthrown or made a separate peace with Berlin.[48]

The assessments by the American and British General Staffs were markedly more pessimistic. Based among other things on the evaluation of Soviet failures during the Finnish winter war of 1939–40, they concluded that the Red Army would be able to resist the Wehrmacht for no longer than one to two months. American military experts were in general agreement with the judgment of their British colleagues, who expected a German victory within no more than eight weeks.[49] Why make strenuous efforts to support an army which was likely to collapse in the near future?

Despite this, and the catastrophic situation of the Soviet Union, Roosevelt and Churchill clung in principle to their course of supporting Stalin, seized the initiative in attempting to form an alliance, and thereby created the foundation for a combination in which the United States, as the leading industrial and economic power in the world, was able to capitalize on its advantages: towards Great Britain, which was increasingly pushed into the role of 'junior partner', and towards the Soviet Union, which had reason to fear that without American and British support, it could not successfully survive the war. Stalin's tacit dependence was to become the basis for Soviet manoeuvres and trials of strength between the Allies, which were finally to culminate in the Cold War.

It would be a gross exaggeration, however, to claim that the long-term policies of the United States were not aimed at preventing a Soviet defeat[50] and that the British government sought refuge in excuses in order to avoid any effective military aid. Equally unwarranted is the claim that in the autumn of 1941 Washington and London had already almost 'written off' the Soviet Union, and that it would have been possible at the end of 1941 for the failure of the German offensive to have been turned into a total defeat for Germany in a relatively short time if all the partners had made the maximum effort.[51] In fact, in the summer and autumn of 1941, and independently of Western promises of aid, the question of whether a final military collapse could be prevented before such aid arrived had to be resolved solely by the Soviet Union.

Between July and September 1941 the American president took measures that already went beyond the limits of 'non-belligerence' and which attempted to engage the Soviet Union as a coalition partner for the overall war. Stalin's appeal for help in his 'deadly danger' on 5 September – the battle in the Kiev area was in full swing – clearly demonstrated his desire for aid from the West, but also the impossibility of a rapid fulfilment of his needs. The declaration of the Atlantic Charter had already aroused Stalin's dissatisfaction, because he felt that he had been ignored in this matter and therefore was only ready to agree to the terms of the Charter during the Allied conference in London on 24 September. However, he then announced grave reservations as to its application, which must cast doubt on his serious intention to respect the 'sovereign rights of nations'. In light of the desperate situation of the Soviet Union and the 'wafer-thin' chances for survival which still remained to him,[52] his stance towards the Western powers appears to be almost self-destructive.

The Soviet Union on the Brink of Collapse: Battle on Two Fronts

STAVKA (Soviet Supreme Military Command) Order No. 270 of 16 August 1941, which was only published by Moscow a few years ago,[53] documents how dangerous the military defeats and losses since the beginning of the campaign had meanwhile become for the Soviet Union. Whereas the order, which blatantly glorifies resistance to date, begins by pointing to the exemplary conduct of a few commanders and formations, it then goes on to condemn sharply the 'inadmissible clumsiness' and 'despicable cowardice' displayed by many commanders and officers to whom the major blame for the defeats is then attributed:

> Can cowards who go over to the enemy and give themselves up, or such commanders, who at the first sign of difficulties at the front, tear off their insignia of rank and desert to the rearward areas, be tolerated in the ranks of the Red Army? No, that is impossible... Cowards and deserters must be destroyed.[54]

The order then decrees that all commanders and political officers who make any attempt during combat to throw off their insignia and give themselves up are to be considered to be deserters, and that their next of kin are to be arrested as 'families of perjurers and treacherous deserters'. All senior commanders and commissars are required to have such deserters 'shot out of hand'. Stalin had thus quite simply introduced the concept of guilt by association. The order goes on to say that any formation or unit that became encircled was required to continue to fight as long as possible, and then to make its way back to friendly lines through the territory held by the enemy. If the situation were to arise that a commander or a unit refused to continue resistance and signify that it intended to go into captivity, then other members of the military had the right and the duty to destroy this commander or unit with 'all available forces on the ground and in the air'. Finally, the order also decrees that commanders of divisions and divisional commissars are required to relieve, demote or even shoot subordinate commanders of regiments or battalions who have shown cowardice in battle or neglected their duties as officers. It should be added that even army commanders, for example Lieutenant General V. J. Katshalov of the Twenty-eighth Army, were stigmatized as deserters and traitors according to a directive from headquarters issued on 12 May 1943 as an extension of this order. It was only many years after the end of the war that hearings were held and victims rehabilitated, and Katshalov was found to have been killed in action.

Stalin's inhumanity towards his soldiers and officers reveals not only a panicky fear of an ultimate breakdown of morale and therefore the collapse of all resistance, but also the desperate bid to put a final end to the mass surrenders by Soviet soldiers. The number of Soviet soldiers who had been captured or had gone over to the Germans had increased to such a level during the first two months of the war as to cause fear of an irreplaceable drain being put on the Red Army. It was also feared that by playing on nationalistic and anti-Bolshevist feelings, the Germans would be able to raise combat units from among their mass of prisoners who would be able to render them inestimable military and political services. Stalin's hostile and pitiless attitude towards all Soviet soldiers who had preferred captivity to death on the battlefield also explains his refusal to accord soldiers who had fallen into German hands the status of prisoners-of-war. According to official doctrine, there were no such prisoners. Even though the Soviet government officially informed Sweden on

17 July 1941 that it was formally prepared to observe the Hague Convention of 1907, in actual practice the respective articles, for example the exchange of lists of prisoners-of-war, were completely ignored.[56]

By the end of the year the number of Soviet prisoners had risen to 3.3 million men and was even to rise to 3.6 million by 1 April 1942.[57] Their care caused enormous problems for the Germans, but from the viewpoint of the Soviet Supreme Command, it offered the Germans unimaginable opportunities. Many people, including Admiral Canaris, General Köstring and Colonel Count Stauffenberg, saw the advantage of setting up numerous combat units out of Russian and non-Russian prisoners, arming them, and using them as allies against Stalin in order to overthrow Bolshevism and liberate their country. From the end of 1941, legions of 'helpers' were formed into companies and battalions; and by 1943 the 'eastern legion' and other 'helpers' numbered at least 400,000 men.[58] Much more important, however, was the formation and deployment of army units who fought on the German side as allies, representing their own national causes.

General Andrei Vlasov, the best-known protagonist of a Russian liberation movement, even believed he could establish himself as a 'third power' between Hitler and Stalin. As late as 1943 Vlasov and his staff were of the opinion that a radical change of German policy in the east would have led to the downfall of the Communist system. In any case, even at the end of 1944 the manpower reservoir of about 1.5 million prisoners of war appeared to be sufficient to set up an independent Russian army of liberation of 30 divisions in alliance with the Wehrmacht. By the end of the war the number of Soviet prisoners-of-war who stood on the side of the Germans in opposition to the Communist regime, and in part fought actively, rose to at least one million men.[59]

That Hitler and Himmler as Reichs Leader SS only came around to recruiting Russian and non-Russian peoples of the Soviet Union as allies towards the end of the war, instead of back in 1941, was a decisive factor in the failure of 'Operation Barbarossa'. There had been no lack of advocates of such a policy of alliance. Stalin's fear that the Germans might exploit the anti-Soviet feelings among Russian citizens, but even more among the non-Russian peoples, is demonstrated by the many brutal measures he took to police the territories behind the front, to control the population and to exterminate ruth-lessly those who were regarded as deserters, subversives, saboteurs and agents. The battle at the front also served Stalin as justification for his bloody and pitiless measures against his own people.[60]

This so-called 'war on two fronts' regarded the fight against the actual or assumed internal enemy as being at least as important as the defeat of the German offensive. Even before 22 June the NKVD had begun to set up the subsequently so infamous NKVD regiments and divisions. These heavily armed formations worked together with the 'back-up units' provided by the armies, which consisted of specially selected dependable soldiers. It was their job to bring home to the fighting forces, even to the individual soldier, that any with-drawal was a hopeless undertaking, and that any attempt to flee would automatically lead to fatal consequences.[61] There were back-up units at regimental and divisional level, the latter being set up as required by the division commanders. As early as June 1941 there were nine regiments and one battalion of the NKVD as well as a back-up unit of the army behind the Soviet southern front.[62]

These back-up units were supported by the so-called 'special formations' of the NKVD, better known as the 'extermination battal-ions', and from 1943 on by the abbreviation SMERSH ('death to the spies'). They, together with other NKVD formations, were instructed to suppress without mercy any sabotage and incitement behind their own lines, even including unrest, panic and defeatism among the population. The assignment to neutralize all agents, spies and para-chutists who attempted to penetrate areas behind the lines on behalf of the Germans served to justify these activities. Moreover, the exter-mination battalions were ordered to destroy all valuable property and equipment that had to be left behind during the retreat. According to Soviet sources, in the summer of 1941 there were already 1755 extermination battalions with almost 330,000 men.[63]

If we look for a moment at the organization of the NKVD,[64] we should direct our attention primarily to the 'Department of Border Troops' and the 'Department of Internal Troops'. Besides these there was the 'Department of State Security' which was responsible for the afore-mentioned 'special formations'. The border troops were not only responsible for border protection but, in cooperation with the regular forces, also for the protection of the areas of operations. In the course of the major withdrawals in 1941 and 1942 the border troops were mainly employed for intelligence, security and purges behind the lines, particularly in areas where the presence of German paratroopers, enemy agents and other 'elements hostile to the state' was suspected. The Germans estimated the strength of a border troop regiment to be 1600 men. Many border regiments were assigned to front-line duties during the course of military operations.[65] In certain instances regiments were consolidated into border divisions. According to German estimates, the total strength of the border troops rose to about 160,000 men in early 1943.

The standing orders for all border troops of the NKVD, which were approved on 25 March 1942, regulated the cooperation between the security forces, the regular forces and the local population in the minutest detail. The following basic rules were set:

The troops must be prepared at any time to proceed against enemy agents and groups of spies and saboteurs who manage to slip through the front line or stay behind in our territories after a withdrawal. They must conduct effective police actions and eliminate the infiltrated agents – spies, saboteurs, parachutists, traitors and wireless operators.[66]

In contrast to this, the formations of 'internal troops' had a mainly political function. This included protection of the organs of the party and the government, and of industrial plants and railways, but also defence against spies, suppression of revolts, and finally the guarding of prisoner transports and camps. They were normally deployed throughout the whole country and were only sent to the front in particularly critical situations. The internal troops were organized into divisions and regiments, with a division normally numbering 8000–9000 men, and regiments on average 1600–1700 men. To these must be added the railway and guard troops, the plant protection troops and the supply units. According to German Intelligence, by the turn of 1942–3 there were about 170,000 internal troops, a number which, from what we know today, is probably too low an estimate.

The back-up formations and extermination battalions were lavishly deployed during the German offensives in 1941 and 1942, and also served to repress anti-Soviet movements and to deter the population from fraternizing with the advancing Germans.[67] In the course of the reorganization of the People's Commissariat for Internal Affairs in April–May 1943, the SMERSH battalions were finally put under the authority of the Ministry of Defence, but with no alterations to their assignments. The NKVD divisions already set up before the war, which within the framework of the original Soviet offensive planning were to have played an important role in controlling conquered territories, grew to a very remarkable size. This can be seen from the fact that in the course of the war 29 NKVD divisions were converted into infantry divisions and transferred to the Red Army.[68] According to some estimates, the NKVD then still retained three-quarters of a million to one million men organized into 53 divisions and 28 brigades, excluding the border troops. In the territories far behind the front, these troops continued the battle for the control and repression of the population.[69]

The extremely harsh measures against his own people were a major component of the 'Great Patriotic War' which Stalin had announced on 3 July, a war that 'knew no pity for the enemy'. They also figured prominently in the incipient 'partisan war'. This war was initiated politically with a decree by the Central Committee of the Communist Party and the Council of the People's Commissioners of 29 June, which was amended on 10 July by the order transferring the agenda for the partisan war to the Supreme Commands of the north-western, western, and south-western sectors.[70] It was only in May 1942 that a central staff for the partisan movement was to be set up in Moscow. The reintroduction of the 'war commissar', otherwise 'political leader', on 16 July 1941, underlines not only the great mistrust of combat morale, but also the efforts by the Supreme Command to strengthen the party's control over its military arm. All of these measures illustrate the concept of 'total' war, which subordinated all of the powers of the state and all sections of the populace to a single goal: resistance at any price.

This radicalization of the battle at the front to include operations both behind the German and also the Soviet lines, went hand in hand with an increase in the hate propaganda, which may partly have been a reaction to German power politics, but which also reflected the desire to stimulate the combat morale of the troops at all costs. This radicalization of the war, which no longer differentiated between combatants and civilians, between German 'dissentients' and regular prisoners – which led to numerous atrocities[71] and reprisals on both sides – not only highlighted a ruthless war of ideologies, but also illustrated the desperate straits in which the Soviet Union found itself. Moscow must have felt itself close to collapse indeed if it had to resort to such desperate measures.

The spiral of violence that led to atrocities and reprisals received its impetus not so much from the notorious Nazi 'criminal orders', but from the direct experience of the soldiers on both sides. From the earliest days of the war, German soldiers became increasingly embittered at finding the mutilated corpses of comrades who had been captured by the Soviets. Confrontation with the victims of Stalin's secret police, who had committed atrocities among political prisoners shortly before the arrival of the German advanced formations, also sparked outrage and desire for retaliation. The dominant feeling in the Red Army was hatred of the invader, who was bringing death and destruction to the country, occupying ever greater areas and beginning to oppress the civilian population. This hatred, incited by the constant, most fiercely polemical propaganda that called for ruthless retaliation against all the 'occupiers', formed the psychological breeding-ground for acts of violence which were to increase substantially during the last two years of the war.[72]

The German chances of winning over large parts the population, even entire racial groups, during the early phase of the war have been graphically confirmed by many witnesses and need not be discussed here.[73] The instability of the Soviet regime was reflected in the disloyal attitude of numerous civilians, and this has to be accorded as much weight as the loss of western Russia and the military defeats during the initial months of the war. The shock of the early German successes must have been considerable, and the report that Stalin, Beria and Molotov attempted to address a peace offer to Gemany at the end of June 1941 must be given some credibility. According to this, the intention was to offer Germany large parts of the western Soviet Union, including the three Baltic states and Bessarabia, and to ask for a cease-fire, using the Bulgarian ambassador as mediator. Molotov in particular allegedly supported this step with his reference to the peace of Brest-Litovsk of March 1918.[74]

In view of the heavy military defeats, the mass surrender of Soviet soldiers, the huge losses of territory, and the inclination of large parts of the population to regard the Germans as liberators, the future of the Communist regime must have looked even more fateful in the summer of 1941 than could be read merely on the military maps. Despite substantial successes in the mobilization of the war economy, in the evacuation of important industrial complexes, and the ruthless application of power in all conceivable areas,[75] in the early autumn of 1941 the overall situation became increasingly fearsome. The serious mistakes that Stalin made as supreme commander during the battle of Kiev, which resulted in the loss of the eastern Ukraine, and whereby, according to German claims, the Red Army lost five armies with 665,000 captured (450,000 according to other sources),[76] not counting the dead and wounded, appeared to have accelerated the descent into catastrophe.

Based on contemporary knowledge, it is hard to accept the claim that Stalin, to all intents and purposes, sacrificed the entire south-western front with its three-quarters of a million men in order to delay the German attack on Moscow. The German victory in the Ukraine favoured the attack against Moscow from the south-west by providing the operational conditions for a flanking attack by Panzer Group 2. In brief, the overall situation on the German-Soviet front was building relentlessly to a climax, and everything depended on whether the Soviet Union would be able to avoid a final collapse before the onset of winter. Hitler, for his part, judged the success in the battle of Kiev to have been crucial. He had pushed through this operation against the advice of the General Staff, and his assessment of its importance for subsequent victory on the eastern front can be gauged from his remarks in mid-September. He reaffirmed the value of the campaign for gaining 'Russian territory' within the framework of overall German strategy, particularly with regard to the United States, as a condition for rendering Europe secure from blockade in the future.[77]

Failure of 'Operation Barbarossa'
before Leningrad and Moscow

When in early September the belated siege of Leningrad began to take shape and the pocket battle of Kiev promised to become a great operational success despite the considerable loss of time involved, those responsible could no longer beg the question of possible final victory in the east during 1941. Had the conditions for a general attack on Moscow been created? Were the German forces strong enough? Was there still sufficient time for such a campaign? Hitler's directive of 5 September on the preparation of this attack reveals that the successes to date on the northern and southern sectors of the eastern front were considered sufficient to warrant a decisive operation against Moscow.

After Army Group North had succeeded in encircling Leningrad in early September, following many weeks of delays, and in cutting the city off from all approaches by land, the objective of the campaign in the north appeared to be within reach. But despite strenuous efforts, the attackers were no longer able to achieve the planned 'close investment', let alone force Leningrad to surrender, and in the ensuing months they had to beat off repeated sorties and attempts at relief from the east. Even though it appeared to require only one final push to take Leningrad, on 15 September, on the orders of OKH, Panzer Group 4, which was deployed to the south of the city, had to withdraw about half of its armour and transfer it as reinforcement to Army Group Centre.[78] With this the direct attack came to an end. Subsequently, the city was to be worn down under the greatest possible conservation of German strength, both because of Hitler's directive forbidding penetration of the city and because there were no longer sufficient forces for a conquest.

Hitler's reasoning in his directive of 12 October not to enter either Moscow or Leningrad was that the defenders had prepared extensive booby traps. Reference was also made to the destruction and loss of life, including that of civilians, that had been caused after the capture of Kiev when a prepared bomb trap had been detonated by remote control on 24 September.[79] Since partisans had also obviously been involved in the devastating attack in the centre of Kiev, the SS, as well as some army commanders, were to seize upon this incident to justify the harshest reprisals which did not even balk at punishing individuals whose guilt could not be clearly established. A further dramatic attack behind the German lines occurred during the night of 14 November 1941 when several districts in Kharkov were blown up with the help of partisans, leading to extensive damage and a huge loss of life among the occupying forces. Lieutenant General von Braun, commander of the 62nd Infantry Division, was also killed in this incident.[80]

The partisan war was soon to develop into a form of secret war in which it became highly difficult for the occupation forces to restrict their military actions to proven partisan fighters while sparing the

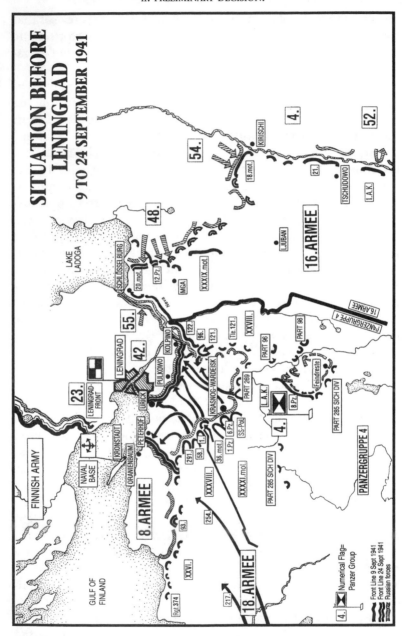

civilian population, because in many instances the partisans used the local inhabitants, including women and children, for their purposes.[81] Because the cruel war conducted by the partisans behind the German lines posed an insoluble security problem for the normally weak occupation forces, in many cases the only effective counter appeared to be ruthless reprisals and threats of the harshest retribution towards civilians. In retrospect, there is a distinction between the legally permissible measures taken by those commanders who attempted to restrict the use of force to genuine partisans and criminals, and those directives which aimed to subdue the entire population by means of terror and oppression. In the case of executions by police units in areas behind the lines of Army Group Centre, Field Marshal von Bock, for example, ordered in early August that punishment was only to be meted out against 'bands that had been taken while armed' and against criminals.[82] That the measure of what was permissible under the laws of war was quickly exceeded, and that the security forces of the SS and SD frequently used the partisan war as an excuse to commit systematically many crimes against civilians that were based on the racial-ideological decrees of the SS leadership, has been extensively documented and does not require further discussion.[83]

We know today that in fact large sectors of both Leningrad and Moscow had been mined. Stalin himself had explicitly approved such mining activities in Leningrad, because from mid-September he seriously reckoned on the impending fall of the city. And Marshal Zhukov, who, as Commander-in-Chief North-west, had been sent by Stalin on 9 September to save the endangered city, and who used draconian measures to stem the decline of combat power and morale, also expected the Germans to enter Leningrad within a few days. The city's fate during those critical days stood on a knife edge.

The successful defence of Leningrad, however, was due less to Zhukov's emergency measures than to the fact that the Panzer Corps deployed in the centre of the line, and the VIII Air Corps which was to support the attack, had to be transferred to Army Group Centre at the very moment when enemy resistance was about to collapse and the fall of the city seemed inevitable. Yet even after the German attack was discontinued, the situation of the encircled forces – three armies – remained so critical that on 23 October Stalin ordered the Supreme Command of the Leningrad Front to conduct a sortie in order to establish a firm corridor to the Soviet forces dug in to the east of the city. Since at the time the Red Army's last reserves were deployed in the battle for Moscow, it was impossible to send any reinforcements to the Leningrad Front. But because Stalin was unwilling to risk the capture of the Leningrad defenders under any circumstances, the encircled armies must at least be able to withdraw to the east if they had to give up the city.[85] The sortie attempts by the defenders, and the relief attempts by the forces concentrated to the east of the siege lines, subsequently led to such hard fighting that the OKH quickly had to bring in several fresh divisions from France and even two regiments of paratroopers. The ruthless nature of the fighting involved during the break-out bids, including the use of civilians in breach of international law, as well as the struggle to establish bridgeheads over the River Neva to the east of Leningrad, were succinctly summed up by one experienced paratrooper of the 7th Air Division with the words: 'Rather Crete seven times over than the Neva front once !'[86]

The underlying reason for the decision in mid-September to transfer large forces from Army Group North was that the strengthening of the central front was now perceived as the priority, even if this meant renouncing an operational solution in northern Russia. Both Hitler and the General Staff saw the major objective of Army Group North as having been more or less achieved with the close investment of Leningrad. Continued employment of the armoured and air forces around Leningrad could have tightened the grip on the city so closely that even supplies by water over Lake Ladoga would have been cut off, thereby bringing capitulation within reach. This advantage, however, was superseded by the more urgent need of Army Group Centre to receive all the armour, motorized and aircraft formations that could be spared from the northern front so as to launch the attack against Moscow in the greatest possible strength.

Despite understandable pleas by the local commanders in front of Leningrad to delay the move, the Army General Staff insisted on the immediate transfer of forces from Army Group North, which began on 17 September. Maximum strength at the focal point of attack was given priority over success, however desirable, in a less important area. The decision to concentrate as many forces as possible in the central sector was correct from the overall military-strategic viewpoint, because the intention was to bring the campaign to a victorious conclusion in 1941. But now the penalty had to be paid for not having been able to take Leningrad in the 'first onslaught' in early August, and also for the fact that reinforcements from Army Group Centre had not been provided for the second decisive attack on the city in mid-August.[87]

The unsatisfactory operational situation in northern Russia put the Germans at a disadvantage for a number of reasons. An entire army, the Eighteenth, facing north, was tied down by the blockade of Leningrad, requiring up to eight divisions, and a further three or four divisions were needed to contain the 'bridgehead of Oranienbaum' south of Kronstadt. Furthermore, valuable forces, including reinforcements, had to be deployed south of Lake Ladoga to defend against relief attacks. Army Group North was therefore unable to spare two armoured and three motorized divisions[88] whose deployment in the centre as reinforcements for the attack against Moscow would have been crucial. Finally, and this weighed most heavily, during the critical months of October and November, Army Group North was unable to support the decisive attack by Army Group Centre with a flanking attack from the north-west. The turn of the war on the eastern front was clearly evident in the northern sector as early as September 1941.

Because of the late conclusion of the battle of Kiev and the time-consuming regrouping and movement of troops from the north and the south as reinforcements of Army Group Centre, preparations for the key attack were only concluded at the end of September. Furthermore, as a result of heavy German losses to date – the armoured forces involved were only up to 45 to 50 per cent of their original combat power[89] – Army Group Centre, for all practical purposes, had to conduct the attack on its own. Army Group North remained tied down on the defensive and, on Hitler's insistence, Army Group South, which could have contributed decisively to the attack against Moscow, had to employ its offensive power for the conquest of the Donetz basin, Rostov and the Crimea. It was absolutely essential that there were still several weeks of dry autumn weather to ensure a victorious conclusion of the campaign.

Despite the advanced time of year, and aware of the approaching autumn mud period, on 30 September the strongly reinforced Army Group Centre launched its decisive attack against Moscow – 'Operation Typhoon' – with its northern flanking army, and followed this

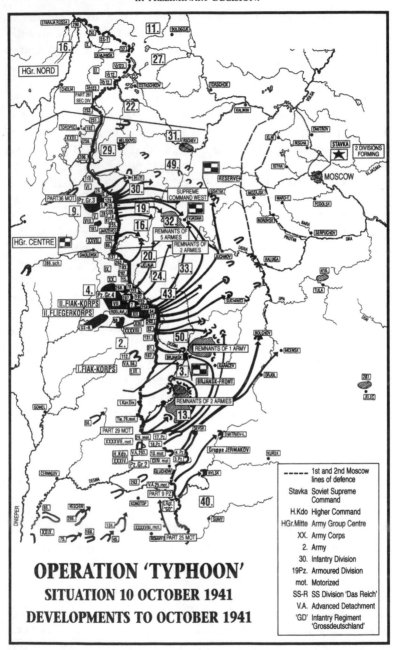

OPERATION 'TYPHOON'

SITUATION 10 OCTOBER 1941

DEVELOPMENTS TO OCTOBER 1941

- - - - -	1st and 2nd Moscow lines of defence
Stavka	Soviet Supreme Command
H.Kdo	Higher Command
HGr.Mitte	Army Group Centre
XX.	Army Corps
2.	Army
30.	Infantry Division
19Pz.	Armoured Division
mot.	Motorized
SS-R	SS Division 'Das Reich'
V.A.	Advanced Detachment
'GD'	Infantry Regiment 'Grossdeutschland'

on 2 October with the mass of its forces. Three armies and three armoured groups, supported by two air corps and two anti-aircraft corps, broke through the strong Soviet front in three places and encircled the mass of eight Soviet armies and parts of three further armies in the Vyazma area, to the north and south of Bryansk.[90] On 19 October the Supreme Command of Army Group Centre proudly announced the capture of 673,000 men, and the destruction or capture of more than 1200 tanks and over 5400 guns. With this the Red Army had suffered a devastating defeat which even surpassed the collapse of the South-west Front in the eastern Ukraine in September.[91] When, only a few days after the start of the new offensive, Reich Press Chief Otto Dietrich announced before the national and international press that with the destruction of Army Group Timoshenko the campaign in the east had been decided, and repeated this statement in a prominently placed newspaper article, it was Goebbels, interestingly enough, who protested to Hitler. He warned of the danger of awakening a premature feeling of victory among the public which would then be disillusioned if its expectations were not fulfilled.[92]

In its elation at victory, when all that appeared to be left was the pursuit of 'enemy remnants' and the occupation of territory, on 14 October the OKH set objectives that went far beyond the gaining of Moscow which was only, for the time being, to be invested. The Ninth Army, with the mass of Panzer Group 3, was redirected towards the north and north-east, in order to intercept and destroy important forces facing Army Group North. The close investment of Moscow was left solely to the Fourth Army and Panzer Group 4. Even though the command of Army Group Centre was far from happy about the redirection of such strong forces, it did nothing to prevent this serious weakening of the main line of attack.[93] The measure of confidence in victory is evident from an order by the OKH to remove an army corps of four divisions from the advance on Moscow and to transport it to France for regrouping.

At about this time, however, i.e. from 14–15 October onward, the onset of the season of autumn mud – the subject of so much discussion – began to slow down Army Group Centre which was in full pursuit, and some of whose spearheads were only about 100 km from Moscow.[94] This distance, measured in terms of the speed of advance in early summer of 1941, would have been covered in only two to three days. In contradiction to the frequently voiced Soviet claim that the stiff resistance by the troops which had escaped from the 'pocket' battles proved decisive,[95] it was primarily weather conditions, but also inconsistencies in the deployment of the pursuing forces, which caused the German advance more or less to become bogged down during those critical days in October. While the German command was aware of the characteristics of the 'mud period', it had completely under-estimated their effect. The further advance on Moscow became a major problem of supply and transportation, compared to which operational leadership receded into the background.

This should in no way detract from the determination of Soviet resistance. Under Zhukov's leadership a new western front was established, so that after the deployment of reserves in mid-October, the defence of Moscow was entrusted to twelve infantry divisions and sixteen armoured brigades.[96] Under normal weather conditions these forces would not have been sufficient for a successful cover of a 300 km-wide front on the 'first Moscow line of defence' between Kalinin in the north and the sector south of Kaluga, and to prevent the Germans from penetrating to the outskirts of the city. However, since the German spearheads were almost completely dependent on the made-up main roads, Zhukov was able to concentrate his forces along these roads and form defensive strongpoints. German Intelligence contributed substantially to the overly optimistic assessment of the situation by claiming in mid-October that the enemy in front of Army Group Centre had been decisively defeated and was no longer able to offer resistance before Moscow. Intelligence believed that the Red Army no longer disposed of any combat-ready reserves 'of greater strength' which it could deploy before the onset of winter.[97] That in October not only Führer Headquarters and the General Staff, but also the command of Army Group North, were confident of victory, can be seen from a statement by Sixteenth Army Command that the enemy was 'at his last gasp' and would be brought down before the beginning of winter.[98]

How deeply German successes during the first half of October troubled the Soviet command, and how precarious the fate of the Soviet state had become, may be judged by the intention of Stalin and his immediate entourage to ask Germany for a cease-fire. A few years ago documents were published in Russia that leave no doubt about

Stalin's and Beria's assessment in mid-October 1941 that the Red Army was facing imminent collapse and that Moscow could not be held. The NKVD under Beria attempted to initiate a negotiated peace settlement with Germany via the Bulgarian ambassador in Moscow and prepared to pay by the cession of extensive territories.[99] The evacuation from the capital, on 16 October, of the central authorities, the diplomatic corps and important armament factories, as well as the preparations for blowing up selected buildings, including Stalin's dacha, underline the fear that Moscow could no longer be held.[100] On 18 October Stalin himself wanted to leave Moscow for a secret headquarters in the Volga region. Many government offices and the diplomatic corps were already on their way to Kuibyshev on the Volga. However, under the influence of his military advisers, he obviously changed his decision and on 19 October had a state of emergency declared for Moscow and its immediate approaches.

Evidence that the Western nations also considered the Soviet military situation to be on the brink of collapse after the German victory in the double battle of Vyazma and Bryansk comes, for example, from transcripts of broadcasts by the BBC in London. According to one British commentary:

Such victories have never before been recorded in history. The Russians are standing with their backs to the wall and are defending themselves as best they are able. Behind this wall, however, stand Great Britain and the United States![101]

Churchill and Roosevelt also saw the danger of a Soviet collapse. On 12 October Churchill sent a personal message to Stalin in which he promised delivery of 3000 trucks, and at almost the same time Roosevelt directed his Chief of Staff General Marshall to give the delivery of war materials to the Soviet Union the highest priority over any other form of aid. Even if these measures had no effect on the outcome of the battle for Moscow, they do illustrate how the situation was assessed.

The Soviet command had to fight the battle for Moscow with those forces left to it after the losses incurred in the 'pocket' battles, and the reinforcements brought into central Russia from the Far East and central Asia since the end of September. In addition, new reserves were formed far behind the lines. The introduction of reinforcements from Russian Asia, which completely escaped the attention of German air reconnaissance, provided the defenders of Moscow with at least thirteen infantry divisions and five armoured brigades by the end of October.[102] Some of these formations were already involved in heavy fighting on the western approaches to Moscow between Borodino and Moshaisk as early as 13 October.

It has occasionally been claimed that the arrival, just in time, of fresh troops from Russian Asia was due partly to the intelligence provided by the secret agent Richard Sorge, and partly to the political assessment by the Soviet leadership of how Japan would react. All things being equal, Sorge's important signal from Tokyo that the Japanese government did not intend to attack the Soviet Union, which has commonly been dated 15 October, would have come too late to form the basis for the decision to move troops from Asia to Moscow. In early October the Japanese leadership, particularly within the army, was strongly of the opinion, with regard to its war plans against the United States, that Germany and the Soviet Union should find a political solution to the war. This was made quite clear to the German ambassador on 4 October. Sorge's signal to Moscow, which was most probably based on this information, might have confirmed Stalin's earlier decision to move troops from the Far East but could not have triggered it. Furthermore, the Soviet leaders would hardly have taken such a momentous decision based only on a single report by one agent.[103]

The subsequent military developments in front of Moscow need only be touched on briefly. Seen in retrospect, the war in the east had already reached its culmination point in mid-October 1941. What then occurred in November and December was only the desperate attempt by the German side to convert the fruits of the summer and autumn battles into a lasting victory. The key factor in deciding to continue the attack was the consideration that to remain in the positions reached would mean handing the initiative to the enemy and be tantamount to admitting the strategic failure of 'Operation Barbarossa'. An alternative to the final offensive attempt would have been to withdraw to a winter position in order to conserve operational strength and facilitate the renewal and reorganization of the exhausted troops.

As many studies have shown, the final attempt, beginning between 15 and 19 November, to invest Moscow with the last remaining forces, was a gamble of the highest magnitude. Despite the onset of frost, the alarming condition of the troops,[104] the unfavourable shape of the front, the absence of support from the air, the bottlenecks in supply and the lack of winter equipment, the Supreme Command of Army Group Centre again went over to the attack, but no longer with the sole objective of capturing Moscow. Against the advice of high-ranking colleagues, Field Marshal von Bock – strongly supported by the Chief of the General Staff[105] – pressed ahead with his plan, even though he knew that he could not count on any support by Army Groups North or South, who both demanded going over to the defensive. But it was not only von Bock who still entertained high ambitions of investing Moscow before the onset of deep winter; other commanders within the army group also favoured the notion of a mid-November attack. This is borne out, for example, by the objectives Colonel General Guderian set for his LIII Army Corps. The two exhausted infantry divisions of this corps were to advance 140 km to Ryasan, on the River Oka, in order to cut Moscow off from the south – an operation that Guderian calculated would take three weeks. There was no intention to relinquish the advantages gained during the summer campaign.[106]

The stance of the Commander-in-Chief of Army Group Centre before and during the final attack remains highly ambivalent, fluctuating wildly between a realistic appreciation of the situation and purely wishful thinking. On the one hand he successfully resisted the General Staff's attempts to set unachievable objectives far to the east of Moscow, while on the other he desperately attempted, after all, to achieve the impossible by means of the close investment of Moscow and the build-up of a defensive front against expected relief attacks to the east of the city. Even though he was already admitting on 11 November that the most that could be hoped for was to reach the Moscow–Volga Canal and the River Moskva to the south-east of the city, he still clung to the concept of attack. Although he personally witnessed the hopeless condition of his troops after the start of the attack – many battalions were being led by lieutenants, and regiments were down to 250 fighting men[107] – and even reported to the OKH on 23 November that it was 'five minutes to twelve', he yet drove forward the few formations still capable of attack in order at least to reach the northern suburbs of Moscow. And having finally come to the conclusion that his forces were no longer sufficient to invest Moscow, he still deployed as a central assault force his last remaining reserves: a single infantry division.

It was only on 1 December that he sent an alarming telex to the OKH requesting a decision as to whether to continue an attack that had become senseless and without objective, whether the army group should go over to the defensive, or even withdraw to rear positions.[108] Von Bock himself took no decisions and allowed the operation to run on. The extremely depleting attack against an increasingly stronger enemy broke through the 'second Moscow line of defence' and on 3 December, in dropping temperatures, came to within 18 km of the north-western outskirts of the city. On 5 and 6 December the Red Army launched a counter-attack with parts of the Kalinin Front, the Western Front and the South-west Front. On his Western Front alone, Zhukov deployed ten armies.[109] At this point Army Group Centre lost its last possible opportunity to break off the attack and to prepare serviceable winter positions without coming under pressure from the enemy.

The risk taken by the Germans with the final attack against Moscow is, with hindsight, evidence that those responsible had mistaken the culmination point of the campaign. It can also be argued that the attempts by several senior commanders to seize the ultimate chance and force a decision against an exhausted opponent with the 'last battalion' were not completely hopeless. What is in no way plausible, however, is the theory that it was Hitler who had insisted on the final attack against Moscow at any price, and that von Bock and Halder had seen no other alternative than to agree to the attack, thereby deliberately bringing about its failure in order to force Hitler to agree to a withdrawal from Moscow.[110]

It should be noted in the first place that during those critical November days Hitler did not exert any particular influence on the final attack against Moscow. After he had admitted on 22 November that the objectives of the campaign had not been achieved, three days later and with winter fast approaching, he assigned priority to the capture of Leningrad and southern Russia and not to the investment of Moscow.[111] Furthermore, this hypothesis ignores the fact that Halder, in agreement with von Bock, had considered Moscow to be the prime objective ever since the beginning of the campaign and had doggedly pursued this objective despite all difficulties. Even as late as the General Staff conference on 13 November, Halder, von

Bock and other commanders had still reckoned on some chance of success and insisted on continuing the attack, even though the representatives of the other two army groups had argued in favour of halting the offensive. That von Bock was driven by the ambition to enter Moscow as a conquerer, as he had entered Paris in June 1940, has been confirmed by important witnesses.[112] Finally, such an intrigue between Halder and von Bock to force a withdrawal would have been a gross irresponsibility towards the troops, who would have been cold-bloodedly exposed to a heavy defeat during the Russian winter.

Army Groups North and South, in their turn, had suffered reverses at the end of November and beginning of December. At the beginning of December Army Group North had finally to abandon the attempt by the Sixteenth Army to link up with the Finnish army in the Tikhvin area. In the south, the attempt to gain further territory south of the mouth of the Don failed when the First Panzer Army had to withdraw from Rostov on 28 November. Hitler's order of 8 December to go over to the defensive along the whole front was not only a reaction to the failure to take Moscow, it was also the admission that the political and military objectives of 1941 had not been achieved. It all made for an irreversible turn of the war at the strategic level.

This turn was the result of the German failure to capture Leningrad no later than in September, and Moscow during October, or at least to have eliminated both targets as power centres. The attack on Leningrad was broken off shortly before the expected victory as a result of military-strategic priority accorded Moscow, to which the secondary objective of Leningrad was subordinated. That the German attack bogged down after the enormous victories in the double battle of Vyazma and Bryansk was mainly due to the lateness of the day, which only permitted an operation of two weeks' duration, due in part to the effect of the seasonal period of mud, in part to the errors committed in the deployment of the pursuing forces,[113] and finally to the under-estimation of the strength of Soviet resistance. All things being equal, an attack date between 20 and 24 September would have offered the possibility not only of destroying the Soviet forces confronting Army Group Centre, but also of taking Moscow before the onset of the autumn rains and the arrival of reinforcements from the Far East. This brings us back to the assessment

II. PRELIMINARY DECISION:

already made that a time-span of between seven and ten days was wanting for a victorious conclusion of the campaign in the east.

Only coordinated and synchronized political and military action, together with the renunciation of any secondary objectives, could have led to ultimate success in 1941. The great military victories of the Wehrmacht during the summer and autumn had not only driven the Red Army to the brink of catastrophe, but had also shaken the Communist regime to the point where the leadership in Moscow sent out feelers for a cease-fire and also entertained fears as to the likely collapse of the home front. A German leadership that would have been prepared to take political as well as military action in order to gain the goodwill of the population and future allies could have brought about Stalin's downfall. At least this would have done much to prevent the Communist agitation, the hate propaganda and the build-up of partisan formations behind the German lines.

A military victory in the form of the capture of Leningrad and Moscow would therefore have needed to occur before the onset of adverse weather conditions in October in order to deprive the Soviet regime of any chance of military and political recovery. The Soviet counter-attack before Moscow, and German reversals on the other sectors of the front, not only enabled Stalin to consolidate his power but also secured his position with Great Britain and the United States. Having achieved victory in front of Moscow against the predictions of several General Staffs, the Soviet Union became, so to speak, 'worthy of an alliance'. Today it is quite clear that despite the successes of the German army in the east, despite all the efforts made by the leadership and the troops, and despite the will to win,[114] in 1941 'Operation Barbarossa' failed due to miscalculation of the time factor as well as political and military blunders by the leadership. In addition, in the winter battle for Moscow the aura of invincibility of the Wehrmacht was shattered. The essence of the failure of Germany's strategy was that it had over-reached itself.[115]

Finally, we must deal with the claim that because of the vastness and condition of Russian space, the climate and the natural resources of the nation, even the best-conducted operation, even the capture of Moscow, would not have given the German army final victory.[116] Such a claim is based on the consideration that 'operations in the classical tradition' would not have been sufficient to force the enemy to surrender as in the other campaigns to date. That such operations were inevitably necessary, however, since they formed the basis for a military-strategic success, has been demonstrated above. That, on the other hand, the German leadership set geographic objectives, both in the planning of the campaign as well as during its course, which went far beyond what was reasonable and achievable – the capture of the city of Gorki on the Volga, for example – indicates to what extent the purely military options were over-estimated, though not that the gaining of such objectives would have been absolutely necessary for a final victory.

It has been established that the German victories in the pocket battles, in the course of the siege of Leningrad, and during the advance on Moscow, proved that the morale of the Soviet soldiers and the civilian population's will to resist could easily be broken. As explained, on several sectors of the front the Soviet leadership was only able to maintain resistance by the most brutal methods. Many Soviet prisoners, including officers of the higher and highest ranks, were counting on victory for the Wehrmacht. Ordinary people, too, proved willing to cooperate with the Germans until well into the autumn. The panic-induced incidents in Moscow after 16 October illustrate the lack of stability in a crisis and refute the propaganda claim that the will to defend Moscow 'indivisibly ruled the minds and hearts of the whole Soviet nation'.[117]

It has been claimed that even a victory culminating in the capture of Moscow would not inevitably have turned the war in favour of Germany.[118] Such a claim is open to doubt. The fall of Moscow would not only have led to decisive military but also political and moral consequences: loss of the capital, in itself an important centre of traffic and arms production, and the destruction of the last remaining forces available for national defence. Soviet transportation and supply problems would have increased immensely after the loss of the 'turn-table' of Moscow. At the least, the Wehrmacht would have gained a vital central region that would have permitted further operations to the north and south. Furthermore, the capture of Moscow by mid-October would have provided sufficient time before the onset of winter for Army Groups North and South to acquire additional territory as well as favourable winter positions along the whole front. It is also highly probable that the fall of Moscow would have led rapidly to the surrender of Leningrad and the consequent link-up with the Finnish army, not to mention the psychological effects of such events on other cities and regions. Even if Stalin had withdrawn behind the central Volga with the remnants of his forces, and the war in the east not ended in the surrender of the Red Army, it would have been highly questionable whether the dictator, under the impact of defeat, would have retained sufficient authority to urge the continuation of resistance at any price. In any case, the Germans would have held strong trump cards which would have been invaluable for reaching a political settlement of the Soviet problem.

Summary: The Turn of the War in December 1941 as Seen within the Framework of Overall Strategy

There are two further reasons why the failure of the campaign against the Soviet Union at the gates of Moscow and Leningrad was significant. 1. The bulk of the Army and the Luftwaffe remained tied down in the east for the unforseeable future and was therefore not available for any 'post-Barbarossa' operations. 2. Entry into the war by the United States after the Japanese attack on Pearl Harbor on 7 December 1941 meant escalation into a world war, with a clear-cut shift of power to the disadvantage of the Axis powers. Was this therefore the all-decisive turn of the war? What prospects and options did Germany and Italy still have after failing to achieve the objectives of 1941, and the United States, the strongest economic power in the world, had joined the ranks of the enemy?

The period of mounting tension in Japanese-American relations from 26 July 1941, the day Great Britain and the United States froze Japanese assets, and 1 August, when an oil embargo was declared against Japan, to 7 December has been sufficiently illuminated by historical research. From the end of July on, and even more clearly from the beginning of October, those circles in Japan who urged a surprise attack against the American Pacific Fleet began to gain the upper hand. The Japanese army, which had still not excluded its original intention of intervening in the war against the Soviet Union, gave in to the opinions of Prime Minister Tojo and Admiral Yamamoto, commander of the fleet, who favoured moving south, with a surprise attack on Pearl Harbor. The fact that several leaders, first and foremost President Roosevelt himself, gained knowledge of the secret instructions to the Japanese diplomats in the United States through the breaking of the Japanese 'code purple' – the deciphered signals of which were designated as 'MAGIC' – supports the belief that the Americans were expecting a surprise attack by the Japanese fleet at any time after 1 December. After all, the Japanese code had been almost completely broken as early as August 1940.[119] That Roosevelt as well as the Secretary of War and the Secretary of the Navy possessed important information about Japanese intentions is at least documented by his warning of the imminent danger of war during the 'war council' held on 25 November. The ultimatum given to Japan on the following day counted upon an early outbreak of war. In any case, Roosevelt wanted the Japanese to begin hostilities so that he could obtain the nation's agreement to enter the war. It is worth considering that a timely withdrawal of the American fleet from Pearl Harbor, or appropriate measures of defence, would probably have persuaded the Japanese to renounce their intentions against Hawaii.[120]

Nevertheless, the allegation that Roosevelt kept the responsible navy and army commanders in Hawaii, Admiral Husband Kimmel and Lieutenant General Walter Short, completely in the dark cannot be maintained. What is of more importance is the fact that over a longer period of time the responsible authorities did not systematically analyse the information provided by MAGIC, and that they adopted the practice of transmitting such information through unwieldy and time-consuming regular channels, with the result that the recipients of these highly secret messages either failed to receive them at all, or at least not in time.[121] Nonetheless, Admiral Stark, Chief of the Naval Staff, had sent three 'war alerts' to the naval commands in the Pacific after 24 November 1941, and on 28 November the 'Rainbow 5' plan, directed against Japan, was activated. Thus the claim that the American leadership had not reckoned with a Japanese attack on Pearl Harbor during these critical days can no longer be upheld.[122] General Arnold, Commander-in-Chief of the USAF, in fact ordered combat alert for the air forces stationed in California. The attack on 7 December by the Japanese fleet, including six carriers with just under 400 aircraft, against the 86 ships of the Pacific Fleet, including eight battleships in Pearl Harbor, was only partially successful, one reason being that the three carriers assumed to be there were either at sea or in harbours on the American west coast.[123]

Roosevelt, who had calculated that Hitler would most probably support Japan in case of war, had thus succeeded at last in effecting a state of war with Germany by the 'back door'. On 4 December Hitler had finally yielded to the repeated requests by the Japanese government to join a war on Japan's side, regardless of who began hostilities. Germany's declaration of war against the United States on 11 December only confirmed the *de facto* state of war between the two nations which had existed since the summer of 1941 because of several incidents at sea,[124] and merely anticipated America's entry into the war alongside Great Britain.

The immediate advantages to Germany included the certainty that the feared agreement between Japan and the USA had become impossible, so that Germany could now count on Japan against the United States, and that the Kriegsmarine was no longer under any restrictions in the sea war. It was hoped that Japan would so effectively tie down America's potential as to rule out an intervention by American forces in Europe and North Africa in 1942, thereby giving Germany a more or less free hand on the eastern front. A more significant warning sign, however, was the fact that in addition to an as yet undefeated Soviet Union, Germany now faced a new opponent in the United States, with her far superior economic and naval power.[125]

Apart from America's entry into the war, the failure of Germany's strategic war plan proved to be the main factor in the turn of the war. Not only did the exhausted eastern army have to suffer heavy fighting to repulse the Soviet winter offensive of 1941–2, and the Afrika Korps was forced to retreat in North Africa, but the coming war on several fronts already cast its shadow on prospects in the areas of arms production and supply of raw materials. Now that the hope of a rapid, victorious conclusion of the war in the east had vanished, Germany's overall strategy had to adjust to the enemy's strategy of attrition. Faced with irreplaceable losses in men and *matériel* in the east, the increasing needs of the Luftwaffe and the Kriegsmarine, and the huge demands on the armaments industry, Germany had to come up with a strategy that somehow reconciled means and objectives.

There is clear evidence that certain individuals on the German side, as for example Fritz Todt, Minister for Armaments and Munitions, as well as the sometimes very perceptive Goebbels, were conscious that as a result of the crisis on the eastern front, an irrevocable turn in the war had occurred. While Todt told Hitler at the end of November that he had fundamental doubts whether the war could still be won militarily,[126] Goebbels had warned in an article on 9 November that an early victory should not be expected and called for a 'gigantic national effort'. Simultaneously he had recommended a comprehensive mobilization of all sectors of the population in order to bolster the military power that was obviously on the decline.[127] He was already expressing the fundamental point of view he was to advocate from then on but not able to realize until February 1943.

By 31 March 1942 the extremely heavy defensive fighting in the east, in the course of which the Red Army made gains of up to 200 km in depth, had led to German losses of 1,108,000 men, killed, wounded and missing. Not counting replacements, this amounted to 34.6 per cent of the average strength (3.2 million) of the army in the east. The total losses in tanks and self-propelled guns rose to 4241 by the end of January, and by the end of March the sixteen armoured divisions deployed in the east could between them count on only 140 operational tanks.[128] The defensive battles in December and January alone cost over 950 armoured vehicles. Losses among other vehicles were equally heavy. In March 1942, an evaluation of the combat value of the 162 divisions deployed in the east came to the conclusion that only 8 divisions were fully capable of attack, 3 others only after reinforcement, and 47 more 'only of limited combat value'. In the Luftwaffe, after the transfer of most of *Luftflotte 2* to southern Italy and Sicily in early December, the three air fleets in action recorded a total loss of 2500 front-line aircraft and a further 1800 damaged machines by the end of December 1941.[129] By the end of March the total losses had risen to 2700 aircraft.

Besides these dramatic losses, the crisis in the Wehrmacht leadership in December and January clearly illustrated the rupture in the inner structures of the organization. The deeply rooted tensions between Hitler and the army command were reflected not only in the dismissal of the Commander in-Chief on 19 December, but also in the voluntary or forced resignations of several commanders of army groups and armies who could not bring themselves to comply with Hitler's extremely harsh and unorthodox demands. Field Marshals von Rundstedt, von Leeb and von Bock were relieved of their commands, and the redistribution of the senior commands in the army revealed contradictions in the operational and tactical thinking of many officers at all levels who had to cope with the extreme and unprecedented challenges of the winter war of 1941–2, frequently in seemingly hopeless situations.[130]

The Soviet offensives between Lake Ladoga in the north and the Crimea in the south had placed the eastern armies in a highly dangerous situation. The Second Attack Army, bound for the relief of Leningrad, had succeeded in achieving a deep penetration across the River Volkhov in January which could only be contained with the greatest difficulty. Attempts to break out from Leningrad continued. Farther south, at the same time, six divisions and 95,000 men of the German II Army Corps were encircled at Demyansk, and this could only be relieved in April. In mid-January three Soviet armies broke through between Army Groups North and Centre and penetrated to a depth of 200 km to the south-west, splitting the inner flanks of the two army groups and creating a lasting threat to the rear of Army Group Centre. In the centre, a two-pronged attack from the north and the south-east at the end of December 1941 attempted to destroy large parts of Army Group Centre, which only escaped this danger in mid-February after extensive losses of ground. Simultaneously the defenders had to endure exhausting battles behind the front with cavalry and airborne forces, the destruction of which dragged on until mid-April. In mid-January Army Group South had barely been able to contain a deep penetration by three Soviet armies over the Donetz south of Kharkov, and in the Crimea the Kerch peninsula had been lost at the end of December.[131]

In view of the highly critical situation, Hitler's controversial 'order to hold' of 16 December 1941 was basically justified, considering the pros and cons as known today, even if the manner in which it was carried out was seriously flawed. The troops were to be forced to offer 'fanatical resistance' where they stood until sufficient reinforcements had been brought up to permit the withdrawal of the front line to shorter and prepared positions. But any anticipatory withdrawal from sectors of the front that were not already under enemy attack was expressly forbidden, and the build-up of reserves for the suppport of threatened neighbouring sectors was for the most part prevented. The catastrophic manpower situation is underlined by the fact that the only remaining tactical reserves of Army Group Centre consisted of two (!) police battalions which were brought up to the front from the rear on 17 December.[132] However, the maintenance of morale, essential for the continuation of dogged resistance, was of far greater importance. Any thought of withdrawal to unprepared positions, together with the irreplaceable loss of equipment, could easily have led to mass flight and brought about a 'Napoleonic conclusion'.[133]

It was only Hitler's agreement on 15 January 1942 to the withdrawal of three armies of Army Group Centre to the so-called 'winter position' which led to a shortening of the front line by over 150 km, thereby eliminating the crisis points and permitting the build-up of the reserves necessary for future operations.[134] Under these conditions, it was only through hard fighting from the end of January that the army group was able to bring the situation under control. Nevertheless, by mid-January 1942, the tactical and operational crises on the fronts of all three army groups had reached a point where a total collapse of the whole eastern front had become a distinct possibility. Quite apart from the psychologically damaging factor of having had to abandon the offensive within sight of Moscow, the troops and their leaders were faced not only with a resurgent enemy, but with crushing temperatures of more than -30°C, for which they were neither mentally nor physically prepared. How close to its limits Germany's manpower potential had already come at the turn of the year 1941–2 is illustrated by the fact that after mid-December 1941 the eastern army could only be reinforced by a mere five infantry divisions, and that VIII Army Corps, which had been transferred to the west in October, already had to be redeployed under Army Group South near Kharkov in January.

Labouring under extreme climatic conditions and irreplaceable losses, the German army in the east brought the Soviet winter offensive to a halt by the end of March 1942, indisputably a military achievement of the first magnitude which even surpassed the achievements of the summer and autumn. It was only this factor which mitigated to some extent the negative effects of the turn of the war in late 1941. Otherwise this would have led to the total defeat of Germany far sooner than was actually the case. In the event, the German command was granted time to make an attempt to regain the strategic initiative in 1942.

III

THE TURN OF THE WAR 1942–1943: THE FINAL LOSS OF THE STRATEGIC INITIATIVE BY THE AXIS POWERS

The Controversial German War Aims for 1942

The reasoning on which the military-strategic and operational objectives for 1942 were based was not only to have substantial influence on the ultimate failure of the war plan as a whole, but also vividly explains why alternative options were not even taken into consideration. The basic conviction of the Wehrmacht leadership, as well as that of the Army and the Luftwaffe, was that only the year 1942 still remained – if that – in which to force a military decision in favour of the Axis powers. Because of the war in the Pacific the United States would be prevented for the time being from intervening in Europe or North Africa with any substantial forces, and Great Britain was also still considered to be incapable of opening a second front in western Europe because of its many other commitments and the drains on its armaments industry. So 1942 still appeared to offer a certain manageable period of time in which the bulk of the Army could be deployed in a single theatre of war in order to reach a decision.

It must be noted, however, that the Luftwaffe was now no longer capable of supporting the operations of the Army on the eastern front as previously. Already in November 1941 *Luftflotte 2* had been ordered to prepare for transfer to the Mediterranean because the reversals of the German-Italian Panzer Group Africa in Cyrenaica, and the dramatic increase in shipping losses, appeared to make it necessary to attack British positions in the central Mediterranean, particularly Malta. The offensive by the British Eighth Army's Lieutenant General A. Cunningham, and subsequently by Major General N. Ritchie, begun on 18 November under the code-name 'Operation Crusader', anticipated Rommel's planned attack to take Tobruk and involved Panzer Group Africa in heavy fighting. While this led to a serious defeat for the British 7th Armoured Division during the first phase of the battle, by 7 December Rommel had decided to give up the siege of Tobruk and withdraw to Cyrenaica.

The main reason for this decision was the fact that by the end of November the Panzer Army only disposed of 57 light and medium German II, III and IV tanks and 30 Italian tanks, and the supply situation no longer permitted offensive action due to British successes in sinking ships.[1] On 24 November, for example, two freighters with valuable equipment for the Luftwaffe had been sunk. Furthermore, Italian Comando Supremo had informed Rommel that he could not count on any substantial supply by sea or air before early January 1942. Even the appointment of Field Marshal Kesselring as Commander-in-Chief South on 2 December 1941 was not able to change this situation in the short term. By the turn of the year the Eighth Army had driven the German-Italian forces back to the El-Agheila position from which Rommel had launched his offensive in March 1941. With this the operational turn in the North African theatre had occurred at the same time as the turn before Moscow, and even if not so dramatically, then still in the sense of a profound change in the situation.[2]

The defeat in Libya also led to the Luftwaffe being called in for quick support in order to stabilize the situation. The transfer of *Luftflotte 2* and II Air Corps was a very difficult decision, because these forces were withdrawn at the very time that the heavily engaged forces in front of Moscow needed all the air support they could possibly get. It is incorrect to suggest that because of the bad weather in the east during the winter of 1941–2, the withdrawal of *Luftflotte 2* had only a negligible effect on the air war.[3] A stabilization of the eastern front would hardly have been conceivable without support from the air, particularly in dropping supplies by air for encircled formations of the Army. All that remained in support of Army Group Centre was VIII Air Corps. After this was withdrawn to southern Russia in early April 1942 the air forces remaining in the centre were Luftwaffe Command East, which had emerged from V Air Corps.[4] The decision to weaken the already heavily endangered front of Army Group Centre at the end of 1941 in order to counter a threatening defeat in another theatre, or at least to minimize it, illustrates the fact that by this time not only the Army but the Luftwaffe as well were suffering from a serious over-taxation of their strength.

The highly endangered supply situation of the German-Italian forces in Libya, particularly the effect of the 'unsinkable aircraft carrier' Malta on Axis shipping, made reinforcement of the Luftwaffe and the Kriegsmarine (among other things 24 U-Boats were to be sent to the Mediterranean) appear inevitable. With the deployment of *Luftflotte 2* the Wehrmacht and the Luftwaffe also intended to form a unified High Command for the entire theatre, but were unable to gain the cooperation of the Italian authorities. All that could be achieved with the Italian ally was an agreement which did not go beyond a partial improvement of the cooperation between the various branches of the services. German claims to leadership had to bow to the Italian Comando Supremo's jealously guarded independence[5]

Nonetheless, by early March 1942, II Air Corps, which had been deployed in Sicily, had succeeded in greatly reducing the impact of the British air forces from Malta on the German-Italian convoys, and also in weakening Malta by attacks on British convoys. By the end of February four Axis convoys reached the ports in North Africa with the loss of only one ship and thereby enabled Rommel to retake Cyrenaica and make preparations for his spring offensive against Tobruk. A further reinforcement of *Luftflotte 2*, which comprised II and X Air Corps as well as the forces of 'Air Command Africa', appeared to be necessary due to its many different tasks. These included, above all, destroying Malta as the central British base, securing the supply routes to North Africa, supporting land operations by the Army and combating the British navy. By early April *Luftflotte 2* was brought up to a list strength of 662 front-line aircraft – of which 397 were serviceable – and 50 transport planes, so that II Air Corps alone was able to deploy 390 aircraft – 268 serviceable – against Malta.[6]

In the course of these developments it again became clear that only the complete elimination of Malta, preferably its capture, would guarantee unhindered supplies for Panzer Group Africa and was therefore the indispensable condition for Rommel's victory in North Africa. The importance of Malta for a military decision in the Mediterranean theatre cannot be over-estimated and was to lead to sharp controversies within the German command. The problem of Malta, in fact, was never to be solved, even though the responsible German and Italian commands did take concrete offensive measures.

Sixteen, and subsequently twenty-four, U-boats – plus an additional five to six submarines in the waters off Gibraltar for the attack against convoys to the British base – were transferred to the Mediterranean at the turn of the year 1941–2. Although some spectacular successes were recorded, this move greatly weakened the attack on supplies in the Atlantic. These measures were taken just at the time when, after America's entry into the war, the German submarine arm was mustering all its forces for the battle against the Anglo-American Atlantic convoys. The transfer of so many submarines to a secondary theatre of war contradicted the axiom of concentration of forces. This led to a controversy between Admiral Dönitz, Commander U-boats, and Kriegsmarine Command, in which Dönitz emphatically protested the transfer of submarines to the Mediterranean which were then lost to the battle in the Atlantic, whereas Kriegsmarine Command felt it had to bow to the requirements of the overall conduct of the war.[7]

At the end of 1941, therefore, the German Supreme Command began to reinforce the Mediterranean by quite considerable forces in order to regain the military-strategic initiative in this theatre, even though the main thrust still lay in the east. Stationing an average of 21 submarines in the Mediterranean during the first three months of 1942 had already shown how narrow the limits were for a shift of force by only one branch of the services, and indicated that the problems facing the entire Wehrmacht, in light of the radically altered overall situation in early 1942, were almost insoluble. The more success the German eastern army enjoyed in bringing the Soviet winter offensive to a standstill, the more pressing was the resolution of the question as to whether during 1942 Germany should continue to seek the decision in the east, or whether a shift of the strategic initiative to the Mediterranean region was to be preferred.

Such a shift would very probably have led to a German victory in the Mediterranean, including the Middle East, with an expenditure of land, air and naval forces that would have been relatively modest compared to the overall military requirements. Deployment of *Luftflotte 2* had already brought remarkable results. Given the luxury of unhindered supplies, transfer of two or three armoured or motorized divisions to North Africa would have given Rommel the superiority he needed to achieve a decision in this theatre as early as 1942. However, the indispensable condition for this was the neutralization or capture of Malta. Such an offensive towards the Middle East, which was emphatically recommended by the Kriegsmarine,[8] would most likely have resulted not only in the capture of the Suez Canal and British positions in the Middle East, but would also have helped to prevent an American landing in North Africa.

It was clear, however, that while such an offensive by the Axis powers would have cleaned up the situation on the strategic southern flank of Europe, it would not have brought about a final military decision in the war against Great Britain and the United States. Furthermore, given the total forces required, the transfer of even two or three armoured or motorized divisions to North Africa would have taxed German strength to such a degree that it might have made it impossible for a decisive eastern front offensive, with far-reaching objectives, to be mounted at all. In the spring of 1942 there were no reserves of any magnitude available. Under these circumstances the only realistic operations would have been attacks with limited objectives, which, although offering chances of success, would have meant having to give up any subsequent major offensive in southern Russia.

A further option which was primarily urged by Admiral Dönitz, the Commander U-boats and future Commander-in-Chief of the Kriegsmarine, lay in concentrating all resources on building submarines and intensifying the supply and tonnage war in the Atlantic. Despite all efforts, during 1941 German submarines had not sunk enough enemy vessels to bring within reach a paralysis of British supplies by sea. The U-boats sank about 2.1 million tonnes of shipping[9] in that year, a total below that achieved in 1940. This relative Allied success in the tonnage war was mainly due to the breaking of the German code by British Intelligence (Ultra), leading to changes in the management and routing of Allied convoys. The shipping space saved from June 1941 through the information gained by Ultra is alleged to have amounted to almost 1.5 million tonnes; in other words, loss of shipping space was reduced by about 65 per cent in the second half of 1941. America's 'undeclared war' from late summer onward also contributed to greater security for the Atlantic convoys.[10]

Under these circumstances Admiral Dönitz believed, optimistically, that during 1942 monthly sinkings of at least 700,000 tonnes would be necessary to neutralize the effect of estimated new construction. Such a figure would therefore need to be exceeded to inflict lasting damage on the enemy. This was still some way off in the first quarter of 1942, when sinkings averaged only 645,000 tonnes per month.[11] Although German submarines did achieve astonishing successes off the eastern coast of the United States during 'Operation Drum-beat', which began in mid-January 1942, having sunk 228 ships totalling 1.28 million tonnes by mid-July, advances in submarine defence made it clear that victory in the tonnage war was still not in sight. Defensive improvements included the introduction of the 'Huff-Duff' direction-finding equipment, increases in the number of aircraft employed in submarine warfare, extension of the surveillance areas of these aircraft, and introduction of improved depth-charge launchers. According to new calculations by Dönitz and other senior naval officers, victory in the battle of the Atlantic would depend on 100–150 front-line submarines being on constant patrol; and given the necessary intervals for repairs, resupply and crew recuperation, a total force of about 300 boats would be required.[12]

Success in the tonnage war therefore depended primarily on submarine construction and repair time. It became evident that, come what might, new construction could not fall below 21 vessels monthly in order to be able to achieve a standing strength of 300 front-line boats. The major problem became the allocation of workers and this could not be solved during 1942 to the satisfaction of Kriegsmarine Command. While there were 249 submarines in service on 1 January 1942, 58 of these were employed for basic training in the Baltic, and 100 for advanced training. Because of secondary missions, only 55 of the remaining 91 front-line boats were available in the Atlantic, and of these a mere 22 were on patrol at any given time. Despite an increase of 80 boats by 1 July 1942, because of training needs and losses incurred in the meantime, the number of front-line boats only rose by 47.[13] Even though submarine repair was given top priority in mid-1942 and new construction increased slightly – 23 vessels in October 1942 – the Kriegsmarine was aware that only the rigorous assignment of labour and technical advances in the 'weapons system' submarine promised any chance of decisively reducing Allied shipping space within a foreseeable time-span. But such a preferential treatment of the submarine arm would have required a telling reduction in arms production for the Army, and this would more or less entail giving up any offensive plans on the eastern front. Eventually Kriegsmarine Command had to recognize that it would only receive the necessary capacities after the successful conclusion of the campaign in the east.

At the turn of the year 1941–2 the situation in the air was equally threatening, so far as the Luftwaffe was concerned. Its problem was not only to provide the strongest possible offensive forces for the support of future army operations in the Soviet Union, North Africa and other theatres, but to build up a home air defence in anticipation of having effectively to counter a 'strategic' bomber offensive by the Western powers. With the deployment of three *Luftflotten* on the eastern front in the spring of 1941, air defence in the west had to make do mainly with only two fighter wings. After 10 August 1941, home air defence became the responsibility of Air Command Centre, consisting of XII Air Corps together with anti-aircraft formations under General Josef Kammhuber.[14] Despite tactical and technical advances in the development of 'bright' and 'dark' night fighting, and a total of 302 night fighters and 358 crews by the end of 1941, the fighter force was already near crisis point. Even though the number of single-engine fighters increased from about 800 in 1941 to over 1300 by the beginning of 1942, this growth was mostly to the advantage of the front-line formations.[15]

Because senior leaders of the Luftwaffe under-estimated the air war potential of the United States and also assumed that for all practical purposes the British bomber arm would only be employed at night, they believed that in 1942 they could still get by with an expanded anti-aircraft defence and improved night fighting. Luftwaffe Command was primarily concerned with the forthcoming battles on the eastern front and in the Mediterranean and was not much worried about air defence over the territory of the Reich. It was only by the end of 1942 that the night fighter arm had increased to five wings with about 650 aircraft, which conducted the battle against the nightly attacks of the British with varying degrees of success.[16] British Bomber Command, which from the end of 1941 possessed an increasing number of heavy four-engined bombers, announced by a major attack on Lübeck on the night of 29 March 1942 that it had begun the 'unrestricted air war' against German cities. According to the directive of the British Air Staff of 14 February 1942, the primary targets were to be the urban housing areas in order to break the working population's will to resist. The first '1000 bomber attack' against Cologne during the night of 31 May 1942 – in fact by 1046 bombers – demonstrated not only the inferiority of the defence (only 52 bombers were lost) but also the magnitude of the growing threat to the home front.[17]

Increasing losses during subsequent attacks and difficulties in marking the targets led, however, to longer intervals between British bombing raids in the strategic air war after August. In 1942 their average loss rate of 5.6 per cent of the bombers employed lay well within acceptable bounds.[18] And since the US 8th Air Force was still in the build-up stage and only began flying occasional missions with limited effect against targets in northern France from mid-August on, Luftwaffe Command still believed it could give priority to the offensive. Before the beginning of the drive in southern Russia in June, 54 per cent of the air forces were on the eastern front. A boost in the increase of fighter aircraft that was being demanded in certain quarters, particularly by the Luftwaffe Chief of Staff, was slow to be realized. It was only in December 1942 that fighter production exceeded 700 per month – a completely unsatisfactory situation given the increased demands.

Far into 1944 the ratio between attack and defence aircraft was to remain at about one to one.[19] The list strength on 30 June 1942 was 1970 fighters against 1995 attack aircraft, i.e. bombers, dive-bombers and high-speed bombers; and one year later, the ratio had only shifted marginally. with about 2400 fighters against 2300 bombers. During the same period the quota of fighters had only increased from 33 per cent to 34 per cent of total aircraft.[20] This indicates how dominant the concept of offensive air war remained at a time when Germany had long lost the strategic initiative. The Luftwaffe had clearly made the shift from the offensive to the defensive far too late. Taking all circumstances into consideration, this shift should have occurred no later than in the autumn of 1942 in order to prepare the defence against the air offensive in 1943.

The basic question, therefore, is whether a turn in the war in Germany's favour could have been achieved at all in 1942, and if so, for which objectives and by what means. Discussion of these points not only provides information about the war aims of the Axis powers, but also helps to resolve the question as to how far the turn of the war in 1942–3 was due to blunders in evaluation and disposition of forces. In this context the only decisive question was whether the available forces of the Army and the Luftwaffe on the eastern front offered a sufficient guarantee that Germany could still bring the war in the east to a favourable conclusion in 1942. This was recognized as the indispensable condition for shifting the strategic and armament focus of the war against the Western powers, who were not expected to intervene in Europe and North Africa before early 1943. The alternative, given the demands being raised by the Luftwaffe and the Kriegsmarine, and the potential represented by the United States, would be to shift the strategic focus to the Mediterranean, renouncing far-reaching offensive plans in favour of limited attacks on the eastern front, and to begin husbanding military strength in anticipation of the future.

The decision as to which theatre of war and which branch of the Wehrmacht should receive priority naturally had a far-reaching effect on armaments policy. As already shown, from the summer of 1940 onward the German arms industry was under great pressure. On the one hand it had to maintain supplies for imminent or ongoing battles, and on the other to prepare for a redistribution of its priorities after the probable ending of the current campaign. The redirection of the war economy in July 1940 towards the requirements of the Luftwaffe and the Kriegsmarine had been followed by yet a further redirection to satisfy the needs of the Army at the end of September 1940 because of the planned campaign against the Soviet Union. This shift, however, had been watered down considerably by the Führer Directive of 20 December 1940. The order that the Luftwaffe and the Kriegsmarine were not to be deprived in any way at the expense of the Army meant that new equipment for the eastern army was not yet at the level required to cover the losses so far incurred. In mid-June, immediately before the beginning of the campaign in the east and in anticipation of a rapid victory over the Soviet Union, the Wehrmacht command again underlined its intentions to shift the weight of arms production to the Luftwaffe as quickly as possible in order to defeat Great Britain, which was now considered the primary enemy.[21]

A few weeks later, the progress of the campaign appeared to justify Hitler's directive of 14 July 1941 concerning a reduction in the arming of the Army in favour of an increase, albeit limited, of armament for the Luftwaffe. Shortly thereafter, the Kriegsmarine was also given assurances with regard to its submarine-building programme. However, there was still no centralized coordination of arms production which could have terminated the rivalries between the different branches of the Wehrmacht. As a consequence, the Army was unable to draw upon the amounts of weapons, equipment and munitions that would have been urgently required to cover the losses incurred during the summer and autumn battles. The already badly weakened eastern army had to fight a costly winter battle for which it was neither prepared in terms of manpower nor equipment. The renewed redirection of the war economy towards the Army, based on Hitler's decree of 10 January 1942, was therefore only a logical consequence of the neglect that had previously been shown to that branch of the Wehrmacht, which was to have decided the issue on the eastern front and thereby the preliminary outcome of the whole war. Under

EASTERN
FRONT
5 DECEMBER 1941
TO 31 MARCH 1942

Front Line on 6 Dec 1941
Front Line on 31 March 1942
II. Army Corps
16. Army
Nord Army Group North
AGr. Army Group
STAVKA Supreme Soviet Command

great time pressure and many shortcomings, the eastern army was now to be sufficiently well equipped and supplied by 1 May 1942 to be able to launch a major offensive with at least a part of its forces.[22]

Yet the commanders of the eastern army knew full well that it could never again reach the level of combat power it had enjoyed on 22 June 1941. The redirection of arms production in favour of a renewed offensive in the east also made it clear that for lack of labour and raw materials, the Luftwaffe and the Kriegsmarine could not count on any increase of their own armaments programmes – with a view to a major war effort – for some time to come. In any event, the order of the day was now to exercise moderation and to bring objectives into line with material means. Yet it would be an over-statement to claim that in early 1942 the shortages of material resources had already brought about an irreversible turn of the war against Germany. Even although in terms of armaments and manpower, the room for manoeuvre had already been greatly reduced by this time, it would still be an exaggeration to claim that the failure of the Blitzkrieg concept at the end of 1941 had marked the crucial turn in the direction of ultimate defeat. There was still sufficient military potential available to initiate action against one or other of Germany's enemies, at least in one of the theatres of war.[23]

The measures taken by Minister Speer from February 1942 onward demonstrated the unused capacities and reserves that could still be mobilized. If the mistakes made so far were to be corrected and further fragmentation of effort avoided, Germany still had a chance of bringing about a situation in which to deny her enemies final success in the war, provided, however, that her resources were concentrated on the key objectives. The situation envisaged had to be one which, if it did not offer the possibility of a German victory, at least excluded a German defeat in the sense of the subsequently raised demand for an 'unconditional surrender'.

The Partial Offensive on the Eastern Front in 1942 as Seen within the Framework of a Strategic Defence

With regard to the military and strategic possibilities that still remained against the Soviet Union, it quickly became apparent that there could no longer be talk of gaining final victory in 'battles of annihilation' leading to the downfall of the enemy. Instead the German command went over to *a strategy of attrition and exhaustion,* the essence of which was to gain new territories with a view to exploiting their strategically important raw materials. In the shift to this strategy of exhaustion lay the admission that even the most overwhelming victory in battle on the eastern front would not force an end to the war. The strategy was intended to deprive the enemy of the resources he required for an extended war and exploiting them oneself, as well as occupying and holding territories which were of key importance in a war on several fronts. Naturally the strategy also included weakening the enemy's military forces as far as possible. With this policy, Germany had gone over to strategic defence.[24]

The strategic intention to conduct a large offensive in order to gain the Caucasus and the lower Volga dated back to the autumn of 1941 and was reaffirmed by Hitler in early January 1942 as well as in an OKH directive of 12 February 1942 entitled 'Directive on the Continuation of the Campaign in the East after the End of Winter', at a time when a successful conclusion of the winter battles was still very much in doubt. Quite apart from the lack of clarity as to which forces would be available at the presumed starting date of the offensive, no consideration was given to the question whether the continuing difficulties on the fronts of Army Groups North and Centre and the conduct of the enemy would even permit a decisive offensive in the south. For Hitler personally, but equally in the interests of the arms industry, the military and the economy at large, the acquisition of the Caucasian oilfields, the coal mines of the eastern Donetz basin, the huge manganese reserves near Chiatura in Georgia, and the extended grain-growing area south of the lower Don, were indispensable objectives.

The calculations and assessments of the raw material reserves and the armaments potential of the Soviet Union contained partially realistic, partially unsubstantiated, inaccurate and contradictory statements, which in essence did not provide any information as to whether or how the Soviet war economy could be decisively damaged by the German military strategy for 1942. The estimated production figures for the more important weapons systems – which could not be accurately verrified by Intelligence and subsequently had to be corrected several times – showed that already the Germans were over-estimating their own potential and under-estimating that of the enemy.[25] As we know today, during the winter of 1941–2 the Soviet war economy suffered a serious decline in production caused by relocation of the arms factories and the immense losses which had to be replaced: in December 1941, for example, aircraft production only reached 39 per cent of plan.[26] From spring 1942 onward, however, remarkable overall results were achieved. In 1941 the Soviet armaments industry produced 24,500 tanks and about 33,000 pieces of artillery including anti-aircraft guns, whereas the Germans had only estimated a maximum of 11,000 and 7800 respectively. According to official figures, Soviet industrial production grew by a total of 19 per cent during 1942.[27]

Because of the actual and anticipated bottleneck in fuel supplies, capture of the oilfields of the Caucasus appeared to be the first priority, particularly since a study in April 1942 had shown that three-quarters of total Soviet oil production came from this source. Even if there were some doubts about this figure at the time, we know today that in all probability over 80 per cent of the estimated 22 million tonnes of oil produced in 1942 came from the Caucasus, so that the capture of this area would have resulted in a deadly danger for the Soviet war economy.[28] However, the following points had to be taken into consideration: 1. At all costs the conquest had to include the most important oil centre of Baku, and this lay about 1200 km away from the southernmost sector of the eastern front. 2. At all costs the oilfields had to be captured undamaged so that the Germans could exploit them for their own needs. 3. The lasting defence of the conquered territory had to be assured. 4. Fuel supplies to the Western Allies had to be prevented or at least hindered. The plan therefore included blocking river traffic on the Volga by which the valuable cargo was transported northwards to the production centres.

The Soviets enjoyed a great advantage in that their defence of the Volga region and the oilfields of Grozny, Machachkala and Baku, would involve the Germans in a time-consuming, exhausting advance without the need for giving battle prematurely. A decisive confrontation to defend these vital areas could be staged behind the line of the River Don and then immediately in advance of the objectives themselves. Success or failure of the German plan of campaign of 1942 therefore depended on being able to destroy large parts of the Soviet army in southern Russia *immediately after the start of the offensive* and preventing their withdrawal to the Volga and the Caucasus.

If the Germans failed to encircle and destroy the bulk of the Soviet Southern and South-western Fronts as well as parts of the opposing Bryansk Front at the very beginning of the attack[29], there was hardly any hope of their taking Stalingrad and the valuable areas in the Caucasus before the onset of winter. Success would depend upon capturing roughly 700,000 prisoners, a figure that would equal the achievement in October 1941 in the double battle of Vyazma-Bryansk. Germany's strategic reserves, who could have supported the attack in depth, had shrunk to a minimum.

The strategic and operational planning, which decisively influenced the course of the campaign during summer and autumn, was based on a discussion held at Führer headquarters on 28 March and finally on Directive No. 41 of 5 April 1942. The overall objective, namely 'to finally destroy the remaining Soviet armed forces and as far as possible to deprive them of their most important sources of economic power',[30] clearly and logically required the destruction of the opposing enemy forces in the south as the *sine qua non* for the success of the campaign. The advance of the German armies by sectors in three phases, the intermediate objective of which was to gain the land bridge between the Don and Volga rivers and Stalingrad, also demonstrates that the German command was well aware of the precarious conditions upon which the success of the summer offensive depended. Furthermore, there was no intention expressed to take Stalingrad, but only to paralyze the vital arms production and supply centre. The advance towards the Caucasus was only to be undertaken after the intermediate objectives had been attained and a secure position along the River Don built up to protect the flank. The Caucasus was clearly defined as the primary objective of the campaign.[31] On all other fronts, efforts were mainly to be concentrated on defence. The only other objective envisaged was the capture of Leningrad and the link-up with the Finnish army, but this was secondary to the offensive in the south.

How realistic, in the circumstances, was Directive No. 41? If the main line of intention had been adhered to and if the plan had been executed resolutely and without any mistakes, then perhaps the projected offensive would have been within the realm of possibility. The big question marks that remained, however, were the likely nature and effect of the expected Soviet counter-attacks in the sectors of Army Groups North and Centre, and the combat worth and dependability of the allied Hungarian, Italian and Romanian armies who were to provide flank protection along the Don. There was enormous time pressure on the German offensive to bring the war in the east to a victorious conclusion in 1942. Speer was only one of many who in the spring had urged mobilization of all resources in order to achieve victory as soon as possible. The war had to be won by the end of October before the onset of the Russian winter 'or we will have lost it for good'.[32]

It is significant to note that although the Chief of Staff and many experts expressed serious doubts about the summer campaign, based on the reduced combat power of the eastern army and the imbalance of the modest means and the far-reaching objectives, nobody proposed a viable alternative option. Even during the situation briefing on 28 March, Halder accepted Hitler's intentions and did not present an alternative plan, even though, according to later published statements, it is possible that such a plan existed.[33] Quite the opposite: Halder subsequently devoted himself to creating the operational, organizational and logistic conditions needed to provide the southern wing of the army in the east with the best possible basis for attack and the greatest possible combat power.

A strategic alternative, such as shifting the focus to the Mediterranean theatre along the lines urged by the Kriegsmarine, was no longer a point for discussion after the spring when Hitler had obviously decided once and for all to seek the decision on the eastern front. As he told Mussolini at their meeting on 30 April 1942, he expected the land war to be decided in the east, where a defeat for the Soviet Union, or its withdrawal from the war, would compel Great Britain to come to terms and seek a political solution. In this context, economic considerations took first place. All other options – Rommel's advance on Egypt, the capture of Malta or the stepping-up of the war in the Atlantic – while contributing substantially to overall success, would not bring about a decision.[34]

Looking back from our present vantage point to consider Germany's military strength and the Soviet Union's military potential, it does appear that German chances of success in the spring of 1942 were far less than was even estimated at the time. The assessment of the manpower potential of the Red Army was already based on index figures which cast doubts on its ability to recover from the enormous losses suffered since 22 June 1941. The manpower reserves were calculated at 1.97 million men (figure of 1 April 1942), which would only permit a maximum reinforcement by 60 divisions before the autumn. To his great surprise, Field Marshal von Bock, the new commander of Army Group South, had been informed at the end of March by Intelligence Department East that he had to reckon with 50-60 newly formed enemy divisions.[35] Colonel Gehlen, the head of the department, declared at the beginning of June that the enemy would most likely never again be able to throw the same potential into the battle as he had been able to do during the winter of 1941-2.[36] In mid-May, however, Intelligence calculated total Soviet strength at 546 major formations, of which no less than 487 were deployed opposite the three German army groups. According to these figures, Army Group South alone would have to deal with 168 enemy formations. In addition, the operational reserves were reckoned to number a maximum of 50 divisions,[37] so that from these estimates alone the growing superiority of the Red Army was becoming apparent. In contrast to this, on 24 June the Wehrmacht was only able to deploy 165½ divisions in the east, not including security divisions:[38]

Army Group North	36⅔ divisions
Army Group Centre	61 divisions
Army Group South	60½ divisions
11th Army (Crimea)	8 divisions
Total eastern front	165³/₂ divisions
(in addition:	12 security divisions)

If we look at the other theatres of war, the forces in Norway and Finland were relatively strong – 17½ divisions, of which 5½ were on the Finnish front – while those in the west had been noticeably 'thinned out' to 27 divisions, including 3 armoured divisions. There were also forces in the Balkans which were being held with only 5 divisions (!), and 3 divisions each in North Africa and on the home front. Therefore, of the Army's total of 234 divisions, including security divisions, 76 per cent were deployed in the east, excluding Finland, and with Finland included the ratio was over 78 per cent. Thus although the numerical strength compared to 1941 – about 73 per cent – appeared to have increased, in terms of quality there was a serious loss of combat power compared to the eastern army of the previous year.[39]

The immediately striking fact about the preparations made by the Soviet command to counter the German offensive in 1942 is the strength of the STAVKA reserves which could only be deployed with Stalin's explicit permission. In June 1942 the STAVKA disposed of operational reserves comprising ten armies, two tank armies, at least fifteen independent armoured corps, numerous infantry, armoured and engineering brigades, as well as many artillery and mortar regiments.[40] The deployment plan for these reserves show that there were no less than two tank armies and one army in the area to the south and south-west of Moscow, as well as a further five armies in the area between the upper Don and the lower Volga. Already during the winter of 1941–2 and in early spring, nine reserve armies had been created, most of which had already taken part in the (admittedly costly) Soviet counter-offensive. The continuing build-up of new 'strategic' reserves had for the most part escaped the attention of the OKH and was to prove one of the reasons for the subsequent defeat of the German summer offensive. The way these reserves were deployed in early summer 1942 confirms that the basic strategic assessment of German intentions by the Soviet command had been that the Wehrmacht would attempt a second major offensive against Moscow from the south-west with parts of Army Groups Centre and South, but that there was no indication as to the likely departure points and possible depth of this encircling attack to the south of the capital. However, there were also four armies being set up in the approaches to the Caucasus.

The deployment of the new Third and Fifth Tank Armies to the south-west of Moscow was intended to repel an expected attack by Army Group Centre from the south, similar to the attack by the Second Panzer Army in autumn 1941. The deployment of two reserve armies on the Volga at Saratov and Stalingrad suggest that Stalin had also considered a wide encircling move through the Stalingrad area northward along the Volga as a possibility. Even at the end of July, at the height of the German offensive, when the Soviets should long have recognized that the major German objective was the Caucasus, Stalin still clung to the opinion that the major danger lay in a German advance to the Volga, to be followed by a turn to the north.[41]

The meeting of the STAVKA and the Committee of National Defence at which the points were set for the summer campaign, took place on 28 March, on the same day that Hitler and the General Staff of the Army agreed the basics of the German offensive. The Moscow meeting agreed, in principle, to conduct a strategic defence and to provide 'strategic' reserves in order to counter the German attack. Simultaneously, however, preparations would be made for attacks with limited objectives on many sectors of the front in order to wear down the enemy and to prevent his withdrawing forces from less threatened areas. Such attacks, for example, were to be conducted to relieve Leningrad, to destroy the pocket of Demyansk, and to cut off German forces in the salients at Rzhev, Orel and Kharkov.[42] Although this had the advantage of the bulk of the Soviet reserves not being committed and dissipated prematurely, it was to result in heavy losses for the South-west Front of the Red Army during its limited attacks. In the course of these actions it became clear that the operational and tactical leadership had learned from the mistakes of the preceding year but that serious deficiencies still existed, for example in the leadership of armoured forces at corps and army level.[43]

In the spring battles in the sector of Army Group South – the recapture of the Kerch peninsula in May, the 'pocket' battle south of Kharkov that ended on 28 May, the battles between the Donetz and Oskol rivers near Volkhansk and Izyum in June, and the capture of the fortress of Sevastopol by early July – the Red Army suffered heavy defeats during which a total of almost 540,000 prisoners were taken. In the battle of Kharkov alone the South-west Front lost more than three armies with about 239,000 men.[44] In view of these defeats the STAVKA decided to forgo further costly operations such as a concentric attack in the area of the Bryansk Front with the object of taking Orel.[45] However, the Red Army had also gained experience in anticipating German encircling attacks, while German operations in advance of the main offensive 'Operation Blue' had cost valuable time so that this was only able to begin on 28 June. The General Staff therefore did not adhere to the originally scheduled date of 18 June, as von Bock had urged, and thereby gave the enemy the opportunity to reinforce and regroup his forces on the South-west Front.[46]

In weighing the relative strengths in mid-June 1942, the overall situation that had developed, the possibilities that existed on both sides, and the time pressure under which the German operation laboured, the question arises today as to whether the offensive towards the lower Volga and the Caucasus actually was the most promising solution for the strategic problem in 1942. The forces available, 60½ divisions of Army Group South and by mid-August an additional 36 allied divisions whose combat value was considered to be significantly lower, already show that whereas for this decisive attack Germany had to make do with about the same number of troops as had been available in early October 1941 for the attack on Moscow, it was aiming at far more distant strategic objectives. The attacking forces only included sixteen armoured and motorized divisions which were facing enormous wear and tear in the approaching battles and the long distances to be covered. Furthermore, on its southern flank, Army Group South was not going to be able to call upon the support of the Eleventh Army with its eight divisions, as had originally been planned.

Finally, the General Staff also had to consider the difficult positions of Army Groups North and Centre whose front lines were unusually jagged, showing many bulges, dents and weak spots, as well as the still uncleared areas of partisan operations in the rear, particularly behind Army Group Centre. Because of the priority given to reinforcing Army Group South, the reserves of the other two army groups were very meagre. It had not yet been possible, therefore, to eradicate the many operational danger spots, for example, to cut off the deep Soviet penetration on the inner flanks of Army Groups North and Centre by a pincer attack and eliminate this threat to the rear of the Ninth Army. In the north, the capture of Leningrad would have been an essential in order finally to free three army corps of the Eighteenth Army from their force-consuming ties. The front in the area of the German Demyansk salient, which could only be supplied through a narrow corridor, also urgently required relief. Furthermore, the Sukhinichi bulge – which it was planned to eliminate – posed a threat for the Fourth Army and the Second Panzer Army.[48]

Under these auspices, the offensive in the south, which under certain conditions might have stood some chance of success, became even more critical. The relationship between the strategic objectives, the available forces and the probable reactions of the enemy, was extremely precarious. It remained questionable whether strong segments of the Red Army could be destroyed in the initial attack. A failure of the offensive would not only lead to impossible over-taxation of the available forces, it would also have adverse repercussions on Army Groups North and Centre. Even if all of the oilfields in the Caucasus were to be captured, an extreme trial of strength would undoubtedly ensue, because the enemy would spare no efforts to retake them.

Under these circumstances a strategic alternative might have been to forgo an offensive in southern Russia, to eliminate instead the most immediate sources of danger along the eastern front and, after a phase of replenishment, to consider local attacks with limited objectives. One such objective, for example, could have been the capture of Leningrad which would finally have freed the bulk of the Eighteenth Army, and also a major part of the Finnish army, for other assignments. Another option might have been several offensive blows in the sector of Army Group Centre, which after eliminating the various threats in the rear, could have served not only to straighten the front but also, under favourable circumstances, to launch a renewed attack against Moscow.[49]

Limited offensives of this nature would not only have caused the enemy heavy losses – in the sector of Army Group Centre alone seven or eight Soviet armies could have been encircled or at least decisively weakened by clever operational leadership – but could also have enabled the eastern army to gain substantial reserves. At least three armies comprising six army corps, including armoured forces deployed on the front, could have been freed in the sectors of Army Groups North and Centre. In addition, the bulk of the Eleventh Army would have become available for other assignments after the capture of Sevastopol. The Wehrmacht could thereby have created a balance of forces and a sufficiently advantageous situation for the mustering of all reserves for a decisive attack against Moscow, which Stalin and the STAVKA were considering to be quite realistic.[50] Furthermore, such self-imposed restraint would have created the timely opportunity to provide armoured forces for the North African theatre.

The alternatives described might be said to provide a reasonable solution 'according to the book', whereas the planned offensive in southern Russia demonstrated the determination to force a strategic decision at all costs in 1942, even if this meant accepting high risks. In the light of the subsequent catastrophe at Stalingrad, it is clear that the German decision to mount the offensive in southern Russia set the scene for an inevitable and crucial show-down. Were the offensive to fail, then a turn of the war in favour of the Axis powers would have become virtually impossible.

Setting the Points:
Operational Fragmentation on the Way to Stalingrad

The summer and autumn campaign of 1942 has of course been discussed and analysed in depth,[51] and the purpose of our study is therefore to examine the more important turning points. The relatively small number (sixteen) of major armoured and motorized formations did not permit simultaneous deployment of the various attack groups, so that the enemy formations not under attack had the advantage of in-depth withdrawal. While the German advance by sectors did serve to conserve strength, it also gave the Soviet Bryansk, South-west and South Fronts an easier chance to predict Army Group South's next operational objective. The Sixth Army, for example, only possessed one Panzer Corps (XXXX) as a 'pincer arm' and was therefore unable to embark rapidly on the all-important drive into the big bend of the Don which would have ensured a deep encirclement of the enemy. So although the first two phases of the offensive on 28 June brought about a breakthrough to the Don at Voronezh, and gained much ground, it did not lead to a collapse of the Soviet south-west front.

At this point it should be noted that while the Soviet Supreme Command had learned about the basic concept of the first stage of the German offensive through a captured document, it did not draw the evident conclusion that the main German attack was aimed at gaining the Caucasus and the lower Volga. Stalin and most of the other senior leaders clung to the belief that the planned German breakthrough at Voronezh was the initial phase of a wide encirclement of Moscow from the south and was additionally designed to cut the lines of communication between central and southern Russia. Obviously the commanders of the fronts involved saw the dangers associated with the German drive to the Don more realistically, but were unable to convince Supreme Headquarters in Moscow.[52] In this respect, the STAVKA's misinterpretation gave the German eastern army an initial advantage, because valuable operational reserves were

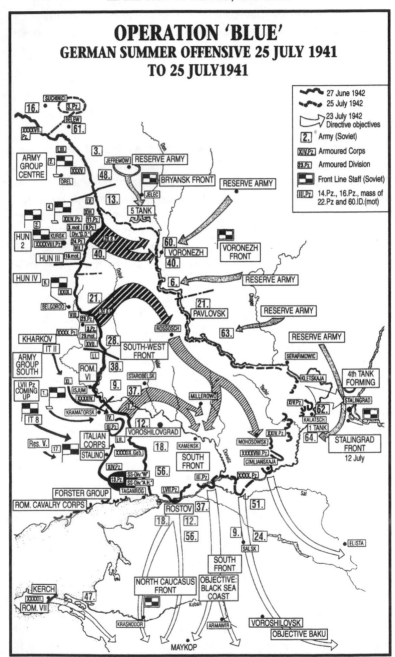

OPERATION 'BLUE'
GERMAN SUMMER OFFENSIVE 25 JULY 1941
TO 25 JULY 1941

held back for the protection of Moscow. In the long run, however, this advantage was lost, because on the one hand there were still sufficient Soviet reserves available to build up a stable line of defence along the Don, and on the other, the Germans lost valuable time in annihilating the Russian southern flank at the moment of its greatest weakness. The tactical surprise achieved during the first days of the offensive was quickly to dissipate.

Let us turn now to the main factors which contributed decisively to the failure of the German offensive:[53]

1. With a view to the rapid capture of the important city of Voronezh, against the opinions of Hitler and the General Staff, but following the tactical recommendations of the local commanders, the leadership of Army Group South retained the Fourth Panzer Army on the upper Don in the Voronezh area for several days from 4 July onward. This seriously delayed the planned attack by the Fourth Panzer Army down river in the rear of the enemy forces retreating before the advance of the Sixth Army.[54] As a consequence, large forces of the Soviet Fortieth and Twenty-first Armies were able to escape from the intended encirclement. Furthermore, only XXXX Panzer Corps was then available for the drive to the south.[55] In the course of these developments, Field Marshal von Bock vacillated between the desires of the local commanders to gain the bridgehead over the Don at Voronezh and the intention to have the armoured forces turn south as quickly as possible to cut off the enemy. This latter objective largely failed. By 11 July only some 88,000 enemy prisoners had been brought in and only about 1000 tanks and 1700 guns destroyed or captured. These were disappointing numbers. Even though von Bock subsequently tried to atone for the previous operational mistakes, particularly to regain lost time, he was held responsible for the failure of the initial phase of the campaign and relieved of his command on 13 July.[56]

2. In the further course of events, the Fourth Panzer Army had to relinquish 9th and 11th Panzer Divisions because these were required as reinforcements for the northern defensive flank. In the attempt to break through this flank at the beginning of July, the Bryansk Front launched heavy attacks by the Fifth Tank Army – which alone comprised over 600 tanks – and two independent armoured corps.

While these led to extremely heavy losses for the Soviets,[57] they did tie down German armoured forces. That the Soviets committed serious operational mistakes can be seen from the fact that in the Voronezh sector in early July, the Bryansk Front enjoyed a strong superiority in armour – the Fifth Tank Army and seven independent armoured corps – but could not prevent the German breakthrough. Far more grievous from the German viewpoint, however, was that after having completed their assignment, the valuable 9th and 11th Panzer Divisions were not returned to the Fourth Panzer Army which urgently required reinforcements. Instead they were put under the command of Army Group Centre in order to participate in a limited local attack. This resulted in a serious weakening of the already meagre attack forces which in mid-July began the decisive attempt to encircle and destroy the Soviet South-west and South Fronts.

3. After completion of the first phase of the attack, a serious conflict broke out between Hitler and the Chief of Staff of the Army and the Commander-in-Chief of Army Group B, which had come into being on 7 July when Army Group South was split into Army Groups A and B. As opposed to the intentions of Army Group B to send the Fourth Panzer Army south-east into the bend of the Don in close pursuit of the retreating enemy, on 13 July Hitler ordered this army to turn south into the Rostov area in order to prevent the clearly obvious withdrawal of the enemy to the south over the lower Don. Army Group A, which consisted of the First Panzer Army and the Seventeenth Army, and which should have formed the southern 'pincer arm' to encircle the enemy according to the original plan, was only given the order to hold. This fundamental change in the operational plan was an indirect admission that the first two stages of the offensive had not led to the planned encirclement and destruction of strong enemy forces. Since only relatively small numbers of prisoners and captured weapons had been reported, the only explanation was a large-scale withdrawal by the Soviet South-west and South Fronts. It was therefore hoped that this could be made up for by a successful 'pocket' battle of Rostov. Hitler's directives of 17 July for the continuation of the operation clearly define this objective.[58]

It is appropriate at this point to discuss in detail the criticism that has frequently been raised in the literature about the 'fatal' turn-off of the mass of the German southern flank in the direction of Rostov and the lower Don. Hitler's decision to reinforce Army Group A by the Fourth Panzer Army and to seek a major battle on the lower Don stood in contrast to Army Group B's intention to push the unreduced bulk of its forces into the big bend of the Don in order rapidly to gain the land bridge between the Don and the Volga to the west of Stalingrad. As opposed to the original Directive No. 41 which had intended to bring about an interim decision by uniting the spearheads in the Stalingrad sector (not in Stalingrad itself!), the focus of the operation was now to be transferred to the south. This also aimed at cutting off as many of the withdrawing forces of the Red Army as possible even if expert opinion was that the enemy would again escape from encirclement.

Attainment of the intermediate operational objective, namely the capture of the *Stalingrad area*, had thus been delayed in favour of concentrating the main force in the direction of the Caucasus and of gaining time, even if this meant weaknesses on the flanks and in the rear of Army Group A in its advance to the south. Whereas the compromise that General Halder brought about on 18 July did make possible the advantageous loosening up of the attack forces of Army Group A in favour of Army Group B, the new assignment now given to Army Group B, namely to 'take Stalingrad by a daring advance', revealed very sharply the competition between the lines of advance both to the Caucasus and to Stalingrad. As yet this had not led to a basic unresolvable contradiction, and as yet the advance south towards the oilfields still had priority, even if this meant forgoing a rapid and resounding success in the Stalingrad area.[59]

Directive No. 45 of 23 July, leaving the bulk of the forces with Army Group A which was to advance into the Caucasus to the distant objectives of Baku and the Black Sea coast, has been much criticized but cannot necessarily be regarded as a strategic error. Although this did lead finally to the divergence of the two main lines of advance, with the advance to the Caucasus designed to occur simultaneously with the capture of Stalingrad, control of the Volga and the subsequent advance to Astrakhan at the mouth of the river, the operational focus remained in the south with Army Group A. There was still the opportunity to sacrifice the costly advance of the Sixth Army towards Stalingrad and make do with the establishment of a protected flank in the bend of the Don in the form, for example, of a tangential line in the Chir sector, which would have maintained the link with the eastern flank of Army Group A south of the Don. The fatal dilemma which was to run its course in the ensuing weeks resulted from the *failure to define the priority of either of the two main objectives of the campaign*. In this context it is impossible to overlook the weeks' long tug-of-war between Hitler and the General Staff of the Army, which was still bent on clinging to its original plan despite all the 'dilutions' that had occurred in the meantime.

Even after 23 July it would not have been too late to declare priority for the objective which had from the very start been in the minds of Army Group B and the General Staff of the Army, i.e. Stalingrad and the lower Volga. And the decision of 23 July, which also took the time factor into consideration,[60] would also have had a chance of success had the advance of three German armies been concentrated on the Caucasus. Directive No. 45 was not the main reason for the dilution of the German attack plan, but rather the decision taken on 30–31 July in which Halder played a major role. Following this decision, the considerable forces of the Fourth Panzer Army were withdrawn from the line of attack towards the Caucasus and placed under the command of Army Group B as reinforcement for the attack on Stalingrad from the south. Only now had the highly questionable situation been created whereby both army groups disposed of roughly equal forces, including evenly divided armoured and motorized troops, so that a hopeless fragmentation of the already very meagre attack forces became evident. From this point on, Army Group B disposed of three armoured corps with a total of four armoured and three motorized divisions as mobile forces for its attack on Stalingrad, whereas for the capture of the oilfields in the Caucasus – originally the most important objective of the campaign – Army Group A was likewise left with only three armoured corps made up of three armoured and three motorized divisions.

Yet even after this decision to weaken Army Group A in favour of Army Group B as it advanced on Stalingrad, a strict concentration of all available forces there would at least have made it possible to gain this objective. However, it would have entailed a yet further weakening of Army Group A and the abandonment of the ambitious objectives in the Caucasus. This consequence – the giving up one of the two key objectives of the summer campaign – was not faced. So

Army Group B had to do without those few armoured forces which might have guaranteed the destruction of the four Soviet armies in the Stalingrad sector and the speedy capture of the city in August.

Further problems were created by the withdrawal of the 'Großdeutschland' Division from the front of Army Group A and its transfer to Army Group Centre, as well as by the decision not to deploy the 'Adolf Hitler' SS Division, which had so far been held in reserve, but to send it to the Channel front in France in expectation of a British landing. By mid-August the mobile forces of Army Group A had shrunk to five German divisions and one Slovak division just when it was fighting for the approaches of the Caucasus and had only taken the oilfield of Maikop.[61]

There were two further factors which proved detrimental to the German offensive. Ever since the directives of 17 July it had been apparent that Hitler did not wish to involve the bulk of the Eleventh Army in the conquest of the western Caucasus. Five divisions from this army were withdrawn from the Crimea in order to take part in the capture of Leningrad which was planned for September. Only two divisions of the Eleventh Army therefore participated in the amphibious operation against the Taman peninsula.[62] As a consequence, the bulk of the Eleventh Army under Field Marshal von Manstein was not available for the decisive battle which could either take place on the Caucasus front or at Stalingrad. Given the meagre forces on the German southern front, this was a fatal decision. One of the problems it caused was that transportation of the forces, especially the siege artillery, from the Crimea to Leningrad took several weeks so that there was no guarantee that the conquest of Leningrad could take place before the onset of the autumn weather. There is much to be said for the supposition that leaving the Eleventh Army on the southern front would have prevented, or at least greatly mitigated, the subsequent catastrophe of the Sixth Army at Stalingrad.[63]

The second unfortunate decision concerned the Italian Alpini Corps which possessed valuable experience in mountain warfare but instead of being deployed in the Caucasus was sent to the bend of the Don at Novaya Kalitva as flank protection. And this took place at a time when the Seventeenth Army still had some hopes of being able to push through over the crest of the Caucasus and reach the Black Sea coast at Tuapse.

Soviet counter-measures

The initial German successes, the heavy losses on the northern wing of the South-west Front, the unsuccessful counter-attacks by the Soviet Fifth Tank Army and the signs of dissolution during the in-depth withdrawals, caused Stalin great consternation lest the initially orderly withdrawal turn into a hopeless flight. Moreover, for many weeks he still feared a gigantic encircling movement by the Germans across the Don and upriver along the Volga. The disintegration of the South-west Front and the simultaneous creation by the STAVKA on 12 July of the Stalingrad Front, initially consisting of three armies,[64] as well as the basic decision to withdraw behind the Don on a broad front to the positions at Stalingrad and the approaches to the Caucasus, indicate the Soviet intention to avoid an annihilating defeat and to concentrate on the defence of vital centres, even if this meant giving up large territories.

The notorious order of the People's Commissioner for Defence No. 227 of 28 July,[65] in which deserters, panic-mongers and cowards were threatened with the harshest punishment, also contained the demand, 'Not one step back!', but served primarily to re-establish discipline and combat morale. Stalin threatened commanders of all ranks, as well as commissars and political functionaries, with imme-diate dismissal and court-martial should they retreat without permis-sion. It is evident from reports of the many dismissals and verdicts in July and August 1942 relating to high-ranking officers that combat morale and the will to resist had sunk to a new low in many forma-tions of the Red Army in southern Russia during this phase, and that numerous incidents of panic-stricken flight and voluntary surrender into German captivity occurred. Minister of the Interior Beria's appearance and actions at the headquarters of the Transcaucasian Front in Georgia on 22 August also testify to the strong mistrust by the political leadership of fighting morale in many sectors.[66]

In mid-July Stalin also had to recognize that he could no longer count on the repeatedly demanded second front in 1942 which the Western Allies were expected to mount on the coasts of occupied western Europe. The planned operations in question were 'Bolero' and 'Sledgehammer' on the French Channel coast, which were to have been conducted mainly by American troops with the objective of drawing 40 German divisions away from the eastern front. When he received a negative response from Churchill, Stalin sent him a very sharply worded letter on 23 July in which he came very close to accusing him of downright betrayal. Stalin also suspected the United States of not making a supreme effort in the context of the Soviet-American agreement of 11 June to support the Soviet Union by all possible means.[67] The suspicion that for years Great Britain and the United States deliberately postponed opening the second front in order to force the Soviet Union to bear the brunt of the war against Germany, even that the USSR had been assigned the role of the 'sacrificial lamb', became a basic tenet of Soviet foreign policy and was to play an important role in post-war politics.

A further accusation addressed to London was that the British navy was not making a sufficient effort to get the convoys with vital war materials for the Red Army through to Murmansk and Archangel. There is conclusive proof, however, that despite grave doubts the British navy was prepared to risk the heaviest losses in order to transport the required goods to northern Russia. Convoy PQ 16, for example, suffered severe losses in the Arctic Ocean at the end of May 1942, while in early July PQ 17 was almost totally destroyed within only a few days as a result of concerted attacks by German submarines and *Luftflotte 5*. Of the 37 mainly British and American ships, 24 were lost.[68] It is a wild exaggeration to claim that the British government used the destruction of convoy PQ 17 as an excuse to reduce the aid shipments to northern Russia, or even to discontinue them for many months.[69]

Despite the continuing battle at the approaches to Stalingrad, the STAVKA realized at the beginning of September there was no danger in the near future of the Germans capturing the important oilfields,[70] nor of their breaking through to the Black Sea coast, nor of their over-running the Soviet positions in the Stalingrad region. Indeed, to all intents and purposes, the German summer offensive had run itself out. On the other hand, the STAVKA had played its trump cards against Army Groups North and Centre. In a battle lasting many weeks, a Soviet relief offensive against the German encirclement at Leningrad had succeeded by the end of August in decimating the important divisions of the Eleventh Army which had been earmarked for the capture of the city. In the area of the German II Corps at Demyansk, twelve divisions remained tied down in an exposed position under the threat of again being cut off. In the area of the German Ninth Army and the Third Panzer Army several attacks conducted by a total of eight Soviet armies had succeeded by the end of July in achieving deep penetrations and forcing the defenders to throw in their last reserves. The Soviet leadership had thereby gained the inestimable advantage of having considerable operational reserves committed long-term to the support of the highly endangered front of Army Group Centre, because Hitler could not see his way clear to a total or partial evacuation of the threatened salients on this front, for example the bulge at Demyansk.[71]

In breach of the principle not to deploy disproportionately strong forces in a secondary theatre to the detriment of the main theatre, on 11 August and with the agreement of Halder, Hitler had begun an offensive action by the Second Panzer Army to cut off the Sukhinichi bulge, for which four infantry and no less than five Panzer Divisions (!) were committed without achieving a breakthrough.[72] The degree to which the division of forces had shifted to the detriment of Army Groups A and B by mid-August could be seen by the fact that both army groups together only disposed of twelve divisions of German mobile forces, so that for its attack on Stalingrad Army Group B had to make do with seven of these. Army Group Centre, on the other hand, could deploy fourteen armoured and motorized (albeit greatly weakened) divisions even though it was only defending a secondary front. Since the infantry reserves were also mostly used up, by the beginning of September the German Supreme Command had practically nothing left with which to bring about the intended turn of the war in 1942.

Interim results

With hindsight, it is clear that at the beginning of September the Germans had lost the strategic and operational initiative on the eastern front, even though the battle for Stalingrad was still to enter its most violent and costly phase. There was no longer any hope of gaining the originally planned objectives on the Caucasus front or on the approaches to the oilfields of Grozny. Only in the Stalingrad area and on the lower Volga was there still a slight chance for the campaign to score a partial success. While the complete capture of the city would have freed some reserves, notably three decimated armoured divisions,[73] given the acute shortage of fuel and ammunition, it still remained highly doubtful whether these reserves, together with a few additional formations, would have been sufficient to support the threatened 650 km-long front on the Don where

Romanian, Italian and Hungarian forces were acting as flank protection and where it had been impossible to prevent the Soviets from gaining several bridgeheads. The outright capture of Stalingrad would have brought the attack to a tactical conclusion in this sector, but this would not have resulted in a turn of the war in Germany's favour. Everything now depended on whether it would be possible to hold the ground gained against all counter-attacks during the winter, despite the over-extended front, the low combat potential of the allied forces, the meagre reserves and the difficulties of supply.

Despite Stalin's fear that the city which bore his name could be lost and that the Germans could thereby cut the principal river highway of the country, the decision was already taken on 13 September to prepare 'Operation Uranus', an encircling counter-offensive against the Sixth Army and the Fourth Panzer Army.[74] After the partial successes that the Red Army had achieved in the northern and central sectors, the STAVKA obviously believed that it could deny the Germans a final victory in the Stalingrad sector as well and that the operational situation offered possibilities for a decisive counter-attack. The more German forces committed to the battle at Stalingrad – which entered its most costly phase only on 11 September – the greater the chances of an attack against the north-western and southern flanks of these forces which were completely denuded of reserves.[75]

The OKW only began to admit with reluctance in the course of September and October that because of the lack of forces and the difficulties of supply, it would no longer be possible to force the desired final decision in 1942. Nevertheless, the numerous subsequently discussed concepts[76] show that the intention was to hold the line reached under any circumstances and to use it as the basis for further conquests in the spring of 1943. The 'September crisis' at headquarters led, on 24 September, to the dismissal of Colonel General Halder, who had long been involved in irreconcilable controversy with Hitler on operational questions.[77] The crucial mistake made by Hitler and other leaders of the Wehrmacht is that because of their misapprehension of the many danger spots on the eastern front and their under-estimation of the enemy's options in the Mediterranean and North Africa, they failed to draw the correct conclusions in the autumn of 1942 and resort to a defensive strategy in line with Germany's potential at the fronts, in the occupied territories and at home. Their insistence on opting to improve the situation offensively destroyed any chance of preventing a turn in the war in favour of the enemy.

The Collapse of the Southern Flank of the Eastern Front and its Consequences

In many respects, the factors that led to a military-strategic turn on the eastern front were determined in the summer and autumn of 1942 by the Germans themselves, by virtue of their mistaken assessments and omissions. Given the decisive battle of Stalingrad, the collapse of the front on the Don and the German withdrawal from the Caucasus, the question that arises is what alternatives the Germans had to avoid this disastrous turn of the war. Since the literature dealing with Stalingrad has provided many interesting revelations,[78] we need not go into details here but may rather concentrate on the key questions.

The intention to leave the German armies in the Caucasus on the lines they had gained depended on their rear and northern flanks being securely protected. In other words, any Soviet breakthrough on the Don or to the north-west or south of Stalingrad would create a deadly danger for Army Group A. Hitler, the new Chief of Staff of the Army, General Zeitzler, as well as the commanders of Army Group B, the Sixth Army and the Fourth Panzer Army, were aware of these threats to their flank positions. The key problem, however, was that the local commanders wanted to break off the incredibly costly battle for the city centre in order to gain reserves for the support of the threatened flanks, whereas Hitler, as we know, insisted, mainly for psychological reasons, that the city be completely taken and made this a condition for the withdrawal of reserves for the flanks. This was based on an operational order by Hitler of 14 October which demanded that the lines reached should be held and stabilized as a departure base for offensive operations in 1943.[79]

It is also clear that at headquarters of Army Group B and the Sixth Army the danger of a Soviet breakthrough in the sector of the Romanian Third Army and the Italian Eighth Army was recognized, and that the Chief of Staff of the Sixth Army even reckoned with the possibility of a temporary encirclement of his army during the winter.[80] However, the counter-measures proposed by these commands did not go beyond tactical measures to strengthen the Romanian Third and Fourth Armies. The provision of local reserves was limited to the 22nd Panzer Division with only 42 tanks (!), parts of the 14th Panzer Division, and the weak Romanian 1st Armoured Division. As a minimal solution the Chief of Staff of Army Group B suggested pulling the Sixth Army back to a line between the bend of the Don and the bend of the Volga south of Stalingrad – a measure which would only marginally have improved the precarious situation of the Sixth Army. A withdrawal to a 'Don–Chir position' which the command of the Sixth Army urged repeatedly during October was also only a partial operational solution and would only have removed the immediate threat.[81]

The question of a major shortening of the front

The reduced combat power of the German forces at Stalingrad, as well as the precarious operational and logistic situation of the Sixth Army and the Fourth Panzer Army, should have demanded a timely withdrawal of these armies as well as the Romanian Third and Fourth Armies to a much shorter and strength-saving position. In the autumn of 1942 important senior officers were in agreement about this and such an assessment is also the majority opinion expressed in the literature.[82] In any case, supply problems and the lack of preparations for the winter alone would have made a withdrawal in depth of the German and allied forces appear to be mandatory. Even before it was encircled, the Sixth Army had already needed to bring in supplies by air from time to time. If Stalingrad was not to be given up under any circumstances, then the solution on offer would have been a withdrawal of Army Group A to the Sal sector or behind the lower Don, while possibly maintaining a bridgehead to the south of Rostov. This would have reduced to a minimum the danger of Army Group A being cut off from the rest of the eastern front in the Rostov area and, furthermore, would have provided reinforcements for Army Group B.

Because of the lack of operational reserves and the weakness of the allied armies, holding on to the positions at Stalingrad *and* in the Caucasus already appeared to be a highly dangerous proposition. But while the recommended withdrawal of parts of Army Group B to a more favourable position along the upper and middle River Chir, for example, would have made it easier to repel Soviet breakthrough attempts on this front, it would not have improved the extremely exposed position of the armies in the Caucasus, especially not the latent threat to their northern flank in the Kalmyk steppe. Only a prompt withdrawal – no later than in early November – of the armies in the Caucasus, regardless of any measures taken in the sector of Army Group B, could have helped to stabilize the whole southern flank of the eastern front.[83] Whereas in the autumn of 1942 senior commanders repeatedly considered the advantages of withdrawing the Sixth Army and the Fourth Panzer Army and giving support to the flanking armies, a far bolder solution would have been required in order to stabilize the whole eastern front. Such a solution would have entailed the withdrawal in depth, for example, of both Army

THE MAJOR SOVIET OFFENSIVE
STALINGRAD FROM 19 NOV. 1942 ON

Groups A and B to as short a line as possible between the Don sector at Voronezh and the river itself at Rostov, or even more radically to a straightened line as held on 28 June 1942 at the beginning of the summer offensive. In addition, relatively small forces could have taken over the protection of the Kerch peninsula. Finally, in the sectors of Army Groups North and Centre, bulges in the front could have been given up to conserve strength.

Such a radical solution would have created the opportunity of permanently stabilizing the whole eastern front; it would have freed numerous reserves, and made possible the repulse of the expected winter offensive by the Red Army. Such a move would basically have meant giving up the strategic conquests made in 1942 and required the German leadership to face the fact that there was practically no hope left of reconquest in 1943. But even without this painful admission, it was already evident that prior to the start of the Soviet offensive on 19 November, Germany stood virtually no chance of repelling the winter offensive and preventing the defeat of the southern flank of the eastern front.

German estimation of the enemy situation

The differences of opinion in the evaluation of the enemy focus and the forces he would employ during his expected winter offensive contributed much to the success of the Soviet attacks of 19 and 20 November, even though they were not decisive. While Hitler expected the main Soviet assault, with operational objectives reaching all the way to the mouth of the Don at Rostov, to take place in the sector of the Italian Eighth and Romanian Third Armies which had been deployed on the left flank of the Sixth Army on 10 October, the Sixth Army command was only expecting more limited targets restricted to the attempt to encircle the German forces in the Stalingrad area. Responsible experts considered a double envelopment of the Sixth Army to be virtually impossible. The Intelligence Department at OKH was of a completely different opinion. For a long time it assumed that the main Soviet attack during the winter offensive would take place on the front of Army Group Centre, and as late as during a briefing on 6 November it spoke of attacks in this sector to cut off bulges in the German front. While Intelligence did reckon with Soviet attacks against the allied positions on the Don, it considered this threat to be of only secondary importance[84] and assumed an attack with the aim of destroying the whole German southern flank to be highly unlikely.

The differences of opinion between the local commanders and Central Intelligence can be seen from the fact, for example, that local radio surveillance had already detected the deployment of the Soviet Fifth Tank Army on the front of the Romanian Third Army on 11 November and had reported this, while Intelligence erroneously claimed that the Fifth Tank Army was deployed somewhere else entirely. The Soviet South-west, Don and Stalingrad Fronts, whose deployment the Germans had at least detected in broad terms, comprised a total of ten armies, including a tank army, with more than 93 divisions and four air armies, while there were a further three armies, including two guard armies, approaching from the north as reserves of the Supreme Command. By November 1942 the Soviets had succeeded in setting up five armies, one tank army, five independent armoured and motorized corps, and 27 infantry divisions as strategic reserves, over and above the reinforcements provided for the front-line formations.[85]

There is no doubt that the Soviet preparations for attack along the Don front and at Stalingrad had been more or less accurately recognized by the local German commands by the end of October/beginning of November, with only a few exceptions. It is also true that – despite the sombre predictions and increasing concerns of the staffs of Army Group B and the Sixth Army – very few preparations were made for the repulse of the Soviet offensive; and due to the lack of sufficient forces, virtually nothing at all was done to counter a decisive attack in the direction of the mouth of the Don.[86] Whereas at OKH there was growing awareness of an impending crisis, the Chief of Staff, Colonel General Zeitzler, had not been able to convince Hitler of the necessity of withdrawing forces from the Stalingrad area. Furthermore, the threat of a Soviet attack in the sector of Army Group Centre was causing bigger headaches. Given the decisions taken, Zeitzler obviously did not take any further steps to make Hitler reconsider and consoled himself with the stop-gaps and meagre reinforcements already described.[87]

The question of a breakout by the Sixth Army

From Moscow's point of view, the Soviet attacks on 19 and 20 November had the overall strategic advantage that *after* the landing by the Western Allies in North Africa, and *after* Rommel's heavy defeat at El-Alamein in early November, the German leadership could no longer give its undivided attention to the happenings on the southern flank of the eastern front. While the Soviet breakthroughs on 19 and 20 November led to the formation of a loose ring of encirclement of the Sixth Army and parts of the Fourth Panzer Army, totalling 250,000 men on 23 November, there were many factors that argued for giving up Stalingrad and rapidly breaking out to the south-west in order to join up with the remaining German and Romanian forces outside the pocket.

The constantly reiterated question as to which factors and considerations ultimately led to Hitler's decision to leave the Sixth Army at Stalingrad and to liberate it by a relief attack from the south, ignores a very important point. To concentrate only on the operational situation in the Stalingrad region is to be blind to the situation of the German armies in the Caucasus. The German leadership restricted its measures for the salvation of the Sixth Army to the forces and means of Army Group B, and later to those of the newly formed Army Group Don, but initially *did not regard the immediate withdrawal of the Caucasus armies* in the direction of the lower Don as the unavoidable condition for the stabilization of the overall situation. The reason for clinging to positions in the Caucasus was that Hitler – and other leaders as well – still nourished the hope of adhering to the original German long-range objective, namely crossing the southern Russian frontier and advancing to the Middle East and Iran with an 'expeditionary force', even if this had to be postponed until spring of 1943.[88]

During the dramatic process of reaching a decision which took place between Hitler, Göring, the General Staff of the Army and the Commands of Army Group B and the Sixth Army, and which concluded temporarily on 24 November with Hitler's order to form a pocket, the demand was frequently and emphatically raised to permit the encircled forces to break out. During these critical days, however, nobody appears to have suggested to Hitler that a breakout by the Sixth Army must be accompanied by an immediate withdrawal of Army Group A to the lower Don, even though Zeitzler did claim after the event that he had already suggested the withdrawal of Army Group A to Hitler at the end of November and had repeatedly come back to this topic.[89] Such a measure would not only have freed the Seventeenth Army and the First Panzer Army from the danger of becoming cut off from their lines of communication over the lower Don, but would have had the added advantage that parts of these armies could have been brought up to support the front to the west and south-west of Stalingrad. There would then have been justifiable hopes of the Sixth Army – if permission to break out were granted – joining up with the First Panzer Army to form a new defensive front. The cooperation of the Seventeenth Army, which was subsquently brought up in January 1943 to form the so-called Kuban bridgehead, would also have been required.

After weighing up all the pros and cons, it is reasonable to conclude at this point that the decision to leave the Sixth Army in the Stalingrad pocket and to await the results of the relief attack was self-damaging and therefore a blunder. Even if one of the key players, namely Field Marshal von Manstein, Commander-in-Chief of the newly formed Army Group Don, attempted to justify this decision after the event,[90] there can be no doubt that the disadvantages far outweighed the advantages. During the initial days of encirclement, the Sixth Army was not yet faced by a stable Soviet front, its physical forces had not yet been weakened by the subsequent defensive fighting, and by the great hardships later endured under siege. There was still great uncertainty as to when, and in what strength, forces could be made available for the relief attack. Finally, the survival of twenty-one German and two Romanian divisions, and numerous other forces, totalling roughly 250,000 men, depended on an adequate and continuous supply by air. Von Manstein's conduct during those critical days in November, incidentally, also show that even outstanding commanders did not think it necessary to subordinate the immediate breakout by the encircled forces to all other options. To be fair, it must be admitted that an early breakout by the Sixth Army would also have entailed considerable risks. First, all the encircled forces to the west and south-west of Stalingrad would have had to be united, which was in contradiction to Hitler's order to hold the city. Second, the lack of fuel would have necessitated leaving a major part of the armour and other vehicles behind, and the problem of transporting several thousand wounded would have had to be solved. Third, in the course of the breakout the Soviet reserves would also have had to be defeated.[91]

In the final analysis, it was the discussions concerning the feasibility of ensuring supplies by air, about which there are many detailed descriptions, that led to Hitler's decision of 24 November.

The mistaken assumption that a daily supply of between 400 and 500 tonnes could be flown into the pocket already lacked any realistic foundation.[92] After meeting his closest advisers, Göring, on 23 November, apparently made his commitment to a daily transport figure of 500 tonnes under the impression that he was dealing only with a *temporary* emergency situation. What was far more fatal, however, was that this mistaken assessment was not corrected after the initial failures of the operation, even though high-level experts had advised against attempting to supply the Sixth Army by air from the very beginning. Had the army been granted the freedom to act there would still have been a realistic chance, up to the final days of November, to save the greater part of the army, leaving immobilized equipment behind. At this point the Sixth Army still possessed some 150 tanks.[93] There was still an opportunity to coordinate the operations of Army Group Don, under whose command the Sixth Army had been placed, with the withdrawal of the two armies in the Caucasus and, finally, of avoiding a catastrophic defeat on the southern wing of the eastern front, albeit with heavy losses.

In considering the controversial question as to whether an opportune breakout or a successful relief attack would have stood a chance of saving the mass of the encircled forces, it is worth pointing to testimony from the Soviet side. The front-line commands had estimated the strength of the forces surrounded at Stalingrad to be in the order of 85,000 to 90,000 men; in other words they greatly underestimated their number. Furthermore, there had been many problems in trying to coordinate the closure of the pocket with the measures taken for the repulse of a German relief attack.[94] Seen from today, 'Operation Winter Storm', the relief attack begun on 12 December primarily with the forces of LVII Panzer Corps, 2½ armoured divisions with 230 tanks, was merely a 'catastrophe solution'. In the event, not only the constantly stiffening Soviet resistance but also the offensive by the South-west and Voronezh Fronts, which began on 16 December and quickly led to the collapse of the Italian Eighth Army on the middle Don, made it essential to break off the relief attack on 23 December. Due to lack of reserves, Army Group Don was required to withdraw parts of the relief force and deploy it against the new acute threat to its left flank.

The often discussed option of having the Sixth Army break out around 19–20 December in its extremely weakened condition, without adequate fuel and food supplies and against Hitler's orders, would in all probability have led to its rapid destruction. At best a few remnants without any combat power could have been saved in the winter steppe to the south-west of Stalingrad. The Sixth Army, after all, was encircled by seven Soviet armies with up to 60 major formations which had made thorough preparations against any breakout attempt. If these seven armies had become free, this would have had catastrophic repercussions for the entire southern wing of the eastern front. The final conclusion, therefore, is that a breakout attempt by the Sixth Army in the initial days after being surrounded would have had a far greater chance of success than any attempt made between 19 and 23 December.[95]

That during these highly dramatic days Hitler and members of the Wehrmacht Operations Staff still believed in a turn for the better and the possibility of resuming the offensive in 1943 can be deduced from a meeting he had on 18 December with the Italian Foreign Minister, Count Ciano. According to this, the objective of the campaign in the east was still to defeat the 'Bolshevik colossus', to prevent its expansion to the west, and to exploit economically the conquered eastern territories. Hitler assumed that the enemy had been so seriously damaged that his situation was becoming critical due to lack of food and raw materials. While he confirmed Soviet successes against the Romanian and Italian fronts on the middle Don sector, he did not in any way describe these as being decisive and pointed to the counter-measures that had been initiated.[96] Even allowing for diplomatic treatment of an important visitor, it is worth noting that in his estimation of the Soviet Union, as well as the overall war situation, Hitler was quite optimistic. Reality, however, was all too soon to catch up with him.

Results and consequences

The sacrifice by the Sixth Army in the Stalingrad pocket at least tied down the enemy Don Front with 55 major formations for many weeks and enabled the bulk of Army Group Don to escape from Soviet encirclement. That it was indeed a sacrifice far removed from any false heroics, and that this sacrifice, under conditions of unimaginable suffering, did gain important operational advantages for the southern sector of the eastern front, cannot be denied.[97] It made possible the eventual withdrawal of Army Group A from the

Caucasus, permission for which General Zeitzler was finally able to wrest from Hitler after bitter controversy on 28 December – much too late.[98] This withdrawal, however, merely led to an unsatisfactory compromise solution. Contrary to the original plan, only half of the First Panzer Army was brought up to reinforce Army Group Don while the rest, together with the strong Seventeenth Army, were to form the subsequent Kuban bridgehead and were therefore not available on the major front. According to most recent calculations, with the surrender of the last remnants of the Sixth Army in the 'northern pocket' on 2 February 1943, about 225,000 out of an original 250,000–260,000 men had been lost, including 170,000 Germans. About 25,000 men were flown out. Some 110,000 Germans and 3000 Romanians went into captivity. *Luftflotte 4* lost almost 500 aircraft during the airlift operations.[99]

After the devastating defeat of the Romanian Third and Fourth Armies, the collapse of the Italian Eighth Army on the Don, and the Soviet breakthrough south of Voronezh in the sector of the extremely combat-weak Hungarian Second Army[100] after 12 January 1943, it was clear that these four armies no longer existed as operational units. By the end of January all four army commands had been withdrawn from the front. The extension of the Soviet winter offensive all the way to the sector of the German Second Army, and the deep Soviet penetrations to the upper and middle Donetz in early February – where for a time there were only a few isolated units defending a 300 km-wide gap – demonstrate the intention of the STAVKA to deal the enemy a crushing blow which would have gone far beyond the catastrophe at Stalingrad. The capture of Kharkov on 16 February and the daring advance by a Soviet armoured group towards the Dnieper at Dnepropetrovsk, with the threat of encircling the main force of Army Group Don from the west, mark the high-points of the Soviet winter offensive.[101]

Several factors, however, including the timely intervention by parts of the First Panzer Army, the arrival of powerful reinforcements from France, von Manstein's superior command abilities, the significant shortening of the front in combination with counter-attacks, the recapture of Kharkov on 14 March and, finally, leadership errors on the Soviet side, made it possible, after dramatic crises, once more to stabilize the situation on the southern sector of the eastern front by the end of March. In the final analysis, it became clear that in its euphoria about the victories achieved so far, the STAVKA over-valued its own operational possibilities and under-estimated the residual combat power of the German eastern army. The operation to encircle the German-Romanian forces and the subsequent battles up to 2 February had cost no less than 155,000 dead and 331,000 wounded.[102]

The stabilization of this sector, which was being defended by the newly formed Army Group South under von Manstein, had also been unusually costly. In view of the loss of four allied armies, of 21 German divisions at Stalingrad, and the extremely high material losses in the fighting during the retreat, it is fair to claim that the devastating defeat of the German southern flank in 1942–3 was *the turn of the war in the east*. But the claim that during the Soviet offensive at Stalingrad, 113 German and allied divisions had been destroyed, of which 68 were totally annihilated, so that more than 1.5 million men were lost, does not equate with the facts.[103] Nor is there reason to believe the statement by former Marshal of the Soviet Union Sergei Akhromeyev that between November 1942 and March 1943 over 100 German and allied divisions had been destroyed for a total loss of 1.7 million officers and men. The actual losses amounted to the equivalent of 55 divisions, of which 21 belonged to the Sixth Army.[104] However, one can agree with the assessment that 'the destruction of the largest enemy strategic grouping' had from the military and political viewpoints, fundamentally changed the situation to the detriment of Germany and her allies.[105]

The Turn of the War in the Mediterranean: Malta, El-Alamein, Tunisia

While the turn of the war on the southern flank of the eastern front was unfolding, the decision in the Mediterranean theatre had already fallen. From the beginning of 1942, until the retreat of Panzer Army Africa to Tunisia, the question of besieging or capturing Malta had been a key problem for the Axis powers in the Mediterranean. In retrospect, Hitler's decision of 22 June 1942 to refrain from taking Malta because of Rommel's great operational successes was to acquire great importance. As many studies have shown, the British position in the Mediterranean and North Africa stood and fell with possession of the naval and air base of Malta. The success or failure of Rommel's army, which on 21 January 1942 again set out to retake Cyrenaica, was directly dependent upon the fall of Malta so as to prevent any interference with the supply by sea of the German-Italian forces.

If one compares British successes against the convoys bound for North Africa with the various German-Italian air offensives against Malta, the causal link between the two becomes clear. British sinkings were always highest during periods when II Air Corps in Sicily was required to undertake other assignments. In May 1942, for example, after heavy raids against Malta, almost 1000 soldiers, 2262 vehicles and approximately 34,000 tonnes of supplies could be brought to North Africa, whereas in August, following the turn in the situation at sea and in the air, the figure was only 17,000 tonnes, and in October – after a slight improvement during September – only 19,300 tonnes could be shipped, and this at a time when the decisive battle of El-Alamein was taking place and Panzer Army Africa had reported an average monthly requirement of 30,000 tonnes.[106]

The overriding importance of taking Malta was not only emphasized by Rommel, Field Marshal Kesselring and the Italian Comando Supremo, but also by the Kriegsmarine, whose Commander-in-Chief tried twice, on 12 March and 13 April, to make Hitler realize the great advantages that lay in capturing Malta. In this context Dönitz declared that to forgo taking the island meant having to continue German air attacks in the present dimensions, because only an 'uninterrupted attack' would prevent the resurgence of British offensive and defensive power.[107] The air offensive conducted by II Air Corps between 20 March and 28 April with all its forces had caused the British on Malta such heavy losses that the base was considered to have been paralyzed and 'ripe for the taking'. During this attack, II Air Corps had flown 5807 bomber, 5660 fighter and 345 reconnaissance missions, thus deploying an average of 300 aircraft per day.[108]

The result was that Malta had been battered to a point where an invasion by air or by sea would have been possible. From March on, Kesselring, Chief of Staff of the Luftwaffe Colonel General Jeschonnek, and the Italian Comando Supremo all began to think about a landing on Malta, even if no concrete preparations were undertaken. The OKW attempted to convince a sceptical Hitler of the advantages of taking the island fortress as soon as possible. As can be seen from his statements on 30 April to Mussolini and Colonel

General Cavallero, Chief of the Italian General Staff, although he was cautiously in favour of the capture of Malta, he agreed with Rommel in giving priority to a German-Italian offensive against the British Eighth Army, after the conclusion of which an operation against Malta could commence.[109]

Even though the Italians, too, argued in favour of giving the capture of Malta higher priority than the offensive in North Africa, because taking the island would secure the supply of Panzer Army Africa, it was agreed to postpone this operation – code name 'Hercules' – until about 18 July. However, the preparations then suffered from a lack of commitment by the Italians who demanded large amounts of fuel from the Germans, and from a renewed reluc-

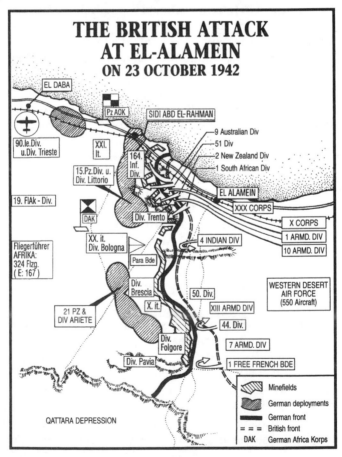

THE BRITISH ATTACK AT EL-ALAMEIN
ON 23 OCTOBER 1942

tance on the part of Hitler who already in May no longer believed in the likely success of the invasion.[110] From then on the Kriegsmarine shifted its operational priorities to attacking British Arctic convoys to northern Russia and treated the supply of the Italian navy with fuel as being of secondary importance. To this was added the dilemma of the needs of the eastern front, the Atlantic front and of Air Leader Africa, so that in early May II Air Corps had to relinquish two fighter groups and Bomber Wing 77, which on 10 May reduced the number of aircraft in Sicily to 255, of which only 142 were operational. This reduced German air power by more than 50 per cent, and it was self-evident that Malta could now no longer be held in check, so that in the ensuing months British offensive power again increased. In the end this was to deal the Axis convoys their death-blow.[111]

Rommel's successful offensive in Libya reached its high-point on 21 June with the lightning capture of Tobruk and the taking of 32,000 prisoners. It demonstrates a curious phenomenon, namely the narrow margin that lay between a turn of the war in favour of the Axis powers and one in favour of the British. It also demonstrates the dependence of an offensive concept on logistics and a correct evaluation of the enemy situation. Neither of these was correctly assessed by Rommel, who justifiably felt himself to be the victor and wanted to capitalize on his triumph by a relentless pursuit of the escaping enemy. Rommel's unilateral decision on 22 June to continue his attack with a view to taking Egypt and the Suez Canal, as well as the decision by Hitler and other senior officers at OKW and the Kriegsmarine to give emphatic support to this operation, constituted a *virtual turn* in the war.

Giving Rommel's highly risky attack top priority meant a *de facto* renunciation of the capture of Malta, even if the operation was officially only postponed for an indefinite time period. This decision not only ignored the strategy of the Italian Comando Supremo, but also cancelled out the plans of the Commander-in-Chief South, who – following the original agreement – now wanted to assign priority to the operation against Malta.[112] Rommel's decision would soon prove to have been a military mistake, but for a time this error was disguised by the concept of a gigantic pincer movement with the objective of toppling the British position in the Middle East by way of an advance through Egypt and a simultaneous advance through Transcaucasia. This concept of an enormous encirclement of the

Middle East, at a time when the German summer offensive on the eastern front had not yet even begun, was not only limited to Hitler but was shared by the Chief of the OKW Operations Staff and within the Supreme Command of the Kriegsmarine. In retrospect, it lay far outside the realities of resources, time and space, and was a major contribution to the 'virtual turn' of the war in the Mediterranean theatre. Only the capture of Malta could have created the conditions for a possible victory by the Axis powers.[113]

It is not the intention here to analyse the dramatic details of the failure of Panzer Army Africa in its advance on El-Alamein; but it is relevant to point out, in the context of defeating the British Eighth Army, how weak Rommel's remaining forces were following the previous battles and the eastward pursuit. After breaking off the attempt to smash through the front at El-Alamein on 4 July, the strength of each of Rommel's three German divisions was down to 1200–1500 men. He possessed only 50 heavy tanks, 20 light tanks, 15 armoured reconnaissance vehicles and 34 batteries of artillery.[114] Rommel's operational failure can in itself already be seen as the turn in the North African theatre, even though it was only the second attempt to defeat the superior Eighth Army in the battle of Alam el-Halfa on 30–31 August to 7 September which visibly and irrevocably put an end to any further offensive ambitions on the part of the Axis powers. British air superiority increasingly became the decisive factor for the outcome of the campaign. After Rommel broke off his attack on 3 September, for example, the Royal Air Force flew 902 missions as against only 171 by Air Command Africa.

Rommel himself also recognized that this costly failure marked the end of his offensive, even though the new commander of the Eighth Army, Lieutenant General Montgomery, had failed to deal Panzer Army Africa an annihilating defeat despite his immense superiority in armour. Nonetheless, the initiative had passed for good to the British.[115] The race between both sides to bring in reinforcements which had been in full swing since mid-July was already clearly going in favour of the Eighth Army. The urgent necessity on the German side to provide air forces for the direct support of Rommel's forces, and simultaneously to attack British convoys to Malta, made it impossible to reduce the island fortress.[116]

It was therefore only a question of time before Montgomery, who was well informed about German planning thanks to Ultra,[117] would, with his far superior forces, deliver the enemy his final defeat. With hindsight, Rommel has been criticized for not deciding to withdraw his army, say, to the Sollum line. However, there were good reasons for this, not the least of which was the tactically favourable defensive position in front of El-Alamein. It was soon to become clear that in desert war it was not the holding of positions on land but command of the air and the sea which were decisive. Montgomery only began the battle after he had achieved an overwhelming superiority. He was able to oppose Panzer Army Africa with its 103,000 men, of which only roughly 60,000 Germans and Italians were actually combat-ready, with a fighting strength of 195,000 men. There were 1100 British tanks opposing about 270 German tanks and only a handful of Italian tanks of comparable combat power. In the air, Air Leader Africa disposed of 324 aircraft, of which 167 were operational, whereas the British had almost 900 aircraft, 550 of which flew in direct support of the ground forces.[118]

The offensive of 23 October, which was planned as a conventional battle to break through head-on, only achieved the final break-through on 4 November after days of wearing down of the defenders and heavy British losses, mainly thanks to British air superiority. Montgomery's unimaginative qualities of leadership again failed to inflict a decisive defeat. Rommel was able to save about 70,000 men from destruction (only one-third of which, however, were fighting fit), and lead them back to the Beurat position east of Tripoli by the end of December without serious interference. Under certain circumstances Panzer Army Africa might still have been powerful enough to prevent the Eighth Army from achieving final victory. However, the Anglo-American landing in Morocco and Algeria on 7 and 8 November under General Eisenhower made it clear that the conquest of North Africa could not be denied to the Allies for very much longer.

This landing, 'Operation Torch', had been undertaken only after bitter controversy between the British and American command staffs, and represented a compromise, completely at variance with Stalin's demands for the opening of a second front in Europe. In the opinion of the American Joint Chiefs of Staff, who considered the risks of crossing the Channel to be acceptable, 'Operation Sledge-hammer', striking at objectives such as Cherbourg or Brest on the French channel coast, should already have been mounted in the summer of 1942. The American navy had just achieved its first great victory over the Japanese carrier fleet in the air-sea battle of Midway on 3 to 6 June, which led to an easing of the pressure in the Pacific. After an intervention by Roosevelt, agreement was finally reached in London on 25 July to give priority to the landing in French North-west Africa in order to strike first at the 'soft underbelly of Europe', in line with Churchill's intentions, and to postpone the invasion of western Europe until 1943. After all, the unhappy and highly costly landing attempt by the Canadian 2nd Division at Dieppe on 19 August 1942, which had been undertaken mainly for political reasons, had just demonstrated the dangers of a limited amphibious operation against a prepared enemy. Losses had amounted to approximately 4000 men, over 100 aircraft and 33 landing craft.[119]

After the successful conclusion of the landings in Morocco and Algeria, which had not come as a surprise to the Axis powers, Hitler – supported by Göring, Jodl and Kesselring – expressed his determination to defend the remaining territory in North Africa, particularly the Tunisian bridgehead, despite the over-taxation of forces this entailed. The bridgehead was even to be extended in order to deny the Allies advancing from the west and south-east the base for an attack against southern Europe. Expectations of such an Allied landing had a negative effect on Franco-German relations and on total German resources so that valuable armoured divisions were diverted to France. In the spring of 1942, for example, not only were three armoured divisions withdrawn from the east and brought up to strength in France, but subsequently the 'Hermann Göring' Division (motorized) and an SS Panzer Corps, comprising three strongly equipped armoured divisions, were set up there.[120] Three divisions from these forces then took part in the occupation of Vichy France from 11 November onward.

At the very time that the desperately embattled eastern army was about to face its greatest crisis, valuable armoured formations were being kept tied down in the west on security and occupation assignments, two of them even being sent to Tunisia and lost. At the end of November 1942 *Luftflotte 2* also grew to its maximum strength with 1532 aircraft, including transport planes, of which 858 were operational, while *Luftflotte 4* in southern Russia only had available 1177 machines at a time when the catastrophe of Stalingrad was visibly looming on the horizon.[121]

Having formed the Tunisian bridgehead and set up the Fifth Panzer Army there, by 10 November the German command had initiated a development which could have led to the salvation of all Axis forces still remaining in North Africa. However, the powers that be considered the reinforcement of the German-Italian forces and the offensive expansion of the bridgehead, even the reconquest of French North Africa, to have priority. Seen in retrospect, such objectives lacked any basis in reality. Against the wishes of Rommel, who had recommended the withdrawal of all soldiers under his command from the Tunisian bridgehead back to Europe, an 'Army Group Africa' was formed which by early April 1943 consisted of two armies with more than eight German and six Italian divisions. After the disastrous defeat on the eastern front and the loss of Tripolitania, the decision not to give up the bridgehead in North Africa was based mainly on political considerations. As late as 9 March, Mussolini sent a very strong letter to Hitler in which he energetically demanded that the 'land base' in North Africa be held and argued in favour of offensive action. The information that Rommel was being replaced reached the Commander-in-Chief South on the same day. Hitler had decided to dispense with the services of probably the most popular German field marshal, who had put military necessity ahead of what was politically desirable.[122]

The political change of direction in favour of regaining what had been lost was revealed in the *Memorandum of the Wehrmacht Operations Staff* of 10 December 1942. On the one hand it admitted the danger of an early invasion of the European mainland by the Western Allies – in the western Balkans and Greece, for example – with the secondary objective of an attack on the Romanian oilfields; on the other hand it clung to the hope of a successful defence against the Western Allies provided the supply situation could be improved, and of 'holding and extending the Tunisian bridgehead for subsequent offensive operations'. Moreover, as far as the war against the Soviet Union was concerned, despite the growing superiority of the enemy, it reiterated the notion of 'again taking the offensive in the east at the earliest possible date, with the object of gaining the Middle East'. The message was that in 1943 Germany was not prepared to remain on the defensive, but would attempt to seize back the initiative by limited offensives. Next to the capture of Leningrad the main targets were to be the sources of raw materials in the

Caucasus, thereby tying down strong British forces in the Middle East. Together with the submarine war, this strategy was still seen as being the key to a victorious conclusion of the war.[123]

That these strategic considerations were not only based on an unrealistic appreciation of the situation, but were also quickly to prove to have been redundant, was brought to the fore by the military catastrophe on the southern flank of the eastern front and the collapse of Army Group Africa. With the surrender of the last troops in Tunisia on 13 May 1943, about 130,000 German and almost 120,000 Italian soldiers went into captivity.[124] In view of the impending invasion of southern Europe, this was an irreplaceable loss. *Luftflotte 2*, which had been reinforced at the expense of the eastern theatre, lost over 2400 aircraft between 1 November 1942 and 1 May 1943, including numerous transport planes. Even if German losses were not as massive as at Stalingrad, the political-strategic consequences of the turn of the war in the Mediterranean were close to those of the turn on the eastern front. The southern gateway to 'Fortress Europe' stood wide open.

IV

THE FAILURE OF THE
OFFENSIVELY CONDUCTED DEFENCE
OF 'FORTRESS EUROPE' IN 1943

Overall Situation and Mobilization of Forces
within the Framework of 'Total War'

In late winter of 1943 the shifts in political and military balance had fundamentally altered the overall strategic situation. Since the war could no longer be won, the only decisive question for the Axis powers was how it could still be brought to a conclusion without defeat. Strategically, on the eastern front they were enmeshed in heavy defensive fighting until von Manstein's victorious counter-offensive led to a temporary breather. In the Mediterranean, ever since the final phase of the battle for the bridgehead in Tunisia, they had to expect landing operations in Sicily, Sardinia, Corsica, the Italian mainland, the Balkans or the Greek islands, without sufficient forces available for the defence of Europe's southern flank. The partisan war against Tito's forces in Yugoslavia, which escaped from encirclement in Bosnia at the end of January 1943 after heavy fighting, was tying down further forces on the 'inner front'. With the first American daylight precision bombing attack against a target within the borders of the Reich, namely against Wilhelmshaven on 27 January, the threat posed by the air war assumed a new quality which placed a hitherto unknown burden on air defence. Only in the Atlantic were the submarines still able to achieve astonishing successes until March, even though a turn in favour of submarine defence was already becoming evident.

On the diplomatic level, after her defeats on the eastern front and in North Africa, Germany had lost much credibility with her allies Italy, Romania and Hungary.[1] The latter two began to extend peace feelers to the Western powers, and in Italy there was apparent danger of a rupture of the alliance should there be a further German defeat. For Mussolini and the Fascist party it was, after all, a question of political survival. Finally, after the first heavy defeats at the hands of the American navy, Japan's strategy clearly signalled that she had no intention of taking part in any joint operations against the Soviet Union, even though on 1 January 1943 Hitler, after much hesitation, had specifically called upon Japan to attack the Soviets.[2] Japan's increasing preoccupation with the east Asian and Pacific theatres demonstrated that the opportunity to wage an effective coalition war by concentrating on a single enemy had long passed.

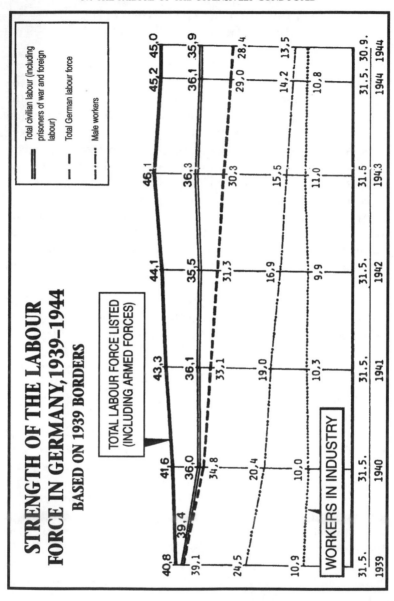

STRENGTH OF THE LABOUR
FORCE IN GERMANY, 1939–1944
BASED ON 1939 BORDERS

Total civilian labour (including
prisoners of war and foreign
labour)

Total German labour force

Male workers

TOTAL LABOUR FORCE LISTED
(INCLUDING ARMED FORCES)

WORKERS IN INDUSTRY

	31.5. 1939	31.5. 1940	31.5. 1941	31.5. 1942	31.5 1943	31.5. 1944	30.9. 1944
Total civilian labour	40,8	41,6	43,3	44,1	46,1	45,2	45,0
Total German labour force	39,1	36,0	36,1	35,5	36,3	36,1	35,9
	39,4	34,8	33,1	31,3	30,3	29,0	28,4
Male workers	24,5	20,4	19,0	16,9	15,5	14,2	13,5
	10,9	10,0	10,3	9,9	11,0	10,8	

Quite apart from these factors, because of the leap in the manpower requirements of the Wehrmacht and the increasing demands on production, the armaments industry was facing an insoluble dilemma. As will be shown, the German leadership was confronted by the fundamental decision either to transfer the defence of Europe to the southern perimeter and consequently put the bulk of the remaining manpower reserves at the disposal of the Wehrmacht, or to give armaments production top priority and therefore adjust the front lines to a reduced Wehrmacht potential. The former option would mean tenaciously defending the peripheral territories at the price of serious attrition of military strength and repudiation of any important boost to vital war industries. The latter alternative would entail the withdrawal from strength-draining positions, giving up costly operations, assigning top priority to the arms industry and accepting the principle of *economy of force*.

Even after Goebbels announced 'total war' on 18 February 1943, the efforts made fell far short of the requirements for total mobilization of all resources.[3] In arms production, for example, it appeared initially as if the shock of Stalingrad had led to the marshalling of previously untapped reserves. Yet, despite remarkable endeavours, what the Minister for Armament and Munitions called 'the total mobilization of the economy' was not achieved. Until far into 1943, the economy remained on a peace-time footing in many sectors, as Speer stated on 6 October 1943.[4] The main issues were to convert production capacities to the needs of the armaments industry, and to increase the work force at the expense of the Wehrmacht, which was itself suffering from a lack of manpower. In 1942, for example, production of consumer goods was only reduced by 12 per cent, and as late as 1944 still commanded a share of 22 per cent of total net industrial production.[5] Speer's attempt to recruit women on a large scale for arms production was only marginally successful, because Hitler was reluctant to adopt radical measures for the mobilization of female labour. The attempt to reduce the size of governmental offices in order to free 200,000 civil servants for the armaments industry was also largely unsuccessful.

Bottlenecks in the recruitment of labour persisted, despite the highly questionable activities undertaken by Sauckel, the 'Plenipotentiary for the Deployment of Labour', and other emergency measures such as the extension of the working week. In 1943 and

1944 the labour force was only increased by 2.1 million foreigners (forced labourers), and 800,000 prisoners of war, even though in 1942 the war economy was already short of about one million workers. Sauckel's plan to 'recruit' a further 500,000 French and 150,000 Belgian workers in August 1943 did not even get off the ground. Figures for the overall deployment of labour show, in fact, that between the end of May 1939 and the end of May 1943, the total number, including foreigners and prisoners of war, declined from 39.4 million to 36.6 million. In the same period the number of German workers decreased from 39.1 million to 30.3 million. Considering that at the end of May 1943 the Wehrmacht comprised 9.5 million men, it is clear that an even more drastic decline in the labour force was only avoided by the recruitment of forced foreign labour and prisoners of war.[6]

Speer's attempt to gain control of arms production for the Kriegsmarine and the Luftwaffe, in addition to that for the Army, was undertaken not only to augment his sphere of power, but also to increase the efficiency of the armaments industry as a whole. While naval armament was given the highest priority in mid-April, it was only on 26 July 1943 that it was put under Speer's ministry, after the war in the Atlantic had turned in favour of the Allies. For the Luftwaffe, an agreement was reached in early March 1944 between Speer and Field Marshal Milch, the Inspector General of the Luftwaffe and Chief of Aircraft Development, according to which arms production for the newly formed 'Fighter Staff' was put under Speer's control. But it was only after overall production for the Luftwaffe was entrusted to Speer on 20 June 1944, at a time when the Allies had long achieved air superiority, that total arms production, apart from the manufacture of the V weapons,[7] was finally united under a single central control.

As will be shown below, because of the intensified air offensive by the Western Allies, concentration of arms production for all three branches of the Wehrmacht did not have the effect in 1943 and 1944 of reducing the enemy's lead in this area. Nevertheless, until mid-1944 German arms manufacture did achieve some noteworthy successes despite the Anglo-American bomber offensive. After production had reached an index value of 242 in early October 1943 – based on January–February 1942 = 100 – it even increased to a high-point of 322 by July 1944, before abruptly declining in the autumn of 1944.

The high-point in aircraft production was also attained during the summer of 1944 before it then began to fall in October. Production of heavy and light tanks and self-propelled guns reached highs in May and October of 1943, and again in July and December of 1944.[8]

As for raw materials, it became increasingly apparent that the occupied territories in the east were not the main sources of iron and other metals, but that production depended mainly on the Balkans and Turkey with their manganese, chromium, copper, lead, zinc and molybdenum, on Swedish iron ore, and on the ores from Lorraine which, together with the Franco-Belgian industrial base, made a major contribution to the German war industry.[9]

In 1943 the German armaments industry still had capacity reserves in manpower and in the fields of organization and technology that were far from exhausted. A total mobilization of the war economy no later than in January 1943 would not only have benefited production, but would also have set manpower free for the Wehrmacht. The demand by the OKW in mid-January for the drafting of 800,000 men during the first half of 1943 had already been preceded by Hitler's decree of 8 January to enlist 200,000 men from certain sectors of industry by March 1943. A further 200,000 men were to be provided for the Wehrmacht by calling up those born in 1901 through 1906. The remaining 400,000 had to be found by additional means, for example by calling up older age-groups, or by recruiting Poles of German descent. But bitter controversy over the fulfilment of the '800,000 man plan' then erupted not only among the various branches of the Wehrmacht, but also between individual departments. It became evident that in view of the numerous exemptions, in favour, for example, of the Reichsbahn (German state railway), the original demand was not going to be met.[10]

Seen overall, an ever-widening gap opened between the remaining manpower reserves and the requirements of the Wehrmacht, the war industry and agriculture, which could only partially be filled by the deployment of foreign labour, prisoners of war, 'Hilfswillige' (lit. 'willing helpers', in effect forced labour), by recruiting volunteers for the Waffen-SS (armed formations of the SS who fought as soldiers), and by setting up volunteer organizations in the east, the so-called 'Eastern Legions' and 'Eastern Battalions'. Considering that roughly 1.5 million foreigners, including almost one million from the Soviet Union,[11] only became active in the Wehrmacht and the Waffen-SS during the second half of the war, it is abundantly clear that the opportunities were missed by not having taken steps to mobilize manpower reserves in time.

Nevertheless, it would not be justified to argue that a comprehensive programme of manpower mobilization in early 1943 could have brought about a turn in the war. The lead in productivity that the United States and Great Britain enjoyed over Germany gave the Western Allies an advantage that could not be overcome. What proved to be decisive were their advances in standardizing production methods and their higher per capita productivity. The Germans, who concentrated more on technological flexibility and qualitative superiority, were left behind in mass production. In the final analysis, German attempts to increase productivity in line with the Americans also failed because of labour policy. For obvious reasons, foreign labour, mainly consisting of forced labour and prisoners of war, and, subsequently, also inmates of concentration camps, were far less motivated than German workers.[12]

Success or failure to increase war production was directly associated with considerations as to how home air defence could be strengthened with the minimal adverse effect on overall productivity. The question was to what extent air defences would need to be reinforced in order to win the air battle over Germany that had already begun. Even before the war, British military doctrine already envisaged the likelihood of strategic terror bombardment;[13] and this could only be practised in the form of 'indiscriminate' bomb warfare from 1942 onward, after the necessary powerful bomber fleet had become available. This concept, primarily advocated by Air Chief Marshal Harris, Chief of Bomber Command, was not based on the idea of reprisal but on the consideration that massive area bombardment by night would not only hit industrial targets but also weaken enemy resolve and damage the morale of the population. The bomber offensive against a combination of economic, military and civilian targets was intended greatly to shorten the war, and in best cases to lead to an early collapse of the enemy.

After massive attacks against cities in the Ruhr were flown from early March 1943, Harris told Sir Charles Portal, Chief of the Air Staff, in April that continuation of this air offensive would quickly deal the enemy a death blow.[14] Harris clung to the concept of area bombardment even after the introduction in early 1944 of improved navigational and aiming instruments which permitted aimed bomb drops and therefore a switch from 'indiscriminate attacks' to 'precision bombing' by day, even if restriction to exclusively military targets was hardly possible.

The air war directive of 21 January 1943, which the American and British staffs had prepared under the eyes of Roosevelt and Churchill during the conference at Casablanca, provided for a 'division of labour' between British Bomber Command and the US 8th Air Force. Attacks against military, industrial and other targets were to be increased to such a degree, and the morale of the German people so undermined, that a decisive weakening of armed resistance was to be expected. In practice, Bomber Command was to continue with its area bombing at night while the 8th Air Force was to fly precision bombing attacks against armaments plants and submarine wharves, fighter aircraft factories, refineries and traffic junctions. In fact, until the spring of 1943 the main targets for the 8th Air Force were the German U-boats.[15]

Even though the expediency of the agreed tactics was still highly controversial, and the debate only superficially glossed over, nonetheless the signal for an intensified air war against Germany had been sounded. With the approval of the so-called 'Pointblank' offensive in mid-May 1943, the coordination of attack methods and schedules was agreed and 76 precision targets in six key industries identified. Night and day attacks were to be flown against such targets whose paralysis would multiply the damage for other key industries. For successful daylight attacks a minimum of at least 300 bombers per mission was set in order to overcome the expected German fighter defence. The estimation was that in the spring of 1943 the Luftwaffe would deploy about 50 per cent of its fighter aircraft against the British and American bombers. Should German fighter defence prove to be even stronger, the planners feared such heavy losses that daylight attacks and in worst cases even night-time attacks would become too costly.[16]

As for the legitimacy of air attacks that did not spare residential areas, it should be noted that all the important air powers had been fully aware since the beginning of the war that 'indiscriminate bombing attacks against the civilian population were not consistent with humanitarian conventional rules of international law'.[17] While there was agreement between the belligerents in 1939 to spare civilians, each side upheld its right to break this agreement if the other side were to violate it. By leaving it to the judgement of the party concerned whether or not to ignore the humanitarian restrictions, the belligerents were in a position to justify their own indiscriminate attacks by pointing at will to precedents set by the other side. During the Battle of Britain, for example, after the first British attacks on Berlin on 4 September 1940, Hitler threatened that he would 'eradicate' British cities as a reprisal. On the other side, Bomber Command adhered to the declaration by the War Cabinet of 18 April 1941 that German cities would continue to be bombed even if the Luftwaffe were to discontinue its attacks against Britain, because such raids were defined as military actions and not as reprisals.[18] The American air force command, on the other hand, favoured systematic daylight attacks against important industrial and military targets, and by an unprecedented air offensive intended not only to keep losses on land as low as possible, but to bring the whole war to an end as quickly as possible.

Future production of the German war economy, the reinforcement of the Wehrmacht, the protection of the civilian population, the supply of materials, even the whole future course of the war, largely depended, therefore, on the success or failure of air defence. Even after the turn of the war in 1942–3, and despite the impairment that resulted from the massive air attacks, the Wehrmacht was still achieving remarkable successes in the field and industry was still able to increase production. Yet if the German air defence had been able to score a decisive victory, the military and industrial successes would have been even greater. From this point of view, the fact that German fighter defence was not stepped up later than the turn of the year 1942–3 – at the cost, if necessary, of the other branches of the Luftwaffe, or even of the Army – appears to be an omission that was decisive for the war. In early 1943 the race between the increasing strength of the Allied bomber formations and the power of German fighter defence had not yet been decided.

That Roosevelt had recognized the decisive effects of an overpowering bomber weapon early on can be seen from statements he made to the effect that reservations based on international law against the application of even the most brutal methods were inadmissible when the issue was the destruction of 'an enemy that had been outlawed'.[19] Large-scale destruction of Germany from the air would make the occupation of the enemy territory much easier after the will to resist had been broken. The primary target for the air attack was Germany's industrial, economic and military foundation – the enemy's 'national structure'. Hand in hand with this objective was the breaking of enemy combat morale.[20] This concept was in line with the demand for 'unconditional surrender' made on 24 January 1943 even if – as is commonly agreed by many observers – this merely strengthened Germany's will to resist.

The air operations during the first half of 1943 revealed that the British and American bomber formations were not yet capable of decisively weakening this national structure. Nevertheless, the Allied staffs in Great Britain continued to prepare for the main air offensive. Even if the battle over the Ruhr from the beginning of March to the end of June 1943 had cost the British 870 aircraft, or almost 5 per cent of the machines employed,[21] these losses were still within acceptable bounds. Whereas in early 1943 Bomber Command had possessed only 480 long-range bombers for its nightly attacks, by May there were already 800; and from mid-year over 1000 four-engine bombers were available, with a combat-readiness of 60–70 per cent.

The Americans depended mainly on the 8th Air Force in southern England and on the 9th Air Force, which initially flew strategic missions from North Africa, and from the autumn of 1943 tactical missions from England. From November 1943, the 15th Air Force flew long-range missions from southern Italy, while the 12th Air Force was reserved for tactical purposes. When the US Air Force began to make an impact within the framework of the 'combined bomber offensive' from mid-June onward, it had already reached a strength of 500 bombers which permitted it to fly missions into central Germany with about 250 aircraft, even though there were still no long-range escort fighters – the P-38 'Lightning' or the P-51 'Mustang' – available. The battle of the bombers against the fighter defence thus entered its decisive phase because the daylight attacks were mainly aimed against aircraft plants and their sub-contractors. The Luftwaffe leadership still believed in the need to reinforce the front-line forces, especially on the eastern front, so as to be able to support the planned offensive battle, 'Operation Citadel', with a major deployment. From this alone it can be seen that strategic air defence had still not been assigned priority. The neglect of air defence in favour of the forces required for the new offensive on the eastern front is the key to the subsequent defeat in the air battle over Germany. There is much to be said for the claim that ongoing losses of over 10 per cent for each mission would soon have brought the American daylight offensive to an end.[22]

It was only 'Operation Gomorrah' – the disastrous air raids on Hamburg, four by night and two by day, between 24 July and 3 August – during which the anti-aircraft defence was reduced to a minimum by the dropping of aluminium strips, that caused a change of mind in the Luftwaffe leadership. At last the emphasis of the air war was shifted to air defence. Although production of fighter aircraft, which had still numbered only 725 in February now rose to over 1000 per month by mid-year, it was already clear by then that this would not be sufficient to meet the needs of both the front and home defence. A glance at the total production figures for bombers and dive-bombers, as compared to fighters, reveals the extremely slow shift from attack to defence aircraft. Whereas in 1942 about 5600 bombers and dive-bombers, as opposed to some 5500 fighters, had been produced, in 1943 the figure for the former was still almost 8000 against 10,900 fighters,[23] aptly demonstrating that a basic redirection in favour of air defence had still only just begun.

The numerical development of the list strength of fighters and night fighters from the end of 1942 to July 1943 can be seen from the following table:[24]

	31.12.42	31.03.43	31.05.43	31.07.43
Fighters:				
Day	1360	1534	1786	1528
Night	389	493	508	577
Totals	1749	2027	2294	2105

The extreme pressure caused by aircraft losses could no longer be eased even by the substantial increase in production. At the beginning of August, Air Command Centre, which had to wage the defensive battle over the territory of the Reich, operated with barely 1000 day and night fighters. By the end of July and beginning of August, even with the additional contribution of some of the 216 fighters belonging to *Luftflotte 3* in western Europe, only about 50 per cent of all fighter aircraft were directly or indirectly deployed for the defence of Germany. Taking into consideration the recommendation made by senior Luftwaffe generals in the spring of 1943 to set up three Fighter Corps with two or three Fighter Divisions consisting of day and night fighters, and with up to 2000 night fighters alone,[25] the conclusion must be that only the abandonment of costly offensives by the Army would at this stage have permitted an 'about-face' of arms production in favour of air defence.

Hitler was also well aware of these alternatives. But by staking everything on a victorious offensive on one sector of the eastern front in order to regain the initiative, he hoped after its successful conclusion to be able to free many fighter formations for the air defence of the Reich. His statement in early July 1943 to General Kammhuber, Commander of XII Air Corps and the man responsible for night fighters, underlines the extremely high risk he was accepting by putting 'Operation Citadel' ahead of all other requirements. Nothing can better illustrate the acid test facing the Wehrmacht in early summer 1943 than Hitler's words to Kammhuber: 'When I have defeated Russia you can have everything for the defence of the Reich. However, then you will no longer need it.'[26]

Developments in the battle of the Atlantic during the spring of 1943 were also important for the impending course of the war. In the war of supply fought in the northern and central Atlantic, German success reached its summit in March, yet the battle was broken off in May. During these months the German navy was able to throw into the fight more submarines than had ever been used previously; but in this same period the technical and tactical advantages enjoyed by the Western Allies also achieved a breakthrough. The events in the Atlantic in the course of the spring bear out the observation that outwardly visible successes are often deceptive, and that more effective underlying counter-measures can be decisive.

At the Casablanca conference of January 1943, the battle against the German U-boats had been put at the head of the list for the Allied conduct of the war, indicating that the British and American leadership considered victory in the supply war to be the most important condition for the attack against 'Fortress Europe' from the west.[27] In March Admiral Dönitz, who since 30 January was also Commander-in-Chief of the Kriegsmarine, finally had a total of 400 submarines at his disposal, sufficient numbers, it would have appeared, to win the battle of the Atlantic. However, this was outweighed by the Western Allies' intelligence and their tactical and technical counter-measures, even if they were slow to take effect. These included the significant British decoding successes of Ultra, which began to make their mark from the end of March, the deployment of 60 Liberator bombers to cover the 'sea gap' south of Greenland, the increase in auxiliary carriers for convoy protection, and the introduction of the H2S aircraft radar, known to the Germans as 'Rotterdam', for detecting submarines on the surface which in their turn lacked any form of effective reconnaissance at sea.

The relatively meagre successes in sinkings in January and February 1943 have mainly been attributed to the manoeuvres by the convoys to evade the 'submarine packs', which were made possible by the rapid decoding of German radio traffic. The great contribution by the British cryptographers was to create the conditions under which the turn in the battle of the Atlantic already became possible in May 1943, rather than in the following autumn, when it would most probably have happened anyway, given the material superiority of the Allies.[28]

The 400 U-boats which were available in early March 1943 were deployed as follows:[29] Of the 222 front-line boats, 182 were stationed in the Atlantic and 40 elsewhere. Of those in the Atlantic, 68 were at base, 44 en route and 70 on combat patrol, with 45 of these patrolling the convoy routes in the North Atlantic. 178 were not on combat assignments but included 52 boats for basic training, 119 for advanced training, plus seven experimental boats.

In the 'great convoy battle' in the North Atlantic which lasted from 16 to 20 March and in which 43 U-boats took part, the Germans once again achieved an impressive victory by sinking 21 ships of almost 141,000 tonnes for the loss of only one submarine. Had such results continued, supplies to Britain would have hung by a thread. However, the total sinkings of 590,000 tonnes achieved in March fell below expectations. In order to overcome new ship production by the Western powers, sinkings of 1.3 million tonnes per month would have been required. Even though there were 65 submarines in the war zone by the end of the month, in April only 276,000 tonnes were sunk for a loss of 15 submarines. The final turn came about in May 1943. Sinkings of only 44 freighters with 226,000 tonnes had to be paid for with the loss of 41 submarines; in other words, the ratio between successes and losses was no longer tolerable. If this is compared with the figures for May 1942 when sinkings of 585,000 tonnes were achieved for the loss of only four submarines, it becomes clear that the supply war had become a battle of attrition which the U-boat fleet could no longer endure. Dönitz's order of 24 May to discontinue the battle of the Atlantic is but the logical consequence that the leadership drew from this realization.[30]

The importance of this turn in the Atlantic war went far beyond the war at sea. It enabled the Western Allies not only to supply Britain more or less without interference but also to build and maintain an air potential that would wage the strategic air war against Germany with increasing power and finally to build up an invasion force for the attack against western Europe in 1944. The strategic alternatives facing the German Supreme Command at the end of May after the battle of Atlantic had been lost were either to give absolute priority to home air defence, gaining command of the air and renouncing any offensive in the east unless it could begin no later than at the end of May, or to make a further attempt to defeat the Soviet Union, which would mean neglecting other military necessities. The Supreme Command chose the second alternative.

The Question of 'Closing Down the Eastern Front' and a Separate German-Soviet Peace

With the catastrophe looming at Stalingrad and the costly withdrawal of the southern wing of the eastern front, leading authorities began to consider how the German-Soviet front could be shortened and strengthened to such a degree that it could resist even large-scale Soviet attacks. With this, the concept of an 'eastern wall' behind which the eastern army could regroup and prepare a permanent and successful defence, again came to the fore. Simultaneous attempts were made on the political and diplomatic level to bring about a separate peace between Germany and the Soviet Union, which would have enabled the bulk of German forces to be withdrawn from the east and all efforts to be concentrated against Great Britain and the United States. Obviously the conclusion of such a separate peace would have given the Axis powers a strong trump card with which to end the war without being defeated.

The fact that in the spring of 1943 the bulk of the Army and 45 per cent of the forces of the Luftwaffe were still tied down in the east clearly indicates that only a radical reduction of the armies in Russia could have made the defence of Europe against the Western powers on land and in the air even possible. On 9 April the four army groups deployed in the east – A, South, Centre and North – comprised 182½ divisions, excluding training divisions and foreign major formations, out of a total force of the Army of 266 divisions, including security, reserve and Luftwaffe ground divisions. In other words, almost 69 per cent of the forces of the Army were still deployed in the east.[31] Compared to mid-June 1942 when roughly 76 per cent of the Army forces, excluding the front in Finland, had been on the eastern front, this represented only a minor decline in the ratio of distribution, and as far as the number of major formations is concerned, even an increase. Until early July 1943, the eastern army grew to 3.14 million men and was therefore even larger than the equivalent deployment on 22 June 1941.[32]

Of the total forces of the Luftwaffe, the quota of the three *Luft-flotten* deployed in the east – LF 1, LF 4 and Luftwaffen Command East[33] – came to 45.9 per cent in March 1943, and in June to 45.2 per cent. From the viewpoint of the Luftwaffe at the beginning of 1943, *war on three fronts* had become a reality when the costly defensive battle over the homeland and occupied western Europe was added to the high requirements of the Soviet and Mediterranean/North African theatres.[34] How fully the air forces in the east were occupied with close support of the ground forces can be seen from the fact that the Luftwaffe was only able to shift to 'strategic air war' in May and June 1943, and to fly missions against railway stations, airfields and important industrial targets in the Soviet hinterland. However, for several reasons, including the brief time-span available for such actions, these mainly successful attacks were not sufficient to inflict lasting damage on the Soviet war industry.

The notion of coming to a political or military solution which would lead to a relief, or even to a comprehensive 'closing down', of the eastern front, touched radically on the fundamental objective of the campaign against the Soviet Union. Should the bulk of German forces continue to be tied down in the east after the military failure of two attempts to defeat the Soviet Union? Should the focus of the war still remain in the east in view of the threatening invasion of southern Europe and the intensifying air war? Or should an effort be made, under the dictates of the actual situation, to revise the 'image' of Russia and to reach a political settlement – even if only temporary – with Moscow?

The military catastrophe at Stalingrad finally caused several departments and authorities to rethink their former positions. Military authorities had already been engaged for some time in the attempt to gain the support of Russians and non-Russians in the battle against Stalin's regime; now it was ministers Rosenberg and Goebbels who attempted to swing German political opinion in favour of a more indulgent attitude towards the Red Army and the Russian people,[35] if for no other reason than their appreciation of the basic change in the war situation. From January 1943 both ministries attempted to persuade Hitler to issue an 'eastern proclamation' which would prohibit any further disparagement of the peoples concerned and lead to a change in the perceived image of the Soviet Union.

The stance of the Minister of Propaganda nevertheless remained highly ambivalent. Whereas in his press campaigns Goebbels continued to advocate the 'crusade against Bolshevism' which had to be waged for the salvation of Europe, he also urged that the 'eastern workers' and the Soviet prisoners of war be treated humanely, and rejected any insults to the 'eastern peoples'.[36] Influenced by a memorandum of the General Staff of the Army which rejected any inhuman treatment of the Slavs and argued in favour of self-government for the Russians, Goebbels drafted an 'eastern proclamation' in mid-February which Hitler was to issue. Any discrimination against the population of the occupied eastern territories was to cease, and these peoples were to be made to understand that a German victory was in their own basic interest. Hitler, however, refused to sign such a proclamation, which he was prepared to consider publishing only after the start of a new major offensive on the eastern front.[37]

In February 1943 Field Marshal von Manstein prepared a comment on the draft of the 'eastern proclamation'. It declared that in view of the threatening military situation, the proclamation should be used to give the people of occupied eastern territories the feeling that they were 'equal partners in a new Europe'. Defamation of the population and the 'colonial methods' had to cease.[38] In the summer of 1943, following a suggestion made by the writer Edwin Erich Dwinger and other authors, Goebbels is alleged even to have toyed with the idea of producing a film on German-Soviet reconciliation in order to support the Vlasov movement.[39]

Among the military departments at OKW and OKH, the counter-espionage department under Admiral Canaris had since 1941 possessed, in the person of Captain Professor Dr Theodor Oberländer, one of the most outspoken advocates of the idea of initially gaining the support of the non-Russian and later also of the Russian people in the fight against Stalin's regime. In his last memorandum, which he completed on 22 June 1943, i.e. on the exact day on which the German-Soviet war had begun two years previously, but before 'Operation Citadel' was launched, Oberländer addressed himself to fundamental political strategy:

The war in the east cannot be won by military measures alone. These must be enhanced and supported by political measures. The war in the east may be compared to a pair of pliers which can only work effectively by the simultaneous application of both the military and the political lever. The situation today is surprisingly similar to the military struggle for the survival of Bolshevism. During the civil war Lenin destroyed the militarily led White Russian armies by clever exploitation of the topics of 'freedom for the people' and 'land for the farmers', by which he took the political wind out of their sails... The shift in eastern policy must be recognizable and total. It would be fatal to spend this sole remaining political option in the form of small change without tangible results. Any partial solution would be seen by the people as an admission of our weakness, would whet their appetite, and lead to new demands being raised.[40]

Oberländer's recommendation culminated in the appeal to seize the chance that still existed, resulting from the treatment of 'Soviet citizens' by the Communist regime, in order to gain the support of the 'population in eastern Europe' for Germany. Quite apart from the question as to whether this was still a realistic opportunity at the time, Hitler refused to consider the basic concept expressed in the memorandum despite the fact that Canaris supported it.[41] Quite obviously Hitler did not want to go beyond his concession of permitting the formation of numerous 'eastern legions' as auxiliary forces from among the non-Russian peoples of the Soviet Union. His attitude towards the ideas expressed in the memorandum, which were being submitted in similar form by many other officers, civil servants and diplomats, was effectively to reject any political commitment which would have required him to recognize autonomous states within the territory of the Soviet Union either during or after the war. Hitler's decision at the Berghof on 8 June 1943 not to form a Russian army of liberation under General Vlasov, which would have given him the status of an ally, must also be seen in this context.[42]

One of Vlasov's closest confidants, Captain Strik-Strikfeldt, expressed his views about the approach to Russia in a lecture he gave at Posen on 6 February 1943 at a training course for Ic (Intelligence section) officers. 'We can detect a highly different picture of the "Russian" when we learn that the Russian will always react with hatred if he is treated as a "sub human", so that it is of primary importance first to appeal to him as a human being in order to be able to overcome this hostility.'[43] The speaker was one of the few people who advocated a reconciliation between Germans and Russians not only for reasons of expediency but also because of inner conviction.

Hitler's negative standpoint on concessions, particularly towards the Russian population, which was also shared by segments of the SS leadership,[44] was motivated primarily by the thought that any such concession could be interpreted as a step back, and it was therefore necessary first to gain an impressive military victory so as to approach Stalin with a view to a possible political settlement from a position of strength. Simultaneously Hitler rejected any idea of discontinuing the economic exploitation of the country, particularly the Ukraine. He believed that it was impossible to compel the local population to supply food and provide mass unpaid labour while at the same time promising an improvement of the situation or even political autonomy. He also voiced the highly controversial argument that any 'mild' administration by the occupation forces would only give a boost to the partisans.[45] Despite the various arguments presented, Germany must adhere to a policy of strength in the east.

This determination to pursue a position of strength under any circumstances is also the key for understanding Berlin's extremely cool reaction to the Soviet peace feelers and mediation attempts from abroad which had been taking place since the spring of 1942.[46] Here the interests of Japan and Italy coincided with the advances made by the Soviet Union, whether these were meant seriously or were only a tactical manoeuvre. While from the very beginning Japan's offers resulted from her intention not to become involved in the war with the Soviet Union so as to be able to concentrate all forces against the United States, Italy only came around to considering the Soviet factor in a new light after the defeat in North Africa and with the approaching catastrophe on the eastern front. Mussolini's attempts, which became tangible in written and verbal form after 6 November 1942 and which were presented to Hitler on 18 December 1942 by Foreign Minister Ciano in the form of appropriate recommendations, were based on the idea of reaching a settlement with the Soviet Union – a second 'peace treaty of Brest-Litovsk'. Mussolini and Ciano argued that within the forseeable future all available forces would be needed to repel the anticipated invasion of Sicily and Italy by the Western powers. If a separate peace with Stalin could not be reached, then the Germans should set up a deeply echeloned, well-fortified line of defence as quickly as possible, where, with the 'deployment of the smallest possible force by the Axis Powers', future Soviet offensives could be crushed. Such a line of defence should preferably take the form of an 'eastern wall'.[47]

Following the defeat at Stalingrad, Mussolini several times returned to the idea of building an eastern line of defence against which the Red Army would exhaust itself. This concept was strongly emphasized in a letter to Hitler on 9 March 1943 in which he argued that after the creation of such an eastern wall, the Soviet Union would no longer be as dangerous as it had been in 1941. This would finally lead to a 'neutralization of the Soviet Union'.[48] The idea of a separate German-Soviet peace, which was discussed by Hitler and Mussolini during their meeting at Kleßheim Castle (Salzburg) from 8 to 10 April, and subsequently again by German and Italian diplomats, received no support from Hitler because he intended to solve the 'eastern problem' by military means. The main argument here, as on other occasions, was that a separate peace entailed an extremely high risk. Even if all of the Soviet territorial demands were granted, Germany would in future have to reckon with a rejuvenated and strengthened Red Army so that it would primarily depend on Stalin's goodwill as to whether the peace treaty was kept, or whether he would again go to war but under more favourable conditions.

This line of reasoning also underlay Hitler's stance towards the exploratory bilateral talks being carried on in Stockholm via various German and Soviet contacts. In particular, the indications of a willingness to mediate, which the agent Edgar Clauß signalled with increasing intensity from late autumn of 1942 onward, and the Soviet peace feelers which the Foreign Ministry and the Intelligence Department took up, appeared to offer a viable basis for negotiations well into the early spring of 1943.[49] In any case, it is probable that the offers made by the Soviets by means of contacts in Stockholm until September 1943 were not just a 'game', but were at least intended to discover how serious Germany was to conclude a separate agreement, on the basis, for example, of a return to the mutual frontiers existing before 22 June 1941. It must be remembered that the Soviet government had suffered two serious political setbacks in the spring. First, the discovery of the corpses of at least 4000 murdered Polish officers at Katyn on 13 April had led to the most serious breach to date between Moscow and London, as well as the Polish government in exile. Furthermore, Stalin had been informed by Churchill and Roosevelt on 4 June that the opening of a second front in western Europe could not be counted upon before May 1944, which led to a further strain on the anti-Hitler coalition.[50]

The decision not to invade western Europe in 1943 had been taken during the Anglo-American conference in Washington from 12–15 May. While the intention was to prepare for this invasion with all due care, after convoluted discussions Roosevelt gave in to the argument advanced by Churchill and his advisers that it would be more advantageous to attack the Italian peninsula next and to force Italy to renounce her alliance with Berlin. What most probably influenced Churchill was the consideration that an attack across the Channel against the fortifications on the French coast was a highly risky operation which would only be appropriate after the Wehrmacht had been substantially weakened on other fronts. To deduce from this that Churchill deliberately intended to provoke complications with the USSR, and that he carried the major share of the blame for the 'grievous breach of faith' resulting from the conference in Washington,[51] is an exaggerated interpretation in the attempt to saddle him with the responsibility for the tensions existing within the anti-Hitler coalition in the spring of 1943.

The issue, therefore, is not whether a termination of the war with Germany as early as 1943 was in line with the concept of the Western powers or not, but whether the actual conditions for such a conclusion to the war in that year existed at all. Judging by the overall situation and the deployment and ratio of forces, there is much to be said for the argument that these conditions could hardly be met within the time available in order to be ready for an attack against the French west coast by the late summer of 1943. In July there were no fewer than 42⅔ divisions, including two paratroop divisions in the occupied western countries, and a further five armoured divisions and four other major formations were in the process of being set up. That Churchill flatly rejected such an operation[52] does not alter the fact that the preconditions for it did not yet exist. On the other hand, it was obvious that in 1944, as Wehrmacht defeats in the east became ever more costly and exhausting, conditions for an invasion would be more favourable.

Seen from this perspective, Stalin's anger and disappointment in early summer 1943 do not appear unfounded. He was also faced with the question as to why the German spring offensive, which he had been expecting since early May, was being so long delayed, and whether this could not be taken as an indication that Berlin was willing to negotiate. It was obvious to the Soviets that they would have to continue bearing the brunt of the battle against the German armies despite all the burdens to date. Was Stalin not justified in questioning the dependability of the Western Allies – whom in his typically mistrustful way of looking at things he even suspected of 'disloyalty'[53] – despite using much more restrained language in his diplomatic correspondence? That the theoretical possibility of a German-Soviet agreement had been recognized by the Western powers indirectly enhanced Stalin's freedom to act. Might not the conclusion of a separate peace with Germany therefore offer the better way out in order to bring the war to a profitable conclusion without further heavy losses? Would not such a peace be more advantageous than a war won by a Pyrrhic victory?

This Soviet perception was opposed by the evaluations of the peace feelers on the German side. These ranged from 'acceptable and useful' to 'superfluous, because disadvantageous and highly tricky'. Quite apart from the element of speculation that accompanied the assessment of their chances of success, Hitler and – to a lesser degree – von Ribbentrop took the position that the Wehrmacht had not yet been so greatly weakened as to consider sacrificing to the enemy all the conquests made since June 1941 as the price for a separate peace. The Wehrmacht still stood deep in Soviet territory, valuable sources of raw material were still being held, and there was still the chance that a successful offensive might bring about a substantial shift in the balance of power in Germany's favour. Under no circumstances was Hitler minded to give up the Ukraine on whose mineral resources the German war economy was largely dependent.[54]

It seems logical, therefore, that such considerations tipped the scales in favour of letting the guns speak before possibly entering into negotiations with Moscow. Nevertheless the Foreign Minister – in a departure from the official party line – did apparently make several attempts at the end of 1942 to bring Hitler around to the idea of a separate agreement with Moscow. In view of the military situation in the spring of 1943, it is difficult, therefore, to sustain the claim that the determining factor in the German decision-making process was 'defeat of the Soviet Union' in the form of a 'campaign of annihilation'[55] based on racial ideology. In anticipation of actual events, it appears that in 1943 Germany could realistically look forward to nothing better than the possibility of a 'draw' on the eastern front. Only if the German leadership no longer expected any improvement in the military situation – in contrast to what historical sources indicate – could it be reproached for not entertaining the Soviet peace feelers. However, since Hitler regarded any German peace overtures as a sign of weakness, the conclusion is that he intended first to gain a position of relative strength and thereby keep all his options open until later.

The afore-mentioned idea urged by the Italians of establishing a deeply echeloned, long-term defensive position in the east, had already been mooted by the German authorities at the end of 1941 shortly after the failure of 'Operation Barbarossa'; and it was again taken into consideration by the General Staff of the Army in the autumn of 1942. At the end of November 1941 Hitler, too, had given thought to erecting an 'eastern wall' consisting of military strong-points after the capture of Leningrad, Moscow and southern Russia.[56] Nearly a year later, Hitler had only accepted the notion of a 'wall' in one respect, namely that a defensive line be set up along the boundary of the current front line on the middle Don and possibly along the Volga downstream from Stalingrad.

The concept of a strongly fortified defensive position behind which the eastern army could be regenerated was a preoccupation, too, of Chief of Staff Zeitzler, who from the late winter of 1943 received support for this from Field Marshal Milch and Armaments Minister Speer. The military leaders, however, were well aware that even a strongly fortified position would not be an insurmountable obstacle for the enemy. In any event, the advocated defensive position should not run close behind the front line, but rather along the Dnieper under the protection of its steep western bank.[57]

The difficulty in convincing Hitler of the advantages of a timely withdrawal to shortened prepared positions was demonstrated by his month-long resistance to the General Staff's plan advocating withdrawal of the bulk of the Sixteenth Army from the pocket of Demyansk and pulling the Ninth Army, the Third Panzer Army and parts of the Fourth Army out of the Rhzev salient back to the so-called 'Buffalo position'. The advantages of these moves would be not only the evacuation of exposed bulges, whose exposed positions invited enemy attack to cut them off, but also the opportunity to gather large numbers of reserves. It was only the extremely pressing need for troops caused by the losses in the southern sector of the eastern front that finally won Hitler around to approving the recommendations made by the Chief of Staff.

On 31 January Hitler agreed to the withdrawal from the heavily contested Demyansk pocket; within ten days this enabled the Germans to pull the twelve divisions that had been tied down there back to a line, about 200 km shorter than previously, south of Lake Ilmen. From the end of February the bulk of these divisions became available for the support of threatened neighbouring positions and as reserves. Hitler's approval on 6 February finally to evacuate the salient south of Rzhev in the sector of Army Group Centre produced a perfect example, between 1 and 21 March, of a planned withdrawal, free of enemy interference. Occupation of the well-prepared 'Buffalo position' east of Smolensk, where the troops were finally given the opportunity to recuperate, also resulted in the shortening of the front line from roughly 500 km to about 200 km. The net result was that one Army Command, five General Commands and 21 divisions, including three armoured divisions, were freed as operational reserves, an unusually high number for the eastern front.[58]

Even though three General Commands and other formations had been deployed by early April to reinforce other threatened sectors of Army Group Centre, there were still eleven divisions, including seven armoured divisions, left as uncommitted reserves. The withdrawal movement by three armies had demonstrated that a successful retreat was not a defeat and could help to restore freedom of action. But Hitler had refused to shorten as well the extremely costly front of Army Group North before Leningrad. In the spring there were still seven army corps with 29 divisions[59] defensively deployed on the River Volkhov, south of Lake Ladoga, in front of Leningrad, and in the Oranienbaum bridgehead, after two Soviet armies had succeeded on 12 January in breaking through the German ring of encirclement on the River Neva and establishing a nine kilometre-wide land link with the defenders of the city. Here, too, it would have made sense to withdraw to a greatly shortened line between the Bay of Kronstadt and the Volkhov near Novgorod and thereby to acquire at least ten divisions as reserves.

How difficult it was in the spring of 1943 to set up an operationally useful back-up position for the bulk of the eastern army is demonstrated by the fact that behind the fronts of Army Groups Centre and South the so-called 'Tiger position', also known as the OKH position, was only inspected but not fortified. This OKH position was to run from the River Dvina north of Vitebsk past Smolensk on the east to the River Desna, then down the Desna to the area of Novgorod-Seversky, from there to the Dnieper, and then downriver to Melitopol. This position, which the General Staff of the Army had ordered to be explored on 24 April 1943, would have been valuable for strengthening the strategic defence. Hitler, however, was obviously not informed about this project because it was known that for psychological reasons he was sceptical of – if not decidedly opposed to – the construction of defensive positions deep in the rear areas.[60]

In the spring of 1943, given the situation that had developed because of the refusal to initiate negotiations for a separate German-Soviet peace agreement, the only remaining option was to gain a quick and effective military victory which would decisively shift the balance of power on the eastern front. It was clear, however, that should this operation fail, Germany would no longer have any chance to build up a position of strength, because the initiative would irrevocably have passed to the Red Army.

The Turn at Kursk: Failure of 'Operation Citadel'

The decision once more to undertake a limited offensive on the eastern front was laid down in Operational Directive No. 5 of 13 March 1943, at a time when von Manstein's successful counter-offensive had not yet been brought to a conclusion. Hitler was in agreement with the Chief of Staff of the Army and the C-in-Cs of Army Groups Centre and South to go over to the defensive in the east, but at least partially to seize the initiative from the enemy. A strategy restricted purely to the defensive did not appear to offer any guarantee that the front line could be held. The intention, therefore, was substantially to reduce the enemy's offensive power by well-prepared limited attacks. The bulge in the front at Kursk, which extended far to the west, appeared to offer an opportunity for such an attack in the form of a double envelopment, and an early date of attack was seen as being advantageous because time was on the side of the Soviet Union. The decision-making process and the preparations for 'Operation Citadel' demonstrate the many weighty factors involved and the various alternatives that had to be considered. A diversity of motives included political, military, economic and psychological elements which interacted and were difficult to evaluate.[61]

From the political viewpoint, a rapid and impressive victory was required in order to convince the enemy coalition of the resurgent strength of the Wehrmacht and the continued power of the Axis.[62] It would demonstrate that an invasion in southern or western Europe would meet the heaviest resistance. It would also greatly improve the conditions under which Germany could respond to the feelers being extended by a Soviet Union that was perhaps ready to make peace. The psychological intention – after the defeat at Stalingrad – was once more to enthuse the nation with reports of victory, but also to rekindle confidence in German arms among her allies, particularly Japan, Italy and Finland. Furthermore, if they were to be available in time, the superiority of newly developed weapons, for example the 'Tiger' and 'Panther' tanks, could be exploited for propaganda purposes.

The economic motives had to do with the expected immense numbers of prisoners and materials, the armaments industry in particular placing great value on prisoners as future workers. Considering that in the event of a resounding success in the battle at Kursk the German General Staff was counting upon the encirclement of eight to nine armies which would promise the capture of 600,000–700,000 men, then the hope of closing the gap in the labour requirements of the armaments industry does not appear to be all that unrealistic. With these prisoners and additional Russian civilians, the Speer ministry was confident that it could cover most of the unfilled jobs. The establishment of 'staffs for requisition and booty' in the three attacking armies underlines the value placed in Soviet prisoners and future forced labourers.[63]

Outweighing all other motives, however, were the military arguments. Despite the successful consolidation of parts of the front in the sectors of Army Groups North and Centre, there were still potential danger spots which could not be eliminated simply by remaining on the defensive. In addition to the exposed position of the Seventeenth Army which was required to hold the so-called 'Goth's Head' position opposite the Kerch peninsula with nine German and five Romanian divisions, these included the salient held by Army Group South for the protection of the Donetz basin and, most importantly, the bulge in front of the Second Panzer Army at Orel and the Soviet salient at Kursk. This extended westwards to a depth of 120 km on a 200 km-wide front and offered the Red Army favourable chances of attack. It was immediately essential, therefore, to straighten the front, either by giving up threatened sectors or by means of offensive missions. Merely to hold on to the existing front line appeared to be both inadequate and unnecessary.[64]

The need had also arisen, particularly in the sector of Army Group Centre, to deal with the mounting threat to zones behind the lines posed by numerous partisan formations, who from early 1943 had been conducting highly embarrassing disruptive actions, primarily blowing up railway lines and bridges, and thereby tying down increasing numbers of security troops. In the summer of 1942 the OKW and the senior commands concerned had already decided to pay increased attention both to the fight against the partisans and to the cultivation of the civilian population. In the directive of 18 August 1942,[65] the troops were ordered to gain the confidence of the people and to offer them incentives for cooperation in order to reduce the partisan threat. A further consideration was not to endanger agricultural production. Even though the lack of regular army formations led to a growing involvement of SS and police units in the fight against the partisans from the summer of 1942 on, it was the local army commanders who were still solely responsible for these actions, even when they drew on SS and police support.[66] The dramatic shortage of manpower behind the lines on the eastern front is illustrated by the setting up of five auxiliary divisions in the sector of Wehrmacht Command East and Ukraine which were to be employed against the partisans. Furthermore, in addition to an increase of the so-called 'local formations', the order was given to transfer an auxiliary organization comprising 50,000 men to the operations area of the Army by the end of October 1942. That the

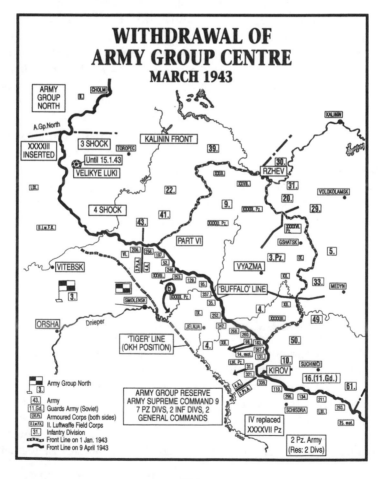

leadership of the most seriously affected Army Group Centre was attempting not to have all members of partisan units indiscriminately treated as criminals, but to differentiate between the 'hard core' and those who were serving under duress, may be seen, for example, by the order of 3 September 1942. This explicitly declared that involuntary members of partisan units were to be dealt with leniently. A decree by the OKW of 11 November 1942, while still demanding harsh measures in the fight against partisans, ordered that deserters and such partisans as surrendered voluntarily were to be treated as regular prisoners of war.[67] It can be proved, therefore, that some command authorities were attempting to defuse the partisan war by forgoing reprisals and by treating prisoners and deserters from the ranks of the partisans correctly.

Commanders of a number of army corps were sufficiently concerned at the potential danger behind their lines that during the preparations for 'Operation Citadel' several actions were conducted against the partisans. In the spring of 1943 no less than 50,000 men, including allies and security forces, were deployed against approximately 100,000 resolute partisans to the rear of Army Group Centre. In the course of 'Operation Marksman' in May, three German divisions, and during 'Operation Gypsy Baron' from 16 May to 6 June, parts of three infantry and two armoured divisions, as well as an Hungarian division and several security formations, were deployed in the sector of the Second Panzer Army in the Bryansk area, but without achieving complete success. There was a similarly disappointing outcome to 'Operation Neighbourhood' in the Fourth Army sector, where the advancing troops ran into strong resistance from prepared positions in the forests.[68] These few examples illustrate the worsening situation in an area through which led the supply lines of many of the formations who were preparing themselves for a major offensive.

In the spring of 1943 intelligence concerning the size and deployment of the enemy indicated that the Red Army was obviously obtaining arms and munitions more rapidly than the Wehrmacht, and was therefore further increasing its material superiority. At the end of March 1943 Intelligence Department East calculated total enemy strength on the European front to be 5.7 million men in 62 armies, three tank armies and 28 armoured and mechanized corps, which comprised a total of almost 400 infantry divisions, 194

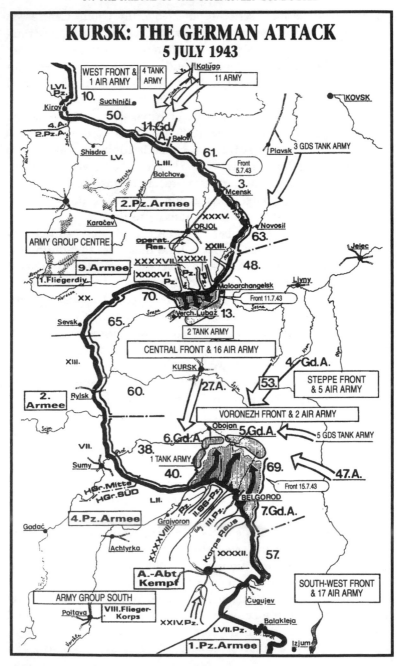

KURSK: THE GERMAN ATTACK
5 JULY 1943

infantry brigades, 171 armoured brigades and 48 mechanized brigades. In March tank production was estimated to be 1500 vehicles per month, to which had to be added deliveries from the United States and Britain. In 1943 actual production is said to have been about 24,000 tanks and self-propelled guns, and 37,000 aircraft.[69] It is not surprising, therefore, that by the end of June the strength of the Red Army along the whole eastern front is given as 6.61 million men, 10,200 tanks and self-propelled guns, and 10,250 aircraft.[70]

For this reason alone it was considered paramount to anticipate the enemy by an attack, to deal him a costly defeat, to draw as many of his operational reserves as possible into the battle, and at the same time to shorten the front drastically by 220 km. The successful execution of 'Operation Citadel' could lead to the destruction of no less than 60 Soviet divisions and five to six armoured corps, and also free many German divisions which could be made available as reserves for other theatres of war as well. After the conclusion of this attack, the preparation of which was initiated by Operational Order No. 6 of 15 April, further operations were envisaged for the renewed encirclement of Leningrad or the protection of the Donetz basin. Von Manstein's much discussed recommendation to give up the Donetz basin voluntarily and then to hit the advancing enemy in a surprise mobile attack, from the 'backhand',[71] so to speak, was certainly the more brilliant solution. But since this would not only have meant temporarily giving up the economically valuable Donetz region, but also evacuating Kharkov and the Orel bulge, Hitler insisted on the frontal attack against the Kursk salient.

The basic question here is whether von Manstein's concept of employing mobile warfare against the enemy on the eastern front, thereby wearing him down sufficiently by mobile warfare in order to force a 'draw', was realistic or only wishful thinking. Some have claimed that the very hope of achieving a 'draw' represented a 'considerable over-estimation of the possibilities remaining to the Reich'.[72] If we agree with this argument, then we cannot speak of a turn at Kursk, because even a victorious conclusion of 'Operation Citadel', including the destruction of at least 60 divisions and five to six armoured corps, would not have brought about a reversal of the strategic situation on the eastern front. And according to this view, a German failure at Kursk would only have reinforced the military decision that had already come about.

Against this is the consideration that the situation on the eastern front offered the Germans several options that did not necessarily depend on a victory at Kursk. These include the voluntary evacuation of areas and salients that were sapping German strength; for example, withdrawing the Eighteenth Army from Leningrad, evacuating the Seventeenth Army from the 'Goth's Head', and relinquishing the Orel bulge, the Kharkov area and the Donetz basin by pulling back to a shorter line with prepared positions. In the latter three instances, mobile counter-attacks against the flanks and rear of the advancing enemy could have caused him severe losses of men and material. Another option was a general withdrawal to the aforementioned 'Tiger position' between Smolensk and the Black Sea at Melitopol, which would not only have freed considerable forces for defence but also have kept economically important areas of the Ukraine under German control. In this case, too, there would have been an opportunity to employ the numerous reinforced Panzer and Panzer Grenadier divisions – Army Group South alone had thirteen such major formations – to inflict heavy losses on the enemy by means of a mobile defence. Furthermore, sufficient fast mobile forces would have been freed for the southern European theatre to help repel an Allied invasion there – a recommendation that accorded wholly with the thinking of the Wehrmacht Operations Staff and which it had already proposed on 18 June.[73]

What was to prove decisive for the outcome of 'Operation Citadel', however, was the massive Soviet defensive strength in the greater Kursk area as well as the selection of a highly unfavourable date for the attack. As is easily proved today, the STAVKA soon learned of German intentions to attack in the Kursk area and by the end of March 1943 had already begun to make extraordinarily elaborate and thorough preparations for defence. Based on a decision of mid-April, counter-attacks with far-reaching objectives were only to be launched after the repulse of the German attack. On the German side, the probable intentions of the enemy were initially unclear, but after the end of May it was assumed that the Red Army was preparing itself simultaneously for defence against the German offensive at Kursk and for decisive attacks in other sectors.[74]

The extremely strong Soviet zone of defence along the Kursk salient consisted of three systems of positions to a depth of up to 40 km in the area held by the armies deployed on the front line, augmented by the 'Voronezh', 'Central' and 'Steppe' Fronts to an added depth of up to 300 km. The defences were based on tank barriers and artillery forces, most heavily concentrated at the likeliest points of attack. According to Soviet statements, a total of eight defence zones had been erected in sequence.[75] In addition, two tank armies, a further army and several independent corps were available as operational reserves. The most important STAVKA reserve was the Steppe Front which by early July had been brought up to a strength of four armies, one tank army and three independent armoured and mechanized corps; it was intended primarily for conducting long-range counter-offensives. The air forces allocated to the three Fronts consisted of 25 air divisions with at least 2500 aircraft.[76] The overall situation was unusual in that the side with superior manpower and *matériel* deliberately remained on the defensive in order to inflict a heavier defeat on the attacker.

This overview is intended to show that when the German offensive at Kursk, which still had a reasonable chance of success in May, began on 5 July, it came up against Soviet dispositions whose defensive power had in the meantime outstripped the German power of attack. During the spring, Germany had managed to increase her combat power to such a degree that from barely 500 tanks and self-propelled guns on the whole eastern front at the end of January,[77] by early May the number had risen to 1620, all fully or almost operational. Of these, Army Groups Centre and South alone disposed of 1450 tanks and self-propelled guns, of which almost 500 were assigned to Army Group Centre's Ninth Army which was to carry out the attack, and 680 to the attacking forces of Army Group South.[78] On 10 June the entire eastern front was up to over 3000 tanks and self-propelled guns, of which almost 2570 were combat ready. By early July the number had risen to 3700, not including light tanks, half-tracks and captured tanks.[79]

Even though it had been possible to increase the armoured attack forces of both army groups to 16⅓ Panzer and Panzer Grenadier divisions with 1900 heavy and medium tanks and self-propelled guns by 5 July,[80] this was still insufficient compared to the progress meanwhile achieved by the Soviets. The enemy's increase in numbers in the Kursk area since mid-April from thirteen to seventeen armies and numerous independent corps was of less importance than the strengthening of the Soviet tactical and operational zone of defence.

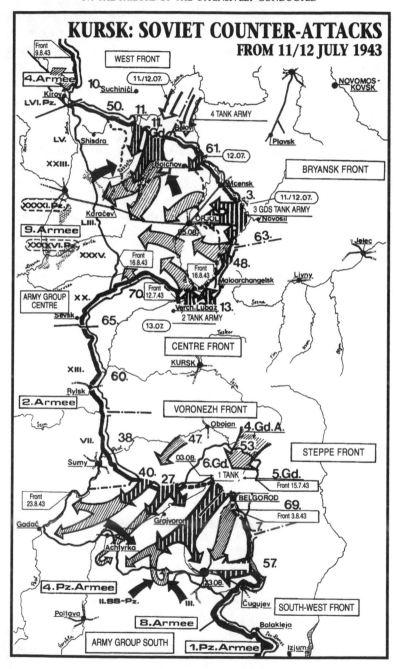

KURSK: SOVIET COUNTER-ATTACKS
FROM 11/12 JULY 1943

Front 9.8.43

WEST FRONT

11./12.07.

4.Armee

10 Suchiniči

NOVOMOS-KOVSK

Kirov

LVI.Pz.

50. 11.

4 TANK ARMY

LV. Shisdra

11. Gd.

Bolov

61. 12.07.

BRYANSK FRONT

XXIII.

Bolchov

Mcensk

3. 11./12.07.

3 GDS TANK ARMY

XXXXI.Pz.

Karačev

Novosil

9.Armee

LIII.

ORJOL

25.06.

63.

Jelec

XXXVI.Pz.

XXXV.

48.

Livny

Front 16.8.43

Front 16.8.43

Maloarchangelsk

ARMY GROUP CENTRE

XX.

70. Front 12.7.43

Verch.Lubaz 13.

2 TANK ARMY

Sevsk

65.

13.07.

CENTRE FRONT

XIII.

KURSK

2.Armee

60.

Rylsk

VORONEZH FRONT

Obojan

4.Gd.A.

VII.

38.

47.

53.

STEPPE FRONT

Sumy

40. 27.

03.08.

6.Gd.

1 TANK

5.Gd.

Front 15.7.43

Front 23.8.43

BELGOROD

69.

Front 3.8.43

Godač

Grajvoron

7.

Achtyrka

57.

4.Pz.Armee

23.08.

II.SS-Pz.

III.

Čugujev

SOUTH-WEST FRONT

Poltava

8.Armee

Balakleja

ARMY GROUP SOUTH

1.Pz.Armee

Izjum

The repeated postponement of the date of attack by Hitler, first from 3 May to 12 June and then to 5 July, was explained in terms of bringing in reinforcements of modern tanks, self-propelled guns and artillery.[81] This was far outweighed, however, by the loss of time. Not only were the Soviets enabled to perfect their defensive and counter-offensive preparations, in case of a successful attack, but the Germans had also lost the time necessary to free their reserves and deploy them for the repulse of the expected invasion by the Western powers in southern Europe.

Given the required preparations, an attack date in mid-May, or at the latest on 25 May, would still have been justifiable, as the commander of the Ninth Army suggested. Judged in retrospect, however, a postponement to early June, which the Chief of the General Staff still found acceptable,[82] cannot be considered to have made sense or offered much chance of success. Since the element of surprise was no longer there and the lapse of time was mainly to the Soviet advantage, the only militarily justifiable solution from early June onward would have been to give up 'Operation Citadel' entirely.

The offensive and defensive potential built up by the German side by early July was considerable. It consisted of 28 infantry and 16⅓ Panzer and Panzer Grenadier divisions; and with the inclusion of the uncommitted army group reserves it produced a total of 48 fresh major formations[83] and numerous support units. Of these, 33 divisions, including all the armoured formations, were earmarked for the attack. *Luftflotten* 4 and 6 supported the attack with over 1800 bombers, fighters, dive-bombers and reconnaissance aircraft.[84] This force, however, was faced by a far larger potential on the Soviet side. According to Russian sources, the Central Front and the Voronezh Front deployed for the immediate defence of the Kursk salient alone disposed of 1.3 million men, about 20,000 guns and mortars, almost 3000 tanks and self-propelled guns, and approximately 2900 aircraft, including long-range aircraft.[85] Added to these were the five armies of the Steppe Front with their 1600 tanks and self-propelled guns, as well as four further armies of the STAVKA reserves in the areas south and south-west of Moscow, which were to form the nucleus of counter-attacks. This rough comparison alone explains the clear superiority of the Red Army, which was further enhanced by the massive defensive fortifications available.

211

The failure of the German attack of 5 July, which after modest gains and despite the most strenuous efforts, came to a halt within only a few days,[86] obviously marks a turn in the war which has received particular emphasis on the Soviet side. What appears equally important, however, is the 'virtual turn' in the war which resulted from the German decision, firstly to refrain from launching a timely attack before 25 May at the latest, and secondly to risk it just the same after an extreme delay. The date selected could not have proved more disadvantageous. The issue of Hitler's directive of 13 July to break off the battle was influenced by the enemy's evidently unbroken resistance, the massive Soviet attacks against the Orel bulge,[87] the heavy German losses, and, to crown everything, news of the landings by British and American troops in Sicily on 10 July. This event in particular highlights the fatal nature of the unfavourable date chosen for the attack.

The 'virtual turn' of the war in the spring of 1943 resides in the fact that the German command, which urgently needed an early and successful outcome to 'Operation Citadel' in order to repel the Allied invasion of southern Europe, had now almost completely lost its freedom of action. To choose the alternative of calling off this operation after the beginning of June[88] would not only have spared invaluable German potential, but also retained the freedom to act, insofar as the major part of the forces committed to 'Citadel' would have become available for other theatres of war. The months-long commitment of almost all of the reserves so laboriously built up for this single operation merely worked to the advantage of the Allied war plan. From mid-July 1943 onward the initiative had therefore clearly passed to the enemy.[89]

Rarely in military history had both sides deployed their best equipped and best prepared troops with the most modern weapons in such a concentration as in the Kursk area. And rarely before had either side staked so much on the result of a single operation. For Germany it was a matter of regaining the initiative, for the Soviet Union a question of setting the seal irrevocably on her superiority and providing the impetus for an all-out push westwards. The significance of the battle to either side can be gauged from the fact that about 50 per cent of all Soviet and 64 per cent of all German armoured forces,[90] including strategic reserves, were concentrated in the Kursk sector. An overwhelming success by the Wehrmacht at

Kursk would not necessarily have resulted in victory over the Soviet Union, but that it had been the last chance to achieve a 'draw' on the eastern front.

To criticize German strategy, with hindsight, as, for example, Hitler's refusal to release von Manstein's XXIV Panzer Corps for the final breakthrough attempt by Army Group South,[91] and to pretend that more intelligent conduct of the battle could still have led to victory, is irrelevant. In the final analysis, it was the Red Army's sheer superiority in manpower and *matériel* that decided the battle. The ongoing or imminent Soviet attacks in other sectors, as well as the necessity of freeing substantial forces for the Italian theatre, hardly left the Germans with any other option than to break off the operation. A further argument, namely the heavy losses suffered by the German side, carries even less weight, for Soviet claims in this respect have proved to be wildly exaggerated. While both German attack groups did suffer high losses, particularly in tanks and self-propelled guns, the actual total losses of 15 per cent to 20 per cent were still within tolerable bounds.[92] The more important factor was that the infantry was not able adequately to protect the flanks of the armoured formations because of its numerical weakness, while the armoured forces could not capitalize on their tactical strength in the deeply echeloned enemy defence system.

The assessment of the battle of Kursk and the subsequent counter-offensive by the Red Army from 12 July, which led to the elimination of the Orel bulge and finally to the capture of Kharkov on 23 August, has for many years been dramatized and overpraised by Soviet historians and commentators. Analysis of the greatly exaggerated figures of German forces and losses cited by the Soviets suggests, firstly, that their intention was to present their victory as having been even more outstanding and glorious than it already was; and secondly, that the Soviet leadership was not all that confident in the success of its overall plan of operations.

Evidence of the former may be seen in the claims made with regard to German losses during the 50 days of the battles around Kursk, Orel and Kharkov, which were alleged to have been about 500,000 men, 1500 tanks, 3000 guns, and over 3700 aircraft.[93] Had they been true, aircraft losses alone would have exceeded by far the total combined complement of just under 2100 aircraft of all three *Luftflotten* on the eastern front!

The latter consideration implies Soviet doubt as to the effectiveness of the measures adopted and the potential defensive strength in the Kursk salient. This may be deduced indirectly from the many motivational tours of the front by senior leaders, including Stalin's personal visit in early August to the West Front.[94]

Even if it is inaccurate to speak of the 'crucible of Kursk' in which the German Panzer arm simply melted away, the importance of the battle can most aptly be summed up as the 'completion of the basic turn' which had begun with the battle of Stalingrad.[95] Moreover, this is the only example in the war of a carefully prepared Wehrmacht offensive failing within such a short time. The forces deployed on the German side, measured in terms of the number of tanks and aircraft, were greater than for the summer offensive in 1942, even though the attack was only directed against a relatively limited sector of the front. The losses suffered by the attacking armies were also far lower than Soviet literature claims. The total losses in tanks during July, August and September were almost completely made good by new production.[96] Yet even though in July 1943 the eastern armies were still capable of launching counter-attacks on the operational level, as the battles in the Ukraine were subsequently to demonstrate, Germany had nevertheless become strategically dependent on the enemy. The Wehrmacht no longer had the chance to reverse the military balance of power.

It would nevertheless appear to be greatly exaggerated and even arrogant to claim that Roosevelt and some of his advisers knew, after the battle of Kursk, that 'the Soviet Union would destroy the Nazi Reich without help from outside'.[97] Germany still required strong forces for defending or even keeping order in the occupied western territories, Norway, Italy and south-eastern Europe. Added to these were the vast human and material resources provided from the autumn of 1943 onward for air defence – AA defence alone absorbed sixteen divisions and brigades! This suggests the enormous potential both of the Wehrmacht and the armaments industry that was tied down by the front against the Western Allies and therefore unavailable in the battle against the Soviet Union.

It seems highly doubtful that the power of the Red Army alone could have defeated the Wehrmacht without the attacks of the Western Allies in Italy and France and without the destructive air offensive against Germany. If the unproven claim had been true that the eastern armies lost 1.4 million men during the summer and autumn of 1943,[98] then the Wehrmacht would have broken down in short order. That the Soviet summer offensive did not lead to rapid and overwhelming victories can be seen in the painful and costly advances against the two German armies in the bulge of Orel, where the Red Army only succeeded in pushing them back to the so-called 'Hagen position' east of Bryansk by 18 August.[99] The subsequent struggle for the Dnieper line in 1943-4, which was costly for both sides, together with von Manstein's counter-blows, do not suggest that the Red Army would have gained the victory all by itself.

The Collapse of Italy

The German defeat at Kursk does gain significance, however, seen in context with its effect on the war in southern Europe. Just at the time when, from 10 July onward, the Western Allies were slowly but surely conquering Sicily, the bulk of the German Panzer and Panzer Grenadier divisions remained tied down on the eastern front. In the ensuing weeks Hitler was unable to decide to withdraw substantial forces from the eastern front in order to deploy them against the expected invasion of Italy or the Balkans. Even the withdrawal of II SS Panzer Corps with two Panzer Divisions, which began on 17 July, was cancelled so as to continue Army Group South's defensive battle with undiminished forces. The alternative to this would have been the rapid withdrawal to shortened lines, for example by giving up the Orel bulge, the Donetz area and the 'Goth's Head' in the Kuban region. Finally, there was still an opportunity to pull back the bulk of the eastern armies to the 'Tiger (OKW) position' where long stretches of the Desna and Dnieper rivers could have served as an obstacle. Since the senior German leadership did not choose this alternative, its operations in southern Europe remained dependent for the time being on improvisations.

The continued concentration of strategic focus on the eastern front offered General Eisenhower, in command of the Allied forces in the Mediterranean, excellent opportunities to achieve a decisive victory over the Axis powers in the Mediterranean in 1943. However, since the beginning of 1943, serious differences over strategic priorities had arisen between the American and British, both on the military and political side. Initially the only decision taken at the conference in Casablanca had been to conquer Sicily ('Operation Husky') after completion of the campaign in Tunisia. The ongoing dispute over the priority of an invasion of western Europe from Britain, according to American plans, or of an attack against Italy or the Balkans, as advocated by Churchill, could only be defused at the 'Trident' conference in Washington from 12–15 May by means of a half-hearted compromise.[100]

According to this, strategic priority would be given to the invasion of western Europe, preparations for which were to be concluded by 1 May 1944; but in practice Churchill and his advisers had won a temporary victory. Because of the preponderance of the British fleet in the Mediterranean and in the armed forces, which comprised almost 30 British or British-led major formations in this theatre as opposed to only nine American and one French, agreement was reached first to force Italy out of the war. No agreement, however, was arrived at for more ambitious plans such as the rapid conquest of the Italian mainland or an amphibious operation on the Greek or Yugoslavian coastline. The message to Stalin that the invasion of western Europe was to be postponed until the spring of 1944 led to serious stresses within the war coalition, as has already been explained. Seen from today, however, this strategic compromise between the Allied leaders was a serious mistake in that they only capitalized on the weakness of the Axis during the summer of 1943 to a very modest degree. Finally, the decision to transfer seven battle-experienced divisions to Britain by 1 November, and therefore not to profit at once, with all available forces, from the advantage gained by the conquest of Sicily, resulted in the Italian campaign of 1943 deteriorating into no more than a strategic half-measure.[101]

After the loss of the Tunisian bridgehead, the situation of the Axis powers had swung in their disfavour for a number of reasons. Not only had 250,000 well-trained and combat-proven soldiers been lost, not only was Germany's Italian ally becoming increasingly less dependable, but the Axis nations now had to prepare themselves to face not only the growing threat of invasion in Italy itself, but also in Sicily, Sardinia and Corsica. Keeping these islands supplied required further efforts. Massive air attacks against southern and central Italy had to be reckoned with. Furthermore, there could no longer be any hope of a forceful intervention by the Italian fleet, the bulk of which had already been withdrawn from Naples to La Spezia in December 1942. Finally, protection of the Balkans and the Greek islands necessitated further land and air forces. In order to improve the air situation, Luftwaffe Command South-east was set up in Salonika in mid-May and rapidly reinforced, so that by 10 July it consisted of no less than 632 aircraft of which 359 were ready for combat.[102] The land forces under Supreme Command South-east in the Balkans and Crete were reinforced, albeit modestly, given the threat of invasion and the size of the territory to be covered, so that by early July there were eleven and one-third German, three Croatian and three Bulgarian divisions deployed there in addition to an Italian formation.[103] Finally, due to several measures of deception by the Allies which suggested that Sardinia and Greece were initially to be the targets for invasion, the Wehrmacht command was in the dark about the real target. All the trump cards were clearly held by the attackers.[104]

While Hitler's statement of 1 July to the commanders on the eastern front that the battle in Tunisia had postponed the 'invasion of Europe' for half a year was basically true, the Germans had done little to increase defensive power in Italy, Sicily, Sardinia or Corsica, apart from the reinforcement of *Luftflotte 2*.[105] The intention to withdraw six to eight armoured divisions and other forces from the eastern front and to deploy them for the battle for the southern fringe of Europe in time, was – as we have seen – put aside in favour of 'Operation Citadel'. Only if these divisions had been brought in would the time gained by the sacrifice of the German-Italian forces in Tunisia have been justified.

The conquest of Sicily, conducted with great effort and superior forces and originally disguised as a feint, which was finally concluded on 17 August, brought no more than a 'text-book' victory over four German divisions and several Italian formations that were hardly committed to fighting any longer. After a cleverly conducted retreat, the defenders withdrew to southern Italy with the bulk of their equipment under the protective cover of the 'AA umbrella' of Messina.[106] Almost 40,000 German and 62,000 Italian soldiers were safely brought back to the mainland. However, the battles in Sicily and in the adjoining waters had again caused *Luftflotte 2* serious losses; it had neither inflicted any appreciable damage on the Allied naval forces, nor had it rendered support to the German ground forces. The rapid gain of aerial superiority – which bordered temporarily on complete command of the air – by the Allies was to become an inevitable feature of the subsequent course of the war in Italy. The total forces of *Luftflotte 2*, including transports, which at the time the attack on Sicily began on 10 July had numbered 958 aircraft, of which 593 were operational, was reduced to 722 aircraft by 31 August, of which 387 were combat-ready, and this despite constant reinforcements, especially in bombers and fighters.[107]

The air battles over Sicily had shown that for all its efforts fighter defence was hardly able any longer to offer effective resistance to the enemy bomber formations. The continual demands for reinforcements made by *Luftflotte 2* demonstrated that in view of the requirements for the air defence of the Reich, the Luftwaffe was facing a dramatically accelerating acid test. On top of this, in August Allied bomber formations set a new marker in the strategic air war when they began flying missions against airfields, cities and armament centres deep in enemy territory from bases in North Africa, Britain and the 'aircraft carrier' Sicily. Air attacks against Milan, Turin, Wiener Neustadt and Rome on 12–13 August, and Foggia on 16 and 18 August, went far beyond the preparations for a landing on the mainland. Defeat in the air in the sector of C-in-C South had visibly begun with the capture of Sicily. The evacuation of Sicily had also signalled the failure of the intention to defend the southern perimeter of the European mainland.[108]

From now on much would depend on whether the weak German forces in Italy would be able successfully to repel invasion attempts against the Italian mainland, something that was made even more difficult when during July Italy's attempts to break away from the Axis became increasingly obvious. How far could Germany still count on dependable Italian formations willing to fight in the defence of Italy and Sardinia? Would she be able, in case Italy defected, to initiate in time her 'Alarich', 'Constantin' and 'Axis' emergency plans?[109] These called not only for the compulsory occupation of large parts of the country by German troops, but also the disarming, dismissal or detention of Italian troops at home as well as in the territories under Italian control. And could the Germans take over the assignments of the 34 Italian divisions abroad, for example that of the Italian Fourth Army which was defending the southern French coast?[110]

Mussolini's downfall on 25 July, the hectic attempts at least to delay Italy's defection (i.e. to practice political 'damage limitation'), the occupation of northern Italy by the newly created Army Group B with eight divisions under Field Marshal Rommel from 26 July onward, the closing of the Alpine passes, and the transfer of the 2nd Paratroop Division from southern France to the area south of Rome, all demonstrated the political and military tensions under which the German strategic build-up in Italy was labouring. That Rommel was preferred over Kesselring – judged to be too much of an 'Italophile' – as 'Commander South' may be deduced from the highly questionable decision of 16 August to split the command by putting Rommel in charge of all German formations north of the line Pisa–Arezzo–Ancona, while leaving Kesselring in command of the remaining forces south of this line.[111]

The fact that the German leadership had an internal battle on its hands until 8 September, when the capitulation by the Badoglio regime was announced, naturally made preparations for defence against an invasion even more difficult. In southern Italy Kesselring only disposed of the 1st Paratroop Division and two armoured corps with five Panzer and Panzer Grenadier divisions.[112] In the Rome area there were only two and one-third major German formations. However, after the launch of 'Axis' on the evening of 8 September, they succeeded within a couple of days and against all expectations in overwhelming the five Italian divisions deployed for the protection of Rome after short and intermittently sharp fighting. The Italians captured in the Rome area were released on Kesselring's orders and Rome was designated as an 'open city'. From the point of view of Supreme Command South, this allayed the extremely dangerous threat of protracted resistance by the Italians, possibly in conjunction with an airborne operation by the Allies, that might otherwise have confronted the German troops in southern Italy.[113]

The operation begun by the American Fifth Army on the morning of 9 September to establish a beachhead in the Bay of Salerno, which then held out with great difficulty against strong German counterattacks,[114] irrevocably underlined the turn of the war in southern Europe. The Allies had succeeded in creating a strong operational base on the mainland; and this, together with the British landings in Calabria and Apulia at the end of September, would facilitate the capture of large parts of southern Italy without German response. But whereas the planned withdrawal of the German Tenth Army to the 'Bernhard Line' in November, and subsequently to the 'Gustav Line', as well as the evacuation of Sardinia and Corsica, extended the territory held by the attackers, there were to be no more decisive victories in this theatre during 1943. Nor did the plan to invade the Balkans receive any further impetus.[115]

As a result of the defensive achievements of the Tenth Army, the German leadership took the decision to halt the retreat and to defend the strong 'Gustav' position energetically with eight divisions, thereby operationally sealing the Italian 'boot' at its narrowest point between Gaeta and Ortona.[116] This also gained valuable time to strengthen the so-called 'Goth Line' in the northern Apennines which was to serve the German forces as the final position from which to defend northern Italy. The attacks launched by the Allies along the approaches to the 'Gustav Line' until the end of the year were only modestly successful. The Allied Supreme Command had neglected to carry out the airborne operation in the Rome area originally scheduled and prepared for early September, probably because of the suspicious conduct of the Italians during the cease-fire negotiations. This not only wasted the chance of gaining a political victory with the occupation of the capital, but also a military one through the inevitable withdrawal of all German forces from central and southern Italy.[117]

With the German defeats on the eastern front during the summer of 1943 and the firm establishment of two Allied armies in southern Italy, Hitler's strategy to defend the borders of Europe by means of decisive offensive actions had also failed. The elaborately prepared attempt to achieve an outstanding operational success in the east had come to an end just as quickly as the attempt to deny the Allies a landing on the European mainland and to deal them a painful defeat as a possible deterrent for the future. The outer wall of 'Fortress Europe' had been deeply breached in several places. Would the inner wall and the roof of this fortress now withstand attack?

V

THE LAW OF GRAVITY 1944

The Air Battle over Germany
and the Economic War in 1943–1944

We cannot discuss the decisive phases of 1943–4 without first determining in what sense these were still turns of the war. It is clear that after the collapse of the German southern flank on the eastern front and the loss of North Africa by the Axis powers, they could no longer hope for victory. Nor, after the withdrawals on the eastern front in the summer of 1943 and the conquest of southern Italy by the Allies, could there be any further talk of defending the 'periphery' of Europe.

How then can the next phase of the war which lasted until June–July 1944 still be characterized as a turn? Was the issue not simply the sealing of an already irrevocable defeat? Or did Germany still have sufficient freedom to mount a strategic defence that would give hope for some conclusion other than the demand for 'unconditional surrender'? How much chance was there still of ending the war by some sort of 'draw'?

In attempting to answer these questions let us first discuss the strategic air war against Germany up to the spring of 1944. In an overall situation that was characterized by defensive fighting in the east and in Italy against ever-growing enemy forces, as well as by increasing battles against partisans – particularly in Byelorussia and the Balkans – the uninterrupted production of arms had to assume decisive importance. One of the most important conditions for this was an air defence which could reduce the effects of the Allied bombing offensive to the barest minimum. The issue was therefore the stability of the 'roof' of fortress Europe. That the Western powers considered this 'roof' to have many holes can be seen from a message to Congress by Roosevelt on 17 September 1943 in which he stated: 'I doubt that fortress Europe is impregnable, because Hitler forgot to put a roof on this fortress.'[1]

As already mentioned, according to the directive for the combined bomber offensive (CBO) of 10 June 1943, British Bomber Command and the American 8th Air Force operated from Great Britain, while the 9th Air Force conducted the strategic air war against southern Germany, Italy and south-eastern Europe from its bases in North Africa, where it was replaced by the 15th Air Force in the autumn.

Despite the outward appearance of unanimity, the leadership of Bomber Command normally refused to give direct support to the 8th Air Force and declined to attack important targets – the destruction of which was not seen as a panacea – in harmony with the Americans. The American bomber formations in their turn insisted on checking results by day and did not take part in the nightly 'crusades' by the British against Berlin from November 1943 on.[2]

It was already apparent during the summer of 1943 that the 8th Air Force, and to a lesser degree the 9th Air Force, were waging their battle against the German fighter arm by attacking its production plants, in particular the ball-bearing factories, and the refineries. Destroying German fighter capacity was considered to be an indispensable preliminary objective, following which other important industrial targets, fuel production and the means and systems of transport were to be attacked. After the battle against the U-boats as primary targets had been discontinued in the early summer of 1943, American attacks were concentrated on six major groups of industry from which a total of 76 individual targets were selected including above all plants making ball-bearings and aircraft engines.[3] At this time long-range fighter escorts, such as the P-51 'Mustang' which with its range of between 800 and 1000 km was capable of protecting the bomber waves throughout their missions, were not yet available, so these daylight raids were flown with a strength of about 300 bombers in order to present the greatest possible defensive power against German fighters.

From the summer of 1943 a double struggle developed: on the one hand the duel for air supremacy between the attacking bombers and the defending forces, on the other the race between German fighter production and the increasing numbers of Allied bombers and escort fighters.[4]

Once German fighter production had been decisively damaged, it was forseeable that the bomber offensive would be turned against other important arms sectors such as production of tanks, self-propelled guns, transport vehicles, anti-tank and AA weapons, and finally the V weapons.

Statistics from 1943 onward for major categories of tank production, excluding command, scout, recovery, light and special tanks, were as follows:[5]

	1943	1944	1945
Panzer IV	3023	3225	438
Panzer V (Panther)	1848	3777	507
Panzer VI (Tiger I)	649	623	(?)
Panzer VI (Tiger II)	NA	376	112
TOTAL	5520	8001	(?)

A glance at the increased production of self-propelled guns with 7.5cm barrel L/48 (type III) and 10.5cm field howitzer (type IV), shows that 3245 such weapons had been produced in 1943 and as many as 5758 in 1944.[6] These numbers indicate that despite the increased bombing, a significant leap forward in the production of armour had been achieved within the framework of the extended tank production programme of 22 January 1943. While Germany did not succeed in reaching the monthly production figure of 1955 tanks of all types envisaged in 1943 by the Inspector General of Armoured Forces,[7] the increase in the number of 'Panthers' and 'Tigers' after mid-1943 shows that Germany was also capable of achieving unexpectedly high production figures which were bound to become even higher if the Allied bomber offensive against the production plants could be repelled.[8]

It should be noted at this point that the air war waged against Germany by the Allied bomber fleets in order to paralyze morale and the war economy did not fulfil expectations despite the huge destruction caused. Neither the attacks on civilian housing areas nor the precision bombing of armament targets led to a collapse of the enemy 'hinterland'. Only 12 per cent of all bombs dropped landed on industrial targets and 24 per cent on housing areas with over 100,000 inhabitants. It was only by the end of the war in 1945 that roughly 50 per cent of the armaments industry, 30 per cent of the steel industry and almost the entire fuel industry had been destroyed.[9] According to official American statements, loss of production due to bombing was calculated at roughly 9 per cent for 1943 and 17 per cent for 1944, whereas British estimates were higher with regard to certain key industries. For the quota of iron and steel production reserved exclusively for arms production, for example, losses in production in the second half of 1943 were estimated at 46.5 per cent and in the second half of 1944 at 39 per cent.[10]

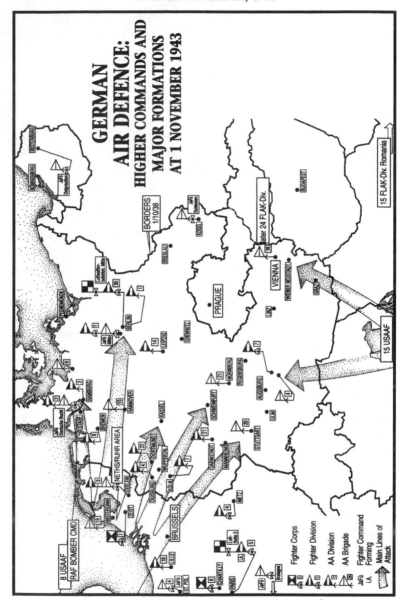

GERMAN
AIR DEFENCE:
HIGHER COMMANDS AND
MAJOR FORMATIONS
AT 1 NOVEMBER 1943

Fighter Corps
Fighter Division
AA Division
AA Brigade
Fighter Command
Forming
Main Lines of
Attack

JaFü
I.A.

The Luftwaffe leadership, for its part, obviously only began to appreciate the threat to German cities posed by the nightly bombing raids after the extremely devastating day and night attacks, from 24–25 July onward, on Hamburg, where fires caused a total of 40,000 dead and left 600,000 homeless.[11] The General Inspector of Aircraft, Field Marshal Milch, was among those responsible for arming the air force who wished to shift the focus of production to fighters as quickly as possible. According to Milch's plan, the current production figure of 1000 fighters per month was to be increased to 3000 per month by the summer of 1944.[12] But since this was to be achieved without any decrease in bomber production, there was no clear shift in balance even at this time. Nor did the monthly production of 1000 fighters primarily benefit the defence of the Reich because the majority of these aircraft were assigned to the *Luftflotten* at the fronts, mainly to *Luftflotte 2*. It was only after 1 October that Milch's Aircraft Programme No. 224 unequivocally gave priority to defensive aircraft; yet the plan still called for a monthly production of 1294 bombers, high-speed bombers, dive-bombers and destroyers right up to September 1945. On the other hand, during the same period, 4105 day fighters, 302 night fighters and 225 twin-engine fighters were to be produced monthly, so that the ratio in favour of aircraft deployed for defence could be brought up to 3.4 to 1.[13]

Whereas compared to Aircraft Programme No. 223 of 15 April 1943, an extraordinary step had been taken in the direction of air defence, it was highly questionable whether the production figures within the envisaged time-scale could be achieved by an industry that was being increasingly damaged by bomb attacks, was suffering from shortages of workers and raw materials, and was also expected to record exceptional results in many other categories of weapons programmes. Milch's staff, for example, calculated the monthly requirement of aluminium for Programme No. 224 at 26,000 tonnes, whereas the actual monthly average available was only 22,000 tonnes.[14]

For tactical reasons alone, the absolute priority of fighter production for the defence of the Reich should have been obvious to all. Experience in the air battles to date had proved that in a given battle fighter defence needed a threefold to fourfold numerical superiority in order to stand any chance of inflicting serious losses on an attacking bomber formation and preventing it from fulfilling its mission.[15] There was the additional necessity of increasing the fighter quota still further in case the bomber formations were escorted by numerous long-range fighters which had to be fought separately. A ratio of 4 to 1, or 5 to 1 in favour of the defenders was therefore to be aimed at. Only if this were achieved would the struggle between bombers plus escorting fighters against defenders enter its decisive dramatic phase.

The numerical weakness of the Reich air defence was further aggravated by problems of organization and partly, too, by lack of manpower. The organizational problem sprang from the failure of the Luftwaffe command to build up a unified air defence over the Reich and the occupied territories in western Europe. No decision was taken for the central defence of the Reich. For too long the leadership clung to the concept of 'peripheral air defence', which required an even distribution of the fighter formations in Holland, Belgium and north-western Germany.[16] In the autumn of 1943 the existing day and night fighter formations were reorganized. Air Commander Centre regrouped his fighter aircraft into I Fighter Corps, with its command centre in Zeist near Utrecht, and 7th and 30th Fighter Divisions, while *Luftflotte 3* in the west assigned its fighters to II Fighter Corps, with its headquarters in Chantilly north of Paris. The projected and urgently required formation of a third fighter corps in southern Germany by reinforcement of 7th Fighter Division, with its command centre in Schleißheim near Munich, did not come about.[17]

That Germany did have plans that corresponded to the realities of the threat from the air can be seen from the intention to assign the defence of the Reich, including the eastern regions and the western territories, to three fighter corps, who in the final stage of organization were to comprise ten fighter divisions plus 'Fighter Leader Brittany'. There is much to be said for the claim that such a decisively reinforced air defence with the required priorities in material and manpower would have stood a good chance in the battle for air supremacy in 1943–4. In the air war such a move would at least have followed the principle of setting one concentration of power against another. It must also be noted, however, that such an armaments programme would have had to recognize the clear priority of the air force over the army, and the decision to wage 'economic' warfare in Italy and on the eastern front, including a withdrawal to a much shorter and more easily manageable front by giving up the Crimea and pulling back to a line between the Bay of Narva in the north and the mouth of the Dnieper in the south.[18]

Another important factor in the battle over the Reich was the marked increase in ground-based air defence. But despite the undisputed efforts made by the AA formations, there was a price to be paid in the disproportionately high manpower and material requirements needed to fight enemy bombers by means of anti-aircraft weapons. Not counting the medium and light AA guns, ground-based air defence in mid-1942 consisted of 1148 heavy AA batteries (increased to 2132 in 1943 and to 2655 in 1944) with which to fight the high-altitude bombers.[19] Normally AA units were equipped with three to four 'heavy' batteries. Already in 1942 the AA arm comprised 1568 heavy and 1237 medium and light batteries.[20] After the turn of the year 1941-2 the majority of the heavy batteries each had six guns. The most important of these were the 8.8cm and 10.5cm gun, of which there were about 14,000 and 2000 respectively by 1944, numbers that were far higher than originally projected in 1942.[21]

Because the AA arm had been given preference for air defence of the Reich from the very beginning of the war, in 1941 and 1942 the AA formations were more rapidly reinforced than the fighter arm, even though the system of electronic detection still had large gaps. After the reorganization of air defence in mid-October 1943 there were a total of nine AA divisions and seven AA brigades deployed within the Reich, in Belgium, the Netherlands and north-western France.[22]

Berlin area	1st Flak Division
Hamburg	3rd Flak Division
Duisburg	4th Flak Division
Cologne	7th Flak Division
Bremen	8th Flak Division
Leipzig	14th Flak Division
North-West France / Lille	16th Flak Division
Darmstadt / Rhine–Main area	21st Flak Division
Dortmund	22nd Flak Division
Munich / Augsburg	4th Flak Brigade
Wismar / Odermüngdung	8th Flak Brigade
Hannover	15th Flak Brigade
Vienna	16th Flak Brigade
Amsterdam / Rotterdam	19th Flak Brigade
Stuttgart	20th Flak Brigade
Nuremberg	21st Flak Brigade

By the autumn of 1943 the effort to heavily protect major cities or particularly endangered industrial centres had led to an extraordinary concentration of AA forces, so that some targets were protected by 100 or more heavy AA guns. In October 1943, for example, there were 23 heavy batteries with about 130 guns of 8.8cm calibre in Schweinfurt. The massed AA guns did cause losses among the attacking bomber forces, and were feared by the bomber crews; furthermore they helped to boost morale. Even so, such a high concentration of AA units, using electronic detection equipment that was often prone to faults, could not prevent the enemy from carrying out aimed bomb drops over their targets.

That the deployment of AA forces was uneconomic may be seen from the fact that on average it required 16,000 shots by the standard 8.8cm Flak 36 and 8000 shots by the improved 8.8cm Flak 41 to shoot down one bomber flying at high altitude.[24] Tactically, only those AA batteries that were deployed directly around the target under attack, or which the bombers flew over, could play a part in the battle; fighters, on the other hand, utilized more flexibly and stationed further apart, were capable of giving battle uninterruptedly to successive waves of bombers.

The extremely high manpower requirements of AA defence, particularly of helpers, who consisted largely of schoolboys but also prisoners of war, can already be seen in the increase from 500,000 men at the time of mobilization to 1.1 million men by the war's end. Towards the end of 1944 there were twelve AA divisions and seven AA brigades in the Reich alone.[25] With the reorganization of brigades into divisions and the setting up of new formations, by the end of the war there were 30 AA divisions, including the railway air defence.[26] In addition to the manning problem there was the extremely high material requirement and production capacity which caused even Hitler and Speer to have doubts about the mass production of the greatly improved 8.8cm Flak 41. The enormous amount of ammunition needed meant a waste of material, as for example the huge quantity of aluminium that was required for fuses.[27]

Besides shifting the focus of air defence to the fighter arm as early as the end of 1942, the only really useful help would have been the rapid development of anti-aircraft rockets such as the 'Rheintochter' and 'Wasserfall'. Only such a high-speed AA rocket programme for both the effective and also economic protection of targets – if begun in 1942 – would have offered a promising alternative to air defence with guns.[28] Even Speer described the failure to develop AA rockets and the concentration instead on mass production of the long-range rocket A4, later known as the V2, a 'massive blunder',[29] which, to make matters worse, also affected fighter production. In this case particularly, Hitler's preoccupation with reprisal, fuelled mainly by his anger at the destruction and losses being caused by the Allied bombers, proved to be self-damaging. If Germany insisted on branding indiscriminate bombing as terrorism and therefore against international law, she herself should not have resorted to similar acts of terror.

In 1943, therefore, air defence of the Reich tied down thousands of AA guns which were needed just as urgently on the eastern front to defend against tanks; and it also tied down hundreds of thousands of soldiers, workers and helpers, who were thus lost to the front, to other branches of the service and to the armaments industry. The manpower, organizational and material requirements of this form of air defence were clearly disproportionate to its effectivity.[30]

The daylight air battles which took place in the second half of 1943 were conducted on the German side by a fighter arm which had neither the numerical nor material power which senior Luftwaffe officers knew to be required to meet Göring's demand that approximately 50 per cent of the incoming bombers were to be destroyed. In early August Air Command Centre had 588 single-engine day fighters and 103 twin-engine fighters for the defence of the Reich, and by the end of August the numbers were 556 and 110 respectively, of which about 70 per cent were operational.[31] The attack against the armaments factories in Schweinfurt and Regensburg by the 8th Air Force on 17 August cost the attackers losses of 16 per cent, with no lasting damage to the plants. The British 'Hydra' attack against the rocket development site at Peenemünde on 17–18 August, however, led to a far more dramatic result. It was most probably the motive for the suicide of Luftwaffe Chief of Staff Colonel General Jeschonnek; and it caused Hitler to take the decision to move the production of the A4 rocket to the so-called 'Mittelwerk' in the Kohnstein mine near the village of Niedersachswerfen in the Harz Mountains and to transfer supervision over testing and production to the SS.[32]

The highpoint of the daylight air battles, i.e. the attack on Schweinfurt on 14 October by 291 American B-17 bombers, cost the attackers 82 machines shot down, crash-landed or irreparably damaged, and also around 640 men, which amounted to a loss quota of 28.2 per cent – considered by US command to be intolerable. Added to the losses suffered shortly before this, it would be fair to say that the 8th Air Force had lost control of the air over Germany at this point.[33] The German fighter arm had thrown roughly 350 aircraft against the attackers in over 880 missions and only lost 33 fighters totally destroyed and 21 damaged – a hint of what might have been achieved had it gone into battle with a threefold numerical superiority. The over-strong concentration of AA forces in Schweinfurt only accounted for eleven bombers shot down,[34] which again indirectly underlines the advantages of superior numbers of fighters. Due to various counter-measures, loss of production in ball-bearings did not amount to Allied expectations.

Nor did the night offensives by Bomber Command against Berlin from 18 November 1943 to 24 March 1944 achieve the desired objective despite the great damage caused, even though Air Chief Marshal Harris had noted before the operation began that Berlin 'could be destroyed from one end to the other' and Germany brought down to final defeat if the American bomber formations were to take part.[35] After the losses in the 'Battle of Berlin' – in total over 520 bombers – Bomber Command suffered its heaviest defeat during its attack on Nuremberg on the night of 31 March 1944 when 107 out of 725 bombers, in other words almost 15 per cent, were lost. How seriously the morale of the attackers had been damaged by this time can be seen, for example, in the recommendation by the responsible tactical staff to discontinue entirely the practice of flying bombers in streams.[36]

The massive daylight attacks by the US 8th and 15th Air Forces, which were flown in conjunction with British night attacks against key industries during the 'Big Week' at the end of February 1944, made it clear that the German fighter arm had lost control of the air and could no longer regain it. The superiority of the American waves of bombers, which were now being protected by numerous P-51 'Mustang' fighters, made itself felt in the dangerously rising number of losses among the defending fighters, whereas the attackers' losses were lower during the daylight battles than in the night attacks.[37] Even the formation of the 'Fighter Staff' at the end of February and beginning of March 1944, while bringing the list strength of fighter aircraft up to more than 3000 machines by the end of September, could no longer break the numerical and technical superiority of the Allies.

One of the final major successes in a daylight battle was achieved on 6 March over Berlin when at the cost of minimal losses German fighter defence was able to inflict losses of 68 bombers and 11 fighters on the 8th Air Force, in other words almost 11 per cent of the bombers involved. Finally the American air offensive against the fuel plants in central Germany, which began on 12 May, hit the German war economy in its obviously most vulnerable spot. Together with the attacks against the transport network, these raids caused irreparable breakdowns in the supply of fuel and energy as well as steel production and also contributed largely to the preparation of the invasion in the west. For Speer these air attacks even signalled 'the end of German armament'.[38]

There is truth, therefore, in the assessment that Germany began her energetic, even desperate, attempts to give priority to the strengthening of the fighter arm and to shift to air defence *approximately one year too late*.[39] A forceful concentration on fighter production at the expense of other forms of weapons, including anti-aircraft, begun at the end of 1942 and beginning of 1943 would have made it possible already in the summer of 1943 to oppose the Allied bomber streams with a numerical superiority of at least 3 to 1 and might still have achieved a turn in the air war. In any event, it is worth noting that until 1942 only 50 per cent of air armament production capacity was only being utilized and that one of the major weaknesses had been the planning of aircraft development.[40]

It has been suggested that if the attempt had not been made to convert the Me 262 jet aircraft from a fighter to a high-speed bomber, and the plane had been produced exclusively as an interceptor, this might have helped to reverse the air war in 1944. The theory, however, is not convincing. The allusion is to Hitler's decision of 26 November 1943 when, after being shown a prototype of the Me 262 at Insterburg, he gave the order to modify this machine and produce it as a 'lightning bomber'. By the end of 1944 production figures for the Me 262 – primarily as a bomber and fighter-bomber – had reached 568, and was to reach 1400 by the end of the war.[41] However, it was not the attempted conversion into a 'high-speed bomber' but other factors which explained why this jet aircraft no longer had any effect. These included technical problems in the production of the turbines, lack of material, shortage of fuel, delays because of bombing attacks, and insufficient time to convert technical superiority into combat power by training as many pilots as possible in refined attack tactics against the bomber formations.[42] At the time of the invasion in Normandy, the Luftwaffe, on whose full power Hitler set great hopes of opposing the landings, had less than 30 Me 262s which were not even tested for combat. Given the fact that production of the trial series had only begun in January 1944, it is evident that here, too, testing and production of this aircraft was begun one year too late in order to achieve a possible turn in the air war.

A summary of the results of the air war over Germany in 1943–4, demonstrates that from late spring of 1944 German air defence was no longer capable of repulsing the Allied bomber offensive. Attacks against the German war economy also began to have such a devastating effect from May 1944 onward that – despite all of the major achievements during the summer and autumn – further production increases could no longer be expected in the longer term. That the armaments industry only collapsed for good at the turn of the year 1944–5[43] is due to feats in repair and improvisation, but also to the fact that the general air offensive against the transportation network only took full effect relatively late in the game. Among the reasons for the relatively modest success – as compared to the gigantic effort – of the Allied air offensive until the spring of 1944, are the following:[44]

1. Lack of consistency in direction, notably the repetition of attacks against key targets, such as ball-bearing plants.
2. Over-estimation of the damage caused.
3. Mistaken assessment of the cause-effect relationship between the targets bombed and potential arms production.
4. Under-estimation of the German reserves in available raw materials as well as the ability to develop substitute materials.[45]
5. Under-estimation of German ability to improvise and to create a 'substitute economy'.
6. Over-estimation of the effect of area bombardment on the enemy's will to resist, and on fighting and working morale. In fact, only the indirect results of the destruction caused were of any importance. This included tying down labour for clearing rubble and making

repairs, the loss of millions of working hours, traffic interruptions, burdening the population and administration with the care of the homeless and the wounded, etc.

Comparison of British and American air strategy indicates convincingly that while the British bomber arm suffered slightly lower losses in its night attacks than the Americans, the precision attacks by the US 8th and 15th Air Forces caused the German war economy far greater damage. The offensive against the fuel industry and the traffic network from May 1944 onward proved a highly important factor for Germany's final defeat in 1945. With a high degree of probability, an earlier start of this offensive would have speeded up the collapse of German defensive power. Simultaneously, the British decision to concentrate on area and population targets rather than concrete industrial targets must be seen as *an admission of failure.*

Out of the total of 2.77 million tonnes of bombs that the Western Allies dropped on Europe, until 1944 the major part fell on area targets, in other words only indirectly damaged the German armaments industry. Even though the economic war against Germany did not prove as decisive as British and American strategists had intended,[46] it did nevertheless make an important contribution to the military collapse of Germany from June 1944 on. In all probability this collapse would have come about sooner if the British bomber arm had lent its full power to the American precision attacks from the very start. It cannot be denied that the greatest effect of the Allied strategic air war was the degree to which it directly damaged the combat power of the Wehrmacht.[47]

The dedicated advocacy of an air offensive against German cities becomes even harder to understand when considering that the British leaders had seen how the German air attacks of 1940–1 had failed to break the will of their own population.[48] Today there is widespread agreement that 'indescriminate' air bombardment in Europe was not decisive for the war. It is also clear that the Allied strategists were unable to step up the air war to such an extent that invasion of western Europe became superfluous. Responsibility for the 'total' bombing war lies not only with the leadership of Bomber Command, but also with the General Staff of the Royal Air Force, and in the final analysis with Churchill and Roosevelt, who were in agreement in assessing the efficacy and permissibility of such bombing attacks. In contrast to this, with very few exceptions, the Luftwaffe continued to differentiate between important military targets and civilian areas. Today there appears to be widespread agreement that despite the existing 'grey area', the precepts of international law of war cannot be reconciled with 'total' bomb warfare.[49]

If one can speak of a turn of the war in the air, this took place in the spring of 1944 after the American bomber formations, protected by sufficiently numerous escort fighters, were able to gain air superiority, and subsequently complete command of the air, over Germany and the occupied western territories. After the defensive successes in late summer and autumn of 1943, the Luftwaffe leadership had neglected to increase fighter defence to full capacity – if necessary even at the expense of other types of weapons – so as to be able in 1944 to counter the inevitable enemy daylight attacks with an approximately 4 to 1 superiority. Even after the 'torch of Hamburg' a radical realignment of arms production towards air defence could still have had a decisive effect on the survival of 'fortress Europe'. In this omission lies *the 'virtual turn' in the air war* in the second half of 1943. The American air offensive in May 1944 against German fuel production brought about the irrevocable decision in the air war, [50] even before the failure to ward off the invasion in the west clearly revealed the defeat of the Luftwaffe.

The Invasion in the West and the Collapse of Army Group Centre in Mid-1944

The argument advanced above is intended to show that until early 1944 Germany still had the chance, if not actually to gain air superiority, then at least to avoid defeat in the aerial battle over the homeland. Such a development would not only have had an important effect on the protection of the civilian population, the arms industry and the supply network, but also on the preparations for repelling the invasion in the west. The air battle over Germany must be seen in direct relationship to the defence of 'fortress Europe', because the invasion preparations by the Americans, British and Canadians were largely dependent on the extent to which the bombers could soften up this 'fortress' for attack. In any case, during late winter 1944, after the 'Big Week', the Allied staffs, including the Chief of Staff of

Supreme Allied Command (COSSAC), became aware that even the increasing successes in the extension of air supremacy would not render an invasion of western Europe superfluous.

The Allied air attacks were largely successful in that they were able to weaken air defence of the Reich to such a degree in the spring of 1944 that Germany could no longer meet the final catastrophic acid test. If the bulk of the fighter forces were to be concentrated in the Reich, then the defence of the occupied western countries, which suffered massively under the preparatory air attacks from mid-April on,[51] would have to be neglected. If, on the other hand, all available fighter and AA forces were sent west, whereas air preparations for the invasion might be seriously impeded, the Allies would gain unrestricted command of the air over Germany. In March 1944 losses of day and night fighters in defence of the Reich were almost 11 per cent, in April 8.8 per cent and in May 10.7 per cent, so the chances were that the Luftwaffe would no longer be able to stand the battle of attrition.[52] The extent of the invasion preparations can be seen from the fact that the 9th Tactical Air Force, for example, flew more than 35,000 missions between 1 May and 6 June in order to destroy the transport network and supply facilities in Belgium and in western and central France. For all practical purposes the plan of the Luftwaffe command now consisted of retaining the mass of the fighter forces in the Reich and only transferring them to the west immediately after the landings began. This compromise solution aptly illustrates the hopeless over-taxation of the fighter arm at the beginning of 1944.

From the viewpoint of the overall strategic situation in the autumn of 1943, the OKW was faced with some basic considerations. According to the Führer directive of 3 November 1943, priority was to be given to augmenting the defensive power of the western army even though the threats on other fronts were not to be neglected. This directive contains some very clear statements:

The danger in the east still remains, but a greater danger is becoming apparent in the west, the Anglo-Saxon landing! In an extreme the depth of space in the east will permit loss of territory even to a greater degree, without mortally touching on the German vital nerve. Quite different in the west! If the enemy succeeds in penetrating our defence here on a broad front the consequences will become unimaginable within a short time![53]

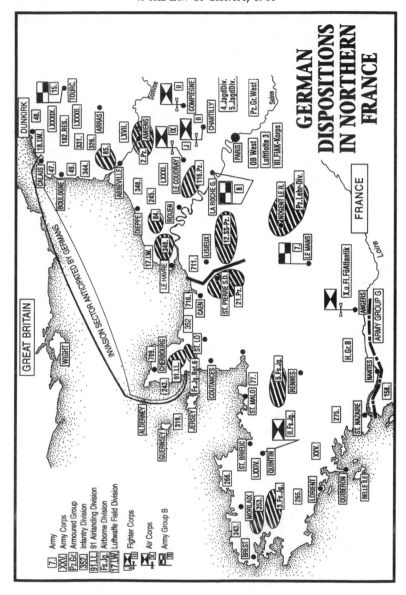

GERMAN DISPOSITIONS IN NORTHERN FRANCE

Hitler himself did not count on an invasion before mid-February 1944 at the earliest, as can be deduced from the briefing on 20 December 1943. Even though this directive had clearly emphasized that the decisive battle would take place in the west during 1944, and might result in a turn in the war, until the spring of 1944 the necessary conclusions were not drawn, either in the allocation of forces nor in the taking of operational measures.

Most of the reserves created with great pains during the winter of 1943–4 were not deployed in the west but were thrown into the focal points of the fighting, in particular on the southern wing of the eastern front and in central Italy, without any means being provided to bringing them back quickly for the reinforcement of the western army. Therefore the 'centrally placed fully mobile operational army' demanded by the C-in-C West, Field Marshal von Rundstedt, which was to serve as his mainstay,[54] was likewise not set up. Since the autumn of 1943 the OKW had also been attempting to create a 'central reserve', something that was particularly strongly advocated by the Chief of the Operations Staff. It was primarily to consist of divisions formed from the 21st to 24th draft calls. However, most of these were subsequently sent to the eastern front.

Of the eight Panzer and Panzer Grenadier divisions, including four SS divisions being set up in western Europe since the summer of 1943, two were temporarily sent to the east, and one was deployed for the occupation of Hungary in March 1944. A further major formation, namely the Paratroop Panzer Division 'Hermann Göring', which was to have been transferred to the west in late January, remained tied down in Italy because of the German formation of a strongpoint opposite the Anzio-Nettuno beachhead. The armoured reserves thus formed had a dual status because they were earmarked both as operational reserves for the western army and also on call as OKW reserves for other war theatres.[55] The allocation of tanks and self-propelled guns between the various fronts also suggests that the west was in no way being given priority. While in February 1944 there were 3050 tanks and self-propelled guns on the eastern front – about half of which were undergoing repairs – the C-in-C West could only call on 1233 such vehicles. In early February there were 481 in combat or in repair in Italy, and in the Reich itself a further 1230 undergoing repairs.[56] It is not surprising, therefore, that in stark contrast to the strategic importance of the western theatre, all that could be deployed there in the way of strategic reserves in early June 1944 were ten Panzer and Panzer Grenadier divisions.

The overall military situation

At the start of 1944, in terms of the overall situation of the fronts, the Wehrmacht was faced with a highly disquieting picture. In Italy, Army Group C had successfully withdrawn to the 'Gustav Line', and from mid-January on was able to repulse several extremely ferocious breakthrough attempts by the American Fifth Army at Monte Cassino and north of the Bay of Gaeta, with heavy losses for the enemy.[57] After the first heavy setbacks at Monte Cassino the very uninspired Allied leadership qualities were demonstrated by their inability to come up with a radical change in their operational approach, for example by shifting the focus to the sector of the Eighth Army or by undertaking several airborne and amphibious landings in the rear of the enemy. The controversy about the continuation of the campaign in Italy in February 1944 again revealed the differences of opinion between the American and British leaders, as in the Americans' refusal to give up 'Operation Anvil', the landing on the coast of Provence, which they saw as being in harmony with 'Operation Overlord', the invasion to take place in north-western France.[58]

Even the landing by the US VI Corps at Anzio-Nettuno on 22 January was only a local success due to the faulty battle plan of the attackers, but also because of energetic German defence. It was only after 11 May that both Allied armies were able to break through towards Rome after they had deployed an overwhelming material superiority. The stiff German resistance in central Italy prevented the simultaneous execution of 'Anvil' and 'Overlord', a circumstance from which, however, the German command was unable to profit. The only real success achieved by the Allies in the war of attrition in Italy was that in mid-April it was tying down 23 German divisions, including two valuable Panzer and four Panzer Grenadier divisions,[59] parts of which were therefore not available for repelling the invasion in the west.

By April 1944, in the south-eastern theatre – i.e. the Balkans from Slovenia to Greece, including Crete and the Greek islands – there were only fourteen German divisions and several independent combat and security regiments, several German-Croatian divisions, and the 1st Cossack Cavalry Division, so that the C-in-C South-east disposed of some twenty-one German-led major formations and seven Bulgarian divisions.[60] Hitler's decree to defend this extended area, including the Greek islands, because of the supply of valuable raw materials, hardly spared any forces for the western front. Even at this late stage of the war Germany did not restrict herself to defence, but continued the attempt to take the offensive against the growing strength of the partisan armies. Examples of this were the airborne operation against the central staff of the Tito partisans near Drvar, 70 km south-east of Bihac, and the almost successful capture of Tito himself by 'Operation Knight's Gambit' on 25 May 1944. Given the size of the partisan forces, which already numbered about 400,000 men, there was no longer any question of being able to achieve a decisive victory.[61]

In mid-April there were twenty-one German divisions in Finland and Norway in the far north, an allocation of forces that appears to have been more than sufficient to defend this sector. This relatively high allocation resulted from Hitler's long-standing fear of a major British landing in Norway and an interruption of the important iron ore deliveries from Sweden.

. On the main front in the east, the Wehrmacht had been compelled to give up huge territories and suffer heavy losses during the winter of 1943/4. Army Group North had had to evacuate its advanced positions near Leningrad and on the River Volkhov following strong Soviet attacks in mid-January and to withdraw behind the 'Panther Line' near Narva and on both sides of Lake Peipus after suffering heavy losses. Having given up much ground west of Smolensk and on its southern flank, Army Group Centre was still holding an extended bridgehead on the far side of the Dnieper, but was deployed along a highly unsatisfactory front line in the form of a salient jutting far out to the east which offered the enemy chances of encirclement from the north and south. However, the heaviest losses had been suffered by Army Groups South and A, who, after costly battles of withdrawal and the encirclement of parts of their forces, for example in the Cherkassy pocket, and following partially successful counter-attacks, by mid-April had been forced to give up most of the Ukraine. On 10 April, Odessa, the most important cornerstone on the southern sector of the eastern front, had been lost.

In mid-April the configuration of the eastern front was most inauspicious. Starting in the north at Narva, it continued to Vitebsk, jutted eastwards to include the Dnieper bridgehead, turned sharply back to the west for about 300 km along the Pripet area, bypassed Kovel into the Kolomea area, touched the eastern edge of the Carpathians and finally formed a protective salient for Romania which extended far to the east. The Seventeenth Army was still defending parts of the Crimea, the evacuation of which Hitler rejected mainly for political reasons. Distribution of forces between the Bay of Finland and the Crimean peninsula shows that in mid-April, excluding allied forces, there were 173 major formations including divisional task forces and security divisions, of which most were depleted and fought out.[62] Forty-nine of these, including six armoured divisions, were in the sector of Army Group Centre which had the almost impossible assignment of defending a front of 1100 km in length. After six Panzer and Panzer Grenadier divisions had been freed as reserves, each remaining major formation had to defend a sector averaging more than 25 km in length.

By and large, the fighting only came to an end in the second half of April after the successful breakout by the First Panzer Army from Soviet encirclement north-east of Czernovitz and the withdrawal of the newly formed Sixth Army to the lower Dniester. The counterattack to liberate the First Panzer Army took place with the help of II SS Panzer Corps which had been specially brought in from France; neither of these élite divisions could be transferred back to the western front at the most critical time, by 6 June.[63] This example alone demonstrates how much the over-extended and embattled eastern front depended on reinforcements which had to be taken from other theatres – a double burden in view of the approaching invasion.

This dependence on forces from outside was also due to Hitler's obstinacy, for despite several recommendations to this effect he still refused to consider a radical shortening of the front in the sectors of several army groups, or even less an overall shortening of the entire eastern front. Von Manstein, for example, had repeatedly demanded that the front be shortened by an immediate withdrawal to the Bug and the Dniester line. Von Kleist, Commander-in-Chief of Army Group A, had advocated evacuating the Crimea in order to free the five divisions tied down there as operational reserves. Chief of Staff

Colonel General Zeitzler had demanded, in addition to the evacuation of the Crimea, the prompt withdrawal of Army Group North to the 'Panther Line'; and in early 1944, before the pressure of the enemy winter offensive had made itself felt, Colonel General Jodl, Chief of the Wehrmacht Operations Staff, is alleged already to have recommended withdrawing the whole eastern front to the shortest possible line, in other words between Riga and Odessa.[64] Presumably this was based on the consideration that such a manoeuvre would free forces for the western European theatre.

It is self-evident that such a withdrawal of the front to a line that ran approximately from Riga, east of Vilna, east of Baranovichi to Berdichev, then east of Vinnitsa and the middle reaches of the Bug to the east of Odessa, together with the evacuation of the Crimea, would have offered substantial advantages. At least two armies would have been freed, not only serving as operational reserves for the eastern front but also as a crucial reinforcement of the western army. The latter army, moreover, would not have had to provide forces for the support of the eastern front. Finally, a fairly straight front line would have been created and the danger of salients being cut off would have been removed. In view of the attrition of forces in the east and the premature commitment of OKW reserves in the late winter of 1944, it does not appear that there was any clear plan to give priority to the strengthening of the western army. In fact, the strategy being followed was becoming more and more dependent on the enemy, quite in contradiction to the axiom of concentration on a focal point. In the final analysis, giving up further territory in the east was of secondary importance in exchange for a decisive victory in the west.

Until mid-May there was no substantial change in the allocation of forces, although five further divisions and numerous combat groups formed out of remnants had to be written off after the loss of the Crimea because they had not been evacuated in time. The eastern army still comprised about 163 divisions and divisional combat groups, including the security forces, with a clear concentration of defensive power in the newly created Army Groups North Ukraine and South Ukraine. The bulk of the Panzer and Panzer Grenadier divisions, nineteen in all (!), was deployed in the sector between the Pripet Marshes and the mouth of the Dniester, partially with the aim of carrying out a local offensive in the sector of Army Group North Ukraine.[65] Disregarding the fact that most of these formations needed replenishment and that one armoured division was soon to be withdrawn to the west, by the end of May there were eighteen Panzer and Panzer Grenadier divisions deployed along a sector of the front where no decision was being sought. Meanwhile, incidentally, Army Groups North and Centre had only been allocated six major armoured formations.

The area south of the Pripet Marshes, therefore, was witnessing a concentration of armoured forces such as had not been seen since the days of the Kursk offensive in 1943. The obvious alternative to this would have been a radical shortening of the front in the sector of Army Group Centre by withdrawing to the Beresina line in order to gather the reserves necessary for the repulse of the Soviet summer offensive. The concentration of forces under Army Groups North Ukraine and South Ukraine makes even less sense considering that the invasion in the west was to be expected at any time after mid-May. The failure to repulse the invasion of Normandy is certainly due in part to the way the German forces were allocated, with preference still being given to the eastern front over the western front as late as May 1944!

According to a 'strategic overview' prepared by the Chief of the Wehrmacht Operations Staff in mid-April 1944, the allocation of forces to the eastern front was too high in view of the forthcoming decisive battle on the coasts of France. Jodl argued that since July 1943 a total of twenty-three divisions had been transferred to the eastern front, including thirteen from the west. In mid-April reserves in the west amounted to only three armoured divisions and five infantry divisions of limited use. Further reserves were as yet in the process of being set up.

In Italy, too, total collapse could occur in the event of a further Allied amphibious operation. Jodl concluded that a withdrawal of the Italian front would make the defence of the peninsula far more difficult, and that a partial evacuation of Greece and the neighbouring islands would create a strength-consuming land front in the Balkans. The greatest danger, however, lay in the west, because the troops available there would not be sufficient to repulse a decisive attack; and a successful Allied landing in Denmark, in the Netherlands, in Belgium or in France which could not be driven back or contained immediately would 'result in the loss of the war in short order'.[66]

Preparations for the repulse of the invasion

It is evident from what has been said so far that German preparations to repel a western invasion depended on the strategic distribution of forces. The actual preparations in the west, which have been researched in detail,[67] are only of interest here insofar as they permit an assessment of the extent to which they might have been successful. The first point to note is that the number of divisions available in the west on 6 June, i.e. 58⅓, says little about the actual combat strength of the western army, because the majority of the infantry divisions were only of local use and could therefore be deployed only for static defence. In addition, there were further weaknesses to be taken into account. Despite the fact that the responsible commanders had introduced many improvisations such as 'weeding-out actions' and the setting up of emergency formations, only very few of the infantry divisions and only six of the ten armoured divisions were up to full strength.[68] Many of the coastal divisions had battalions that consisted of 'eastern volunteers', considered to be of doubtful combat value.

Another problem that had only been insufficiently solved by compromises related to the command structure and cooperation between the naval artillery and that of the army units deployed for coastal defence. Differences in tactical concepts and rivalries between Army and Kriegsmarine stood in the way of a mutually satisfactory solution for the whole coastal sector along the Channel, the Atlantic and the Mediterranean, which would have entailed the establishment of a unified command capable of coordinating the battle against targets at sea with the battle against enemy landings.[69]

The so-called 'Panzer controversy' was to assume even greater importance and lead to a disparity in operational concepts. This controversy is personified in Rommel, who had been put in command of Army Group B between the Netherlands and the mouth of the Loire in mid-January 1944, and General Geyr von Schweppenburg, Commander of Panzer Group West. In simple terms, in view of the strong enemy air superiority, Rommel advocated deploying all available Panzer and Panzer Grenadier divisions as close to the coast as possible so that they could be launched against the landing forces at the moment of their maximum weakness and thereby wreck the invasion from the very outset. In contrast, Geyr von Schweppenburg wanted to deploy only small armoured forces in the forward battle zone and keep the bulk of them back until the focal point of the landing was revealed; the invasion would then be destroyed with massed forces in conjunction with forces brought in from secondary fronts.[70] This argument was not restricted to the two main exponents, but was debated among many commanders on the operational level, so that in the spring of 1944 there was nothing like a unified concept of defence on the western front.

As it happened, neither of the two recommendations were applied, because the C-in-C West, Field Marshal von Rundstedt, decided on a compromise solution whereby he put only three of the six armoured divisions stationed north of the Loire at Rommel's disposal. The tactical results achieved on 6 June by the 21st Panzer Division, which had been deployed relatively close to the coast, tend to support Rommel's concept. Nevertheless, despite the plan, the other two divisions were not near enough to the scene to intervene within a few hours of the landings being detected. Taking everything into consideration, Rommel would have needed at least two to three armoured divisions along the coast of Normandy to have any chance of successfully eliminating the Allied beachheads on 6 June.[71]

The main cause of the controversy, however, lay in the acute shortage of forces, particularly in the lack of well-equipped and trained infantry formations for coastal defence. This handicap, together with the weak points of the Atlantic Wall, which only possessed strong defences on a few sectors,[72] resulted in the operational leadership having to use a part of the valuable armoured divisions for assignments which otherwise could have been carried out by the tactical commanders with local armoured reserves.

These short comments are intended to demonstrate that in view of the long time available for preparations, not enough had been done, either in terms of allocation of forces or in the selection of strategy, to face up to the requirements of the impending decisive battle. If the second half of 1943 marked the 'virtual turn' of the air war, then as far as repelling the invasion in the west is concerned, such a turn took place between December 1943 and March 1944.

Apart from the considerable German failings in the allocation of forces and strategy, an almost equally important role was played by the question of the probable invasion point and the state of the tides. Both the C-in-C West as well as Rommel and his staff regarded the sector north of the Seine, particularly the stretch between Le Havre and Boulogne, as the most likely landing area, although Normandy and Brittany came under increasing consideration from the spring onward. The leadership, however, did little to adjust to this changing evaluation of the situation, and the Norman and Breton sectors were not at any subsequent time given priority in defensive preparations.[73]

It was Hitler himself who, in several meetings and discussions from February 1944 on, designated the Cotentin peninsula in Normandy, with the important port of Cherbourg on its northern coast, and alternatively Brittany, as the most probable sectors for the invasion. In April he even demanded that the defensive positions on the northern coast of Normandy be strengthened as quickly and vigorously as possible,[74] but without weakening the sector from Calais to south of Boulogne. The considerable differences of opinion as to the probable landing sector came to a head on 6 May when von Rundstedt flatly turned down Rommel's recommendations to strengthen the defences on the Cotentin peninsula and in Brittany. Jodl responded immediately – apparently as Hitler's mouthpiece – that the Cotentin peninsula 'would be the first objective of the enemy'.[75] Despite this, one cannot agree unreservedly with the statement that for Rommel 'the western bay of the Seine increasingly became the probable landing area'.[76] Had this been the case, the energetic commander of Army Group B would certainly have taken steps to provide sufficient reserves on and behind the coast of Normandy. Rommel's intention to move the 12th SS Panzer Division and the Panzer Lehr Division nearer to the coast would, however, have required von Rundstedt to release these divisions to Army Group B since they were a part of the OKW reserves.

Other leaders, too, expected the main landing in Normandy, particularly on the Cotentin peninsula. They included General Erich Marcks, Commander of LXXXIV Army Corps, and the commander of Fortress Engineer XIX in the sector of the Seventh Army, Colonel Max von Stiotta, who already in the spring of 1943 had prepared a detailed study in which he designated the sector between the mouth of the Seine and the city of Brest as the most advantageous landing area for the Western Allies.[77] He also recommended the C-in-C West to give priority to the fortification of the Norman coast, particularly the Cotentin peninsula, and was supported in this by General Marcks and other senior officers. Furthermore, the fact that Cherbourg was almost completely spared from air attacks indicated that the Allies probably intended to land in this sector and to use the port for their own purposes. The destruction of the bridges over the Seine and the Loire from the end of May onward also clearly pointed to the probable landing area.[78] In any case, the Seventh Army defending Normandy and Brittany was not given sufficient men and materials before the invasion began in order to fortify the Norman coast to the same degree as the straits of the Channel.[79]

A further factor that was to contribute to the success of 'Operation Overlord' was the pattern of elaborate deceptions practised by the British and Americans, underlining their superiority in the 'war of the secret services'. Based on the experience of the landing operation at Dieppe, the German command did not sufficiently appreciate that the Allies would only land on open coasts and not in ports. The defenders were also surprised by the subsequent landing at the onset of the flood tide, because they had not counted on the troops being encouraged to storm ashore across a wide beach without any cover instead of being landed closer to shore at high tide.[80] But far more important for the result of the operation was the elaborate manoeuvre of deception which was conducted under the code-names 'Fortitude North' and 'Fortitude South' and which proved an unqualified success for the invading Allies.

This deceptive policy, the details of which are known today, was intended to make the enemy believe in the existence of a fictitious British Fourth Army in Scotland and a fictitious American First Army Group (FUSAG) in south-east England. While the Fourth Army was to simulate a landing in Norway, the purpose of the make-believe army group in south-east England, with a strength of twelve to fifteen divisions, was to persuade the Germans that the main invasion would take place in the Channel straits. After the landing in Normandy, it was to simulate a landing near Boulogne.[81] It was hoped that German Intelligence would not recognize on 6 June that the threat from south-east England was only a deception and that the delusion of a second landing operation could be maintained as long as possible.[82]

This deception was totally successful before and after the day of the invasion on 6 June. In mid-April the Wehrmacht Operations Staff was reckoning on 65 enemy divisions, and the C-in-C West, in agreement with the OKW, assumed on 23 May that the enemy had 70–80 divisions and that a fairly clear picture was emerging about their deployment and organization.[83] At the end of May/beginning of June Intelligence Department West even assumed 90 operational divisions, including 16 armoured and 9 airborne divisions, and an additional 22 brigades, to be in Great Britain.[84] The coordination of all of these Allied deceptions, which included the use of double agents and spurious agents, was carried out by a department of Military Intelligence in London, which depended quite heavily on the analysis of German radio signals decoded by Ultra. Without the assistance of Ultra, the checking of German reactions as to whether or not the threat of the Anglo-American 'ghost army' in south-east England was genuine, would hardly have been possible. The discovery of the deceit, even immediately before the invasion began, would still have permitted the German command to shift forces to the threatened coastal sector in Normandy. Eisenhower and Montgomery, the designated commander of the forces undertaking the invasion, therefore owed a great deal to the British decoding experts. Taking these factors into consideration, one can agree with the statement that the success of the Allies on 6 June was based on a 'very narrow margin'.[85]

That Rommel and von Rundstedt still believed in the existence of this imaginary army group well into July – and Intelligence West of the Army General Staff even longer – appears incredible; but of far greater importance was the fact that, based on this assumption, the German commanders did not order any shifting of forces into Normandy before 6 June.[86] Moving major forces from the sector north of the Seine on the first or second day of the invasion, in order to turn events in Germany's favour, was then no longer possible because of enemy superiority in the air and the badly damaged traffic network.

As for the defensive preparations of the Luftwaffe, these were the responsibility of *Luftflotte 3*, which from the beginning of the year had been attempting, on Hitler's orders, to fly reprisal raids against industrial towns and port facilities, albeit with meagre results. Up to April the rate of losses was 8–10 per cent. The troop concentrations in ports along the British south coast had been more or less correctly identified by the end of May; but in view of previous losses and the strength of Allied air defence, the forces available were not sufficient for massed air attacks against the detected ships. Due to growing attacks on their ground installations, the nine fighter groups remaining in the west had suffered mounting losses during the spring. In May the Allied air offensive in the west increased to 2000 missions a day.[87] After heavy air raids on coastal defences in the Boulogne–Calais area at the end of April, from the second week in May these attacks were shifted to the bridges over the Seine between Paris and the sea, most of which were destroyed. But during March and April the railway network in northern and central France had already experienced heavy damage through air raids and sabotage, which by early May had resulted in a backlog of almost 1600 trains. The hope of the local German air staffs for the period following the invasion was that they would receive massive reinforcements from the 'Luftflotte Reich', even if this meant running a high risk for home air defence. On 5 June *Luftflotte 3*, which was hopelessly inferior to the strength of the Allied air forces, comprised only 481 aircraft of which 100 were fighters.[88]

Why could success or failure of the Allied invasion in northern France still assume the fateful and dramatic importance of a turn in the war at this late date? Considering that both Churchill and Eisenhower, as well as other senior commanders of the invading forces, saw 'Operation Overlord' as fraught with risks, then the consequences of a failure become quite evident. Churchill in particular – who still remembered the heavy defeat at Dieppe – had grave doubts.[89] If the invasion were to succeed, then the way was open for the all-out attack against the German heartland; moreover, the Wehrmacht would be stripped of the reserves needed on the eastern front where a major offensive was also in the offing. However, if the Germans were to win a complete defensive victory and throw the invading forces back into the sea, then the danger of a further invasion would have been allayed for a long time to come and the Wehrmacht could send numerous forces to the east in order to build up a stable defence. Would Stalin launch his major offensive at all if he were to find himself alone? The Soviet Supreme Command had already more or less completed its preparations by the beginning of June. Could one expect Stalin to attack first and thereby 'pull the chestnuts out of the fire' for the Western Allies? Had not the Red Army already paid enough in blood sacrifices?

It was therefore not only in Berlin, but also in the estimations of Churchill, Roosevelt and Stalin that the landing in Normandy assumed the character of a turn of the war, which in the event of a German defensive victory, followed by the application of astute strategy, would have allowed the Reich to avoid 'total' defeat. But already on the very first day of the invasion – the 'longest day' – the balance had shifted conclusively in favour of the Allies, and the pendulum of fortune swung against Germany. Eisenhower's overwhelming forces[90] comprised 37 divisions, 5100 bombers of all types, 5400 fighters and 2300 transport aircraft, all supported by a gigantic fleet; and whereas only five reinforced major formations initially spearheaded the assault, several additional factors worked decisively to the Allied advantage. These included the almost wholly successful element of surprise in timing, and the resulting failure of the Germans to give early warning to their defence forces, even though Intelligence had correctly detected the imminent invasion.[91] In addition there was the overpowering air superiority enjoyed by the Allies, who on 6 June flew more than 14,670 missions with a loss of only 133 aircraft, whereas *Luftflotte 3* was only able to fly 319 missions.[92]

The dramatic events of 6 June, in particular the defensive tactical victory that the Germans almost achieved in the 'Omaha' landing sector, and the successful counter-attack by the 21st Panzer Division, which had been stationed near the coast, offer proof that Rommel's defensive concept had only partially been fulfilled. Because the Germans were not even able to bring their two armoured divisions into action in the vicinity of the invasion sector and to launch a coordinated counter-attack by the evening of the following day, it is fair to claim that 6 and 7 June were the decisive days of the entire operation.[93] From this point onward the combat power of the Allied beachhead grew so rapidly that all subsequent German attempts to attack it failed. That the Allied armies were finally able to break out of the beachhead at the end of July 1944 is partly due to extremely courageous and tenacious rearguard fighting by the Germans, as was admitted even by their former enemies,[94] but also to Montgomery's very mediocre leadership which cost his troops high casualties and almost lost him his command.[95]

The suggestion that the belated and partially uncoordinated German counter-measures and the slow, listless advance of the Allied troops in Normandy were based on some kind of secret political *rapprochement*[96] seems very far-fetched. So, too, are allegations that the responsible commanders of the western army conspired deliberately to open a gap in the front for the Allies in order to force a political ending of the war in the west, or that the Allied commanders were justified in hoping for an early surrender by Army Group B. The apparent passivity of the American, British and Canadian troops was due mainly to a cautious, methodical procedure which avoided any risks and was intended to keep losses as low as possible. Furthermore, after the successful Allied break-out at Avranches, the victorious battle in central France and the invasion in southern France ('Operation Dragoon'), heavy conflicts broke out among the senior commanders as to the best way of continuing the campaign. These differences were the major reason why the strategic options on offer were largely not exploited: *'Vincere scis, Hannibal; victoria uti nescis!'*...

A chance, albeit slight, of damaging the supply line of the invasion troops over the Channel would have been to employ the V1 flying bomb against port facilities in southern England and ship concentrations at sea. However, the use of this weapon against London, which began on 13 June 1944 and rose to 25 launchings per day by the end of June,[97] was mainly political and psychological in intent. In June and July, the British, who were well prepared for defence against the flying bomb, succeeded in shooting down about 40 per cent of all V1s. It is possible that had the new weapon been employed exclusively for military purposes, and provided it had been ready in time, a mass employment of V1s against the invasion fleet on 6 June could have had a decisive effect. As it was, by the time the ground-based bombardment of England was discontinued on 1 September because the invasion troops had meanwhile advanced to the firing sites between Calais and Rouen, no less than 8617 flying bombs had been launched.[98]

The attack with the A4 rocket (V2) which began on 8 September against targets in Great Britain and France also brought few military advantages, even though initially the effect on civilian morale in the target areas was considerable. Because of the wide fall-out (inaccuracy) of the weapon and inconsistent targeting, which in addition to London and Norwich brought a number of cities in France and Belgium under fire, the effects fell far below expectations. After 12 October, use of the V2 was concentrated on London, Antwerp, Brussels and to some extent Liège; and by 5 April 1945 some 2050 V2s had been launched against the last three targets; but because of technical faults in the weapon itself and appropriate defensive measures, no important interruptions in the Allied supply system were achieved.

It was soon apparent that the technical state of development of both weapons, while permitting their employment against area targets, only made them useful against military targets to a very limited degree. In a complete misapprehension of the facts, the SS departments responsible for the weapon clung to the concept of retaliation, as most fervently advocated by Goebbels,[99] in the hope that the V weapon could wear down Britain's morale and force her to make peace. Consequently Greater London remained the main target even though the Germans should have known from experience that indiscriminate attacks from the air could hardly have the desired effect. By the time the bombardment was discontinued on 27 March 1945, the largely senseless V2 terror attacks against England had cost the population 2724 dead and almost 6500 badly injured.[100]

The destruction of the eastern front

After the victory of the Allies in France, the collapse of Army Group Centre in Byelorussia in June–July 1944 ended any German hopes of still being able to defend the eastern front without bringing in reserves. Since the turn in the west had already irrevocably decided the outcome of the war, the catastrophe of Army Group Centre was merely its final confirmation. Because of a mistaken assessment by Intelligence Department East, the focus of the Soviet summer offensive had been expected in the sector of Army Group North Ukraine between the Pripet Marshes and the Carpathians,[101] whereas 'Operation Bagration', the major offensive begun on 22–23 June, struck the German central front which was hopelessly inferior due to its inherent weakness and the extreme anomalies of its front line. Army Group Centre, which had to hold a front of almost 1000 km in length with four armies, comprised only 41⅔ divisions,[102] of which only four major formations of varying strength, including one armoured division, formed the operational reserves. To the rear there were an additional three security divisions, a training division and four weak Hungarian divisions, three of which were deployed as security troops. The three German armies which had to bear the brunt of the main attack by four Soviet Fronts deployed 29 divisions on the line,[103] so that on average the defence perimeter of each division was 25 km wide.

Against this the Red Army had massed a total of 18 armies, including a tank army, comprising 166 divisions and 9 brigades with 5200 tanks and self-propelled guns, 31,000 guns and mortars, and supported by more than 6000 aircraft. The superiority in artillery along the roughly 690 km-long front permitted concentrations of up to 204 guns per kilometre.[104] Over 4000 tanks and self-propelled guns were provided for the main line of attack alone. After extensive planning, the STAVKA had decided in the second half of May to conduct the first decisive summer offensive in Byelorussia and to destroy the German armies deployed there. In order then to capitalize on the expected success, supporting offensives were to be launched against the German army groups in Galicia and Romania. While there were no delays in the preparations for the offensive, the date for the attack had still only been set for 22 June, primarily for political-strategic reasons. STAVKA intended to await the development of the situation in Normandy.

Hitler had denied the defenders the withdrawal to more suitable positions before the attack began, such as the line Polozk–Lepel–middle Beresina–Bobruisk, which the Commander-in-Chief of the army group had recommended on 20 May.[105] This would have shortened the front by roughly 160 km and the evacuation of operationally unfavourable positions. It was therefore no surprise that the offensive, conducted with overwhelming forces and supported by effective partisan actions, turned into a military catastrophe for the defenders within two weeks. As a result of deep penetrations and encirclements, the defeat was even greater than at Stalingrad. Despite desperate attempts by parts of the encircled Fourth and Ninth Armies to fight their way out, both of these armies, as well as large parts of the Third Panzer Army, were almost completely destroyed by 8 July with a loss of 28 divisions. Of the 380,000 soldiers deployed on the front of the army group almost 300,000 were either killed or captured.[106] On the eastern front there was now a gap approximately 350 km wide, in which only eight German divisions were still operating. In the subsequent battles in Byelorussia and eastern Poland another 100,000 men were lost during the next six weeks. That the remnants of Army Group Centre, together with meagre reinforcements provided at great risk by neighbouring armies, were able once more to form a loose but consecutive front on the borders of East Prussia, the Narev and along the Vistula by the end of August was almost a military miracle.

The additional heavy defeat of Army Group North Ukraine in Galicia after 13 July, and the collapse of the weakened Army Group South Ukraine in Romania at the end of August, which ended in the loss of sixteen divisions and 180,000 men belonging to the Sixth and Eighth Armies,[107] placed a further extreme burden on the overall situation. Despite a renewed stabilization of the front north of the Carpathians and in the Pannonian region, the balance of power no longer offered any hope of being able to defend the east unless the Supreme Command decided on a fundamental change of strategy. To top things off, the loss of the Romanian oil fields was a very severe blow. The military catastrophes on the eastern front in the summer of 1944, which when measured in terms of losses were heavier than those of the western army, should not disguise the fact that the irrevocable turn in the war had already come about during the first two days of the invasion in the west. When Field Marshal Rommel wrote in his dramatic 'considerations on the situation' of 15 July 1944 that the troops were fighting heroically everywhere, but that the unequal battle was approaching its end,[108] he did so with the intention of forcing Hitler to draw the political conclusions. These 'considerations' may also be seen as the admission that the final unalterable turn of the war had passed.

The Ardennes Offensive of 1944–1945: A Missed Opportunity to Turn the War?

After the western, south-western and eastern fronts had, thanks to the most laborious efforts, again been stabilized, Germany's overall situation in the autumn of 1944 can best be summarized by a remark of the Chief of the Wehrmacht Operational Staff in March 1946: 'In a desperate situation the only possible hope lies in a desperate decision,[109] Jodl's statement aptly pinpointed the dilemma that faced Hitler and other prominent leaders: how to achieve, at the very least, a substantial improvement in the military situation so as to avoid having to accept the demand for unconditional surrender which they all rejected. The attacks with the V2 weapon must be seen in this context, in that they reflected the hope – be it ever so faint – that they might induce the enemy to reconsider his stringent demand for surrender or even compel him to negotiate. This was accompanied by the illusory hope, retained until April 1945, that a slackening or even a split of the Allied coalition might occur.[110]

The actual issue under discussion within the Wehrmacht leadership, however, was whether the final reserves of the Army and the Luftwaffe, which had been created under the most difficult conditions during the summer of 1944, should be used for a major offensive or whether they should be deployed as reserves behind the most threatened sectors of the fronts, particularly in the east where the Red Army had been preparing a major attack for some time. In view of the ratio of forces, the extended eastern front hardly offered any

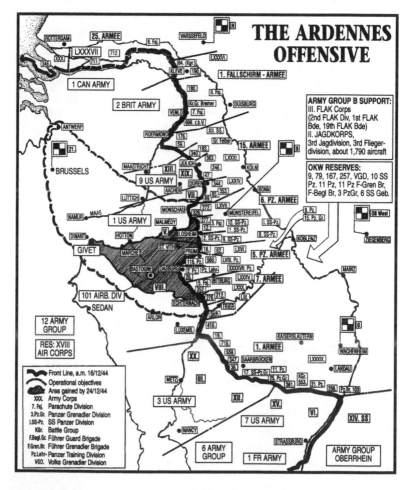

chance for a successful counter-offensive, so that it was only in the western theatre that such an operation appeared at all feasible. The alternatives, therefore, were either to distribute the existing and prospective reserves along the most endangered sectors, i.e. remain on the strategic defensive, or to concentrate all available forces for a final major attack. Whereas the first option offered the possibility of defending 'Fortress Germany', together with a glacis of variable depth for some time to come, and of countering threatened penetrations by shifting forces along the 'inner line', it could not lead to a substantial improvement in the situation, let alone bring about the desired turn in the war. The second alternative, although a calculated risk which, if it failed, would see the wastage of the final operational reserves, offered some enticing advantages should it succeed: encirclement of strong enemy forces, large territorial gains, a radical shortening of the western front and the acquisition of reserves.[111]

The decision in favour of the Ardennes offensive, 'Operation Watch on the Rhine', subsequently 'Autumn Fog', not only illustrates how narrow the margin for action had become for the German leadership in the late autumn of 1944, but also shows the close military-strategic interdependence of the different theatres of war. Any setback in one area that could not be corrected by local means implied that valuable reserves would have to be withdrawn from - or denied to – another area. On the other hand, any major success on one front offered the chance of freeing reserves for despatch to another front where they were more urgently needed. The advantage of the 'inner lines', however, was partially offset by the continuing heavy damage to the traffic network from the air. To this must be added the direct and indirect damage to the armaments industry caused by the Allied air offensive, even though in December 1944 in some sectors – as for example tanks and self-propelled guns – production records were again achieved. In any event it was predictable that in view of enemy air superiority a decisive drop in production, particularly in weapons and fuel, had to be expected. Paralysis of the Ruhr traffic system in the autumn of 1944 had been an alarm signal of the first magnitude.[112]

While Hitler had already mentioned the idea of a counter-offensive against the advancing Allies in August, preparations for a major offensive on the western front, which first became evident in the directive to set up the Sixth Panzer Army as the nucleus of the attack force, began in mid-September. The discussion between Hitler, Keitel and Jodl on 25 September underlines the intention to use the time-lag until the expected Soviet winter offensive in order to bring about a radical change in the balance of forces in the west by means of a successful attack. According to their calculations, an attack carried out with about 30 divisions would be bound to inflict such heavy losses on the American and British armies that the situation in the west could be fundamentally stabilized. Provided this attack were to take place between 20 and 30 November and lead to a rapid victory, it would then be possible to withdraw numerous reserves and transfer them to the eastern front. Until then the risk of a serious inferiority of forces in the sectors north and south of the Carpathians had to be accepted. The decree published on 18 October called for the formation of the *Deutsche Volkssturm* (lit. People's Storm), consisting of men above call-up age and schoolboys who were sent to fight without any training or proper equipment; such a force was hardly likely to augment the defensive power of the eastern front. In any case, the attack was to take place during a period of bad weather in order to prevent air attacks against the advancing troops.[113]

Hitler decided on a line of attack which would take the bulk of his forces from the Eifel sector through the Ardennes to the River Meuse and from there to Antwerp in order to destroy all enemy troops north of the breakthrough point – the British 21st Army Group and at least one American army. Since total Allied strength in the west at the end of September had been calculated at 60–61 major formations,[114] which would not increase substantially by the time of the attack, a successful offensive could count on destroying or capturing at least 30–35 divisions. In the context of the western front, however, the operation ran a risk because the bulk of the German forces had been tied down since early October by heavy Allied attacks, above all by the Americans, in the Aix-la-Chapelle sector, in the Hürtgen Forest, in the Metz area, in northern Alsace and on the border to the Palatinate. Thus there was tension between the local commanders, who wanted to use incoming reinforcements for countering crisis situations, and Hitler and Jodl, who planned to hold back all newly established reserves for the offensive and were prepared to accept further losses of territory. How great the depletion of forces had been on the western front can be seen from a report by the C-in-C West, who put the losses between 6 June and the end of September at 363,000 men for the Army and 29,500 men for the Luftwaffe, so that of the 51 divisions and 4 brigades deployed in the west on 6 September, only 16 divisions and 2 brigades were listed as being 'at full combat strength'.[115]

Although in accordance with Jodl's suggested plan of operation, Hitler decided on 9 October that the main thrust through the Ardennes to Antwerp was to be accompanied by a secondary attack to the south from the area north of Aix-la-Chapelle, in the subsequent planning by the OKW only the attack through the Ardennes was prepared in detail. Field Marshal Model, commander of Army Group B, in agreement with the C-in-C West, believed that the operational objectives had been set too far and on 29 October submitted a plan for an encircling attack against the American forces in the Aix-la-Chapelle sector. It was a 'small solution',[116] dictated not only by limited German troop strength, but also the difficulties of supply and movement in the attack area, not to mention Allied command of the air. However, this realistic plan of attack was immediately rejected by Hitler and Jodl, and the army group was informed that it would have to adhere, under all circumstances, to the more far-reaching objective. Even though the OKW admitted the disparity between the available forces and the extent of the terrain, in the present situation there was no other alternative than to stake everything on one throw of the dice. This fundamental concept found expression in the OKW deployment orders of 10 November and was to remain in force until the beginning of the attack despite all protests by Model and von Rundstedt.[117] Senior officers on the western front at the time, as well as later observers, agree in seeing an attack with limited objectives against the American Ninth Army and parts of the American First Army to the north and south of Aix-la-Chapelle as the operation standing the best chance of success. It was in line with the existing situation, it could have been concluded in a relatively short time, it would have caused the enemy heavy losses and it would have helped to shorten the front. But it could not have improved the situation as fundamentally as could 'Operation Watch on the Rhine'. The major motive for the decision was therefore to accept the greatest risks in favour of an option which, in the event of a rapid and complete success, would have offered the desired military freedom of action. Even then, however, it would hardly have led to a turn in the war. The advanced date of the attack, plus the existing transportation problems, make it very doubtful that reserves for the eastern front could have been released in time; and given the overwhelming Soviet superiority, it is unlikely that their arrival would have made contribution to a decisive defensive victory. As the new Chief of Staff of the Army, Colonel General Guderian, noted, the very late date of the attack was the greatest disadvantage of the Ardennes offensive.[118] Finally, it is highly speculative that even a heavy defeat of the Western powers would have led to a faltering of their war effort, let alone a split of the war coalition.

It was quite astonishing that the Germans managed to create a relatively strong offensive potential on the western front despite all the difficulties. Originally twelve Panzer and Panzer Grenadier divisions and eighteen infantry divisions were earmarked for the attack, while the Luftwaffe was to provide about 1500 fighters. In mid-November the Wehrmacht Operations Staff even counted upon a total of 38 refurbished divisions of which five, however, soon had to be withdrawn for the repulse of the enemy offensive at Metz. In early December 1944 there were a total of 5423 armoured vehicles on all the fronts of the Army, including command, anti-aircraft and rescue tanks.[119] Before the attack the C-in-C West reported 1427 combat-ready tanks, including about 750 'Panthers' and 250 'Tigers'. The three largely refitted attack armies, who initially comprised seven armoured and thirteen infantry divisions,[120] were faced by about four and a half American divisions. In addition, Army Group and OKW reserves consisting of three Panzer, two Panzer Grenadier and four Volks Grenadier divisions, one Mountain division and two Panzer Grenadier brigades, were provided, of which seven divisions and both brigades later saw action. Of the armoured forces, nine Panzer divisions took part in the battle. During the offensive a total of 1350 tanks and self-propelled guns, not counting replacements, were employed.[121] Artillery support for this noteworthy attack force consisted of 3420 guns, including mortars, so that there were 31 guns per kilometre along a front just under 110 km long.

The fuel reserves had originally been calculated by the OKW at 17,000m^3 above normal requirements. However, by the start of the attack only 50 per cent of the required fuel had been delivered. Therefore several armoured divisions only had fuel reserves for a distance of 60–80 km when they set off, because fuel consumption had been abnormally high during deployment.[122] This amount was barely sufficient to enable the attackers to gain the crossings over the Meuse. Together with the limited supply of ammunition, the scarcity of fuel for the fast mobile forces was one of the greatest handicaps for the operation. For the support of the attack from the air a total of 1800 aircraft, including almost 1500 fighters, were provided under the command of II Fighter Corps. An AA division and two AA brigades took over air defence for the three attack armies. The relative strength of the air forces is explained by the fact that General Galland had been attempting since the summer of 1944 to build up a 'fighter reserve' of 2000–2500 aircraft so as to be able to throw them into a great defensive battle against the waves of Allied bombers.[123] Since Hitler had forbidden such an action, many of them were available for the support of the Ardennes offensive.

The success of the operation obviously depended not only on thorough preparation but also on favourable conditions. It is thus an exaggeration to accuse the planners of lacking 'a rational, general staff-like calculation base'. The designation of the operation as a 'Blitzkrieg without fuel' also appears to be too harsh a verdict.[124] From the operational viewpoint, a surprise attack through the Ardennes in the direction of Antwerp did stand a reasonable chance of success given able and energetic execution, continuing bad weather and exploitation of the enemy's weaknesses. On the other hand, seen strategically, the risks taken verged on military irresponsibility, because far too little time had been allowed for the successful conclusion of the operation and the withdrawal of the reserves who were then to be sent to support the eastern front. The postponement of the attack date from 10 to 16 December was in itself an error that could hardly be rectified. Only if the enemy front could be penetrated at the first blow, the Meuse crossed within a few days and Antwerp reached in seven days without interference by the enemy air forces, could an overwhelming victory have been expected. Only then would there possibly be a chance of withdrawing important forces in time and shipping them to the eastern front. There was an increasing probability of a Soviet offensive at any time after the turn of the year 1944–5.

Due in part to careful German preparations, but also to the gross under-estimation by the Allies of the residual combat strength of the western army,[125] the attack on the morning of 16 December led to remarkable initial successes. But these could not be converted into a definitive breakthrough because of tactical errors and operational blunders as well as rapid counter-measures on the part of the Allies. The decisive mistake proved to be the failure to shift the focus of the operation as rapidly as possible to the fluently advancing Fifth Panzer Army, and the insistence instead on trying to force a breakthrough by the Sixth Panzer Army which had met stiff resistance. A further omission was not to give quick reinforcement to the Seventh Army which had been assigned to covering the operation on the southern flank and extending the bulge of attack, but which rapidly bogged down because of lack of forces. Compared to these factors, the tenacious defence of the traffic junctions of St Vith and Bastogne by US forces did not play the key role often attributed to it, because it contributed little to slowing down the German advance.

Besides the difficulties of the terrain and the shortage of fuel, the weakness of the German infantry and artillery formations was of more importance for slowing down the impetus of advance. On the tactical level it became evident that it was not so much the ratio of forces on both sides, but rather the concentration of troops on the front line that tipped the scales. The German armoured forces held in reserve were not able to make the expected impact because, due to road conditions and lack of fuel, they did not reach the front in time to force a decision during the initial days of the battle. Success or failure of the offensive therefore rested mainly on the shoulders of the infantry, which depended on strong support by the artillery. Given the density of forces, the ground conditions therefore favoured the defenders, who were also able to concentrate superior fire power and quickly bring in reserves to the endangered sectors. Furthermore, the defending armour contributed more to the outcome than its attacking counterpart.[126]

Although the spearheads of the Second Panzer Army did approach to within five kilometres of the Meuse near Dinant on 23 December, thereby almost reaching the intermediate objective in this sector, the turn still took place on that day. The counter-attacks by US III Corps caused the southern flank of the German attack increasing difficulties, and in addition, because of an improvement of the weather, the Allied air forces were able to assert a superiority which in the following days interfered seriously with German movements, leading to a near-collapse of the German supply system. On 24 December the German attack had clearly failed. Even a change in dispositions, in order to achieve a partial success along the lines of the 'small solution' that Field Marshal Model was still considering, was no longer realistic. The following day the C-in-C West drew the conclusions from the situation: he recommended breaking off the offensive and withdrawing the forces behind the West Wall.[127]

At this point there was still a chance, albeit minimal, of saving the reserves not yet committed, of withdrawing a part of the valuable armoured forces and also some infantry without enemy pressure, and of sending all of them to the eastern front. The Chief of Staff of the Army had approached Hitler on this several times, most recently on 24 and 31 December. In sometimes heated disputes he drew attention to the virtually completed Soviet deployments between the Baltic and the Carpathians and their enormous superiority over the defenders, as ascertained by Intelligence. His demand was immediately to free all available forces and transfer them behind the threatened eastern front.[128] However, Hitler and Jodl refused this request for the reason that they did not want to renounce the military initiative in the west which had been won with so much difficulty. Even if the original objectives could not be achieved, the intention was to tie down as many enemy forces as possible, and also to conduct a second attack ('Operation North Wind') from the Bitsch-Weissenburg sector in northern Alsace southwards towards Zabern in order to cut off the enemy forces stationed further east. However, this attack by two army corps, launched during the night of 1 January, failed after only a few days and resulted in an additional fatal waste of forces.

The Allies, who from 3 January 1945 onward were advancing against the German bulge in the Ardennes from the north and the south, expended great effort in pushing the three German armies back towards the West Wall. Initial consternation among the Allied command staffs, who had not believed the Germans still capable of such an offensive, was quickly overcome. Nonetheless, in the Battle of the Bulge the Allies had lost about 77,000 men. It was only on 8 January that Hitler decided to withdraw from the most endangered areas in order to avoid the encirclement of parts of the Fifth and Sixth Panzer Armies. At the same time the order was given to free the bulk of the Sixth Panzer Army as operational reserves in order to counter focal points of enemy attacks. This decision came too late to be able to regain the initiative. This now clearly lay with the US First and Third Armies, while by the end of January the Germans had to withdraw to their starting positions under heavy losses, especially of equipment.[129]

The Ardennes offensive was neither a missed turn of the war, nor yet a decisive battle. A missed turn it could not be, because there was no triumphant victory beckoning at the end which was only lost because of clumsiness or blunders. Even the quite considerable operational successes up to 23 December had not laid any foundation for a victorious conclusion of the offensive. From the very start it would have needed a combination of extremely favourable circumstances – continuing foggy weather and usable roads – and the avoidance of any tactical errors by the attackers, in order to reach Antwerp, surround some 30 enemy divisions, and thereby score a complete victory. But the fact that everything depended on capturing undamaged the important bridges over the Meuse west of Liège within only a few days underlines the enormous pressure under which the whole operation lay. Finally, the extremely late date for the attack meant that even in case of a victorious conclusion of 'Operation Watch on the Rhine' there was very little leeway left for releasing a larger number of reserves and transferring them to the eastern front. Nor was the Ardennes offensive a decisive battle, because all the Allies could do was to force the German attackers to retreat, in other words, to inflict on them a 'normal' defeat. It did nevertheless speed up the subsequent collapse of the western front and thus hasten the end of the war.[130]

The failure of the defensive strategy in the east

Seen from the viewpoint of overall strategy, the fatal role of the Ardennes offensive was indirectly to weaken the eastern front. It tied down in the west the last valuable forces which shortly thereafter were so crucially lacking for the repulse of the general offensive by the Red Army on 12 January 1945. From this perspective alone, and in view of the high risk that even an earlier start of the Ardennes offensive entailed, the urgent requirement would have been to abandon this operation completely. The alternative could have been a timely encircling attack with limited objectives against the US Ninth Army in the Aix-la-Chapelle sector. This could have inflicted telling losses on the enemy, achieved a shortening of the line and stabilized the western front, in all probability releasing fifteen to twenty divisions, including seven to nine invaluable armoured divisions. According to estimates by Guderian, who was also attempting to acquire further reinforcements by giving up the greatly extended 'Courland bridgehead' as well as other exposed sectors of the front in East Prussia, such an increase of forces would have been a primary condition for any successful repulse of the Soviet winter offensive.[131]

The struggle to establish a defensible eastern front between the Baltic and the Beskid mountain ranges, and to create the operational conditions for a successful defence in 1944–5, is an extremely dramatic chapter in the final phase of the Second World War. Colonel General Guderian regarded the approaching defensive battle in the east as an unavoidable fight for survival which should take priority over all other military-strategic decisions. In this sense he, together with the commanders of Army Groups Centre and A, was attempting to build up a defensive potential that might even withstand the most massively powerful Soviet attacks, by creating a deeply echeloned defence system along the front line and in the hinterland, by reinforcing formations and by acquiring operational reserves. This last condition was to prove the primary weakness of the entire concept. At the end of December 1944 there were only 145 major formations along the whole length of the eastern front between Courland and Lake Balaton. The sectors of Army Groups Centre and A between the Baltic, including the Memel bridgehead, and a point to the north-west of Miskolc in northern Hungary, extended for 1340 km and was being held by 82 major formations. Many of these were in the process of reorganization or being newly set up and were therefore of relatively low combat value. Both army groups comprised of only 12½ Panzer and Panzer Grenadier divisions as operational reserves between Königsberg in the north and the confluence of the Pilica and the Vistula in the south, of which one was being reorganized and one just being established.[132]

From the spring of 1944 a conflict had been developing between the OKH on the one hand and Hitler and the OKW on the other. Since Army Groups Centre and A, which had borne the major burden of defending the eastern front, had lost about half of their combat power between 22 June and 8 October 1944 and had only received insufficient replacements, the Operations Department in the General Staff of the Army came to the conclusion that the focus of the war now had to be unequivocally shifted to the east.[133] But because of the preparations for the Ardennes offensive and the need for forces in Hungary, the two army groups had had to relinquish six major formations of their valuable armoured forces by early January. At Army Group A alone, which was defending a front of 760 km against which the major offensive of the Red Army on the Vistula would be conducted, the average length of line defended by a single division was 24.5 km, a factor that made a successful defence virtually impossible.

Guderian had therefore been advocating the evacuation of the extended bridgehead in Courland, which since mid-October was being defended by the Sixteenth and Eighteenth Armies with 32 major formations, including 5 armoured formations,[134] and the deployment of the forces thus gained behind the most endangered sectors of the eastern front. This large bridgehead was the result of Hitler's refusal to withdraw Army Group North from the Baltic States across the Dvina in time and then use the troops for the defence of the Reich. Even though, in view of the collapse of Army Group Centre, the Chief of Staff of the Army had been pressing for its withdrawal behind the Dvina since early July, and since mid-October the evacuation of the Courland bridgehead as well, Hitler had continued to reject these recommendations. On the one hand he justified this decision by claiming that holding on in Courland was tying down strong Soviet forces; on the other hand he was reiterating the arguments of the Kriegsmarine who feared repercussions on submarine training in the Baltic and threats to the ore transports from Sweden if the bridgehead were evacuated.[135] Even taking into account that many 'Courland divisions' were not up to full strength, such an increase in forces on the main front between the Memel and the Beskids would greatly have improved the chances of a successful defence. There were also several exposed sectors of the front in East Prussia and in eastern Slovakia that could have been withdrawn in order to free additional forces. Together with the reinforcement from the west of at least fifteen divisions, not only could the rear lines have been more heavily manned but numerous operational reserves could also have been set up.

Furthermore, a deeply echeloned 'battle zone' had been created directly behind the front line, the backbone of which was a 'main line of resistance' designed to offer protection from the expected overwhelming preparatory bombardment and to resist the initial tactical attack of the enemy. In the hinterland there were numerous additional strongpoints as well as lines of retreat – the so-called a, b, c and d lines – which were to cover the sector between the lower Vistula and the Carpathians up to a depth of 300 km. An elaborately designed and partially proven defensive tactic known as the 'major battle procedure'[136] was to prevent the enemy breaking through the forward defence zone, to inflict heavy losses, and facilitate the deployment of operational reserves for counter-attacks.

Military Intelligence had detected a huge concentration of forces on the enemy side, of which 114 infantry divisions, 10 cavalry divisions, 22 infantry brigades, 74 armoured brigades and 51 regiments of self-propelled guns, with a total of 3600 armoured vehicles, were assumed to be facing Army Group A alone. In fact, Army Group A was confronted by 16 armies, 4 tank armies and 9 independent corps with 6460 tanks and self-propelled guns, and over 32,000 pieces of artillery. There were more than 5000 front-line aircraft provided as support from the air. While the General Staff of the Army estimated the total of Soviet tanks and self-propelled guns along the whole front to be 7200,[137] the actual numbers were approximately 12,100.[138] On the sectors selected for the breakthrough in the three bridgeheads on the Vistula, the Soviets had a numerical superiority of 10 to 1 in infantry, 9–10 to 1 in artillery and 10 to 1 in armour. A well-devised and minutely planned method of attack was to make the penetration of the defensive zone easier. According to official figures, in early 1945 the total strength of the Red Army on the German-Soviet front consisted of 55 armies, 6 tank armies and 35 armoured and mechanized corps, with 6.29 million men on land, whereas the total military forces numbered 7.11 million men.[139]

The German General Staff seriously under-estimated enemy strength and organization; but even based on these figures alone, Soviet superiority was still so overwhelming that only the most radical measures would have held out any hope of success. Only the immediate concentration of strong forces and the transfer of the two armies from the Courland bridgehead, as well as numerous divisions from the western front – as, for example, the entire Sixth Panzer Army – would have made a defensive strategy possible. Confronted by the menacing deployment of the Red Army, Guderian had repeatedly demanded that the Ardennes offensive be broken off, had alerted Hitler and Jodl to the overpowering Soviet superiority, and had warned that if the eastern front were to be penetrated at any single spot it would crumble like 'a stack of cards'. As late as 29 December Guderian had telephoned Wehrmacht headquarters at Ziegenberg and demanded that 'everything be thrown to the east'.[140]

Based on various items of intelligence and the statements of prisoners, the Germans expected the start of the offensive between 11 and 16 January, whereas according to Soviet sources preparations for the attack were to be completed between 15 and 20 January. On 22 December Major General Gehlen was still debating the possible reasons for delaying the attack. He considered that the Soviets were waiting for more favourable ground conditions and that the Soviet leadership might be thinking of using the Ardennes offensive for some 'political horse-trading' with its western Allies.[141] Churchill's letter to Stalin of 6 January 1945, asking for information about Soviet military intentions, could easily be interpreted as a request for an early start of the offensive,[142] but most probably had no influence on Stalin's decision. At the time the letter was written the Western Allies had already thrown back the German forces in the Ardennes single-handed, indicating that they did not need any assistance. What is far more likely is that once the Soviet winter offensive began, Churchill and Eisenhower were expecting a large-scale withdrawal of German forces from the western front which would have facilitated a speedy Allied advance to and over the Rhine. On the other hand, it is only logical that Stalin and STAVKA should have welcomed the tying down of valuable German divisions on the western front as long as possible in order to prevent the transfer of these forces to the German-Soviet front, thus enabling their own offensive to make rapid progress towards Berlin. The setting of the Soviet date of attack for 12 January was therefore probably based exclusively on military considerations.

The terrifyingly powerful attack in the early morning hours of 12 January out of the Vistula bridgehead of Baranov, and the follow-up assaults on 13 and 14 January, struck Army Groups A and Centre with such force that the front between Warsaw and the upper Vistula collapsed completely within only a few days. The Germans had neither been able to occupy their 'main line of resistance' in time to escape the destructive enemy barrages, nor had the operational reserves been sufficient to launch counter-attacks to prevent the Soviet armoured corps from breaking through in depth. Because of the lack of reserves to establish zones of resistance along the numerous defensive lines in the rear, and the relentless, penetrating pursuit by the enemy, the bulk of two armies of Army Group A were encircled and quickly annihilated. After sore deprivation, only a few weak splinter groups in the form of 'moving pockets' succeeded in regaining the German lines at the end of January. When Warsaw fell into the hands of the attackers on 17 January and the spearheads of the First Ukrainian Front were close to the borders of Upper Silesia, the fate of the defenders in the great bend of the Vistula was finally sealed. Immediately thereafter the battle for the Reich began. The same was true for East Prussia when parts of the Fifth Guards Tank Army, after having destroyed the Second Panzer Army, reached the coast of the Frische Haff north of Elbing on 26 January and thereby cut off East Prussia by land. In the centre of the front Soviet spearheads reached the Oder near Küstrin and Frankfurt at the end of January.

The overall picture of the military catastrophe between the Baltic and the foothills of the Sudetes was so shattering that even the faint hope – which might have existed before the start of the Ardennes offensive – of being able to stabilize the situation was demolished. What remained was a desperate final battle, militarily quite hopeless, but which in the east still served to save countless elderly men, women and children from the cruel and horrible excesses perpetrated by the soldiers of the Red Army. The climactic battles in East and West Prussia, in Pomerania, Silesia and eastern Brandenburg were no longer being conducted as military operations but, thanks to great sacrifices by the troops, with the aim of keeping open the internal road network of the Reich – path to salvation for the fleeing civilian population. A defensive battle conducted according to clear operational rules would, for example, have had the objective of evacuating East and West Prussia and subsequently eastern Pomerania as quickly as possible, and of rescuing any surviving troops heading west from threatened encirclement. Instead, both the leadership and the fighting men were resolved to hold on, even in the most hopeless positions, in order to save millions of Germans from death or deportation to the Soviet Union. Even the week-long, virtually hopeless defence of 'strongpoints' such as Graudenz, Breslau, Küstrin and Posen served the purpose of splitting up the attacking Soviet armies and of tying down as many forces as possible.[143]

The numerous acts of violence committed by the advancing Soviet troops were not so much the product of indiscriminate crimes of a soldiery drunk with victory, as the consequence of the systematic hate propaganda which had been preached by the authorities with Stalin's encouragement, and which now began to develop its own horrific dynamics. The cruelty displayed by the Soviet soldiers went far beyond the worst fears of atrocities that might be expected from a brutal, undisciplined fighting force.[144] In this context, Ilya Ehrenburg's immoderately worded appeals to give free rein to revenge and destruction served as the pattern for many provocative orders by field commanders,[145] which, together with the long years of anti-German hate propaganda, triggered countless acts of horror. Ehrenburg welcomed the advancing Red Army to 'the land of the murderers' in the role of a pitiless executioner, while morally condemning the whole German nation. His appeals culminated in the slogan: 'We do not bring revenge, we bring justice!'[146]

There is also much to be said for the claim that Stalin was using the acts of violence already committed during the first advance into East Prussia in October 1944 as a calculated means of setting off a huge mass exodus among the civilian population. This would have been a radical solution to the problem of having to deport the German population to the east of the Oder-Neiße Line, which he was already considering as the western frontier of the new Polish state.[147] It was only after the start of the Soviet winter offensive, however, that the massive refugee movements occurred, because the responsible German authorities had refused to evacuate the threatened territories in time. The expulsions and mass flights, which invariably took place under terrible conditions, led to enormous civilian casualties. According to reliable calculations, the total number of Germans expelled or deported in all of the eastern territories, including the German ethnic groups in Poland, Czechoslovakia, Hungary, Romania, Yugoslavia and the Baltic states, came to 14 million, of whom more than 1.7 million died. If one includes the German ethnic group in the Soviet Union, the death figure rises to 2 million.[148]

That the Wehrmacht was still capable of a final effort in spite of the catastrophe in the German eastern territories, without this bringing about any results in the sense of a military-strategic turn, can be seen from the fact that between the beginning of the Soviet offensive and 12 February, 33 divisions were transferred to the eastern front.[149] From the Courland bridgehead alone, ten major formations were shipped out by 1 March 1945. The heavily embattled western army also had to relinquish fourteen major formations including nine Panzer and Panzer Grenadier divisions to the eastern front by the same date. However, the still relatively strong Sixth SS Panzer Army, which had been withdrawn from battle at the end of January, was not sent to the sector east of Küstrin and Frankfurt/Oder, as Guderian had vehemently demanded, but was transported to Hungary on Hitler's orders. There it was to form the nucleus of a new offensive for the relief of Budapest, which had been invested since 25 December 1944.[150] Even the greatly weakened south-western front in northern Italy had to supply three divisions.

Including the numerous reinforcements and locally created formations, by early March there were again approximately 180 divisions, divisional battle groups and independent brigades in the east between Courland in the north and the Drau in the south.[151] Even considering that most of them were extremely weakened and exhausted formations, this was still a considerable fighting force. So one can get some idea of the forces the Wehrmacht could still have mustered in the east in early January 1945 if the Supreme Command had decided to forgo the Ardennes offensive, evacuate all exposed positions and concentrate all available forces for the defence of the eastern front between Königsberg and Lake Balaton. In the failed offensive on the western front in December 1944, the final substance of the Wehrmacht was thrown away and shortly thereafter it was no longer able to fight a defensive battle in the east despite the willingness of the troops involved to sacrifice themselves.

Note: War losses of the Soviet Union 1941 to 1945

Among the many problems with which historic research of the Second World War has to deal is the investigation of losses suffered by the Soviet Union, which is also a subject of 'the politics of history'. For many years the dominating school of thought clung to Stalin's round figure of 20 million dead, as he claimed in 1946. Since 1988, however, in the Soviet Union and subsequently in Russia, voices have been raised which cast increasingly strong doubts on this figure and demand a fundamental revision of the historical picture of the entire war. During an historical symposium in Moscow in April

1988 on current matters of historical research, there was a demand for a final assessment of the actual total number of war victims. The crucial question was also raised as to whether one could speak of a Soviet victory at all. 'But how did we win? If I look at the centre of our Russia today, the empty rural Russia which was the main supplier of common soldiers, then I gain the impression that we were the losers.'[152]

In similar statements the claim was made time and again that the exact losses of soldiers and civilians were not known, but that the price of victory had been 'unimaginably high'.[153] Although on the Soviet side the figure of 7 million military dead was claimed for many years, it never became clear if this meant the soldiers killed in battle and dying of their wounds, or if it also included those who starved to death or were otherwise killed as German prisoners of war. Stalin allegedly also mentioned a figure of 15 million soldiers killed in battle or otherwise done to death.[154] Yet recent estimates according to which the USSR suffered over 40 million – and in one case even 46 million – military and civilian deaths, raise doubts as to whether such a figure is confined to the direct or indirect victims of the war. Even after 1938 the population in the Soviet Union, particularly the non-Russian inhabitants, suffered from purges, deportations and reprisals. One must also take into account that even during the war the death rate in Soviet penal colonies was very high, a phenomenon solely associated with Stalin's policies of oppression. A reliable estimation of Stalin's political victims after he came to power in 1924 puts the figure at 40 million dead. To which accounts are these deaths to be assigned?

At a commemoration ceremony on 9 May 1990, former State President Gorbachev gave a figure of 8.53 million military and 18.4 million civilian dead – a total of about 27 million.[155] A similar statement speaks of 27.6 million victims of which roughly two-thirds had been civilians.[156] While this is again a 'political' figure, the fact that Gorbachev could rely on recently published results of historical research argues in favour of greater credibility in comparison with Stalin's former claims. Apart from the problem caused by gaps in personnel statistics and the fact that the method of data collection has not been revealed, it would appear to be most appropriate to start from those figures that have been relatively well documented. The figure of about 7.5 million military dead as victims of combat is more or less uncontroversial.[157] But there is the matter of the additional losses among the partisans. It has not been verified how many partisans were killed in active fighting and how many were put to death by the occupation forces during reprisal actions. There is also the problem of double counting, because many Soviet prisoners of war were listed as missing, in other words as irretrievably lost, even if they returned home after 1945. Furthermore, it is still impossible to categorize the losses of the 'Vlasov army', of the numerous 'eastern legions' and other 'helpers' who fought on the German side, or the casualties among the almost two million forcibly 'repatriated' at the end of the war. Finally, the after-effects of the deprivations suffered by the civilian population must also be taken into account.

Given these considerations, the number of 8.53 million military dead, including those who died in German captivity, assumes a fairly high degree of credibility. However, the stated number of 18.4 million civilian dead would only appear to be realistic if it also includes the victims of Stalin's oppressions, as for example a substantial proportion of the ten to twelve million people who were condemned to labour camps after 1939. If there were accurate statistics of the casualties among this group and among those who died as a result of deportations, then a relatively clear picture of the number of civilian dead would emerge. It must be remembered that including the Volga Germans, at least 1.65 million people – and according to other claims even four to five million, were forcibly resettled.[158]

The statistics become even more believable if the 2.5 million men who died of their wounds are added to the military dead, as well as the 2.6 million who starved to death or died by violence as prisoners of war. Starting from the afore-mentioned figure of 7.5 million, we would then arrive at 13.6 military dead in the broadest sense, so that the difference between that and the total number of approximately 27 million war victims would be more easily explainable. The Soviet Union would therefore have lost about 13.4 million civilians during the war, a number that appears realistic if it includes Stalin's victims.[159]

It is incontestable that the Soviet Union suffered by far the greatest loss of human lives in the course of the Second World War. The human suffering that this entailed and which cannot be expressed in numbers, still affects the present. 'Historical politics' should not attempt to capitalize on this. Even critical voices who accuse the former Allies of belittling the decisive contribution to victory made by the Soviet Union question the sense of these multitudes of victims. They also ask with great bitterness why the major powers did not learn from their experiences and unleashed the Cold War only a few years later, from which the Soviet Union apparently emerged as the loser in 1990.[160] In the spring of 1997, more than 50 years after the end of the Second World War, it seems only too understandable that the survivors of the war in Russia, Byelorussia, the Ukraine and other CIS states demand as true an accounting as possible of those former events. Only a victory for truth will save us from a new 'dictated' picture of history.

VI

FINAL CONSIDERATIONS

The German Reich lost the Second World War on the intellectual plane before it was defeated on the material plane. This is the conclusion that should have become clear from this discussion. It would be too simple to attribute Germany's defeat solely to its enemies' numerical superiority in soldiers and weapons and to their technical and economic superiority. It would be equally naïve to accuse the General Staffs of the Army, Luftwaffe and Kriegsmarine of having waged the war according to outdated doctrines and with the wrong objectives. And only a belief in predestination could support the claim that Germany's defeat had already been sealed in September 1939 with the declaration of war by Great Britain and France.

While there were military blunders committed both by the German leadership as well as by that of its enemies, the major turns of the war in 1940, 1941 and 1942–3 were the results of an intellectual misconception. Germany believed that by making supreme military efforts it could compensate for the mistakes it made in the formulation of basic policy and the structuring of the administrative and economic systems within its sphere of power. What was lacking from the very beginning was the definition of ideological war aims and the identification of the major adversary. The deployment of the great majority of all German forces in the battle against the Soviet Union and the concentration of the focus of German military effort in the east for many years lead to the conclusion that Hitler and his advisers regarded the Soviet Union as the principal enemy. The ideological and propagandistic confrontation with Moscow also tends to underline this conclusion.

On the other hand, the reluctance to reduce efforts in the other theatres of war and the plans made for the period after the victorious conclusion of the campaign in the east suggest that the outcome of the eastern operation was regarded as being merely a preliminary necessity. But in this event it would have been essential to convince Great Britain and the United States that after such a decisive success in the east, Germany held enough trump cards to be able to repulse any subsequent intervention by the Western powers. The ambiguities and uncertainties concerning the kind of future a victorious Germany would offer the peoples of Europe went hand in hand with the vacillating concepts of the ideological and political 'final objectives'. Was a military victory at any price really a sufficient foundation for the subsequent peaceful restructuring of Europe?

Germany's fundamental mistake was to take the second step before the first and not to concentrate all forces on the main strategic objective. Arms production was therefore repeatedly realigned with a view to the confrontation with the next adversary before the decision vis-à-vis the current adversary had been reached. The frequent losses of time proved particularly fatal for the Wehrmacht. Such a delay occurred, for example, in the second half of 1940, when Germany and her Italian ally failed to overwhelm British positions in the Mediterranean at a time when the enemy was preoccupied with the Battle of Britain and awaiting a German invasion. In many respects, this period between summer of 1940 and late spring of 1941 was the most fateful phase of the whole war.

The German leadership also omitted to begin the campaign against the Soviet Union seven to ten days sooner, which in all probability would have led to its victorious conclusion back in the autumn of 1941. It is clear, however, that military victories alone would not have been sufficient to overthrow the Soviet Union. Given Germany's far-reaching objectives, her operational blunders and the resourceful management of the Red Army, the summer campaign of 1942 was similarly begun too late to be able to bring it to a successful conclusion before the onset of winter and to prepare a defence against counter-offensives.

This is not to claim that purely military victories would have brought about a turn of the war in Germany's favour. But there is much to be said for the claim that a political strategy designed to build confidence, combined with military success, would have dealt a punishing blow to Soviet Communism as early as 1941. There was good reason for Stalin, Molotov and Beria to fear defections among their own people and the internal collapse of the multi-national state just as much as they did the victories of the Wehrmacht. Proof of this comes from the extremely brutal actions taken by the Soviet regime against those unwilling to fight, those suspected of intending to go over to the enemy and other 'internal enemies'. Not least of all, an impending revolt by those officers who had barely escaped execution or labour camps in 1937–8 must have caused Stalin considerable headaches.[1] During the summer and autumn of 1941 the advancing Wehrmacht experienced such massive manifestations of sympathy and cooperation among large sections of the population that Stalin must have seen his worst fears about the stability of the Communist system confirmed. During this period the fate of the Soviet Union most probably hung by a thread.[2] But Hitler, Himmler and other leading personalities had no time for a policy that would have promised the Russian and non-Russian inhabitants of the Soviet Union a satisfactory future.

Even if Stalin had continued resistance in the hinterland after the loss of Moscow, Leningrad and the industrial areas in southern Russia, an ideologically and materially constructive eastern policy on the part of Germany would have improved her position immeasurably and given grounds for anticipating a victorious conclusion of the war in the east and the disintegration of the Soviet Union. Even in the autumn of 1942 Germany would still have had several important political options, ranging from an acceptable compromise peace with Moscow to a complete Soviet collapse, had the campaign in southern Russia been successfully concluded and the Caucasus gained. The theory sometimes expounded that the vast size of Russia in itself precluded the collapse of the Red Army cannot be upheld. No space, be it ever so immense, can save an army – or a nation – from defeat if it does not want to fight, or if it accedes to the enemy's conditions. The conclusion must be, therefore, that a victory over the Soviet Union was within the realm of possibility, though not by military means alone.[3] If you cross the Bug you will destroy a great empire...

A mental attitude that made the fate of Germany – and Europe – dependent entirely on a victory with its own weapons was bound to fail the moment the fortunes of war turned against those weapons. It would be unfair to accuse Germany of failing, in the latter half of 1940, to attempt the political and economic restructure of Europe. Given the uncompromising stance of Great Britain and the ambitions of the Soviet Union, her scope for action was, to say the least, narrow. Berlin's foreign policy at the time was still preoccupied with the conflicting interests of Germany's allies, the conquered lands and the third-party nations, i.e. neutrals and 'non-belligerents'. Furthermore, there were still open questions relating to the conduct of the war which urgently required decisions, so that it appeared reasonable to postpone the restructuring of Europe until after the desired victory. Nevertheless, the campaign against the Soviet Union offered the unique opportunity to combine the military defeat of the nation with a policy of political and ideological liberation, to renounce the concept of exploitation and humiliation, and to convert the conquered into allies. The intention to win a 'Weltanschauungs war' solely by military power is a contradiction of the truism that while it is possible to vanquish an ideology, this can never be achieved by force alone. That the Russian and non-Russian peoples were denied the status of liberated and potential partners from the outset and stamped as subhuman for reasons of racial ideology constitutes a German defeat on the intellectual plane for which there could be no redress.[4]

In our discussion certain events and breaks have been identified as actual or 'virtual' turns of the war. Such a 'virtual' turn can be seen in the second half of 1940 when the Axis powers refrained from seizing the military initiative that was on offer in the Mediterranean, particularly in North Africa. A second such turn took place in the summer of 1941 when the German Supreme Command omitted to concentrate all available forces against the still undefeated main adversary, the Soviet Union, and instead began to hold back newly established forces for subsequent campaigns, and even to redirect armaments production for use against the Western powers in expectation of an imminent entry into the war by the United States.

Important as the turn in December 1941 may have been, and although it may have reduced the chances of a German victory, it must still be recognized that a final decision against the Axis powers had not yet occurred. The break of 1941–2 did not yet signify an irrevocable turn in the overall situation in the sense of an unavoidable collapse of Germany's war potential. While it was clear that Germany now had only a very narrow margin in which to regain the strategic initiative, at the end of the winter battles of 1942 the Wehrmacht and the armaments industry had not yet been weakened to the point that there was no longer any chance of reversing the fortunes of war. The central criterion of the impending turn of the war, however, lay in the fact that having decided to adopt the most dangerous military solution in 1942, the OKW renounced more modest but more 'feasible' objectives, such as a local victory in the Mediterranean and North Africa, and the bolstering of the eastern front by means of limited, strength-conserving offensives. Even a renewed attack against Moscow was within the range of possibility. Along with this, the opportune shift from an offensive to a defensive air strategy would have been practicable. One gains much if one is satisfied with little...

Hitler's decision at the end of July 1942 to attack the Soviet positions in the Stalingrad sector and the oilfields in the Caucasus *simultaneously* with divided forces, in which the armoured spearheads made up only a fraction of the original attacking power, was a further 'virtual' turn in the war. It was not the decision to attack the Caucasus region before first building up a flank protection near Stalingrad and on the lower Volga that proved fatal, but the decision to weaken even further the already under-strength armies advancing towards the Caucasus by launching the attack against Stalingrad. This decision of late July 1942 was a breach of the principle of setting priorities. Even if Hitler had given up one of the two major objectives of the summer offensive, an appropriate husbanding of forces could still have led to a partial success, either the rapid capture of Stalingrad in August or a determined breakthrough to the oilfields on the northern edge of the Caucasus. The catastrophe of Stalingrad was merely the end result of a sequence of military compromises, misjudgements and omissions.

The situation of the German eastern front in early November 1942 was an invitation to the Soviet enemy to launch an offensive with far-reaching objectives – the encirclement and destruction of major German forces. The fact that by then the German Supreme Command no longer had any operational reserves worth mentioning to support the endangered sectors of the front underlines its predicament. Either it clung to the existing line and provoked a catastrophic development of the situation, or it withdrew to an appropriate depth and evacuated threatened positions in order to avoid defeats and simultaneously gain sufficient reserves. The turn of the war in 1942–3 on the eastern front had therefore already arrived because of the mental attitude adopted long before the Soviet attack of 19–20 November began.

The most advantageous decision the Germans could have taken was the timely withdrawal of the forces along the middle Don, in and around Stalingrad, and on the approaches to and in the Caucasus itself, to a greatly shortened line between Voronezh and Rostov. This would have meant giving up the territories captured during the summer and would have been an admission of failure. Nevertheless, despite the numerical superiority of the Red Army, Germany would have stood a good chance of defeating the Soviet winter offensive from a stabilized, greatly shortened line, while keeping back considerable reserves and sparing its allies. Breaks in the alliance would then have been far more unlikely than they became after the destruction of large parts of four armies belonging to the allied Hungarians, Romanians and Italians. An eastern army that emerged victorious from the winter of 1942–3 after beating back a Soviet offensive would have had the opportunity to follow this up with a successful flank attack and even to initiate a separate peace with Stalin. If such a strategy had been adopted, it might still have been possible to prove to the enemy that he stood no chance of achieving a decisive victory over the German eastern army.

The least important turn of the war, namely the defeat of Panzer Army Africa at El-Alamein and the landing of the British-American forces in Morocco and Algeria in November 1942, finally culminated in the surrender of the German-Italian forces in Tunisia in mid-May 1943. But already in the summer of 1942 a virtual turn in the war had occurred because of the omission to take the island fortress of Malta, possession of which eventually and decisively determined the supply situation. The fateful decision to hold on to the Tunisian bridgehead was not so much due to the Axis fear of losing North Africa as to the fact that senior leaders considered a permanent defence of Tunisia to be feasible and therefore neglected the timely evacuation of Army Group Africa when it was still opportune.

The loss of about 250,000 German and Italian soldiers in Tunisia was of far greater importance than the abandonment of the last positions in North Africa. Apart from the strain this put on the relationship with the Italian ally, the highest priority should have been given to saving so many proven 'Africa fighters', including the soldiers of four German armoured divisions, in view of the urgent need to provide sufficient forces for the repulse of the Allied invasions in southern and south-eastern Europe. Because it was clear that the forces on all fronts and at home were becoming over-taxed, the German Supreme Command was then faced with the dilemma of how to organize the defence of Italy, Sicily, Sardinia, Corsica and the Balkans after having suffered such heavy losses.

The defeats at Stalingrad, on the Don front, at El-Alamein and in Tunisia became the most significant, irrevocable turns of the war. The breaking off of the battle against the convoys in the Atlantic in May 1943 marks the irreversible turn of the war at sea. This was an example of what may be termed a clash of disparate development.

While the Germans concentrated on the numerical increase of their front-line submarines, the Allies attempted to convert their predominance in technology and Intelligence into a tactical superiority, which finally achieved a breakthrough in May 1943. The turn of the war in 1942–3, including victory for the Western powers in the Battle of the Atlantic, was therefore the most important break in the Second World War.

From this point on the only question remaining for Germany was whether she could achieve a political and strategic 'draw', and if so in what form, or whether she was heading inevitably towards total collapse. Field Marshal von Manstein, among others, believed that a slight chance still remained of bringing about such a draw; seizing the chance, however, depended not only on the forces deployed by the enemy, but also on Germany's ability to pursue as 'economic' a strategy as possible, by saving her own resources and inflicting such high losses on her opponents as to make them willing to accept some form of compromise peace.

In view of the demand for 'unconditional surrender', which had been announced on 24 January 1943 at Casablanca, the best possibility for Germany to reach a political solution lay with the Soviets. Seen from today, such an accord or separate peace between Germany and the Soviet Union, in which Stalin had been displaying interest since the autumn of 1941 and increasingly so since March 1942, offered the German side a realistic chance – albeit one difficult to evaluate – of reaching a political settlement in the east, in order then to be able to deploy all available forces against the Western powers for the defence of Europe's southern and western flank. Though such a gambit must have appeared fraught with risks, given German assessment of the trustworthiness of the Soviet Union, the threat of invasion in southern Europe, in view of the intensification of the air war and the extremely critical situation in Germany itself, it was still a solution worth considering which would not have run contrary to German interests. Such a solution was not only one of Mussolini's prime objectives but was also probably in accord, too, with Stalin's pragmatic calculations. Stalin was well aware of the price that the Soviet Union would have to pay, for despite the losses already incurred, she would have to continue to bear the major burden of the war, and was still awaiting a firm commitment for the opening of a second front in western Europe.[5]

That the Soviet Supreme Command did not at the time regard the destruction of the Sixth Army at Stalingrad as the decisive turn of the war may be deduced from the strategic conduct of the Red Army during the first half of 1943. The operational successes of Army Group South under Field Marshal von Manstein in February and March 1943, which helped to stabilize the southern sector of the eastern front, made Stalin realize the degree of power the German armies could still unleash even after the defeat at Stalingrad. Furthermore, the Soviets had been unable to prevent the planned German withdrawal from exposed positions on the front in the sectors of Army Groups North and Centre. The decision by the Soviet Supreme Command to remain on the defensive during the summer of 1943, even though it certainly had the numerical superiority to launch a major offensive, reflects its respect for the combat strength the German eastern army had regained.

In any event, before the beginning of the battle of Kursk, the Germans still held several military trump cards which could also have been played politically. For the first time since the summer of 1941 the eastern army again disposed of considerable operational reserves, particularly in armoured forces. They also had the option of evacuating endangered, strength-wasting sectors of the front such as the 'Goth's Head' in the Kuban area, thereby gaining additional forces. A mobile form of warfare which would, for example, have given up embattled sectors voluntarily in order to tempt the enemy into making deep advances and then to cut him off by counter-attacks, would have been a good means of inflicting the greatest possible losses. Forgoing the attack at Kursk would also have offered the option of releasing numerous reserves, sending them to Italy and the Balkans in time, and deploying them together with other reserves in anticipation of the Allied invasion. In parallel to these measures, the occasion demanded the quickest and most energetic reinforcement of the air forces, if necessary at the expense of other types of weapons, in order to defend against the strategic bombing war.

The virtual turn of the war in the early summer of 1943 was not to have launched 'Operation Citadel' in time, but then to have persisted with it anyway. Because it took place too late, the chance was missed to improve quite considerably the ratio of forces in Germany's favour, but also to be able to withdraw considerable forces for the southern European theatre. Abandoning the operation entirely would have made it possible to spare substantial forces and still to build up a successful defence on the eastern front by applying the appropriate tactics. In the attempt to wear down the enemy, Germany exposed herself to the danger of being worn down in her turn. What proved most fatal, however, was that in the east Germany had become irrevocably dependent on the enemy's strategy while tying down valuable reserves just at a time when every division and every squadron that could have been spared was needed for the defence of Sicily, Italy and the Balkans.

Whereas the loss of Sicily in mid-August and of southern Italy by the end of September was of great advantage to the Allied air offensive, it did not have any decisive effect on the overall situation of the war. This was mainly due to the fact that in view of the impending invasion of France in the spring of 1944, the American and British staffs could not see their way clear to capitalizing in time on the political collapse of Italy. In this context the renunciation of an airborne operation in the Rome area was of double importance, because not only was a vital opportunity lost to support the Bagdolio government which was prepared to surrender, but also of taking pressure off the US Fifth Army's beachhead at Salerno after 9 September. If the Allies were prepared to tie down two armies and a tactical air force in southern Italy, and to renounce a landing in the Balkans for good reasons, then General Eisenhower should at least have looked at two options: first, a landing with strong forces, as early as possible, to the rear of the German front, in the sector south of Rome, for example, in order to bring about the fall of the 'Gustav Line' already in the autumn of 1943: second, a major landing in southern France with at least one army, while leaving just sufficient forces in southern Italy to tie down the Germans. Such a landing operation, based on Corsica and Sardinia, would most probably have been able to bring the war in France to an end in 1944.

The successful landing at Salerno, combined with an advance by the British in Calabria and Apulia, defeated the slim chance that still existed in early September of the Germans driving the Allied forces back into the sea and thereby defeating the first invasion attempt in southern Europe. The successful defence of the 'Gustav Line' southeast of Rome from late autumn 1943 only resulted in a costly mutual tying down of forces without any chance of bringing about a decision. With the German withdrawals on the eastern front in July and

August and the capture of Sicily and southern Italy by the Allies, the turn of the war in 1943 had been sealed. The attempt by the Wehrmacht to defend the perimeter of 'Fortress Europe' by means of offensive measures had failed.

On the German side, the final irrevocable turn of the war had its deepest roots not only in the 'legacy' of the previous heavy defeats, but also in the failure in the autumn of 1943 to concentrate all the resources still available for the defence against the Allied air offensive and the repulse of the invasion in the west. Despite recognition of the fact after the inferno in Hamburg at the end of July 1943, that only a radical redirection in favour of defensive air armament could offer any respite – even if this meant neglecting the interests of the other branches of the services – fighter production was not given the necessary priority. That a decisive defensive victory might have been possible, given a superiority of fighters against bombers of at least 3 to 1, can be indirectly deduced from the successes achieved by fighter defence against the daylight attacks in the autumn of 1943, where in many cases the margin of superiority of the fighters was only very narrow. The formation of the 'Fighter Staff' at the end of February 1944 took place at a time when the actual and irreversible turn in the air war had already occurred.

In addition to these significant changes in the overall situation, the preparations for the repulse of the invasion suffered from a self-inflicted disadvantage. Even though the fundamental decrees and orders by the OKW from November 1943 onward demanded that priority be given to the reinforcement of the western army, and Hitler was expecting the invasion at any time after February–March 1944, the focus of the war during the winter of 1943–4 clearly remained in the east. By continuing to send the arduously created reserves to the eastern front for months, where they remained tied down or could not be withdrawn in time, the German leadership destroyed its last chance of being able to convert a defeat of the invasion into a favourable turn of the war. This would have required a strong and well-prepared defensive potential in the west, which could have been gained by forgoing costly defensive battles in the east and by a withdrawal in depth to as force-conserving a position as possible, for example, the shortest line between the Baltic and Odessa.

In view of the fact that the bulk of the armoured reserves were still in the east in May 1944, it is safe to state that the German Supreme

Command did not take all the important measures that would have been necessary for bringing about a decision in the west. Therefore the western army embarked upon a defensive battle under numerically unfavourable conditions and also without any agreement among the senior commanders as to the best strategy. The failed attempt to drive the Allied landing forces back into the sea at the time of their greatest weakness, or at least no later than on the second day, was the final turn of the war, even if this was not yet evident to many of the leading protagonists. That the outcome of the battle was in no way regarded as being certain in the various headquarters in east and west, is underlined by the conduct of Stalin, who only launched the summer offensive in Byelorussia two weeks after the invasion began and after victory for the Allies had been assured. How much more shattering would have been a close coordination of the invasion in the west with a major offensive by the Red Army in the east!

The almost total collapse of Army Group Centre in Byelorussia in June–July 1944 is a prime example of the dictum that victory for one side depends to a large degree on the blunders of the other side which contribute substantially to such a victory. In June 1944 a tenacious and successful defensive battle, preventing enemy breakthroughs, would still have been possible given a fundamentally 'economic' strategy that included a radical shortening of the front and the timely evacuation of the Baltic areas north of the Dvina. After the almost total destruction of three German armies in Byelorussia and after the costly defeats in the southern sector of the eastern front, the historian is faced by the hardly explicable phenomenon that the eastern army was again able, by the beginning of autumn, to form a loose but resistant front north and south of the Carpathians. A large part of this achievement is due to the high morale and combat power of the forces that were still intact, to the leadership and its ability to improvise at the tactical and operational level, and to the timely arrival of reinforcements.

In view of the temporary stabilization of the fronts in the west and the east, it appears to have been an irresponsible strategic risk to have neglected the reinforcement of the troops in the eastern theatre and instead to have thrown the final operational reserves into an offensive battle in the west where a telling success could have been expected only under the most fortunate circumstances. When Hitler and Jodl decided against a modest operation in the Aix-la-Chapelle sector and staked everything on a breakthrough to Antwerp, they did upset the plans of the Western Allies, but they also withheld valuable reinforcements from the armies on the eastern front which were urgently needed for the repulse of the Soviet winter offensive. Since the German Supreme Command had also failed to acquire additional reserves by evacuating secondary positions such as the bridgehead in Courland, the eastern front collapsed like a stack of cards during the initial days of the Soviet attack in January 1945. The sole strategic objective of the defensive battles in the ensuing weeks was to rescue large segments of the population from the Red Army's acts of violence.

The spectrum of decisive events, leadership decisions and options extends from early summer 1940 to the summer of 1944. In the attempt to discuss leadership decisions, particularly those on the German side, against the background of the combinations, ratios of forces and available alternatives, the viewpoints and motives of senior leaders were often at the centre of our considerations. Correct decisions or blunders resulted, as they always do, not only from the evaluation of the concrete situation, in other words from facts, information and circumstances, but also from the weighing-up of possible actions and reactions which stemmed from the options on offer. The role played in this by experience and intuition should not be underestimated.

Out of the 'imaginary life' of these political and strategic alternatives the possibility of real life may well develop, and the ability to recognize them is just as much a part of the responsibility of the politician as is the leadership decision itself. The purpose of this discussion has been to contribute to the perception of how far the German leadership realized, did not sufficiently realize, or completely disregarded, these alternatives during the course of the war. One of the major factors of German strategy during the Second World War was the precedence that military action took over political action, as Goebbels, for example, bemoaned in July 1943 with the words: 'We wage too much war and do not engage in enough politics.'[6] However, the alliance of the Western powers and Stalin's Communist Russia, in their attempts to bring Germany down, also mainly pursued military and not political objectives. The appropriate written comment of Karl von Clausewitz may serve to characterize the results of such a preponderance of the military element:

The greater and stronger the motives for the war are, the more they permeate the whole being of the nations;the higher the tension is which precedes the war, the more the war will approach its abstract form; the more the only issue will be to bring the enemy down, the more the military and the political objectives are in unison; the more purely military, and the less political the war will appear to be.[7]

The failure of German strategy was not only due to misjudgements, omissions and neglect of alternatives, nor simply the negative development of the ratio of forces. Another major cause lay in a mental attitude which sought, even attempted to force, a military decision in situations where political initiatives would have been more appropriate. In closing, this aspect of Germany's strategic outlook may be underlined by the statement of a famous general and military theoretician from an eastern culture, who said:

Therefore fighting one hundred times and winning one hundred times is not best... The one who will win is the one who knows when to fight and when not to fight.[8]

NOTES

(For details of literature cited here, see Bibliography)

I

1. Schultz-Naumann, *The Final 30 Days*, p. 130.
2. A first attempt to illuminate the German-Soviet war on the basis of new Soviet documents was undertaken by the author in 1991. See *New Insights into 'Operation Barbarossa'*, p. 441 et seq.
3. Presentation by Prof. Dr Erika Weinzierl at the commemorative symposium for the year 1938 held in Vienna on 20 January 1988. (The author was present on this occasion.)
4. See the concurrent statements by Schlie in *No Peace with Germany*, p. 16.
5. The reference is to a dispute with the highly respected historian Eduard Meyer within the framework of the extensive work *Kritische Studien auf dem Gebiet der kulturwissenschaftlichen Logik* (Critical Studies on the Subject of Cultural-Scientific Logic) in *Gesammelte Aufsätze zur Wissenschaftslehre* (Collected Essays on Scientific Theory), ed. Johannes Winckelmann, University Handbook No. 1492, Tübingen, 7th ed. 1988, p. 266 et seq.
6. Ibid, p. 273. On the application of political alternatives see Mastny, *Moscow's Road to the Cold War*, p. 3.
7. Hillgruber, *The Second World War*.
8. Max Weber, *Der Sinn der 'Wertefreiheit' der soziologischen und ökonomischen Wissenschaften* (The Meaning of the 'Impartiality' of the Social and Economic Sciences), in *Collected Essays on Scientific Theory*, p. 503.
9. Carr, *What Is History?*, p. 129.
10. Jakob Burckhart, *Historical Fragments*, p. 227. This quotation closely resembles the famous statement by Johan Huizinga: 'History is the intellectual form in which a culture renders account for its past.'
11. Brechtken, *Case Barbarossa*, p. 18 et seq.
12. See, for example, Akhromeyev, *The Basic Turns of the Second World War*, p. 10 et seq.
13. Falin, *Second Front*.

14. Frieser, *'Blitzkrieg' without a 'Blitzkrieg Concept'*, p. 13. See also his assessment that Germany had 'already lost the war strategically' before it had begun operationally in *Blitzkrieg Legend*, p. 380.
15. Concerning German hegemony in Europe in the summer of 1940 and the popular sense of victory, see among others, Hillgruber, *Hitler's Strategy*, p. 65 et seq; Fest, *Hitler*, p. 868; Jacobsen, *The Second World War in Chronology and Documents*, p. 463.
16. According to a trustworthy report, General Jodl already coined the phrase of 'the war has been won' on 24 May 1940 in connection with the controversy over the 'order to halt' at Dunkirk. See von Loßberg, *Member of the Wehrmacht Operations Staff*, p. 61.
17. Schlie, op.cit., p. 198 et seq.
18. Ibid, p. 354 et seq.
19. Ibid, p. 355. However, in his argument Schlie entangles himself in several contradictions. He proves convincingly that even at the time of its greatest peril, namely during the battle of Dunkirk at the end of May 1940, the British government was not prepared to entertain peace feelers (p. 203 et seq.) and that British strategists misread Hitler's intentions, which were not the destruction of the British Empire (p. 201). Yet he makes the criticism that after the rejection of his offer, Hitler had no 'concept prepared against England' (p. 356). This leads to a causal chain of argument whereby the author intends to show that obviously Hitler's only remaining strategic option was to attack the Soviet Union (p. 356).
20. John Lukacs, *Der achtzigtägige Zweikampf* (The Eighty-Day Duel), in *Frankfurter Allgemeine* of 5 May 1990, supplement, p. 1 et seq.
21. Schlie, op. cit., p. 245.
22. Krumpelt, *Material and War*, p. 63.
23. See in detail, Boog, *The Luftwaffe Leadership*, p. 93 and p. 176 et seq.; also Gundelach, *Considerations at Luftflotte 2 during 1938/39 about Waging an Air War against England*, p. 41 et seq.

24. Krumpelt, op. cit., p. 63 et seq.; A similar argument can be found in von Loßberg, op. cit., p. 90.
25. See in detail Frieser, *Blitzkrieg Legend*, p. 63 et seq.
26. Ibid, p. 374 et seq.
27. Meier-Welcker, *The Decision to Halt the Geman Armoured Forces in Flanders 1940*, p. 111.
28. Frieser, op. cit., p. 368.
29. Heusinger, *Orders in Conflict*, p. 92.
30. Hitler's directives and orders show that after the 'order to halt' he was still attempting the destruction of the encircled British. The number of British and French rescued between 27 May and 4 June came to more than 338,000 men. If one includes those evacuated before 27 May, then a total of almost 370,000 Allied soldiers were able to escape captivity. See MGFA, *The German Reich and the Second World War*, vol. 2, p. 293 et seq.; also Meier-Welcker, op. cit., and Warlimont, *At Wehrmacht Headquarters*, p. 112 et seq.
31. Most authors agree on this point. See Fest, *Hitler*, p. 870; Zitelmann, *Adolf Hitler*; MGFA, op. cit., vol. 2, p. 369, Hillgruber, *Hitler's Strategy*, p. 144.
32. Churchill, *The Second World War*, vol. II, p. 141.
33. Quoted according to Gellermann, *Secret Paths to Peace with England*, p. 32.
34. Ibid, p. 36.
35. According to von Tippelskirch, *History of the Second World War*, p. 95.
36. Hubatsch, *Hitler's Directives*, p. 54.
37. Hill, *The Weizsäcker Papers*, p. 204 et seq.
38. Warlimont, op. cit., p. 122.
39. Wagner, *Briefings by the Commander-in-Chief of the Kriegsmarine*, pp. 104, 107.
40. For details see Deighton, *Battle of Britain*, p. 104 et seq., 281; for the planning of the invasion see Klee, *Operation 'Sea Lion'*.
41. MGFA, op. cit., p. 373; von Loßberg, op. cit., p. 91.
42. See Boog, op. cit., p. 97; Klee, *Battle of Britain*, p. 67; also Irving, *The Tragedy of the Luftwaffe*, p. 159.
43. For details see Dönitz, *German Strategy at Sea*, p. 66.
44. Hillgruber, op. cit., p. 161; von Loßberg, op. cit., p. 87 speaks of 1942 as

the probably decisive phase of the 'siege'.
45. Lund and Ludlam, *Night of the U-boats*, pp. 204 et seq.; for the tonnage war see Dönitz, op. cit., p. 67.
46. Fest, op. cit., p. 874.
47. See basically Salewski, *German Naval Leadership*, vol. 1, p. 271. For critical discussion on the points made see Reuth, *Decision in the Mediterranean*, p. 18 et seq. In favour of a priority for the Mediterranean strategy: Baum and Weichhold, *The War of the 'Axis Powers'*; also: B. P. Schröder, *Germany and the Middle East in the Second World War*, p. 30 et seq.
48. Reuth, op. cit., p. 22; Warlimont, op. cit., p. 126.
49. For the continental blockade concept, which was primarily endorsed by Foreign Minister Ribbentrop, see Michalka, *Ribbentrop and German World Politics*, p. 255 et seq.; Hillgruber, *Hitler's Strategy*, p. 178 et seq.
50. Hillgruber, *The Second World War*, p. 45. Hillgruber's interpretation centred on the USA appears to be exaggerated.
51. See in detail U. Volkmann, *British Air Defence*; Klee, *The Battle of Britain*; Maier, *The Battle of Britain*, p. 85 et seq.; also Deighton, op. cit.
52. Irving, op. cit., p. 161; U. Volkmann, op. cit., p. 162.
53. Hillgruber and Hümmelchen, *Chronicle of the Second World War*, p. 41; slightly different numbers in U. Volkmann, op. cit., p. 138, who gives the total number of operational front-line Luftwaffe aircraft on 10 August 1940 as 2651, and on 17 August as 2452.
54. For British fighter production see MGFA, op. cit., p. 403; Bekker, *Attack Altitude 4000*, p. 226, (Me 109 fighter production: July 1940: 220; August: 173; September: 218); Deighton, op. cit., p. 216.
55. In summary see: U. Volkmann, op. cit., p. 187.
56. The man in question is Major General Hoffmann von Waldau; see Halder, *War Diary II*, p. 128, entry of 7 September 1940; see also Boog, op. cit., p. 107 et seq.
57. U. Volkmann, op. cit. p. 199.
58. This was Admiral Dönitz's opinion: see Dönitz, op. cit., p. 81.

59. For details see Grinell-Milne, *The Silent Victory*. To the question of successful radio interception by the British: the contribution to the defensive victory made by British decoding experts, whose highly important information was classified as 'ultra' secret, is not fully clear. Even if one may justifiably speak of 'substantial help' for British defence, from what we now know Ultra was not of decisive importance during the summer and autumn of 1940. See U. Volkmann, op. cit., p. 283 et seq.; Lewin, *Did Ultra Decide the War?*, p. 96 et seq. It was only the capture of German submarine U-110 on 8 May 1941 and seizure of its decoding machine and codes that led to the so-called 'Ultra breakthrough' in the war of the intelligence services.

60. Fest, op. cit., p. 872.

61. In this sense, Schlie, op. cit., p. 244 et seq.; also on the question of the 'détour theory', though with reservations: Cecil, *Hitler's Bid for Russia*, p. 80.

62. See Hillgruber, *The Second World War*, p. 44; a similar argument which emphasizes Hitler's fixation on the east is in von Loßberg, op. cit., p. 83.

63. For Soviet reaction to the Battle of Britain see Irving, *Führer and Chancellor*, p. 333 et seq.

64. In detail see Topitsch, *Stalin's War*, p. 56; also Friedrich, *The Law of War*, p. 277.

65. On maritime support of Britain by the USA see Rohwer, *The USA and the Battle in the Atlantic*, p. 86.

66. Kinsella, *Leadership in Isolation*, p. 142; also: Schwabe, *The Roosevelt Government*, p. 130.

67. See above all Bavendamm, *Roosevelt's War*; in addition: Nisbet, *Roosevelt und Stalin*; Gleasson, *The Undeclared War*.

68. Report of a meeting of Hitler with the chiefs of the Wehrmacht on 14 September 1940 based on the notes of Field Marshal Milch, in Irving, *Führer and Chancellor*, p. 333.

69. In summary: von Lindheim, *How Hitler Tried to Prevent the USA Entering the Second World War*, p. 87 et seq.; Hillgruber, *The American Factor in Hitler's Strategy*.

70. For 'Operation Rheinübung' see MGFA, op. cit., vol. 6, p. 373 et seq.; Rohwer, op. cit., p. 90 et seq.

71. See in detail Maser, *The Broken Word*, p. 201 et seq.

72. Repeatedly and in several variations, Hillgruber, *Hitler's Strategy*, p. 575; also Bianca Pietrov who speaks of a 'racial war of extermination' in *Frankfurter Allgemeine* of 3 September 1986, p. 6.

73. Ernst Nolte, *Fascism in its Era*, p. 436.

74. Ueberschär and Wette, *Operation Barbarossa*, p. 16.

75. Schlie, op. cit., p. 245, quoting from Fest, op. cit., p. 881.

76. Haffner, *From Bismarck to Hitler*, p. 289.

77. See above all Maser, op. cit.; MGFA, op. cit., vol. 4; Ueberschär and Wette, *The German Attack against the Soviet Union*; Stegemann, *History and Politics*, p. 73 et seq.; Wegner, *Two Roads to Moscow*; Suvorov, *The Ice Breaker*; Töpitsch, op. cit.; Hillgruber, *Once Again*, p. 214 et seq.; Magenheimer, *On the German-Soviet War*, p. 51 et seq.

78. *Izvestiya*, 16 January 1993.

79. Participants in the conference on 16 April 1995 were, among others, historians V. L. Doroshenko, Irina V. Pavlova and Tatyana Bushuyeva who had discovered the document mentioned in the Centre for the Collection of Historic Documents, a special archive of the former USSR, f. 7, op. 1, d. 1223.

80. Tatyana Bushuyeva, 'Versuchen Sie mich zu verstehen, während Sie mich verdammen...' ('Try to understand me, while you condemn me...'), in *Novyj Mir* 12/1994, p. 232 et seq.; Carl Gustav Ströhm presented this talk in detail in *Die Welt* of 16 July 1996. Gabriel Gorodetsky (*Die Welt*, 31 August 1996) claims that this is a clever forgery of 23 December 1939 by the French secret service. However, this is decisively contradicted by the fact that in his interview with *Pravda* on 30 November 1939 it would have been impossible for Stalin to deny the contents of a document and declare it to be a forgery, of which he could not have had any knowledge at the time. The date of the *Pravda* interview has been confirmed by Eberhard Jäckel, see 'Über die angebliche Rede Stalins vom 19. August 1939' (On Stalin's alleged speech on 19 August 1939), *in Vierteljahreshefte für*

Zeitgeschichte 4/1958, pp. 380–9.
81. Statement by former General Günther Kießling in *Welt am Sonntag* of 4 September 1994, p. 27, 'Unternehmen Barbarossa' – Präventivkrieg gegen Stalin? ('Operation Barbarossa' – Preventive War against Stalin?).
82. Maser, op. cit.; Rühl, *Rise and Fall of the Russian Empire*, p. 473 et seq.; Topitsch, op. cit.; Richard R. Raack, *Stalin's Role in the Coming of The Second World War*, p. 198 et seq. and the same author's *Stalin's Drive to the West*; see also articles on this by Günther Gillessen in *Frankfurter Allgemeine* of 4 March 1993, p. 14, 16 January 1995, p. 10, 10 October 1995, p. 14.
83. Furet, *The End of the Illusion*, p. 403.
84. Ibid, p. 416. Similar argument by Malia in *Dementia Implemented*, p. 320.
85. Halder, op. cit., p. 21.
86. Warlimont, op. cit., p. 129.
87. Hubatsch, op. cit., p. 87 et seq.
88. Thus the reply by Gerd Ueberschär to statement by Joachim Hoffmann in *Frankfurter Allgemeine* of 31 October 1986, p. 11.
89. In detail see Stegemann, op. cit., p. 88 et seq.
90. For similar argument see Seraphim and Hillgruber, *Hitler's Decision to Attack Russia*, p. 246; Stegemann, op. cit., p. 89.
91. Maser, op. cit., p. 208.
92. Ibid, p. 201 et seq. ; also Suvorov, op. cit., p. 47. German forces on the Soviet frontier numbered 23 divisions on 20 July and were increased to 33 divisions by end September 1940.
93. Irving, op. cit., p. 333 et seq.
94. Karl Gustav Ströhm, 'Fürchtete Hitler Sowjet-Einmarsch?' (Did Hitler Fear Soviet Attack?), in *Die Welt* of 27 September 1989, p. 12, with reference to an article in *Politika*; in summary, Becker, *Battle for Europe*, p. 123.
95. In summary, Reuth, *Goebbels*, p. 465.
96. Hillgruber, *The Second World War*, p. 47.
97. Topitsch, op. cit., p. 97; Klee, *Prehistory of the Russian Campaign*, p. 586; Maser, op. cit., p. 238.
98. For Stalin's position in detail see Hoffmann, in Wegner, op. cit., p. 373 et seq.; on the 'inevitability' of the war: Rühl, op. cit., p. 484; in addition: Volkogonov, *Stalin*, p. 497; for Stalin's ideological war aims: Becker, op. cit., p. 227.
99. Danilov, *June 1941*, p. 3.
100. Topitsch, op. cit., pp. 106, 111; Becker, op. cit., p. 217 et seq.; Suvorov, op. cit. On the assessment of the treaty of 23 August 1939: Ahmann, 'The Hitler-Stalin Pact', in Michalka, *The Second World War*, p. 93 et seq.
101. On military doctrine: Hoffmann, in Wegner, op. cit., p. 369; Suvorov, op. cit., p. 169 et seq.
102. Tarleton, *What Really Happened to the Stalin Line?*, p. 210.
103. Danilov, *Did the Red Army General Staff Prepare a Preventive Blow against Germany?*, p. 43.
104. On Soviet preparations for an attack: Maser, op. cit., p. 265 et seq.; Post, *Operation Barbarossa*; Suvorov, op. cit., p. 90 et seq.; Magenheimer, op. cit., p. 51 et seq. According to the article by Valery Danilov cited above (note 103), the Soviet offensive deployment consisted of 258 divisions, including strategic reserves, divided into four fronts and supported by 165 air regiments, while in May 1941 total strength amounted to 303 divisions and 218 air regiments. Based on contemporary knowledge there were a total of 24,000 tanks and 20,000 front-line aircraft available. The plan foresaw two phases in which the bulk of the German eastern armies were to be encircled and annihilated by superior forces, first in the area between the Carpathians and Warsaw and then also in East and West Prussia.
105. Danilov, op. cit., p. 47; Topitsch, op. cit., p. 112. The assumption that Stalin did not approve the 'Zhukov-Timoshenko plan' of May 1941 but only the preparations for defence may safely be discarded. From end of December 1940 on, Stalin knew about Directive No. 21 of 18 December 1940 ('Operation Barbarossa') through an act of treason and during the first half of 1941 received a total of 84 warnings of a German attack. According to newest research, the claim by Soviet authors that Stalin had ignored these warnings can no longer be maintained. His basic intention had been to avoid any provocation in order to gain the necessary time for the completion of Soviet offen-

sive deployment. For comparison see: 'War die faschistische Aggression ein Überraschungsüberfall?' (Was the Fascist Aggression a Surprise Attack?), in *Voennij Vestnik* of April 1990, pp. 1-6; Suvorov, op. cit., p. 236 et seq.
106. *ÖMZ* 1/1993, p. 49 et seq.
107. See statements in *Europäische Sicherheit*, 5/1996, p. 54.
108. Helmdach, *Surprise Attack?*, p. 66 et seq.; Suvorov, op. cit., p. 383 et seq.
109. Günther Gillessen in *Frankfurter Allgemeine* of 4 March 1993, 'Krieg zwischen zwei Angreifern' (War Between Two Aggressors); somewhat at variance: Suvorov, op. cit.,, p. 429.
110. 'Ja Voina' (The War) in *Der Spiegel* of 17 September 1951.
111. See for example 'Der Kompromiß' (The Compromise), essay by Gregor Schöllgen in *Frankfurter Allgemeine* of 20 November 1996 which was heavily criticized in letters to the editor in the issue of 29 November 1996.
112. Vladimir Karpov, 'Schlafende Aggressoren' (Sleeping Aggressors) in *Der Spiegel*, 22/1990. p. 170; Volkogonov, *Stalin*, p. 546, mentioning an offensive plan without detailed explanations; Kirshin, 'Soviet Forces on the Eve of the Great Patriotic War' in Wegner, op. cit., p. 398 et seq.
113. See *Vojenno istoritshenskij shurnal* (Military Historical Review), vol. 12/1991, 1/2/1992; also *ÖMZ* 1/1993, p. 41.
114. Compare Post, op. cit., p. 209.
115. 'Die Abwiegler' (The Appeasers) in *Süddeutsche Zeitung* of 16 Feb. 1996, p. 14.
116. Danilov, 'Did Stalin Prepare a Surprise Attack on Germany?', in *Komsomolskaja Pravda* of 4 January 1992; also *ÖMZ* 1/1993, p. 41 et seq.
117. *ÖMZ* 1/1993, p. 43; on initialling see *ÖMZ* 1/1995, p. 120 et seq.
118. Mercalov, *22 June 1941*, p. 31.
119. Reference is to 'Did Stalin Prepare a War of Aggression Against Hitler? An Unplanned Discussion.' Collected material (in Russian), published by Grigory Bordyugov and Vladimir Neveshin, AIRO-XX Moscow 1995; the quote is on page 142 (author Mikhail Meltyukov); see also 'Der letzte Sowjetmythos' (The Last Soviet Myth) in *Frankfurter Allge-*

meine of 10 April 1996.
120. Meltyukov, *We Will Destroy the Enemy Even in Enemy Territory*, p. 67 et seq.
121. Weinberg, *A World in Arms*, p. 229.
122. Ingeborg Fleischhauer, 'Stalin Rejected Preventive War' in *The Standard* of 22 June 1991, p. 4.
123. See the extensive treatment by Vladimir Neveshin, 'The Pact with Germany and the Idea of an "Offensive War" (1939–1941)' in *The Journal of Slavic Military Studies*, December 1995, p. 824 et seq.
124. Reference is to statements in Bordyugov and Neveshin, op. cit.
125. Krienen, 'Thunderstorm' or 'Barbarossa', p. 124.
126. Ibid, p. 128 et seq.; also Pietrov-Ennker, 'Germany in June 1941' in Michalka, op. cit., p. 587 et seq.
127. Maser, op. cit., p. 249.
128. These accusations were already voiced in 1986 in connection with an attempted re-evaluation of the German-Soviet war: see, for example, Rolf-Dieter Müller in *Frankfurter Allgemeine* of 16 October 1986, p. 16; Bianca Pietrov in *Frankfurter Allgemeine* of 13 November 1986, p. 8; and, more recently, Wolfram Wette, 'Kampfschrift gegen die Wahrheit' (Polemical Document against the Truth), in *Das Sonntagsblatt* of 22 March 1996, p. 8; Wette's accusation is addressed to Werner Maser, Ernst Topitsch, Joachim Hoffmann, Viktor Suvorov and Walter Post.
129. Kaiser, *Enlightenment or Denunciation?*, p. 455 et seq.
130. Wolfgang Kasack in a review of Suvorov's *Der Tag M* (Day M), in *Osteuropa* 4/1996, p. 15.
131. Of the mass of literature on the ideological, racial, territorial and economic objectives – particularly those of the SS leadership – in connection with the conquest in the east, see the following selected works: Krausnick and Wilhelm, *The Forces of the Weltanschauungs War*; Ley, *Genocide and Hope of Salvation*, p. 236 et seq.; MGFA, op. cit., vol. 4, p. 98 et seq., p. 413 et seq., (contributions by Rolf-Dieter Müller and Jürgen Förster); Umbreit, 'German Occupation Policy', in Wegner, op. cit., p. 2 et seq.; Friedrich, *The Law of War*, p.

320 et seq., p. 412 et seq.
132. Von Bock, *War Diary*, p. 181.
133. Ibid, p. 193.
134. Stegemann, op. cit., p. 87.
135. See the profound discussion by Rauh, *History of the Second World War*, vol. 2, p. 384 et seq.
136. On the Task Forces see Ogorrek, *The Task Forces and the 'Genesis of the Final Solution'*; Friedrich, op. cit. On the multiple facets of the German perception of the threat and the enemy and a sharp criticism of the racial policies, see contributions by Manfred Weißbecker and Wolfram Wette in H.-E. Volkmann, *The Image of Russia in the Third Reich*. For the assessment of these controversial orders and directives one must also bear in mind the threat as perceived in western and central Europe, resulting from the numerous reports by emigrants about the criminal acts of the Bolshevists and the Communist commissars during the Russian civil war as well as by members of the International Brigade during the Spanish civil war. In this sense, the German-Soviet war could be regarded as a resumption of the Russian civil war: see Nolte, *The European Civil War 1917–1945*, p. 3 et seq.
137. Rauh, op. cit., p. 407; Warlimont, op. cit., p. 172.
138. Volker Ulrich in *Die Zeit* of 4 November 1994, p. 17.
139. The main proponents of this school of thought are Andreas Hillgruber (with reservations), Wolfram Wette, Gerd Ueberschär, Jürgen Förster, Bianca Pietrov-Ennker, Erich Volkmann and Gabriel Gorodetsky. On the objective of economic exploitation and the planned repression of the native population, see Müller, *The Door to World Power and Hitler's Eastern War*; Wasser, *Himmler's Territorial Planning in the East*; Rössler and Schleiermacher, *General Plan East*.
140. According to General Halder's notes, on 30 March 1941 Hitler said: '... battle of two Weltanschauungen... We are dealing with a battle of annihilation...', Halder, op. cit., p. 443; whereas in *A World in Arms*, Weinberger writes on Hitler's speech of 30 March 1941, that a 'campaign of annihilation was in the offing...'

141. Von Bock, op. cit., p. 191.
142. Reuth, *Goebbels*, p. 478 et seq.
143. On von Weizsäcker's critical attitude towards the campaign against the Soviet Union, see Jacobsen, *The Road to Partitioning the World*, p. 110; even a sharp critic of German strategy towards the Soviet Union admits the doubts these persons had about the campaign in the east: see Falin, op. cit., p. 257.
144. Hillgruber, *Hitler's Strategy*, p. 373 et seq.; on the sceptical stance of Field Marshals von Bock and von Leeb, see Hillgruber, 'German Military Leader's Perception of Russia', in Wegner, op. cit., p. 177; Schellenberg, *Notations*, p. 170.
145. See Oberländer, *Six Memoranda*; Fröhlich, *General Vlassov*; von Herwarth, *Between Hitler and Stalin*, particularly p. 241 et seq.; Hoffmann, *The Eastern Legions*.
146. One of the severest critics of the 'theory of preventive war' is Pietrov-Ennker: see 'Germany in June 1941', in Michalka, op. cit., especially p. 589 et seq.; also the same author's 'Es war kein Präventivkrieg' (It Was Not a Preventive War) in *Die Zeit* of 24 February 1995.
147. Ströbinger, *Stalin Decapitates the Red Army*; Conquest, *The Great Terror*, p. 211 et seq.; Morozov, *The Hawks in the Kremlin*, p. 174 et seq.
148. This assumption was expressed by politician and publisher Alexander Dugin: see *Elementy* 10/1994, p. 11.
149. See in detail Conquest, op. cit., p. 247, 509 et seq.; on the backgound of the 'Tukhachevsky Case' see Ströblinger, op. cit., p. 281 et seq.
150. Weinberg, op. cit., p. 247.
151. Von Bock, op. cit., p. 177.
152. Halder, op. cit., p. 353.
153. Boog, 'The Luftwaffe' in MGFA, op. cit., vol. 4, p. 653.
154. Heydorn, *Soviet Deployment in the Bialystok Salient*, p. 77; Maser, op. cit., p. 346 et seq.
155. Reuth, *Goebbels*, p. 484; see also the statement by Guderian in *Memoirs of a Soldier*, p. 172; on the under-estimation of the Soviet air forces, see Boog, *The Luftwaffe Leadership*, p. 112 et seq.
156. Haffner, *Comments on Hitler*, p. 113.
157. Zitelmann, 'Explanation of the "Lebensraum" Motive in Hitler's

Weltanschauung', in Michalka, op. cit., p. 560; see also Müller, *Hitler's Eastern War*.

158. Entry of 17–18 September 1941 in Jochmann, *Monologues at Führer Headquarters*, p. 62.
159. On this, see Schustereit, *Risk*, p. 13 et seq.
160. Ibid, p. 21.
161. MGFA, op. cit., vol. 4, p. 263.
162. Maser, op. cit., p. 130 et seq.; Schustereit, op. cit., p. 24.
163. Milward, 'The Second World War' in *History of World Economics in the 20th Century*, p. 47; Fest, op. cit., p. 841; Kroener, 'The Frozen Blitzkrieg' in Wegner, op. cit., p. 135.
164. Frieser, *Blitzkrieg Legend*, p. 8 et seq.
165. Schustereit, op. cit., p. 25.
166. Halder, op. cit., p. 422; MGFA, op. cit., vol. 4, p. 269.
167. Ibid, p. 272.
168. Schustereit, op. cit.,38.
169. MGFA, op. cit., vol. 4, p. 188.
170. Halder, op. cit., entry of 7 October 1940.
171. Milward, 'Labour Policy and Productivity in the German War Economy' in Forstmeister and Volkmann, *War Economy and Armament 1939–1945*, p. 7 et seq.; in addition, Zitelmann, *Hitler*, p. 149 et seq.
172. Baum and Weichold, *The War of the Axis Powers*, p. 77; Hillgruber, *Hitler's Strategy*, p. 180 et seq.; Guderian, op. cit., p. 123 (Actually Guderian meant sending four to six armoured divisions to North Africa.)
173. Reuth, *Decision in the Mediterranean*, p. 29 et seq.; Baum and Weichold, op. cit., p. 110 et seq.; Warlimont, op. cit., p. 144.
174. B.-P. Schröder, *Germany and the Middle East During the Second World War*, p. 63 et seq.
175. In summary: MGFA, op. cit., vol. 3, p. 510 et seq.; on the controversy about the 'missed opportunity' after the end of the Balkans campaign and the capture of Crete, see Gundelach, *Luftwaffe in the Mediterranean*, vol. 1, p. 261 et seq.
176. This assessment is emphatically propounded in Baum and Weichold, op. cit., p. 414 and in MGFA, op. cit., vol. 3, p. 163.

II

1. Compiled on the basis of numerous calculations. See, for example, MGFA, *The German Reich and the Second World War*, vol. 4, pp. 275, 312; map supplement in FA/MA, situation map east, 1:2,500,000, 1/5D, 1/6D; Halder, *War Diary III*, map supplement; Danilov, *Did the General Staff of the Red Army Plan a Preventive Blow against Germany?*, p. 41 et seq.; Heydorn, *Soviet Deployment in the Bialystok Salient*, map supplement.
2. According to author's calculations and statements by Kirshin in Wegner, *Two Roads to Moscow*, p. 389 et seq.; *Voenniy Vestnik*, special edition, 7–8/1990, p. 6. There are even higher figures given for certain categories of weapons. Artillery, for example, is alleged to have comprised 148,600 guns; see Hoffmann, *The Soviet Preparations for Attack*, p. 369.
3. The number of 303 divisions is not first mentioned by Danilov, but can already be found in Reinhardt, *The Turn Before Moscow*, p. 24.
4. The statements are taken from a Soviet technical journal of 1978, quoted according to Tarleton, *What Really Happened to the Stalin Line?*, part 1, p. 213, note 3.
5. Kirshin, *Soviet Forces on the Eve of the Great Patriotic War*, p. 400.
6. Danilov, op. cit., p. 44.
7. Kipp, *Barbarossa*, p. 200.
8. A German infantry division numbered between 15,000 and 17,900 men, depending on list strength and manning quota. A Soviet front-line infantry division actually numbered between 10,000 and 12,000 men. Its list strength was 14,483 men, 294 guns and mortars, 16 tanks, 13 armoured vehicles, 558 other vehicles and 99 tractors; see Kipp, op. cit., p. 201.
9. In early March 1941 the staff of 4th Army which belonged to Army Group Centre still counted upon only 100–104 infantry, 24–25 cavalry divisions and 31 motorized-mechanized brigades. It was assumed that mobilization would provide about 50 additional divisions; see Meier-Welcker, *Notes of a General Staff Officer*, p. 106.
10. Halder, *War Diary II*, p. 461. For the situation on the Soviet side, which

confirms German assumptions in many respects, see: 'Documents of the Directorate of the Western Military District and Field Directorate of the Western Front' in *The Journal of Soviet Military Studies* 1/1991, p. 152 et seq.

11. Becker, *The Battle for Europe*, p. 235 et seq.

12. These 'mechanized corps' had a list strength of two armoured divisions, one motorized division, 1031 tanks (including 546 modern KW and T-34 tanks), 268 armoured vehicles, 358 guns and 36,000 men. However, at the time of the German attack, the corps had only received about 50 per cent of their armour: see: Dick, *Operational Employment of Soviet Armour*, p. 8.

13. Halder, *War Diary III*, p. 170; for the deficiencies of German radio surveillance, see Heydorn, *Intelligence (East) and Soviet Army Wireless Service*, p. 76 et seq.

14. These were 16th, 19th, 20th, 21st, 24th and 28th Army; see Chor'kov, 'The Red Army in the Initial Phase of the Great Patriotic War', in Wegner, op cit., p. 432.

15. Compare Connor and Poirier, *Soviet Ground Force Mobilization Potential*, p. 218.

16. *Hitler's Political Testament*, p. 79; in addition, Hillgruber, *Hitler's Strategy*, p. 506, note 26.

17. In detail, Philippi, *The Pripet Problem*, p. 18.

18. In summary, Zapantis, *Hitler's Balkan Campaign*, p. 86 et seq.

19. See the largely polemical portrayal with remarkably overstated numbers for the German eastern army and understated numbers for the Red Army in Falin, *Second Front*, p. 204. According to this the Wehrmacht (including Luftwaffe, Kriegsmarine and SS) allegedly disposed of 4.6 million men, whereas Soviet forces in the five western military districts only numbered 2.78 million men.

20. Stripp, *Reflections on British Wartime Codebreaking*, paper read at the conference on 'The Importance of Secret Intelligence for the History of the Second World War', Cologne, 24 June 1994, p. 8.

21. A detailed description of how the 'doctored' reports on the enemy situation came about is given by Grigorenko, *Memoirs*, p. 201 et seq.; on the misinterpretation of the information on the imminent German attack see Gordievsky and Andrew, *KGB*, p. 335 et seq.

22. Suvorov, *The Ice Breaker*, p. 109.

23. 'Marshal of the Soviet Union Georgi Zhukov on the Soviet Leadership on the Eve and During the Initial Days of the Great Patriotic War' (first publication) in *Military Bulletin No. 20*, October 1987, p. 10; for a detailed portrayal, Volkogonov, *Stalin*, p. 556 et seq.

24. OKH/Army General Staff/Intelligence Department East, 'Soviet tank and self-propelled gun situation, assumed development since beginning of the war', FA/MA, H3/1522, undated, probably a document from early 1945.

25. MGFA, op. cit., vol. 4, p. 654.

26. This is the untenable claim made by Besymenski in *Special File 'Barbarossa'*, p. 299; in his later book, *The Taming of the Typhoon*, he still holds to this misleading claim; a similar opinion can be found in Chor'kov, op. cit., p. 441; in refutation of this claim, Rauh, *History of the Second World War*, vol. II, p. 415. On the expediency of a breather after the battle of Smolensk, Schüler, 'The Campaign in the East as a Problem of Logistics and Supply' in Wegner, op. cit., p. 209.

27. Compare Chales de Beaulieu, *The Advance of Panzer Group 4 on Leningrad*, pp. 82, 139.

28. Compare Philippi, op. cit., p. 54.

29. Von Bock, *War Diary*, p. 240.

30. Compare Rauh, op. cit., vol. II, p. 420.

31. On the directives in question see Hubatsch, *Hitler's Directives*, p. 140 et seq. For Hitler's indecisiveness on the expediency of continuing the operation after the victorious initial phase see also von Kotze, *Army Adjutant to Hitler*, p. 107 et seq.

32. *OKW War Diary 1940–1941*, vol. 2, p. 1062 et seq.

33. MGFA, op. cit., vol. 4, p. 507. Attention must briefly be drawn to the following facts: Army Group North disposed of only two Panzer Corps (three armoured divisions and three motorized divisions), who, it was hoped, would take Leningrad in the shortest possible time without needing

to draw on the support of parts of Army Group Centre. In the end, this allocation of forces proved to be insufficient. On the other hand, Army Group South disposed of three Panzer Corps (five armoured divisions, four motorized divisions and one motorized brigade), which soon also proved to be too weak to beat the opposing Soviet forces and quickly gain a crossing over the Dnieper with the infantry. Both AG North and AG South were therefore not able to gain their objectives under their own power. Since AG Centre needed all of its mobile forces in order to achieve its objectives, the only options would have been to reinforce AG North with mobile forces from AG South, or vice versa. By this means, the rapid capture of Leningrad by early August would most probably have been achievable.

34. Masson, *The German Army*, p. 182; the same argument can be found in Reinhardt, *The Turn Before Moscow*, pp. 59–60. In contrast to this, Rauh, op. cit., vol. II, p. 423 et seq., proposes the somewhat daring theory that despite the unsatisfactory operational situation, General Halder had prepared a promising plan which called for an attack on 10 August with the combined forces of Panzer Groups 1 and 2 in the eastern Ukraine, to be followed by an advance against Moscow from the south-west.
35. Hubatsch, op. cit., p. 136 et seq.
36. Schustereit, *Risk*, p. 44
37. *OKW War Diary 1940-1941*, vol. 2, p. 1048.
38. Ibid, p. 1022 et seq.
39. On this in detail, Rössler and Schleiermacher, *The General Plan East*; Müller, *Hitler's War in the East*; *OKW War Diary 1940–1941*, part 2, p. 1029 et seq.
40. Compare Hillgruber, 'Highpoint of the Second World War' in Paper No. 65, Institute for European History in Mainz, Wiesbaden, 1977, p. 16 et seq.
41. Wilson, *The First Summit*, p. 173 et seq.; in summary, Mastny, *Moscow's Road to the Cold War*, p. 53; Hans-Jürgen Schröder, 'The Underestimated Giant' in *Frankfurter Allgemeine* of 21 June 1991, p. 12.
42. Hillgruber, *Soviet Foreign Policy during the Second World War*, p. 69.

43. Von Herwarth, *Between Hitler and Stalin*, p.188; Knipping, *American Policy towards Russia*, p. 31.
44. Ibid, pp. 34 et seq., 120.
45. Ibid, p. 178. The man in question was the attaché for trade and commerce at the American Embassy in Berlin who had received this information from Dr Erwin Respondek, an acquaintance of the Chief of Staff of the Heer; see Bavendamm, *Roosevelt's War*, p. 388.
46. Dippel, *Two Against Hitler*, p. 49.
47. Conquest, *The Great Terror*, p. 531; in addition, Gordievsky and Andrew, op. cit., p. 290.
48. Bavendamm, op. cit., p. 170 et seq.; Nisbet, *Roosevelt und Stalin*, p. 50.
49. Bavendamm, op. cit., p. 169. Roosevelt's adviser Harry Hopkins also counted upon the defeat of the Soviet Union even though he was in favour of long-term support for Stalin; see Kimball, 'They Do Not Appear Where You Expect Them' in Wegner, op. cit., p. 592.
50. Falin, *Second Front*, p. 236.
51. Ibid, p. 247.
52. Mastny, op. cit., p. 50.
53. Order from Headquarters of the Supreme Commander of the Red Army, 16 August 1941, in *Military Bulletin No. 17*, September 1988 (by permission of the editorial staff of the *Military-Historical Review*); see the version in *Osteuropa 89* (1989), p. 1035 et seq.; a captured version in Russian is in the FA/MA, sig. H 3/152; in detail, Hoffmann, *History of the Vlasov Army*, p. 132 et seq.; in addition, Bonwetsch, 'Repression of the Military and the Combat-Worthiness of the Red Army in the "Great Patriotic War" ' in Wegner, op. cit., pp. 404–24; Conquest, op. cit., p. 307.
54. *Military Bulletin No. 17*, September 1988, p. 11.
55. Ibid, p. 12 et seq.
56. Tolstoy, *The Betrayed of Yalta*, p. 41 et seq.; Hoffmann, *History of the Vlasov Army*, p. 135 et seq.
57. Wilhelm, *Predictions of Intelligence Department East*, p. 32.
58. Compare Hoffmann, *The Eastern Legions*, p. 172; same author, *History of the Vlasov Army*, p. 14.
59. Neulen, *On the German Side*, p. 342; here the total number of volunteers is

given as 962,000; in addition, Münter, *The Eastern Volunteers*, p. 207 et seq.

60. Tolstoy, *Stalin's Secret War*, p. 249.

61. Excerpt from Intelligence Report 3 of 30 March 1943, Pz. AOK 2 (FA/MA H 3/74); Volkogonov, 'Stalin as Supreme Commander' in Wegner, op. cit., p. 490.

62. Suvorov, op. cit., p. 84.

63. Morozov, *The Hawks in the Kremlin*, p. 252.

64. See the summarized analysis: OKH/General Staff of the Heer/Intelligence Department East (IIb) No. 10/43 secret: Troop formations and paramilitary organizations of the NKVD, 16 January 1943 (FA/MA H3/398).

65. As an example see telex by Army Command 6 of 30 May 1943 (testimony by prisoner), file 27a (FA/MA H3/74).

66. Document cited in note 64. This decree was approved by the Deputy People's Commissar for Internal Affairs, Major General Appolonov, and distributed to the border troop regiments of the NKVD down to battalion command level. The decree covers assignments from the platoon to the regimental level.

67. Hoffmann, *Caucasia 1942/43*, p. 392 et seq.

68. Suvorov, op. cit., p. 89.

69. Gordievsky and Andrew, op. cit., p. 394; Dziak, *Chekisty*, p. 112 et seq.

70. For details see Hesse, *The Soviet-Russian Partisan War*, p. 55 et seq.; for the Soviet view of the partisan war see Sudoplatov and Sudoplatov, *The Henchmen of Power*.

71. De Zayas, *The Wehrmacht Investigation Board*, p. 273 et seq.; a detailed report by a witness about a massacre of German prisoners can be found in Frank, *The 23rd of July 1941*, p. 709 et seq.

72. For details see Zeidler, *The End of the War in the East*, p. 118 et seq.; in his book the author dedicates a lengthy chapter to Ilya Ehrenburg's propaganda activities.

73. Andrei Vlasov can be cited as a prominent witness; see Fröhlich, *General Vlasov*, p. 81 et seq.; in summary, Oberländer, *Six Memoranda*.

74. Volkogonov, *Stalin*, p. 565.

75. Harrison, ' "Barbarossa". The Soviet Answer' in Wegner, op. cit., p. 443 et seq.

76. In the course of the battle of Kiev which ended on 26 September, the Soviet 5th, 21st, 26th, 37th and 38th Armies were encircled and almost completely destroyed, while the 6th and 40th Armies suffered heavy losses. In contrast to earlier Soviet publications which only spoke of 225,000 captured, Volkogonov in his chapter 'Terrible Losses' in *Stalin*, p. 586, puts the number of encircled at 452,270. The military catastrophe in the south was so grave that a completely new South-west Front had to be created.

77. Jochmann, *Monologues at Führer Headquarters*, p. 62.

78. War Diary Army Group North, entry on 15 Sept. 1941 (FA/MA 22 506).

79. MGFA, op. cit., vol. 4, p. 515; *OKW War Diary 1940–1941*, vol. 2, p. 1070. The bomb attack in Kiev was used by the SS police authorities as an excuse for the terrible mass murders at Babi Yar on 29–30 September 1941.

80. Hesse, op. cit., p. 108.

81. Ibid, pp. 118, 121. Gangs of children were used to blow up bridges, while women were infiltrated into German staffs in order, for example, to commit murders by poisoning wells.

82. Von Bock, op. cit., p. 239.

83. See one of the more recent publications about breaches of international law in German occupied territories: Oggoreck, *The Special Task Forces and the 'Genesis of the Final Solution'*.

84. MGFA, op. cit., vol. 4, p. 741.

85. Volkogonov, op. cit., p. 594.

86. War Diary Army Group North, vol. IV, entry of 31 October 1941. (FA/MA, sig. 22 927).

87. On this controversial question see Chales de Beaulieu, op. cit., p. 124.

88. The formations involved were the 8th and 12th Panzer Divisions, the 18th and 20th Infantry Divisions (motorized), and the 'Totenkopf' SS Division. Withdrawing these units in favour of reinforcing Army Group Centre, which urgently required an armoured attack force on its northern flank, would only have been possible if the siege of Leningrad had been given up, freeing the forces by shortening the front.

89. Reinhardt, op. cit., p. 55.

90. Ibid, p. 63 et seq. for details.

91. War Diary Army Group Centre, vol. IV, entry of 19 October 1941, FA/MA, sig. III H 371/4; see also von Bock, op. cit., p. 297 et seq.

92. Reuth, *Goebbels*, p. 488.

93. Von Bock, op. cit., pp. 288, 294.

94. The autumn mud period had already set in with rain and snowfall on the night of 7 October, but the ensuing week had again brought tolerable weather conditions for military operations. See Wagener, *Moscow 1941*, p. 82 et seq.; Reinhardt, op. cit., p. 73. Field Marshal von Bock states that the first snow and hail fell within the sector of his army group on 10 October.

95. See Besymenski, *Taming the Typhoon*, p. 118 et seq.; Samsonov, 'The Battle in Front of Moscow' in Rohwer and Jäckel, *Turn of the War, December 1941*, p. 189.

96. Reinhardt, op. cit., pp. 76, 79. Zhukov states that in mid-October the strength of his Western Front was about 90,000 men.

97. OKH/General Staff of the Heer, Intelligence Department East (II) No. 3905/41 secret; the situation report east No. 129 can be found in *War Diary Army Group Centre*, vol. IV, p. 135.

98. Von Kotze, op. cit., p. 113.

99. Gordievsky and Andrew, op. cit., p. 346; Conquest, op. cit., p. 316; Harrison, *'Barbarossa', The Soviet Answer*, p. 448.

100. Volkogonov, op. cit., p. 596; in addition, Reinhardt, op. cit., p. 88.

101. *War Diary Army Group Centre*, vol. IV, entry of 10 October 1941.

102. In summary, Reinhardt, op. cit., p. 94.

103. Krebs, 'Japan and the German-Japanese War', in Wegner, op. cit., p. 577.

104. Between 2 October and 15 November 1941 the losses by Army Group Centre increased by 87,400 men and reached a total of 316,569 men since the start of the campaign; see Reinhardt, op. cit., p. 146.

105. Colonel General Halder's insistence on 15–17 November 1941 that the attack against Moscow should continue is passed over in many portrayals or only mentioned as an aside; see, for example, Gräfin Schall-Riaucour, *Revolt and Obedience*, p. 172.

106. Discussion between Colonel General Guderian and the Commanding General of LIII Army Corps, General Karl Weisenberger, on 14 November 1941; see Lammers, *Reports*, p. 345.

107. Von Bock, op. cit., p. 325.

108. Ibid, p. 334.

109. Zhukov, *Memories and Thoughts*, p. 340.

110. Rauh, op. cit., p. 467.

111. Von Kotze, op. cit., p. 116.

112. This was the derogatory evaluation by the Commander-in-Chief of the Heer on 16 November 1941; see von Kotze, op. cit., p. 114.

113. The subsequent criticism by senior officers involved was primarily directed against the fact that an armoured corps belonging to Panzer Group 3 which had freedom of movement after the Vyazma pocket had been closed, was not immediately sent east towards Moscow but rather north-east to Kalinin; furthermore that important armoured forces of Panzer Group 4 were held back on the southern front of Vyazma for a relatively long time to guard against breakout attempts, instead of being sent in pursuit towards Moscow as quickly as possible; see Chales de Beaulieu, *Colonel General Erich Hoepner*, p. 200 et seq.

114. Blumentritt, *Overcoming the Crisis Before Moscow*, p. 108.

115. In summary, Reinhardt, 'Failure of the German Blitzkrieg Concept Before Moscow', in Rohwer and Jäckel, op. cit., p. 207.

116. See, for example, Meier-Welcker, *Notes by a General Staff Officer*, Introduction p. 18.

117. Samsonov, *The Battle for Moscow*, p. 193.

118. Jacobsen, *The Road to Partitioning the World*, p. 105.

119. Korkisch, *Pearl Harbor*, p. 243; in addition, Herde, 'Japan, Germany, and the United States', in Rohwer and Jäckel, op. cit., p. 52.

120. Bavendamm, op. cit., p. 410.

121. Lewin, *Did Ultra Decide the War?*, p. 283; also Post, *Pearl Harbor 1941*, p. 279.

122. Ibid, p. 279 et seq.

123. Of the five battleships sunk or run aground, only two had to be written off as a total loss. The remaining three battleships were heavily damaged. A

NOTES

total of 2335 officers and men were killed; see Korkisch, op. cit., p. 246 et seq. For a good summary see MGFA op. cit., vol. 6, p. 234 et seq.

124. One of the prime incidents was the duel between *USS Greer* and *U-652* on 4 September. See Rohwer, *The USA and the Battle in the Atlantic*, p. 95.

125. Syring, 'Hitler's Declaration of War Against America', in Michalka, *The Second World War*, p. 689 et seq.

126. Rohwer and Jäckel, op. cit., p. 209.

127. Reuth, op. cit., p. 492.

128. Reinhardt, op. cit., p. 258.

129. MGFA, op. cit., vol. 4, p. 699.

130. For Hitler's taking over supreme command of the Heer and the disputes within the officers' corps, see Heusinger, *Orders in Conflict*, p. 154 et seq.; Warlimont, *At Wehrmacht Headquarters*, p. 226 et seq.

131. MGFA, op. cit., vol. 4, p. 605 et seq.

132. Von Bock, op. cit., p. 354.

133. Reinhardt, op. cit., p. 221; Blumentritt, *Overcoming the Crisis Before Moscow*, p. 114.

134. *OKW War Diary 1942*, vol. 2, p. 1268 et seq.

III

1. Von Taysen, *Tobruk 1941*, p. 303.

2. Gundelach, *The Luftwaffe in the Mediterranean*, vol. I, p. 309 et seq.; MGFA, *The German Reich and the Second World War*, vol. 3, p. 622 et seq.

3. See statement by von Lüttichau in Rohwer, *Turn of the War December 1941*, p 179.

4. In comparison, MGFA, op. cit., vol. 6, p. 873.

5. Gundelach, op. cit., p. 336.

6. Ibid, p. 354.

7. See in detail, MGFA, op. cit., vol. 6, p. 331 et seq.

8. Salewski, *German Naval Leadership*, vol. II, p. 82 et seq.; Reuth, *Decision in the Mediterranean*, p. 150 et seq.

9. Contribution by Rahn in MGFA, op. cit., vol. 6, p. 337; another statement even claims losses of over 2.17 million tonnes; see Brennecke, *The Turn in the U-boat War*, p. 52.

10. Rohwer, *The USA and the Battle in the Atlantic*, p. 99.

11. MGFA, op. cit., vol. 6, p. 301.

12. Rahn, *Combat Readiness and Combat Power of German Submarines*, p. 74.

13. Ibid, p. 80.

14. Völker, *German Home Air Defence*, part I, p. 93.

15. Contribution by Boog in MGFA, op. cit., vol. 6, p. 493.

16. Völker, op. cit., p. 96 et seq.

17. MGFA, op. cit., vol. 6, p. 515.

18. Völker, op. cit., p. 97.

19. Boog, *The Luftwaffe Leadership*, p. 140.

20. For the deadline on 30 June 1943 the number of twin-engine fighters has not been taken into separate account, because these were listed in a single category together with bombers, so that the numerical split between offensive and defensive aircraft cannot be determined; see *List Strength of the Luftwaffe*, various tables in FA/MA, RL 2 III, 707, 713, 716–22.

21. Schustereit, *Risk*, p. 43.

22. Ibid, p. 67; in addition, Warlimont, *At Wehrmacht Headquarters*, p. 240.

23. See Rohde's detailed commentary to Reinhardt's book *The Turn Before Moscow*, in *Wehrwissenschaftliche Rundschau* 5/1977, p. 176.

24. For comparison, Wegner, 'From Life-Room to Death-Room' in J. Förster, *Stalingrad*, p. 19.

25. Wegner in MGFA, op. cit., vol. 6, p. 813.

26. Harrison, *Barbarossa*, p. 453 et seq.

27. Rühl, *Rise and Fall of the Russian Empire*, p. 502.

28. Wegner in MGFA, op. cit., vol. 6, p. 809.

29. From north to south, the following armies were involved: 40th (Bryansk Front), 21st, 28th, 38th, 9th, 37th, 12th, 18th and 56th.

30. Hubatsch, *Hitler's Directives*, p. 184.

31. MGFA, op. cit., vol. 6, p. 768; but Doerr, *Campaign to Stalingrad*, p. 9, already speaks of the Caucasus as having been the main objective.

32. Speer, *Memories*, p. 229.

33. See also the report on this meeting in Heusinger, *Orders in Conflict*, p. 176 et seq.; Heusinger, who was Chief of the Operations Department at the time, gives the impression that Halder had strongly argued in favour of an attack on Moscow in combination with the subse-

quent option of an attack on Leningrad. Such and similar considerations can also be found elsewhere in the literature, but do not stand up to critical evaluation. At best they can be regarded as a reflection of the normal informal discussions that went on within the General Staff, but in no way as the foundation of a formal, strategic-operational study prepared with the intention of making Hitler give up his Caucasus plan.

34. Hillgruber and Förster, *Two New Notations on 'Führer' Briefings*, p. 119.
35. Von Bock, *War Diary*, p. 408.
36. This is a presentation given by Gehlen to members of the War Academy on 9 June 1942 (FA/MA RH 2/2445).
37. MGFA, op. cit., vol. 6, table on p. 802.
38. Calculated according to 'Organization of the German Heer on 24 June 1942', in *OKW War Diary*, vol. II, part 2, p. 1372 et seq. In a calculation of forces on 15 June 1942 prepared by the General Staff, almost the same number of 165 2/2 divisions appears, see Appendix to OKH/op.Dept. (III) No. 420383/42, secret, Chief only, of 15 June 1942, in FA/MA RH 2/v. 429).
39. Without counting the security divisions, the quota of the divisions on the eastern front, including those on the Finnish front (total 172), came to over 77 per cent of the total potential (222 divisions). The overview by the General Staff lists total potential of 233 1/2 divisions on 15 June 1942, see FA/MA RH 2/v. 429.
40. Kasakov, *The Defensive Battles of the Soviet Bryansk Front*, part II, p. 530, note 28; Kerr, *The Mystery of Stalingrad*, p. 49 et seq.
41. Knyazkov, 'Soviet Strategy in 1942' in J. Förster, *Stalingrad, Event, Effect, Symbol*, p. 47.
42. Ibid, p. 44.
43. Kasakov, op. cit., part II, p. 530.
44. The drama of the battle of Kharkov is well presented in von Bock, op. cit., p. 429 et seq.
45. Kasakov, op. cit., part II, p. 528.
46. Von Bock, op. cit., pp. 441, 445.
47. Until mid-August 1942 Hungary provided 10 divisions, Italy 9 1/3 divisions, Romania 16 divisions and Slovakia one mobile division. When the campaign began on 28 June, there were only 29 divisions on the front or moving up. The German General Staff calculated the combat power of an allied division as being half that of a German division.
48. For details see Magenheimer, *Background and Roots of the Turn of the War 1942–43*, p. 151.
49. In fact, only the commander of the Eighteenth Army tried in the spring of 1942 to win over Hitler for an attack on Leningrad with an abandonment of the operation in the south, see: MGFA, op. cit., vol 6, p. 777; the sources do not reveal any concrete intentions by Supreme Command of Army Group Centre to conduct an offensive against Moscow, with certain limited local offensive intentions to stabilize and straighten the front ('Operation Derfflinger', 'Operation Tornado').
50. The advantage of a renewed attack on Moscow after the conditions had been prepared would also have been to force the bulk of the Soviet operational reserves into battle, and not to give the enemy the chance to withdraw in depth except by giving up Moscow. Furthermore, because of the relatively short distance to the objective, the logistic conditions would have been far better than was the case for the offensive in the south. After an offensive to clear the ground between the German Ninth and Sixteenth Armies, after linking the spearheads south of the Valdai Heights, and after cleaning up the partisan areas to the rear of Army Group Centre there would have been sufficient operational reserves (including the Eleventh Army) to carry out an attack against Moscow, for example, from the sector of the Second Army and the Second Panzer Army.
51. The more important descriptions include Wegner in MGFA, op. cit., vol. 6; Kehrig, *Stalingrad*; Doerr, *Campaign to Stalingrad*; J. Förster, op. cit.; Erickson, *Stalin's War with Germany*, vol. 1; Kerr, op. cit. I have refrained from citing the many popular articles and essays on this topic.
52. Kasakov, op. cit., p. 531; on Stalin's fears about an attack on Moscow, see Volkogonov, *Stalin*, p. 620.

53. In summary, Magenheimer, op. cit., p. 154.

54. The statement by Wegner in MGFA, op. cit., vol. 6, p. 880 that the attacking German armies were generally suffering from a lack of fast mobile forces is correct. At the time the only choice remaining was to give up a minor advantage in favour of a major one.

55. Wagener, *Advance of XXXX Panzer Corps*, p. 395 et seq.

56. Von Bock, op. cit., p. 470 et seq.

57. For the failure of the Soviet counter-attack and the extremely costly fighting see: Kerr, op. cit., p. 72; it is even claimed that the Fifth Tank Army was destroyed.

58. *OKW War Diary 1942*, part 2, p. 1284.

59. See the still valid summary of the operational planning in Doerr, op. cit., p. 21 et seq.

60. Wegner, 'From Life-Room to Death-Room', in J. Förster, *Stalingrad*, p. 29.

61. In total, after having released the Fourth Panzer Army in early August, Army Group A still comprised the First Panzer Army, the Seventeenth Army and, until early September, also the Romanian 3rd Army, which was then transferred to Army Group B. Reduction to five mobile German divisions came about through the release of the 'Großdeutschland' Division and the 22nd Panzer Division at the end of July to OKH, and later to the Sixth Army. See 'Organization of the German Heer on 12 August 1942' in *OKW War Diary 1942*, part 2, p. 1378 et seq.

62. Of the five divisions released, one was sent to reinforce Army Group Centre, which was engaged in heavy defensive fighting in August, and one, the 22nd Infantry Division, was to be converted to an airborne formation.

63. Egger, *Fortress Sevastopol*, p. 237.

64. Subsequently, two tank armies were added, namely the First and Fourth.

65. See Volkogonov, op. cit., p. 621 et seq.

66. See in detail, Hoffmann, *Caucasia*, p. 71 et seq.

67. On this, with harsh criticism of Churchill's and Roosevelt's policies, Falin, *Second Front*, p. 312 et seq.

68. Irving, *Battle in the Arctic Sea*, p. 381.

69. This is the accusation made by Falin, op. cit., p. 307.

70. III Panzer Corps took the oilfields and refineries at Maikop on 9 August. However, these had been so expertly destroyed that there was no possibility of exploiting them in the medium term.

71. For the defensive battle fought by Army Group Centre, see Conrady, *Rzhev 1942–43*; MGFA, op. cit., vol. 6, p. 906 et seq. In the case of the bulge in the front at Rzhev and Vyazma, a partial evacuation, for example to the line Cholm–Chirkovsky–Vyazma–Ugra, would have freed considerable forces as operational reserves.

72. Hermann, *68 Months of War*, p. 26. The author describes the deployment of the task force in unfavourable, restrictive terrain as 'a tactical milling about without compare'.

73. These were the 14th, 16th and 24th Panzer Divisions, to which the German 22nd and the Romanian 1st Panzer Division, as well as one or two motorized divisions, could have been added. On this question, see in detail Kehrig, op. cit., p. 96 et seq.

74. Volkogonov, op. cit., p. 627; Chor'kov in J. Förster, op. cit., p. 55.

75. For comparison, Zhukov, *Memories and Thoughts*, p. 374; during the extremely bitter fighting for the city centre, twelve German divisions had suffered such high losses by mid-November that they were considered to be 'burned out'.

76. These plans included, for example, the destruction of those Soviet armies which were conducting relief attacks against the northern flank of the Sixth Army in the bridgehead between the Don and the Volga, the elimination of the large Soviet land bridge on the southern bank of the Don, and 'Operation Heron' – the advance by armoured forces to take Astrakhan at the mouth of the Volga.

77. Schall-Riaucour, *General Halder*, p. 175.

78. Besides Kehrig's standard work see also his shorter summaries in J. Förster, op. cit., pp. 76–110 and *Stalingrad 1943*, p. 22 et seq. Among the many reports by survivors on the divisional level, see Löser, *Bitter Duty*.

79. Kehrig, op. cit., p. 97.

80. Kehrig in J. Förster, op. cit., p. 77.

81. Kehrig, op. cit., p. 95; in summary,

Philippi and Heim, *The Campaign against Soviet Russia*, p. 167.

82. See a summary of these discussions in MGFA, op. cit., vol. 6, p. 992 et seq.

83. See the still valid evaluation of the situation in Philippi and Heim, op. cit., p. 166.

84. Wilhelm, *Predictions of the Intelligence Department East*, pp. 47–8; Kehrig, op. cit., p. 101.

85. Cited according to G. Förster, *Queries about the Art of War*, p. 11. The army in question taken out of the front was the Third Panzer Army.

86. On 3 November Hitler had ordered bringing in the 6th Panzer Division and two infantry divisions from the western front to Army Group B, but because of the time required for their transportation, this measure came too late to support the threatened flank of the Sixth Army.

87. Heusinger, op. cit., p. 214; for comparison, Masson, *The German Army*, p. 240.

88. In summary, MGFA, op. cit., vol. 6, p. 958 et seq.

89. Zeitzler, *The First Two Planned Withdrawals by the German Army*, p. 110. It appears that during the first half of December Field Marshal von Manstein supported the withdrawal of the Caucasus army, and requested that III Panzer Corps with two armoured divisions be added to the forces that were to conduct the relief attack towards Stalingrad.

90. Von Manstein, *Lost Victories*, p. 334 et seq.

91. In summary, see Glantz and House, *When Titans Clashed*, p. 134.

92. An initial calculation by Army Group B of the quantity of supplies (particularly ammunition, fuel and food) required came to roughly 500 tonnes per day. On 24 November the Command of Army Group Don requested a daily supply of 400 tonnes in fuel and ammunition alone. Apparently Göring had promised 500 tonnes per day, whereas the Luftwaffe staff believed that 350 tonnes per day might be possible for a limited period. There is also a calculation according to which 940 tonnes per day would have been required. See in summary, J. Fischer, *On*

the *Decision to Supply Stalingrad by Air*, p. 7 et seq.; Kehrig, op. cit., p. 218 et seq.

93. Originally the breakout of the army was scheduled for 25–26 November, even if strong doubts were expressed about its success and the losses to be expected. See MGFA, op. cit., vol. 6, p. 1025 et seq.; Kehrig, *Sixth Army in the Stalingrad Pocket*, p. 91.

94. G. Förster, *Queries about the Art of Waging War*, p. 14; in addition, Volkogonov, op. cit., p. 629.

95. In summary, MGFA, op. cit., vol. 6, p. 1062. The former commander of the Soviet 62nd Army, W. I. Chuikov, came to a completely negative conclusion about a breakout as early as 23 November 1942 and believed this would have led to the destruction of the Sixth Army. See 'In den Steppen ohne Chancen' (In the Steppes with No Chance) in *Süddeutsche Zeitung* of 10 February 1978, p. 13.

96. Cited after Jacobsen, *The Road to Partitioning the World*, p. 219 et seq.

97. Masson, op. cit., p. 249; Philippi and Heim, op. cit., p. 196.

98. Zeitzler, op. cit., p. 111.

99. Numbers and designations from Overmans, 'The Other Face of War', in J. Förster, *Stalingrad*, p. 422; Kehrig, op. cit., p. 109. On the German side, five General Commands, fourteen infantry, three armoured and three motorized divisions, the 9th AA Division, the Romanian 20th Infantry Division and the 1st Cavalry Division as well as a Croatian infantry regiment took part in the surrender.

100. Combat power and morale of the Hungarian 2nd Army were far below that of the Romanian 3rd Army and were also assessed as very low by the Germans. The assessment of combat power and morale of the Italian 8th Army was similarly low. See von Kotze, *Army Adjutant to Hitler*, p. 132 et seq.; also J. Förster, *Stalingrad*, p. 55 et seq.

101. See Schwarz, *The Stabilization of the Eastern Front after Stalingrad*; and in summary, Schwarz, 'Between Stalingrad and Kursk', in J. Förster, *Stalingrad*, p. 113 et seq.

102. Glantz and House, op. cit., p. 142; based on new Russian information,

Schwarz, *The Stabilization of the Eastern Front after Stalingrad*, p. 234.

103. Falin, op. cit., p. 339.

104. In addition to the twenty-one German divisions destroyed, there were ten Hungarian, nine Italian and fifteen Romanian major formations which were either captured or almost completely annihilated.

105. Akhromeyev, *On the Basic Turn of the Second World War*, p. 6.

106. Gundelach, op. cit., vol. 1, pp. 364, 411, 426.

107. Wagner, *Briefings by the C-in-C of the Kriegsmarine*, p. 361.

108. Gundelach, op. cit., vol. 1, p. 357.

109. Hillgruber and Förster, op. cit., p. 119 et seq.; in addition: Reuth, *Decision in the Mediterranean*, p. 181 et seq.

110. *OKW War Diary*, Vol. 2, part 1, p. 373, entry of 21 May 1942.

111. In summary, Reuth, op. cit., p. 190.

112. Ibid, p. 20 et seq.

113. Very strongly accentuated in Baum and Weichold, *The War of the Axis Powers*, p. 231 et seq.

114. Gundelach, op. cit., p. 391.

115. At the beginning of the battle, Panzer Army Africa was only able to deploy 234 German tanks plus a handful of Italian tanks of equal value against 700 British tanks. See Hinrichs, *40 Years Ago*, p. 359 et seq.; Reinhard Stumpf in MGFA, op. cit., vol. 6, p. 681 et seq.

116. In summary, Magenheimer, *Turn of the War in the Mediterranean*, p. 229.

117. Santoni, *Ultra Wins in the Mediterranean*, p. 171 et seq.

118. Gundelach, op. cit., p. 438; MGFA, op. cit., vol. 6, pp. 694, 698. Panzer Army Africa consisted of the following German forces: two Panzer divisions (15th and 21st), one light motorized division (90th), one infantry division (164th), and one paratroop brigade which had originally been earmarked for the capture of Malta, and was in tactical command of 19th AA Division. Italian forces comprisd two armoured, four infantry, one paratroop and one motorized infantry division.

119. Salewski, op. cit., vol. II, p. 164.

120. These were the 6th, 7th and 10th Panzer Divisions and the subsequent SS Panzer Divisions 'Adolf Hitler', 'Das Reich' and 'Totenkopf'. On Paratroop Division 'Hermann Göring', see Kurowski, *From Special Police Troop 'Wecke' to the Paratroop Armoured Corps 'Hermann Göring'*, p. 59 et seq.

121. Gundelach, op. cit., vol. 1, p. 461.

122. Baum and Weichold, op. cit., p. 321.

123. J. Förster, *Strategic Considerations by the Wehrmacht Operations Staff*, p. 105.

124. The Germans lost three Panzer divisions, two light motorized divisions, two infantry divisions, the bulk of the 'Hermann Göring' and 'Von Manteuffel' divisions, two AA divisions (19th and 20th), and one paratroop brigade. The Italians lost three infantry divisions and one infantry, one armoured and one paratroop division. See also *OKW War Diary 1943*, part 1, p. 262; Gundelach, op. cit., vol. 2, p. 583.

IV

1. In summary, J. Förster, *Stalingrad*.

2. Martin, 'Japan and Stalingrad', in J. Förster, op. cit., p. 240.

3. Janssen, *The Speer Ministry*, p. 119 et seq.

4. Speer, *Memoirs*, p. 325.

5. Milward, *The Second World War*, p. 106.

6. Wagenführ, *German Industry during the War*, p. 46.

7. For details see Bornemann, *Secret Project Mittelbau*, p. 45 et seq.

8. In detail: index points in May 1943, 465; in October 1943, 454; in July 1944, 589; in December 1944, 598. In summary, Wagenführ, op. cit., p. 178 et seq.

9. Magenheimer, *The Air War over Germany*, p. 123.

10. To be noted in addition is Hitler's decree of 13 January 1943 on 'the comprehensive employment of men and women for the defence of the Reich'; see in summary, Klink, *Initiative to Act*, p. 34; *OKW War Diary 1943*, p. 64; Speer, op. cit., p. 264.

11. Neulen, *On the German Side*, p. 18 et seq.

12. Milward, 'Labour Policy and Productivity of the German War Economy' in Forstmeier and Volkmann, *War Economy and Armament*, p. 82; for the lead in

productivity enjoyed by Germany's opponents, see Zins, *Operation Citadel*, p. 14 et seq.

13. Boog, *The Strategic Bomb War*, p. 26.
14. Middlebrook, *The Night the Bombers Died*, p. 30.
15. MGFA, *The German Reich and the Second World War*, vol. 6, p. 536.
16. Verrier, *Bomber Offensive against Germany*, p. 327.
17. Boog, *Legends of the Bomber War*, p. 28.
18. War Cabinet Defence Committee Meeting of 18 April 1941, cited in Boog, *Legends of the Bomber War*, p. 29.
19. Bavendamm, *Roosevelt's War*, pp. 226, 333 et seq.
20. Boog, *Strategic Bomber War*, p. 27.
21. Middlebrook, op. cit., p. 30.
22. Völker, *German Home Air Defence*, part I, p. 99; *Luftflotte 8* lost 11 per cent of its complement in April, 9 per cent in June and 10 per cent in July 1943.
23. Bekker, *Attack Altitude 4000*, p. 514.
24. List strengths of the Luftwaffe 1941/42/43, FA/MA RL. 2III, pp. 707, 713, 716–28.
25. This was a recommendation by General Josef Kammhuber which was also supported by Adolf Galland, General of Fighter Forces, and Field Marshal Milch; see in detail, Golücke, *Schweinfurt and the Strategic Air War 1943*, p. 115.
26. Ibid, p. 115. Because of his energetic intervention in favour of the requirements of the night fighters, General Kammhuber fell into disfavour with the Luftwaffe leadership, was dismissed from his post as General of Night Fighters in mid-November 1943 and was transferred to Norway.
27. Schofield, 'The Role of the Admiralty Trade Divison' in Rohwer and Jäckel, *Radio Intelligence*, p. 164; Brennecke, *The Turn in the Submarine War*, p. 324.
28. Rohwer, 'The Effect of German and British Radio Intelligence on Convoy Operations' in Rohwer and Jäckel, op. cit., p. 193.
29. Brennecke, op. cit., p. 367.
30. Ibid, p. 409. This can already be seen from the fact that in May 1943 Dönitz was reckoning with a planned production of 30 submarines per month. During a briefing held on 31 May, Hitler increased this number to 40 submarines per month. However, given the war and armaments situation, particularly the lack of workers, this directive came too late. See Salewsky, *German Naval Leadership*, vol. II, p. 283 et seq.
31. Calculated according to *OKW War Diary* 1943, part 1, p. 262.
32. MGFA, op. cit., vol. 4, p. 270.
33. On 11 May 1943 Luftwaffe Command East was redesignated Luftwaffe Command 6; see Klink, op. cit., p. 191.
34. Gundelach, *The German Luftwaffe in the Mediterranean*, vol. 2, p. 584.
35. Weißbecker, 'If Germans lived here...' in H.-E. Volkmann, *The Image of Russia in the Third Reich*, p. 45 et seq.
36. Boelcke, 'Do You Want Total War?', p. 451. It should be pointed out in this context that from time to time Goebbels also favoured a peaceful solution with the Soviet Union, as is suggested by some of his statements, for example on 28 July 1942, or his discussion with Hitler on 23 September 1943.
37. Reuth, p. 517 et seq.
38. H.-E. Volkmann, *The Vlasov Operation*, p. 124, note 30.
39. Fröhlich, *General Vlasov*, p. 152.
40. Oberländer, 'Alliance or Exploitation', Memorandum 6 of 22 June 1943, copy in the possession of the author; see also Oberländer, 'Six Memoranda from the Second World War'.
41. In early 1943 Captain Oberländer was relieved of his position as Commander of Special Formation Bergmann and discharged from the Wehrmacht on 11 November 1943. It was only towards the end of 1944 that he found a new position on the staff of General Vlasov. Canaris's defence of Oberländer allegedly cost the Intelligence Chief much of Hitler's confidence.
42. H.-E. Volkmann, op. cit., p. 126.
43. Talk by Strik-Strikfeldt before Ic officers in Posnan on 6 February 1943. The author is grateful to Dr Elmar Walter, Graz, for kindly giving him a copy of this talk.
44. It is remarkable, however, that in 1942–3 a change of attitude towards the peoples of the Soviet Union, in the sense of better treatment, became apparent within the ranks of the SS leadership. For example, the setting up

of an Ukrainian volunteer force was initiated, for which almost 80,000 Ukrainians had applied by June 1943. In actual fact, only the 14th Galician SS Volunteer Division was set up in the summer of 1943. See Bihl, *Ukrainians as a Part of the Armed Forces of the German Reich*, p. 28 et seq.

45. Hesse, *The Soviet Partisan War*, p. 195 et seq.
46. In summary, Fleischhauer, *The Chance for a Separate Peace*, p. 81 et seq.
47. J. Schröder, *Attempts to Eliminate the Eastern Front*, p. 18 et seq.
48. *OKW War Diary 1943*, part 1, p. 213; J. Schröder, op. cit., p. 21.
49. Martin, *Negotiations about Separate Peace Agreements*, p. 101 et seq. The German-Soviet feelers were continued until October 1943. By a note of 12 November Molotov informed the Western Allies of the Soviet feelers via representatives in Stockholm. It appears that Stalin took this step in order to strengthen his political position vis-à-vis Great Britain and the USA. From this point on, however, there could no longer be talk of a serious intention by the Soviets to negotiate a separate peace with Germany.
50. Martin, op. cit., p. 112, note 90; Mastny, *Moscow's Road to the Cold War*, pp. 91 et seq., 98, whereby Stalin's willingness to negotiate is portrayed against the backdrop of maintaining the appearance of a correct conduct towards the Western Powers.
51. Falin, *Second Front*, p. 356 et seq.
52. Ibid, p. 374, where the claim is made that 'the Prime Minister did not tire of sabotaging all plans which contained any intention of crossing the Channel in the period between June and August of 1943'.
53. On the 'lack of fidelity by the British', Fleischhauer, op. cit, p. 103; compare Hillgruber, *Soviet Foreign Policy*, p. 83 et seq.
54. Compare Fleischhauer, op. cit., p. 122.
55. J. Schröder, op. cit., p. 23; with similar argument, p. 33.
56. Von Kotze, *Army Adjutant to Hitler*, p. 116.
57. Speer, op. cit., p. 282.
58. Zeitzler, *The First Two Planned With-*

drawals by the German Army, p. 116 et seq.; Klink, op. cit., p. 82, speaks of 22 divisions that could have been freed in the course of a withdrawal. However, a study in detail shows that besides fifteen infantry divisions, only 2nd, 5th and 12th Panzer Divisions, 14th and 36th Motorized Divisions, and the SS Cavalry Division were freed.

59. These were 28 German divisions (including four Luftwaffe field divisions), the Spanish 250th Division and an SS brigade of the Eighteenth Army. See schematic organization of 29 March 1943 according to MGFA, op. cit., vol. 6, p. 1085.
60. For details see Klink, op. cit., p. 84.
61. Heusinger, *Orders in Conflict*, p. 247; Klink, op. cit., p. 57 et seq.
62. For background information see Heinrici and Hauck, *Citadel*, part I, p. 469; in summary, Ostertag, *The Greatest Tank Battle in History*, p. 421.
63. Klink, op. cit., p. 95.
64. Heinrici and Hauck, op. cit. part II, p. 544; with similar argument, Ostertag, op. cit., p. 422.
65. Führer Decree No. 46: Directives for the increased fight against armed bands in the east, 18 August 1942, in Hubatsch, *Hitler's Directives*, p. 201 et seq.
66. Hesse, op. cit., p. 192.
67. Ibid, p. 195.
68. Ibid, p. 248 et seq.
69. Klink, op. cit., p. 52 et seq.
70. Solovjov, *The Battle of Kursk*, p. 15. Even though this is a propaganda-type brochure, the facts listed are similar to those contained in most Soviet literature.
71. Von Manstein, *Lost Victories*, p. 482; Heinrici and Hauck, op. cit., p. 473. The operational idea was to withdraw both southern armies of Army Group South to the lower Dnieper and then attack the advancing enemy in the right flank with a strong Panzer army to be deployed in the Kharkov area and encircle him by an advance towards the Sea of Azov. According to von Manstein's calculations, however, this would have required far stronger forces than the army group possessed.
72. MGFA, op. cit., vol. 6, p. 1081 et seq.
73. Warlimont, *At Wehrmacht Headquar-*

ters, p. 347; Heinrici and Hauck, op. cit., part II, p. 534.

74. Klink, op. cit., p. 194 et seq. However, the estimations provided by Intelligence Department East were mainly restricted to listing Soviet options and remained vague; see Wilhelm, *Predictions by Intelligence Department East*, p. 55.

75. Pron'ko, 'Soviet Strategy in 1943', in J. Förster, op. cit., p. 318; Solovjov, op. cit., p. 29; Heinrici and Hauck, p. cit., p. 533, note 47.

76. In summary, Klink, op. cit., p. 204 et seq.; compared to this the figures given by Piekalkievicz, *Operation Citadel*, p. 111, appear to be too high. It should be added that including the operational and strategic STAVKA reserves, in the Kursk area in early July there were seventeen armies, including three tank armies, and numerous armoured and motorized corps with large supporting forces. To the north of these, in the Orel bulge opposite the German Second Panzer Army there were five Soviet armies in the front line and four further armies, including two tank armies in reserve, awaiting the best opportunity to attack the advancing German Ninth Army in its rear.

77. *OKW War Diary 1943*, part 1, p. 66.

78. Army Group South's attack forces consisted of the Fourth Panzer Army and Army Unit Kempf, out of which the Eighth Army was later formed; numbers according to Heinrici and Hauck, op. cit., p. 531, note 41; Klink, op. cit., p. 142.

79. Calculated according to Hahn, *Weapons and Secret Weapons of the German Army*, vol. II, p. 237; also: Middeldorf, *Operation 'Citadel'*, part II, p. 502.

80. Calculated according to Klink, op. cit., pp. 112, 121, 208. In addition to these there were the reserves of both army groups consisting of five armoured divisions (5th, 8th, 17th, 23rd and SS division 'Viking'). If one includes the 23rd Panzer Division and the 'Viking' Division, the number of tanks and self-propelled guns deployed rises to about 2050. In early July the total number of available combat-ready tanks (excluding Panzer II, scout and captured tanks) in both army groups was about 2000, and the number of available operational self-propelled guns was 742 (there were a further 47 in repair). See Hahn, op. cit., vol. II, p. 237.

81. These were mainly the 'Panther' tank, of which 196 were deployed during the operation, the 'Tiger I' heavy tank and the 'Ferdinand' light tank with its 8.8cm gun (deployed in the Panzerjäger formations 653 and 654), furthermore, self-propelled guns such as the 15cm 'Hummel' (Bumblebee) howitzer mounted on the chassis of Panzer III/IV, the 10.5cm 'Wespe' (Wasp) howitzer on the chassis of Panzer II, and the heavy 8.8cm 43/41 'Hornisse' (Hornet) anti-tank gun on the chassis of Panzer III/IV.

82. Heinrici and Hauck, op. cit., part II, p. 531 et seq.; according to Heusinger, op. cit., p. 256, the General Staff even considered a postponement to 12 June as being acceptable.

83. In addition to the attack forces of the Ninth Army, the Fourth Panzer Army and Army Unit Kempf, the Second Army deployed on the western edge of the Kursk salient had the assignment of tying down the enemy. In the sector of Army Group Centre the bulk of the 36th Panzer Grenadier Division, and in the sector of Army Group South, the 23rd Panzer and SS 'Viking' Divisions, were being held in reserve as reinforcements or for the repulse of counter-attacks. On 9 July, the 198th Infantry Division, which had been freed by the First Panzer Army to reinforce Army Unit Kempf, was added to these forces. Also see *OKW War Diary 1943*, part 2, p. 732 et seq.

84. Klink, op. cit., p. 191 et seq.; these were VIII Air Corps of *Luftflotte 4* and 1st Air Division of *Luftflotte 6*.

85. Pron'ko, op. cit., p. 317; Ostertag, op. cit., p. 423; among the air forces there were two air armies, parts of the Fifth Air Army (belonging to the Steppe Front), and of the Seventeenth Air Army (belonging to the South-west Front), plus parts of the long-range flying forces and the home defence forces.

86. See in summary, Battle Reports of the Ninth Army and the Second Panzer Army about the Battle in the Orel Bulge from 5 July to 18 August 1943,

published by Army High Command 9, FA/MA, sig. H 14-25/6; Klink, op. cit., pp. 242, 262; Zins, Operation Citadel, p. 131 et seq.; Piekalkievicz, op. cit.
87. Battle Reports ..., p. 2 et seq.
88. Colonel General Guderian, Inspector General of Panzer Forces, had already urgently warned Hitler on 10 May against undertaking 'Operation Citadel'. See: Guderian, *Memoirs of a Soldier*, p. 280.
89. See in summary, Heinrici and Hauck, op. cit., part III, p. 582.
90. The numerical calculation of German tanks and self-propelled guns only reflects the operational vehicles and does not include the light tanks (Panzer II), captured tanks (T34) or scout tanks, for which reason a certain margin for error still has to be accepted.
91. Von Manstein, op. cit., p. 503; furthermore, on 13 July one-third of the forces of VIII Air Corps had to be released for the support of the Second Panzer Army and the Ninth Army, both of which were under heavy pressure by the Soviets on the Orel bulge.
92. See the 'experience report' of the Fourth Panzer Army for the period of 5–22 July in Heinrici and Hauck, op. cit., part III, p. 589, note 91; however, the combat-ready strength of the armoured formations dropped to 40 per cent to 50 per cent of initial strength. The exaggerated Soviet claims can be seen, for example, in that the number of German tanks and self-propelled guns which allegedly took part in the 'tank battle of Prochorovka' on 12 July were given as 650–700 (against 850 on the Soviet side); it was only Marshal Vasilevsky in 1983 who gave a more accurate number, namely a total of roughly 1200 armoured vehicles on both sides; cited in Pron'ko, op. cit., p. 320.
93. Solovyov, op. cit., p. 60.
94. Pron'ko, op. cit., p. 325.
95. Akhromeyev, *The Basic Turn in the Second World War*, p. 9.
96. In comparison, Middeldorf, op. cit. part II, p. 503.
97. Falin, op. cit., p. 376.
98. Ibid, p. 376.
99. Battle Reports ..., p. 6 et seq.
100. For the war plans of the Allies see

Baum and Weichold, *The War of the Axis Powers*, p. 331 et seq.
101. In detail, Ben Arie, *The Battle of Monte Cassino*, p. 24 et seq.; Wilhelmsmeyer, *The War in Italy*, p. 19.
102. Gundelach, op. cit., p. 605.
103. *OKW War Diary 1943*, part 2, p. 735.
104. Wilhelmsmeyer, op. cit., p. 21 et seq.
105. Baum and Weichold, op. cit., p. 328.
106. Gundelach, op. cit., part II, p. 647 et seq.
107. Ibid, pp. 597, 605.
108. In comparison, Baum and Weichold, op. cit., p. 330; Warlimont, op. cit., p. 335.
109. In summary, J. Schröder, *Italy's Exit from the War*, p. 176 et seq.
110. Ben Arie, op. cit., p. 40.
111. *OKW War Diary 1943*, part 2, p. 1451.
112. This was the bulk of the 16th and 26th Panzer Divisions, the Paratroop-Panzer Division 'Hermann Göring', and the 15th and 29th Panzer Grenadier Divisions; of these forces, two divisions were deployed in the Calabrian area and three in the Salerno–Naples–Gaeta sector; the 1st Paratroop Division secured parts of Apulia.
113. Wilhelmsmeyer, op. cit., p. 140. In comparison see Ben Arie, op. cit., p. 56. After the disarming of Italian troops in northern and central Italy Army Group B reported 415,000 prisoners.
114. Wilhelmsmeyer, op. cit., p. 163 et seq.
115. While the British were still considering an amphibious landing in the Balkans, this was opposed by the political intentions of the American leadership and by Stalin's demand for a second front which he had emphatically raised at the conference in Teheran. See A. Fischer, *Teheran–Yalta–Potsdam*, p. 27 et seq. In contrast to this, Hitler regarded the south-eastern area as being especially threatened, particularly from the summer of 1943 on, and intended to defend it totally despite the growing partisan activities.
116. Ibid, pp. 62, 72. This defensive line had an overall length of just under 135 km and was based on terrain particularly well suited for defence. See Wilhelmsmeyer, op. cit., p. 196. See also Jackson, *The Battle for Italy*, p. 130.

117. On the question of an airborne landing near Rome, Baum and Weichold, op. cit., p. 360; Ben Arie, op. cit., p. 53.

V

1. Korkisch, *The Strategic Air War in Europe and Asia*, part II, p. 211.
2. Murray, *Reflections on the Combined Bomber Offensive*, p. 76.
3. In detail, Golücke, *Schweinfurt and the Strategic Air War*, p. 32 et seq.
4. Also see Völker, *German Home Air Defence*, part I, p. 99 et seq.
5. Hahn, *Weapons and Secret Weapons of the German Army*, pp. 43, 52, 60, 64.
6. Ibid, pp. 80, 83.
7. Guderian, *Memoirs of a Soldier*, p. 179.
8. It must be underlined that the German arms industry suffered from limitations that were not only due to damage to production facilities. These included lack of workers, particularly skilled workers in certain sectors, shortage of some raw materials, the narrow margins by which productivity could be increased, and the time pressure under which research and development were placed. Without interference by air attacks, it has been estimated that German productivity could only have been increased by about 20 per cent.
9. Korkisch, op. cit., p. 208.
10. Milward, *The Second World War*, p. 320.
11. For details see Heitmann, *'Gomorrah'*, p. 1 et seq.
12. Irving, *Tragedy of the Luftwaffe*, p. 300.
13. Gundelach, *Luftwaffe in the Mediterranean*, part II, p. 713; however, this does not include twin-engine fighters. If these were to be included the ratio would be 3.6 to 1.
14. Ibid, p. 719.
15. Golücke, op. cit., p. 113, claiming General of Fighters Adolf Galland as his source.
16. For the deployment of the German fighter forces in 1942–3 see MGFA, *The German Reich and the Second World War*, vol. 6 (contribution by Horst Boog), map according to p. 540.
17. For organization see Völker, op. cit., part I, p. 105 et seq.
18. Such a radical shortening of the front was being considered and repeatedly recommended by senior commanders including von Manstein for Army Groups South and A. See von Manstein, *Lost Victories*, pp. 529 et seq., 544, 552.
19. Koch, *Flak*, p. 651.
20. MGFA, op. cit., vol. 6, p. 552.
21. Cited according to Golücke, op. cit., p. 154, referring to Blöthner, *German AA in the 2nd World War*, p. 534 et seq. The production figures for the 8.8cm, 10.5cm and 12.8cm AA were about 5930 (1943), about 7730 (1944) and about 900 (1945), see Hahn, *Weapons and Secret Weapons of the German Army*, vol. 1, p. 208.
22. Golücke, op. cit., p. 169.
23. For details see Tuider, *The Luftwaffe in Austria*, p. 55 et seq.
24. Blöthner, op. cit., p. 537.
25. ÖMZ 3/1985, p. 206; at this point there were a total of 28 AA divisions and 15 independent AA brigades.
26. Tessin, *Formations and Troops of the Wehrmacht and Waffen SS*, vol. 1, p. 365.
27. Speer, *Memoirs*, p. 291.
28. For details see Ludwig, *German AA Rockets during the Second World War*, p. 90; Boog, *The Luftwaffe Leadership*, p. 207.
29. Piekalkiewicz, *The Air War 1939–1945*, p. 606; for comparison see Murray, op. cit., p. 90; Speer, *The Slave State*, p. 289 et seq.
30. For comparison see: Boog, *Strategic Bomber War*, p. 27; also Boog, *The Luftwaffe Leadership*, p. 208 et seq. in which the limited efficiency of AA guns compared to AA rockets and fighters is illustrated.
31. Golücke, op. cit., p. 198, chart 18.
32. Hölsken, *The V Weapons*, p. 101; Bornemann, *Secret Project Mittelbau*, p. 45; Speer, *Memoirs*, p. 380.
33. Cited according to Golücke, op. cit., p. 385; Koch, op. cit. p. 250.
34. Golücke, op. cit., p. 292.
35. Verrier, *Bomber Offensive*, p. 186.
36. Middlebrook, *The Night the Bombers Died*, p. 239.
37. Koch, op. cit., p. 255.
38. Speer, *Memoirs*, p. 357; in addition: Murray, op. cit., p.79.
39. Boog, *The Luftwaffe Leadership*, p. 140 et seq.
40. Boog, *Luftwaffe and Technology*, p. 69.
41. Nowarra, *German Air Armament 1933–1945*, vol. 3, p. 225.

42. Kosin, *Development of German Fighter Aircraft*, p. 194.
43. Speer, *Memoirs*, p. 431.
44. For summary see Wolf, *Air Attacks against German Industry*.
45. See for example the measures taken to limit damage after the heavy destruction of the ball-bearing plants in Schweinfurt on 14 October 1943, in Golücke, op. cit., p. 357 et seq.
46. Milward, op. cit., p. 314.
47. Golücke, op. cit., p. 411.
48. See the conclusions drawn at an international symposium held in Freiburg in September 1988 in which British and American historians of the air war took part, in Günther Gillessen, *Bomben auf Städte* (Bombs on Cities), *Frankfurter Allgemeine* of 22 September 1988, p. 12.
49. Ibid. Similarly, but less vociferous, Boog, *Strategic Bomber War*, p. 28. The occasional claim that the Luftwaffe began the bombing war against the civilian population with the raids against Coventry on 14–15 November 1940 cannot be upheld, because the German attacks were aimed at the twelve armaments plants there, particularly the aircraft plants. Also see *Coventry war ein Rüstungszentrum erster Ordnung* (Coventry was an arms centre of the first magnitude) in *Frankfurter Allgemeine* of 16 January 1995, p. 8.
50. Korkisch, op. cit., part II, p. 210; Völker, op. cit., part 1, p. 111. The main issue was the decisive reduction in the production of aircraft fuel, with grave repercussions on training and deployment of the Luftwaffe.
51. In comparison, *OKW War Diary 1944/45*, part 1, p. 306.
52. Gundelach, *Threat from the West*, p. 312.
53. Hubatsch, *Hitler's Directives*, p. 233.
54. Warlimont, *At Wehrmacht Headquarters*, p. 431.
55. Wegmüller, *Repulse of the Invasion*, p. 132 et seq.
56. Middeldorf, *Operation 'Citadel'*, part II, p. 503.
57. For details see Wilhelmsmeyer, *The War in Italy*, p. 206 et seq.
58. Ben Arie, *The Battle of Monte Cassino*, p. 232 et seq.
59. Schematic war organization on 15 April 1944, FA/MA, sig. RH 2/v.353.

Originally two armoured divisions were to have been freed and sent to France. In addition, two valuable airborne divisions remained tied down in Italy.
60. Ibid, last page. By mid-May forces had risen to 24 divisions including the Croatians. It should be noted that the claim by some British historians made after the summer of 1991 that from 1943 on the Germans had 30 divisions deployed in Yugoslavia to combat the Tito partisans is false or misleading. Only if one includes all German-led Croatian formations, the Cossack division and the two Bulgarian corps with seven divisions does the number add up to 28 major formations in mid-April. However, these were spread throughout the whole south-eastern area including Crete.
61. Forstner, 'Partisan war', in Schmidl, *Enemy or Friend?*, p. 139 et seq.; in addition: Wiener, *Partisan War in the Balkans*, p. 120.
62. Schematic war organization on 15 April 1944, FA/MA, sig. RH 2/v.353.
63. After the success of the invasion in Normandy Hitler deplored the absence of II SS-Panzer Corps as operational reserve. There is much to be said for the claim that if these two powerful armoured divisions had been deployed in a favourable area and utilized together with the other armoured reserves, they could have contributed much to a defeat of the invasion.
64. Philippi and Heim, *Campaign against the Soviet Union*, p. 227; in summary, Magenheimer, *The Law of Gravity*, p. 22.
65. Schematic war organization on 15 April 1944, FA/MA, sig. RH 2/v.353. The picture presented is as follows: LVI Panzer Corps (belonging to Second Army) with 4th and 5th Panzer Divisions; Army Group North Ukraine: 1st, 7th, 16th, 17th, 19th Panzer Division and battle groups from 6th and 8th Panzer Divisions, 9th and 10th SS-Panzer Divisions, 20th Panzer Grenadier Division; Army Group South Ukraine: 3rd, 13th, 14th, 24th Panzer Divisions, SS-Panzer Division 'Totenkopf', Panzer Grenadier Division 'Großdeutschland', 10th Panzer Grenadier Division.
66. 'Strategic Overview and Distribution of the Total Forces of the German Army,

13 April 1944', published in Jung, *The Ardennes Offensive 1944/45*, p. 270 et seq.; in addition: *OKW War Diary*, vol. 4, part 1, p. 301 et seq.

67. See, for example, Wegmüller, op. cit; Ose, *Decision in the West*; Ruge, *Rommel and the Invasion*; Rückbrodt, *The Invasion in Normandy 1944*, p. 85 et seq.

68. Ose, op. cit., p. 72.

69. Wegmüller, op. cit., p. 122 et seq.

70. For details on the 'Panzer controversy' see Wegmüller, op. cit., p. 133 et seq.; Ose, op. cit., p. 47 et seq.; Irving, *Rommel*, p. 469.

71. See Ruge, op. cit., p. 510 and again in *Europäische Wehrkunde 4/1980*, p. 196. The author gives the impression that Rommel intended to move two armoured divisions that were not under his command to the coast.

72. Zimmermann, *The Atlantic Wall from Dunkirk to Cherbourg*, with exact descriptions of all the fortifications.

73. Rückbrodt, op. cit., p. 190.

74. Warlimont, op. cit., p. 438 et seq.; Irving, op. cit., pp. 455, 460, 467 et seq.; Ruge, op. cit., p. 149; also see Gerhard Weinberg, *'Unternehmen Overlord'* ('Operation Overlord'), in *Die Zeit*, 3 June 1994, extra, p. 39.

75. *OKW War Diary*, vol IV, part 1, p. 303.

76. Ruge, op. cit., p. 512.

77. Von Stiotta, *The Atlantic Wall*, p. 270. The author wishes to thank Herrn Hofrat Dr Peter Broucek for his advice and permission to look into the archives cited.

78. Ose, op. cit., p. 84.

79. Von Stiotta, op. cit., p. 280 et seq. Von Stiotta's report is a valuable source of information not only for the defensive preparations in the sector of the Seventh Army; he also gives many details on the assessment of the situation by Rommel and the Inspector General of Armoured Forces, Colonel General Guderian. The conclusion that emerges is that only very few of the senior commanders paid Normandy the attention it deserved as the main landing area of the Allies.

80. This procedure was selected to spare the landing craft the losses which would have been expected had they run into the many prepared obstacles at high tide.

81. For details see Lewin, 'Radio Intelligence and Radio Deception during the Allied Invasion in Normandy' in Rohwer and Jäckel, *Radio Intelligence and its Role in the Second World War*, p. 202 et seq.

82. Hastings, *Operation Overlord*.

83. *OKW War Diary*, vol. IV, part 1, p. 298.

84. Gaull, *The Luftwaffe during the Invasion*, p. 136.

85. Lewin, op. cit., p. 214.

86. Ibid, p. 220; also: Rückbrodt, op. cit., p. 192; Irving, *Rommel*, p. 510; Ose, op. cit., p. 81.

87. *OKW War Diary*, vol. IV, part 1, p. 305.

88. Gaull, op. cit., p. 139.

89. Weinberg, *A World in Arms*, p. 720.

90. Ose, op. cit., p. 79; the existing 37 divisions were subsequently to be reinforced by a further 40 US divisions.

91. For this ticklish topic which caused so much controversy, see Rückbrodt, op. cit., p. 190 and reply by Oscar Reile in *Wehrwissenschaftliche Rundschau* 3/1979, p. 82; also Ose, op. cit., p. 101.

92. Hillgruber and Hümmelchen, *Chronicle of the Second World War*, p. 214 et seq.

93. According to other expert opinion, 9 June was the decisive day on which the elimination of the beachhead by offensive means finally failed. See Warlimont, op. cit., p. 458.

94. Hastings, op. cit., p. 356 et seq.

95. Weinberg, op. cit., p. 729.

96. This emphatic thesis is propounded by Falin, *Second Front*, p. 427 et seq.

97. For details see: Hölsken, op. cit., p. 107 et seq.

98. Ibid, pp. 109, 117.

99. Reuth, *Goebbels*, p. 542 et seq.

100. Hillgruber and Hümmelchen, op. cit., p. 235.

101. Wilhelm, *Predictions by Military Intelligence East*, p. 59 et seq.

102. For details see Niepold, *Central Eastern Front June '44*, pp. 13, 33. The shortening of the front of Army Group Centre by roughly 1000 km is due to command of LVI Panzer Corps having been transferred to Army Group North Ukraine at the end of May.

103. In summary see Schematic War Organization on 15 May 1944 in FA/MA, sig. RH 2/v.353.

104. Caspar, *Collapse of Army Group Centre*, p. 472.

NOTES

105. Niepold, *Central Eastern Front*, p. 20.
106. Caspar, op. cit., p. 475; Niepold, *Leadership of Army Group Centre*, p. 468. There are also claims of losses of up to 350,000 men. For comparison see 'Forces of Army Group Centre' in Hinze, *Drama on the Eastern Front*, p. 424 et seq.
107. For comparison see *OKW War Diary*, vol. IV, part 1, p. 15. Of these, 150,000 men were taken prisoner.
108. Cited according to Ose, op. cit., p. 335.
109. Jung, *The Ardennes Offensive*, p. 201.
110. Warlimont, op. cit., p. 514.
111. For comparison: Fest, *Hitler*, p. 981 et seq.
112. Speer, *Memoirs*, p. 421.
113. Jung, *The Ardennes Offensive*, p. 103 et seq.
114. *OKW War Diary*, Vol. IV, part 1, p. 387.
115. Ibid, p. 376 et seq.
116. Wagener, *Controversial Questions on the Ardennes Offensive*, p. 48.
117. Jung, op. cit., p. 112 et seq.
118. Guderian, *Memoirs of a Soldier*, p. 338.
119. Müller-Hillebrand, *The Heer. Development of its Organizational Structure*, vol. III, table opposite p. 274.
120. These were eleven Volksgrenadier and two paratroop divisions, the former not having the combat power of normal infantry divisions.
121. According to a calculation based on Jung, op. cit., p. 136 et seq., 343 et seq. The 1700 armoured vehicles mentioned on p. 138 could be correct if one includes all self-propelled guns, light tanks and mobile anti-tank guns, including the self-propelled guns of the Volksgrenadier and infantry divisions as well as those at corps and army level and those belonging to the Waffen-SS. The number of replacement tanks allotted was about 125.
122. Jung, op. cit., p. 133, where he analyses the war diary of C-in-C West, note of 15 December 1944 concerning the fuel situation.
123. Masson, *The German Army*, p. 444; in addition, Speer, op. cit., p. 415.
124. Frieser, *Blitzkrieg Legend*, p. 440.
125. Wagener, *Controversial Questions on the Ardennes Offensive*, p. 26.
126. For details see: Schinzer, *Concentra-*

tion of Troops and Success in Attack, p. 130 et seq.
127. Jung, op. cit., p. 172.
128. Guderian, op. cit., p. 347 et seq.
129. Jung, op. cit., p. 190 et seq.
130. Wagener, op. cit., p. 54.
131. In comparison, Guderian, op. cit., p. 351 et seq.
132. Schematic Organization on 31 December 1944, General Staff of the Heer/Operations Department III; FA/MA III H 410/4.
133. Note of 8 September 1944, OKH/General Staff of the Heer/Operations Department Ia to War Diary vol. 3, FA/MA III H 402/3.
134. Organization of 26 November 1944, *OKW War Diary*, vol. IV, part 2, p. 1884 et seq.
135. For details see XXX *Defensive Battles on the Northern Flank*, p. 104 et seq.
136. In summary, Duffy, *Storming the Reich*, p. 78; Middeldorf, *The Defensive Battle in the Baranov Bridgehead*, p. 187 et seq.
137. 'Assumed forces facing the German eastern front', 8 January 1945, OKH/General Staff of the Heer/Intelligence Dept. (I), excerpt from a briefing note, FA/MA, H 3/196.
138. *History of the Second World War 1939-1945*, twelve volumes, group of Soviet editors, German translation, East Berlin 1982, vol. 10, p. 49; slightly at variance, Zeidler, *The End of the War in the East*, p. 81.
139. *History of the Great Patriotic War of the Soviet Union*, vol. 5, East Berlin, 1967, p. 36. Compare, Organization of the Soviet Field Army, 25 December 1944, OKH/General Staff of the Heer/Intelligence Dept., FA/MA H 3/80.
140. Jodl, 'War Diary, 29 December 1944', quoted according to Jung, op. cit., p. 182.
141. OKH/General Staff of the Heer/Intelligence Dept. East (I), No. 4640/44, secret, reply to question on possible change in Soviet overall operational objectives, situation: 22 December 1944, FA/MA III H, 402/11.
142. Falin, op. cit., p. 457.
143. The military importance of the defence of the strongpoints is explained in detail by Duffy, op. cit., p. 225 et seq.
144. Duffy, op. cit., p. 299; Hillgruber, *Two Different Downfalls*, p. 34. For

details see Nawratil, *Crimes of Deportation against Germans*, p. 101 et seq.

145. See for example the hate-filled proclamation by Marshal Zhukov, C-in-C of the 1st Byelorussian Front, of 6 January 1945, FA/MA RH 19 XV.

146. For the protracted reprisal propaganda of Ilya Ehrenburg see Zeidler, op. cit., p. 114 et seq., particularly p. 120; also Duffy, op. cit., p. 299; Friedrich, *The Law of War*, p. 555.

147. This basic thesis is advanced with convincing arguments by Zeidler, op. cit., pp. 65, 207.

148. Reichling, *Numbers of Expelled Germans*, p. 29 et seq. It should be noted, however, that according to other calculations the losses were as many as 2.8 million, see Nawratil, op. cit.

149. *OKW War Diary*, vol. IV, part 2, pp. 1150, 1306 et seq.

150. The garrison of 'Fortress Budapest' consisted of the IX SS-Mountain Corps and the Hungarian I Army Corps comprising approximately 70,000 men. Before the Sixth SS-Panzer Army could advance to the attack, the garrison surrendered on 12 February 1945. Only small groups succeeded in breaking out.

151. These are the combined forces of Army Groups Courland, North, Vistula, Centre and South, calculated according to wartime organization on 1 March 1945, *OKW War Diary*, vol. IV, part 2, p. 1895 et seq. At this time Army Group Courland still comprised 22 major formations.

152. *Auseinandersetzung mit der Geschichtsschreibung über den letzten Krieg* (Discussion of historic writing about the last war), in *Osteuropa* 5/1989, A 207. On the symposium of the historians, see also Afanassiev, *Russia – Despotism or Democracy*, p. 57.

153. Volkogonov, *Stalin*, p. 598.

154. *Voenny Vestnik* (Military Bulletin), special issue April 1990, p. 11.

155. Gorbachev, *Stalin schuld an Millionen von Toten* (Stalin Guilty of Millions of Dead), in *Süddeutsche Zeitung* of 10 May 1990, p. 1.

156. Falin, op. cit., p. 495.

157. 'This is how the lie is being sustained' in *Sovjetskaja Rossija* of 14 February 1988, German translation by Novosti press agency.

158. *UdSSR: Massenrepressalien, Bevölkerungsverluste und Deportationen seit 1917/1918* (USSR: Mass reprisals, losses of population and deportations since 1917/1918 in *ÖMZ* 6/1991, p. 542.

159. Overmans, *Fifty-five Million Victims of the Second World War?*, p. 112.

160. Falin, op. cit., p. 497.

VI

1. From several indications given by General Vlasov one may deduce the existence of a group of opposed officers within the Red Army; see Fröhlich, *General Vlasov*, pp. 57, 63.

2. See the perceptive estimation by Malia, *Dementia Implemented*, p. 323.

3. Ibid, p. 325.

4. For a summary of the overall problem see: H.-E. Volkmann, *The Vlasov Operation*, p. 117 et seq.

5. In this respect the author is of the same opinion as Hillgruber, *The Second World War*, p. 101.

6. Goebbels, *Diary*, entry of 28 July 1943, quoted by Jung, *The Ardennes Offensive*, p. 91.

7. Carl von Clausewitz, *On War*, p. 109.

8. Quoted from Sun Tzu; Clavell, *Sun Tzu, The Art of War*, p. 38.

BIBLIOGRAPHY

Out of the great mass of publications and sources dealing with the Second World War only those documents, anthologies, monographs and essays from periodicals have been listed that are directly connected to the present discussion. Contributions in dailies or weeklies, with only a few exceptions, have been omitted.

Unpublished sources

Extensive source material from the General Staff of the Supreme Command of the German Army (OKH), various Army Commands, official war diaries, maps and other official documents from the Bundesarchiv/Militärarchiv (Federal Archives/Military Archives) of the Federal Republic of Germany in Freiburg (cited: FA/MA).

Max von Stiotta, *Der Atlantikwall* (The Atlantic Wall), from *Als Österreicher im dritten Reich* (An Austrian in the Third Reich), from the estate, Österreichiches Staatsarchiv/Kriegsarchiv (Austrian State Archives/War Archives), Vienna, collected estates vol. B/923, No 26.

Published sources and literature

Atanassiev, Juri, *Rußland – Despotie oder Demokratie* (Russia – Despotism or Democracy), Düsseldorf, Vienna, New York, Moscow, 1993.

Ahmann, Rolf, *Nichtangriffspakte: Entwicklung und operative Nutzung in Europa 1922–1939* (Treaties of Non-Aggression: Development and Operational Use in Europe 1922–1939), Baden-Baden, 1988.

Aigner, Dietrich, *Hitler und die Weltherrschaft* (Hitler and World Rule) in Wolfgang Michalka (ed.), *Nationalsozialistische Außenpolitik* (National Socialist Foreign Policy), Darmstadt, 1978.

Akhromeyev, Sergei, *Zum grundlegenden Umschwung im Zweiten Weltkrieg* (The Basic Turns of the Second World War), in *Militärwesen* 11/1984, East Berlin.

Bartov, Omer, *Hitlers Wehrmacht*, Reinbeck near Hamburg, 1995.

Baum, Walter and Weichold, Eberhard, *Der Krieg der 'Achsenmächte' im Mittelmeerraum. Die 'Strategie' der Diktatoren* (The War of the Axis Powers in the Mediterranean Theatre. The Dictator's Strategy), Göttingen, Zurich, Frankfurt/M., 1973.

Bavendamm, Dirk, *Roosevelts Weg zum Krieg. Amerikanische Politik 1914–1939* (Roosevelt's Road to War. American Policy 1914–1939), Munich, Berlin, 1983.

– *Roosevelts Krieg 1937–1945 und das Rätsel von Pearl Harbor* (Roosevelt's War 1937–1945 and the Mystery of Pearl Harbor), Munich, 1993.

Becker, Fritz, *Im Kampf um Europa. Stalins Schachzüge gegen Deutschland und den Westen* (The Battle for Europe. Stalin's Gambits against Germany and the West), 2nd ed., Graz, Stuttgart, 1993.

Beer, Albert, *Der Fall Barbarossa. Untersuchungen zur Geschichte der Vorbereitungen des deutschen Feldzuges gegen die Union der Sozialistischen Sowjetrepubliken* (Case Barbarossa. Research on the History of the Preparations of the German Campaign against the USSR), Ellwangen, 1978.

Beesly, Patrick, *Very Special Intelligence in Germany*, Berlin, 1977.

Bekker, Cajus, *Angriffshöhe 4000* (Attack Altitude 4000), Oldenburg, Hamburg, 1964.

Ben Arie, Katriel, *Die Schlacht von Monte Cassino 1944* (The Battle of Monte Cassino, 1944), Freiburg i. Br., 1985.

Besymenski. Lev, *Sonderakte 'Barbarossa'. Dokumente, Darstellung, Deutung* (Special File 'Barbarossa'. Documents, Description, Interpretation), Stuttgart, 1968.

– *Die Zähmung des Taifuns* (Taming the Typhoon), East Berlin, 1981.

Bihl, Wolfdieter, *Ukrainer als Teil der Streitkräfte des Deutschen Reiches im Zweiten Weltkrieg* (Ukrainians as Part of the Armed Forces of the German Reich during the Second World War), in *Österreichische Osthefte* 1/1987.

Blöthner, Hans, *Deutsche Flak im 2. Weltkrieg* (German AA during the Second World War) in *Wehrkunde* 10/1969.

Blumentritt, Günther, *Die Überwindung der Krise vor Moskau im Winter 1941-42, dargestellt an der 4. Armee* (Overcoming the Crisis before Moscow in the Winter 1941–42, using the Fourth Army as an Example), in *Wehrwissenschaftliche Rundschau* 3/1954.

Bock, Fedor von, *Zwischen Pflicht und Verweigerung. Das Kriegstagebuch* (Between Duty and Refusal. The War Diary), ed. Klaus Gerbet, Munich, Berlin, 1995.

Boelcke, Willi A. (pub.), *'Wollt ihr den totalen Krieg?' Die geheimen Goebbels-Konferenzen 1939–1943* ('Do You Want Total War?' Goebbels's Secret Conferences 1939–1943), dtv-Dokumente No. 578, Munich, 1969.

– *Deutschlands Rüstung im Zweiten Weltkrieg. Hitlers Konferenzen mit Albert Speer 1942–1945* (Germany's Arms Production during the Second World War. Hitler's Conferences with Albert Speer 1942–1945), Frankfurt/M., 1969.

Bonatz, Heinz, *Seekrig im Äther 1939–1945. Die Leistungen der deutschen Marine-Funkaufklärung* (Naval War in the Ether. Achievements of German Naval Radio Intelligence), Herford, 1980.

Bonwetsch, Bernd, *Die Repression des Militärs und die Einsatzfähigkeit der Roten Armee im 'Großen Vaterländischen Krieg'* (Repression of the Military and the Red Army's Ability to Fight in the 'Great Patriotic War'), in *Zwei Wege nach Moskau* (Two Roads to Moscow), ed. Bernd Wegner, Munich, Zurich, 1991.

Boog, Horst, *Die deutsche Luftwaffenführung. Führungsprobleme, Spitzengliederung, Generalstabsausbildung* (The Luftwaffe Leadership. Leadership Problems, Organization of the Top, General Staff Training), Stuttgart, 1982.

– *Das Problem der Selbständigkeit der Luftstreitkräfte in Deutschland 1908–1945* (The Problem of the Independence of the German Air Forces 1908–1945) in *Militärgeschichtliche Mitteilungen* 1/1988.

– *Luftwaffe und Technik 1935–1945* (Luftwaffe and Technology 1935–1945) in *Truppenpraxis* 1/1987.

– *Der strategische Bombenkrieg* (The Strategic Bombing War) in *Militärgeschichte* 2/1992.
– *Bombenkriegslegenden* (Bombing War Legends) in *Militärgeschichte* 2/1995.
Bordyugov, Grigori and Neveshin, Vladimir (pub.), *Hat Stalin einen Angriffskrieg gegen Hitler vorbereitet? Eine ungeplante Diskussion. Sammelband von Materialien* (Did Stalin Prepare a War of Aggression against Hitler? An Unplanned Discussion. Collected Material), in Russian, AIRO-XX Moscow, 1995.
Bornemann, Manfred, *Geheimprojekt Mittelbau. Vom Zentralen Öllager des Deutschen Reiches zur größten Raketenfabrik im Zweiten Weltkrieg* (Secret Project Mittelbau. From the Central Oil Depot of the German Reich to the Largest Rocket Factory during the Second World War), 2nd new and extended edition, Bonn, 1994.
Bradley, Dermot and Schulze-Kossens, Richard (pub.), *Tätigkeitsbericht des Chefs des Heerespersonalamtes, General der Infantrie Rudolf Schmundt* (Activities Report of the Chief of the Army Personnel Office, General of Infantry Rudolf Schmundt), Osnabrück, 1984.
Brechtken, Magnus, *Fall Barbarossa. Wendepunkt in der europäischen Geschichte* (Case Barbarossa. A Turning Point in European History) in *Information für die Truppe* 6/1991.
Breithaupt, Hans, *Zwischen Front und Widerstand. Ein Beitrag zur Diskussion um den Feldmarschall Erich von Manstein* (Between Front and Resistance. A Contribution to the Discussion about Field Marshal Erich von Manstein), Bonn, 1994.
Brenneke, Jochen, *Die Wende im U-Bootkrieg. Ursachen und Folgen 1939–1943* (The Turn in the Submarine War. Causes and Effects 1939–1943), Heyne Pocket Book No. 7966, Munich, 1991.
Breyer, Siegfried, *Kampf und Untergang der 'Bismarck'* (Battle and Sinking of the *Bismarck*) in *Soldat und Technik* 6/1981.
Brown, Anthony Cave, *Die unsichtbare Front. Entschieden Geheimdienste den 2. Weltkrieg?* (The Invisible Front. Did Secret Services Decide the Second World War?) Munich, 1976.
Buck, Felix, *Geopolitik 2000. Weltordnung im Wandel* (Geopolitics 2000. The Changing Order of the World), Frankfurt/M., Bonn, 1996.
Bullock, Alan, *Hitler und Stalin*, Berlin, 1991.
Burckhardt, Jakob, *Historische Fragmente* (Historical Fragments), Stuttgart, 1957.

Carell, Paul, *Stalingrad. Sieg und Untergang der 6. Armee* (Stalingrad. Victory and Downfall of the Sixth Army), Berlin, Frankfurt/M., 1992.
Carr, Edward Hallett, *Was ist Geschichte?* (What Is History?), Urban Book No. 67, Stuttgart, 1963.
Carr, William, *Von Polen bis Pearl Harbor: Zur Entwicklung des Zweiten Weltkrieges* (From Poland to Pearl Harbor. The Development of the Second World War), Hamburg, Leamington Spa, New York, 1987.
Caspar, Gustav Adolf, *Der Zusammenbruch der deutschen Heeresgruppe Mitte im Sommer 1944* (Collapse of German Army Group Centre in Summer 1944) in *Truppenpraxis* 7/1984.

Cecil, Robert, *Hitlers Griff nach Rußland* (Hitler's Bid for Russia), Graz, Vienna, Cologne, 1977.

Chales de Beaulieu, Walter, *Der Vorstoß der Panzergruppe 4 auf Leningrad – 1941* (The Advance by Panzer Group 4 on Leningrad, 1941), Neckargemünd, 1961.

–*Generaloberst Erich Hoepner. Militärisches Porträt eines Panzer-Führers* (Colonel General Erich Hoepner. Military Portrait of a Tank Commander), Neckargemünd, 1969.

Chor'kov, Anatoly G., *Die Rote Armee in der Anfangsphase des Großen Vaterländischen Krieges* (The Red Army in the Initial Phase of the Great Patriotic War) in *Zwei Wege Nach Moskau* (Two Roads to Moscow), ed. Bernd Wegner, Munich, Zurich, 1991.

–*Die sowjetische Gegenoffensive bei Stalingrad* (The Soviet Counter-Offensive at Stalingrad), in *Stalingrad*, ed. J. Förster, Munich, Zurich, 1993.

Churchill, Winston S., *The Second World War*, London, 1949.

Clark, Allan, *Barbarossa. The Russian-German Conflict 1941–1945*, London, 1995.

Clausewitz, Carl von, *Vom Krieg* (On War), 16th ed., Bonn, 1952.

Clavell, James (pub.), *Sunzi. Die Kunst des Krieges* (Sun Tzu. The Art of War), Munich, 1988.

Clemens, Detlev, *Herr Hitler in Germany. Wahrnehmungen und Deutungen des Nationalsozialismus in Großbritannien 1920–1939* (Herr Hitler in Germany. (Perception and Interpretation of National Socialism in Great Britain 1920–1939), Göttingen, Zurich, 1996.

Connor, Albert Z. and Poirier, Robert G., *Soviet Ground Force Mobilization Potential: Lessons of the Past and Implications for the Future* in *The Journal of Soviet Military Studies* 2/1988.

Conquest, Robert, *Stalin. Der totale Wille zur Macht* (Stalin. Total Will for Power), Munich, Leipzig, 1991.

– *Der grosse Terror. Sowjetunion 1934–1938* (The Great Terror. Soviet Union 1934–1938), Munich, 1992.

Conrady, Alexander, *Rshew 1942/43*, Neckargemünd, 1976.

Costello, John and Hughes, Terry, *Atlantikschlacht. Der Krieg zur See 1939–1945* (Battle of the Atlantic. The War at Sea 1939–1945), Bergisch-Gladbach, 1978.

Craig, William E., *Die Schlacht um Stalingrad. Der Untergang der 6. Armee: Kriegswende an der Wolga* (The Battle of Stalingrad. The Downfall of the Sixth Army: Turn of the War on the Volga), Vienna, Munich, 1977.

Dahms, Hellmut Günther, *Die Geschichte des Zweiten Weltkrieges* (History of the Second World War), Munich, Berlin, 1983.

Danilov, Valery, *Hat der Generalstab der Roten Armee einen Präventivschlag gegen Deutschland vorbereitet?* (Did the General Staff of the Red Army Prepare a Preventive Strike against Germany?) in *ÖMZ* 1/1993.

– *Juni 1941: Früchte einer falschen Konzeption* (Fruits of a Mistaken Conception), pub. in Russian in *Poisk* (The Search) 25/1996.

Deighton, Len, *Luftschlacht über England* (The Battle of Britain), Heyne Pocket Book No. 5985, Munich, 1982.

Dick, Charles J., *The Operational Employment of Soviet Armour in the Great Patriotic War*, Sandhurst, October 1988.

Dimt, Peter, *Die Pantherlinie. Bausoldaten zwischen Peipussee und Finnenmeer*
(The Panther Line. Engineers between Lake Peipus and the Finnish Sea),
Berg am See, 1988.

Dippel, John, *Two Against Hitler. Stealing the Nazis' Best-kept Secrets*, New York,
London, 1992.

Doerr, Hans, *Der Feldzug nach Stalingrad 1942/43* (Campaign to Stalingrad
1942/43), Darmstadt, 1955.

– *Kriegführung, Besatzungspolitik und Partisanen* (War, Occupation Policy and
Partisans) in *Wehrwissenschaftliche Rundschau* 6/7/1951.

Douglas, Gregory, *Geheimakte Gestapo-Müller – Dokumente und Zeugnisse aus
den US-Geheimarchiven* (Secret File Gestapo-Müller – Documents and Testimony from US Secret Archives), Bremen, 1995.

Dönitz, Karl, *Deutsche Strategie zur See im Zweiten Weltkrieg. Die Antworten des
Großadmirals auf 40 Fragen* (German Strategy at Sea During the Second
World War. Answers by the Großadmiral to 40 Questions), Frankfurt/M.,
1972.

Duffy, Christopher, *Der Sturm auf das Reich. Der Vormarsch der Roten Armee
1945* (Storming the Reich. The Advance of the Red Army, 1945), Munich,
1994.

Dziak, John J., *Chekisty. A History of the KGB*, Lexington, Mass., 1988.

Egger; Martin (pub.), *Die Festung Sewastopol. Eine Dokumentation ihrer Befesti-
gungsanlagen und der Kämpfe 1942* (Fortress Sevastopol. A Documentation
of its Fortifications and Battles 1942), Bern, 1995.

Engelmann, Joachim, *Zitadelle. Die größte Panzerschlacht im Osten 1943*
(Citadel. The Greatest Tank Battle in the East 1943), Friedberg, 1980.

Erickson, John, *Stalin's War with Germany*: Volume I: *The Road to Stalingrad*,
London, 1975.

Fabry, Philipp, *Balkanwirren 1940–1941. Diplomatische und militärische
Vorbereitungen des deutschen Donauüberganges* (Balkan Confusion
1940–1941. Diplomatic and Military Preparations for the German Crossing
of the Danube), Darmstadt, 1964.

– *Mutmaßungen über Hitler. Urteile von Zeitgenossen* (Speculations About Hitler.
The Verdicts of Contemporaries), Athenäum Droste Pocket Books on
History, Kronberg, Düsseldorf, 1969.

– *Die Sowjetunion und das Dritte Reich. Eine dokumentierte Geschichte der
deutsch-sowjetischen Beziehungen von 1933–1941* (The Soviet Union and the
Third Reich. A Documented History of German-Soviet Relations
1933–1941), Stuttgart, 1971.

Falin, Valentin, *Zweite Front. Die Interessenkonflikte in der Anti-Hitler-Koalition*
(Second Front. The Conflicts of Interest in the Anti-Hitler-Coalition),
Munich, 1995.

Fest, Joachim, *Hitler. Eine Biographie* (Hitler. A Biography), Ullstein Book No.
33089, Frankfurt/M., Berlin, 1987.

Fischer, Alexander (pub.), *Teheran–Jalta–Potsdam. Die sowjetischen Protokolle von den Kriegskonferenzen der 'Großen Drei'* (Teheran–Yalta–Potsdam. The Soviet Transcripts of the War Conferences of the 'Big Three'), 2nd ed., Cologne, 1973.

Fischer, Johannes, *Über den Entschluß zur Luftversorgung Stalingrads* (On the Decision to Supply Stalingrad by Air) in *Militärgeschichtliche Mitteilungen* 2/1969.

Fleischhauer, Ingeborg, *Die Chance des Sonderfriedens – Deutsch-sowjetische Geheimgespräche 1941–1945* (The Chance for a Separate Peace. Secret German-Soviet Talks, 1941–1945), Berlin, 1986.

Foerster, Roland (pub.), *'Unternehmen Barbarossa'. Zum historischen Ort der deutsch-sowjetischen Beziehungen von 1933–1941* ('Operation Barbarossa'. On the Historic Position of German-Soviet Relations, 1933–1941), Munich, 1993.

Förster, Gerhard, *Einige Fragen der Kriegskunst während der Stalingrader Schlacht* (Some Questions on the Art of War During the Battle of Stalingrad) in *Militärgeschichte* (East Berlin) 1/1983.

Förster, Jürgen, *Stalingrad. Risse im Bündnis 1942/43* (Stalingrad. Rifts in the Alliance 1942/43), Freiburg, 1975.

– *Strategische Überlegungen des Wehrmachtsführungstabes für das Jahr 1943* (Strategic Considerations by the Wehrmacht Operations Staff for the Year 1943) in *Militärgeschichtliche Mitteilungen* 1/1973.

– *Zur Rolle der Wehrmacht im Krieg gegen die Sowjetunion* (On the Role of the Wehrmacht in the War against the Soviet Union), in *Aus Politik und Zeitgeschichte* of 8 Nov. 1990.

Förster, Jürgen (pub.), *Stalingrad. Ereignis, Wirkung, Symbol* (Stalingrad. Event, Effect, Symbol), Piper Series No. 1618, Munich, Zurich, 2nd ed. 1993.

Forstmeier, Friedrich and Volkmann, Hans-Erich (pub.), *Kriegswirtschaft und Rüstung 1939–1945* (War Economy and Armanent 1939–1945), Düsseldorf, 1977.

Forstner, Franz, *Partisanenkrieg am Beispiel Jugoslawien 1941–1945* (Partisan War, Using Yugoslavia 1941–1945 as an Example) in Erwin A. Schmid (pub.), *Freund oder Feind? Kombattanten, Nichtkombattanten und Zivilisten in Krieg und Bürgerkrieg seit dem 18. Jahrhundert* (Friend or Enemy? Combatants, Non-combatants, and Civilians in War and Civil War Since the 18th Century), Frankfurt/M., Berlin, Bern, 1995.

Frank, H. K., *Der 23. July 1941* (23 July 1941) in *Allgemeine Schweizerische Militärzeit-schrift* 10/1951.

Frankland, Nobel, *The Bombing Offensive against Germany. Outlines and Perspectives*, London, 1965.

– *Bomber Offensive – The Devastation of Europe*, New York, 1970.

Friedrich, Jörg, *Das Gesetz des Krieges. Das deutsche Heer in Rußland 1914 bis 1945. Der Prozeß gegen das Oberkommando der Wehrmacht* (The Law of War. The German Army in Russia 1914 to 1945. The Case against the Wehrmacht Supreme Command), Munich, Zurich, 1993.

Frieser, Karl-Heinz, *'Blitzkrieg' ohne 'Blitzkriegs'-Konzept* ('Blitzkrieg' without a 'Blitzkrieg' Concept) in *Militärgeschichte* 1/1991.

– *Blitzkrieg-Legende. Der Westfeldzug 1940* (Blitzkrieg Legend. The Campaign in the West 1940) in *Operationen des Zweiten Weltkriegs* (Operations during the Second World War), vol. 2, Munich, 1995.

Fröhlich, Sergei, *General Wlassow. Russen und Deutsche zwischen Hitler und Stalin* (General Vlasov. Russians and Germans Between Hitler and Stalin), ed. Edel von Freier, Cologne, 1987.

Funke, Manfred (pub.), *Hitler, Deutschland und die Mächte. Materialien zur Außenpolitik des Dritten Reiches* (Hitler, Germany and the Powers. Material on the Foreign Policy of the Third Reich), Athenäum Droste Pocket Books on History No. 7213, Kronberg, Düsseldorf, 1978.

Furet, François, *Das Ende der Illusion. Der Kommunismus im 20. Jahrhundert* (The End of the Illusion. Communism in the 20th Century), Munich, Zurich, 1996.

Gannon, Michael, *Operation Paukenschlag. Der deutsche U-Boot-Krieg gegen die USA* (Operation Drumbeat. The German Submarine War against the USA), Ullstein Book No. 33171, Frankfurt/M., Berlin, 1994.

Garlinski, J., *Deutschlands letzte Waffe im 2. Weltkrieg. Der Untergrundkrieg gegen die V1 und V2* (Germany's Final Weapon in the Second World War. The Underground War against the V1 and V2), Stuttgart, 1981.

Gaull, W, *Die deutsche Luftwaffe während der Invasion 1944* (The Luftwaffe during the Invasion of 1944) in *Wehrwissenschaftliche Rundschau* 3/1993.

Gellermann, Günther W., *... und lauschten für Hitler. Geheime Reichssache. Die Abhörzentralen des Dritten Reiches* (... and Listened in for Hitler. Top Secret. The Centres of Radio Surveillance in the Third Reich), Bonn, 1991.

– *Geheime Wege zum Frieden mit England* (Secret Paths to Peace with England), Bonn, 1995.

Gerlach, H., *Die verratene Armee* (The Betrayed Army), Munich, 1989.

Geyer, Dietrich (pub.), *Die Umwertung der sowjetischen Geschichte* (Soviet History Re-evaluated), Göttingen, 1991.

Glantz, David M. and House, Jonathan, *When Titans Clashed. How the Red Army Stopped Hitler*, University Press of Kansas, Lawrence, Kansas, 1995.

Gleasson, William Everrett, *The Undeclared War*, New York, 1953.

Golücke, Friedhelm, *Schweinfurt und der strategische Luftkrieg 1943. Der Angriff der US Air Force vom 14. October 1943 gegen die Schweinfurter Kugellagerindustrie* (Schweinfurt and the Strategic Air War, 1943. The Attack by the US Air Force on 14 Oct. 1943 against the Schweinfurt Ball-bearing Industry), Paderborn, 1980.

Gordievski, Oleg and Andrew, Christopher, *KGB. Die Geschichte seiner Auslandsoperationen von Lenin bis Gorbatschow* (KGB. The History of its Foreign Operations from Lenin to Gorbachev), Munich, 1990.

Görlitz, Walter, *Model. Strategie der Defensive* (Model. Defensive Strategy), Wiesbaden, 1975.

Gorodetsky, Gabriel, *Stalin und Hitlers Angriff auf die Sowjetunion* (Stalin and Hitler's Attack on the Soviet Union) in *Zwei Wege nach Moskau* (Two Roads to Moscow), ed. Bernd Wegner, Munich, Zurich, 1991.

– *The Myth of the Ice Breaker*, Moscow, 1993.

Grabmann, Walter, *Geschichte der deutschen Luftverteidigung 1933–1945* (History of German Air Defence 1933–1945), Manuscript in Bundesarchiv/Militärarchiv, Freiburg, sig. LW 11/b.

Greiselis, Waldis, *Das Ringen um den Brückenkopf Tunesien 1942/43. Strategie der 'Achse' und Innenpolitik im Protektorat* (The Struggle for the Tunisian Bridgehead. Axis Strategy and Internal Policies in the Protectorate) in *Europäische Hochschulschriften*, series 3, vol. 67, Frankfurt/M., Bern, 1976.

Grigorenko, Pyotr, *Erinnerungen* (Memoirs), Munich, 1981.

Grinell-Milne, Duncan, *Der stille Sieg. Schicksalhelfer September 1940* (The Silent Victory. September 1940, Turn of Fate). Tübingen, 1958.

Gruchmann, Lothar, *Die 'verpaßten strategischen Chancen' im Mittelmeerraum 1940/41* (The 'Missed Strategic Chances' in the Mediterranean Theatre 1940/41) in *Vierteljahreshefte für Zeitgeschichte* 18 (1970).

Guderian, Heinz, *Erinnerungen eines Soldaten* (Memoirs of a Soldier), 4th ed. Neckargemünd, 1960.

Gulyakevich, Lyudmilla, *Zum Tode verurteilt* (Condemned to Death) in *Imja* (The Name) of 7 June 1996.

Gundelach, Karl, *Drohende Gefahr West. Die deutsche Luftwaffe vor und während der Invasion 1944* (Danger in the West. The Luftwaffe Before and During the Invasion of 1944) in *Wehrwissenschaftliche Rundschau* 6/1959.

– *Gedanken über die Führung eines Luftkrieges gegen England bei der Luftflotte 2 in den Jahren 1938/39* (Considerations during 1938–9 at *Luftflotte 2* on Fighting an Air War against England) in *Wehrwissenschaftliche Rundschau* 1/1960.

– *Der Alliierte Luftkrieg gegen die deutsche Flugtreibstoffversorgung* (The Allied Air War against German Air Fuel Supplies) in *Wehrwissenschaftliche Rundschau* 12/1963.

– *Die deutsche Luftwaffe im Mittelmeer 1940-1945* (The Luftwaffe in the Mediterranean, 1940–1945), 2 volumes, Frankfurt/M., Bern, Cirencester, 1981.

Hackl, Othmar, *Operative Führungsprobleme der Heeresgruppe Don bzw. Süd bei der Verteidigungsoperation zwischen Donez und Dnjepr im Februar und März 1943* (Operational Leadership Problems at Army Group Don and South during the Defensive Operation between the Donetz and the Dnieper in February and March 1943) in *Truppenpraxis* 26/1982.

Haffner, Sebastian, *Anmerkungen zu Hitler* (Notes on Hitler), Fischer Pocket Book No. 3489, Frankfurt/M., 1987.

– *Von Bismarck zu Hitler. Ein Rückblick* (From Bismarck to Hitler. A Retrospective), Munich, 1987.

Hahn, Fritz, *Waffen und Geheimwaffen des deutschen Heeres 1939–1945* (Weapons and Secret Weapons of the German Army, 1939–1945), vols I and II, Koblenz, 1986, 1987.

Halder, Colonel General, *Kriegstagebuch. Tägliche Aufzeichnungen des Chefs des Generalstabes des Heeres 1939–1942* (War Diary. Daily Notes by the Chief of Staff of the Army 1939–1942), ed. Hans-Adolf Jacobsen, Stuttgart, 1962–4.

Harris, Sir Arthur T., *Despatch on War Operations. 23rd February 1942 to 8th May 1945*. With an Introduction by Horst Boog, London, 1995.

Harrison, Mark, *'Barbarossa': Die sowjetische Antwort, 1941* ('Barbarossa': The Soviet Answer, 1941) in *Zwei Wege nach Moskau* (Two Roads to Moscow), Bernd Wegner (ed.), Munich, Zurich, 1991.

Hartmann, Christian, *Halder. Generalstabschef Hitlers 1939–1942* (Halder. Hitler's Chief of Staff 1939–1942), Paderborn, 1991.

Hastings, Max, *Bomber Command*, 2nd ed., London, 1980.

Heideking, Jürgen and Mauch, Christoph (pub.), *Geheimdienstkrieg-gegen Deutschland. Subversion, Propaganda und politische Planungen des amerikanischen Geheimdienstes im Zweiten Weltkrieg* (Secret Service War against Germany. Subversion Propaganda and Political Planning by the American Secret Service during the Second World War), Göttingen, 1993.

Heitmann, Jan, *'Gomorrah'* – The Hamburg Firestorm in *After the Battle* No. 70, London, 1990.

Helmdach, Erich, *Überfall? Der deutsch-sowjetische Aufmarsch 1941* (Surprise Attack? German–Soviet Deployment 1941), Berg am Starnberger See, 5th ed., 1979.

Heinrici, Gotthard and Hauck, Friedrich Wilhelm, *Zitadelle. Der Angriff auf den russischen Frontvorsprung bei Kursk* (Citadel. The Attack against the Russian Bulge at Kursk), parts I, II and III in *Wehrwissenschaftliche Rundschau* 8/9/10/1966.

Herbert, Ulrich, *Best. Biographische Studien über Radikalismus, Weltanschauung und Vernunft 1903–1989* (Some Biographical Studies on Radicalism, Weltanschauung and Reason 1903–1989), Bonn, 1996.

Herde, Peter, *Pearl Harbor 7, Dezember 1941: Der Ausbruch des Krieges zwischen Japan und den Vereinigten Staaten und die Ausweitung des europäischen Krieges zum Weltkrieg* (Pearl Harbor, 7 December 1941: Start of the War between Japan and the United States and Extension of the European War into a World War), Darmstadt, 1980.

– *Japan, Deutschland und die Vereinigten Staaten im Jahre 1941* (Japan, Germany and the United States in 1941) in *Kriegswende Dezember 1941* (Turn of the War, December 1941), (ed.) Jürgen Rohwer and Eberhard Jäckel, Stuttgart, 1984.

Herhudt von Rhoden, Hans-Detlef, *Die Luftwaffe ringt um Stalingrad* (The Luftwaffe Fights for Stalingrad), Ullstein Book No. 34995, Frankfurt/M., Berlin, 1993.

Hermann, Carl Hans, *68 Kriegsmonate* (68 Months of War), Vienna, 1975.

Herwarth, Hans von, *Zwischen Hitler und Stalin. Erlebte Zeitgeschichte 1931–1945* (Between Hitler and Stalin. Contemporary History Experienced 1931–1945), Ullstein Book No. 33048, Frankfurt/M., Berlin, 1985.

Hesse, Erich, *Der sowjetrussische Partisanenkrieg 1941–1944 im Spiegel deutscher Kampfanweisungen und Befehle* (The Soviet-Russian Partisan War 1941–1944 Reflected in German Combat Directives and Orders), Göttingen, Zurich, 2nd ed., 1993.

Heusinger, Adolf, *Befehl im Widerstreit. Schicksalsstunden der Deutschen Armee* (Orders in Conflict. Fatal Moments of the German Army), Tübingen, 1957.

Heydorn, Volker Detlef, *Nachrichtennahaufklärung (Ost) und sowjetrussisches Heeresfunkwesen bis 1945* (Short-range Radio Intelligence (East) and Soviet Army Signals Section up to 1945), Freiburg i.Br., 1985.

– *Der sowjetische Aufmarsch im Bialystoker Balkon bis zum 22. June 1941 und der Kessel von Wolkowysk* (Soviet Deployment in the Bialystok Salient up to 22 June 1941 and the Volkovysk Pocket), Munich, 1989.

Hildebrand, Klaus, *Vom Reich zum Weltreich. Hitler, NSDAP und koloniale Frage 1919–1945* (From the Reich to World Empire. Hitler, NSDAP and Colonial Questions 1919–1945), Munich, 1969.
– *Das Dritte Reich* (The Third Reich), Munich, Vienna, 1979.
– *Deutsche Außenpolitik 1933–1945. Kalkül oder Dogma?* (German Foreign Policy 1933–1945. Calculation or Dogma?), Stuttgart, Berlin, Cologne, Mainz, 5th ed., 1990.
– *Die Entfesselung des Zweiten Weltkrieges und das internationale System* (The Unleashing of the Second World War and the International System) in *Historische Zeitschrift* 251 (1990).
Hildebrandt, Karl-Heinz, *Die Front am Ärmelkanal. Dieppe 1942* (The Channel Front. Dieppe 1942) in *Militärgeschichte* 4/1992.
Hill, Leonidas E. (pub.), *Die Weizsäcker-Papiere 1933–1950* (The Weizsäcker Papers 1933–1950), vol. 1, Frankfurt/M., Berlin, Vienna 1974.
Hillgruber, Andreas, *Deutsche Großmacht- und Weltpolitik im 19. und 20. Jahrhundert* (German Power and World Politics in the 19th and 20th Centuries), Düsseldorf, 1977.
– *Sowjetische Außenpolitik im Zweiten Weltkrieg* (Soviet Foreign Policy during the Second World War), Athenäum Droste Pocket Books on History No. 7222, Königstein, Düsseldorf, 1979.
– *Die gescheiterte Großmacht. Eine Skizze des Deutschen Reiches 1871–1945* (The Great Power that Failed. A Sketch of the German Reich 1871–1945), Düsseldorf, 1980.
– *Hitlers Strategie. Politik und Kriegsführung 1940–1941* (Hitler's Strategy. Politics and War Leadership 1940–1941), Munich, 2nd ed., 1982.
– *Zweierlei Untergang. Die Zerschlagung des Deutschen Reiches und das Ende des europäischen Judentums* (Two Different Downfalls. The Destruction of the German Reich and the end of European Jewry), 3rd ed., Berlin, 1986.
– *Die Zerstörung Europas. Beiträge zur Weltkriegsepoche 1914 bis 1945* (The Destruction of Europe. Contributions to the World War Era, 1914 to 1945), Frankfurt/M., Berlin, 1988.
– *Der Zweite Weltkrieg. Kriegsziele und Strategie der großen Mächte* (The Second World War. Objectives and Strategy of the Great Powers), Stuttgart, Berlin, Cologne, Mainz, 6th ed., 1996.
– *Der Faktor Amerika in Hitlers Strategie 1938–1941* (The American Factor in Hitler's Strategy 1938–1941) in *Aus Politik und Zeitgeschichte* of 11 May 1966.
– *Noch einmal: Hitlers Wendung gegen die Sowjetunion 1940* (Once Again: Hitler's Turn against the Soviet Union 1940) in *Geschichte in Wissenschaft und Unterricht* 33 (1982).
– *Der Zenit des Zweiten Weltkrieges. Juli 1941* (Zenith of the Second World War. July 1941, Presentation No. 65 at the Institute for European History in Mainz, Wiesbaden, 1977.
– *Endlich genug über den Nationalsozialismus und Zweiten Weltkrieg? Forschungsstand und Literatur* (Finally Enough on National Socialism and the Second World War? Status of Research and Literature), Düsseldorf, 1982.
– *Das Rußlandbild der führenden deutschen Militärs vor Beginn des Angriffs auf die Sowjetunion* (The German Military Leaders' Image of the Soviet Union

Before the Attack) in *Zwei Wege nach Moskau* (Two Roads to Moscow), ed. Bernd Wegner, Munich, Zurich, 1991.

Hillgruber, Andreas and Förster, Jürgen, *Zwei neue Aufzeichnungen über 'Führer'-Besprechungen aus dem Jahre 1942* (Two New Notes on 'Führer' Briefings from 1942) in *Militärgeschichtliche Mitteilungen* 1/1972.

Hillgruber, Andreas and Hümmelchen, Gerhard, *Chronik des Zweiten Weltkrieges* (Chronicle of the Second World War), Athenäum Droste Pocket Books on History No. 7218, Königstein, Düsseldorf, 1978.

Hinchliffe, Peter, *The Other Battle*, Shrewsbury, 1996.

Hinrichs, Hans, *Kriegswende Stalingrad. Das Operativwerden der Roten Armee* (The Stalingrad Turn of the War. The Red Army Becomes Operational) in *Europäische Wehrkunde/WWR* 2/1983.

– *Vor 40 Jahren: Kriegswende in Nordafrika. Die Schlacht von Alem Halfa 30. 8. bis 7. 9. 42* (40 Years Ago. Turn of the War in North Africa. The Battle of Alem Halfa 30 August to 7 September '42) in *Europäische Wehrkunde* 8/1982.

Hinze, Rolf, *Das Ostfront-Drama 1944. Rückzugskämpfe der Heeresgruppe Mitte* (The Drama on the Eastern Front 1944. Withdrawal Battles of Army Group Centre), Stuttgart, 1987.

Hitlers Lagebesprechungen. Die Protokollfragmente seiner militärischen Konferenzen (Hitler's Briefings. Fragments of the Minutes of his Military Conferences), ed. Helmut Heiber, Stuttgart, 1962.

Hitlers politisches Testament. Die Bormann-Diktate vom Februar und April 1945 (Hitler's Political Testament. The Bormann Dictations of February and April 1945), Hamburg, 1981.

Höffkes, Karl, *Deutsch-Sowjetische Geheimverbindungen* (Secret German-Soviet Connections), Tübingen, 1988.

Hoffmann, Joachim, *Die Ostlegionen 1941–1943* (The Eastern Legions 1941–1943), Freiburg, 1976.

– *Die Geschichte der Wlassow-Armee* (History of the Vlasov Army), Freiburg, 1984.

– *Kaukasien 1942/43. Das deutsche Heer und die Orientvölker der Sowjetunion* (Caucasia 1942/43. The German Army and the Oriental Peoples of the Soviet Union), Freiburg, 1991.

– *Die Angriffsvorbereitungen der Sowjetunion 1941* (The Soviet Union's Preparations for Attack 1941) in *Zwei Wege nach Moskau* (Two Roads to Moscow), ed. Bernd Wegner, Munich, Zurich, 1991.

– *Stalins Vernichtungskrieg 1941–1945* (Stalin's War of Destruction 1941–1945), Munich, 3rd ed., 1996.

Hölsken, Dieter, *Die V-Waffen. Entwicklung und Einsatzgründsätze* (The V Weapons. Development and Principles of Employment) in *Militärgeschichtliche Mitteilungen* 2/1985.

Howard, Michael, *The Mediterranean Strategy in the Second World War*, London, 1968.

Hubatsch, Walter (pub.), *Hitlers Weisungen für die Kriegsführung 1939–1945. Dokumente des Oberkommandos der Wehrmacht* (Hitler's Directives for the Conduct of the War 1939–1945. Documents of the OKW), Koblenz, 2nd ed., 1983.

Irving, David, *Die Tragödie der Deutschen Luftwaffe* (The Tragedy of the Luftwaffe), Ullstein Book No. 3137, Frankfurt/M., Berlin, Vienna 1975.
- *Rommel. Eine Biographie* (Rommel. A Biography), Hamburg, 1978.
- *Schlacht im Eismeer. Der Untergang des Geleitzuges PQ 17* (Battle in the Arctic Ocean. The Destruction of Convoy PQ 17), Heyne Book No. 6387, Munich, 1984.
- *Führer und Reichskanzler Adolf Hitler 1933–1945* (Führer and Chancellor of the Reich Adolf Hitler 1933–1945), Munich, Berlin, 1989.
Iststärke der Luftwaffe 1941, 1942, 1943 (List Strength of the Luftwaffe 1941, 1942–3, Federal Archives/Military Archives RL III, 699, 707, 713, 716–22, 723–34, 1007, partially published in *Militärgeschichte* 3/1978.

Jäckel, Eberhard, *Hitlers Weltanschauung. Entwurf einer Herrschaft* (Hitler's Weltanschauung. Blueprint of a Regime), Tübingen, 1969.
- *Hitlers Herrschaft* (Hitler's Regime), Stuttgart, 1986.
Jackson, William G. F., *The Battle for Italy*, London, 1967.
Jacobsen, Hans-Adolf, *1939–1945. Der Zweite Weltkrieg in Chronik und Dokumenten* (1939–1945. The Second World War in Chronology and Documents), Darmstadt, 4th ed., 1959.
- *Nationalsozialistische Außenpolitik* (National Socialist Foreign Policy), Frankfurt/M., 1968.
- *Der Weg zur Teilung der Welt. Politik und Strategie 1939–1945* (The Road to Partitioning the World. Politics and Strategy 1939–1945), Koblenz, Bonn, 1978.
- *Zur Struktur der NS-Außenpolitik 1933–1945* (On the Structure of Nazi Foreign Policy 1933–1945) in Manfred Funke (pub.), *Hitler, Deutschland und die Mächte* (Hitler, Germany and the Powers), Kronberg, Düsseldorf, 1978.
Jacobsen, Hans-Adolf and others (pub.), *Deutsch-russische Zeitenwende. Krieg und Frieden 1941–1995* (German-Russian Turning-points in History. War and Peace 1941–1995), Baden-Baden, 1995.
Jacobsen, Hans-Adolf and Rohwer, Jürgen (pub.), *Entscheidungsschlachten des Zweiten Weltkrieges* (Decisive Battles of the Second World War), Frankfurt/M., 1960.
Janssen, Gregor, *Das Ministerium Speer* (The Speer Ministry), Frankfurt/M., Berlin, Vienna, 1968.
Jochmann, Werner, *Adolf Hitler. Monologe im Führerhauptquartier 1941–1944* (Adolf Hitler. Monologues at Führer Headquarters 1941–1944), Hamburg, 1980.
Johnson, Brian, *Streng Geheim. Wissenschaft und Technik im 2. Weltkrieg* (Top Secret. Science and Technology during the Second World War), Stuttgart, 1983.
Jukes, Joffrey, *Stalingrad. Die Wende im Zweiten Weltkrieg* (Stalingrad. The Turn in the Second World War), Rastatt, 1982.
- *Die Schlacht der 6000 Panzer. Kursk und Orel 1943* (The Battle of 6000 Tanks. Kursk and Orel 1943), Rastatt, 1982.
Jung, Hermann, *Die Ardennen-Offensive 1944/45. Ein Beispiel für die Kriegsführung Hitlers* (The Ardennes Offensive 1944/45. An Example of Hitler's Art of Waging War), Göttingen, Zurich, Frankfurt/m., 1971.

Junker, Detlef, *Kampf um die Weltmacht. Die USA und das Dritte Reich 1933–1945* (Battle for World Power. The USA and the Third Reich 1933–1945), Düsseldorf, 1988.

Kageneck, August von, *Examen de Conscience* (Test of Conscience), Paris, 1996.

Kaiser, Gerhard, *Aufklärung oder denunziation? Zur Ausstellung 'Vernichtungskrieg- Verbrechen der Wehrmacht 1941–44'* (Enlightenment or Denunciation? On the Exhibition 'War of Destruction – Crimes of the Wehrmacht 1941–44') in *Merkur* 5/1996.

Kasakov, M., *Die Abwehrkämpfe der sowjetischen Brjansk-Front vor Voronezh im Juni-Juli 1942* (The Defensive Battles of the Soviet Bryansk Front before Voronezh in June-July 1942), translated and introduced by Wilhelm Arenz, three parts, in *Wehrwissenschaftliche Rundschau* 8/9/10/1966.

Kehrig, Manfred, *Stalingrad. Analyse und Dokumentierung einer Schlacht* (Stalingrad. Analysis and Documentation of a Battle), Stuttgart, 3rd ed., 1979.

– *Die 6. Armee im Kessel von Stalingrad* (The Sixth Army in the Stalingrad Pocket), in *Stalingrad*, ed. J. Förster, Munich, Zurich, 1993.

– *Stalingrad 1943* in *Information für die Truppe* 2/1983.

Keilig, Wolf, *Das deutsche Heer 1939–1945. Gliederung, Einsatz, Stellenbesetzung* (The German Army 1939–1945. Organization, Deployment, Manning), 3 volumes, Bad Nauheim, 1956–70.

Kerr, Walter, *Das Geheimnis Stalingrad* (The Mystery of Stalingrad), Heyne Book No. 5599, Munich, 1979.

Kershaw, Ian, *Hitlers Macht. Das Profil der NS-Herrschaft* (Hitler's Power. The Profile of Nazi Rule), Munich, 1992.

– *Der NS-Staat. Geschichtsinterpretationen und Kontroversen im Überblick* (The Nazi State. Overview of Historic Interpretations and Controversies), new and amended edition, rororo non-fiction book No. 9506, Reinbeck near Hamburg, 1994.

Kimball, Warren F., *'Sie kommen nicht heraus, wo man sie erwartet': Roosevelts Raktion auf den deutsch-sowetischen Krieg* ('They don't come out where you expect them': Roosevelt's Reaction to the German–Soviet War) in *Zwei Wege nach Moskau* (Two Roads to Moscow), ed. Bernd Wegner, Munich, Zurich, 1991.

Kinsella, W. E., *Leadership in Isolation. F.D.R. and the Origins of the Second World War*, Cambridge, Mass., 1978.

Kipp, Jacob W., *Barbarossa. Soviet Covering Forces and the Initial Period of War: Military History and Air-Land Battle* in *The Journal of Soviet Military Studies* 2/1988.

Kirshin, Yuri J., *Die sowjetischen Streitkräfte am Vorabend des Großen Vaterländischen Krieges* (Soviet Forces on the Eve of the Great Patriotic War) in *Zwei Wege nach Moskau* (Two Roads to Moscow), ed. Bernd Wegner, Munich, Zurich, 1991.

– *Die sowjetische Militärdoktrin der Vorkriegszeit* (Pre-war Soviet Military Doctrine), Novosty Agency, Moscow, 1990.

Klee, Karl, *Das Unternehmen 'Seelöwe'. Die geplante deutsche Landung in England 1940* (Operation 'Sea Lion'. The Planned German Landing in England 1940), Göttingen, Berlin, Frankfurt/M., 1958.

- *Die Luftschlacht um England 1940* (The Air Battle for England 1940) in *Entscheidungsschlachten des Zweiten Weltkrieges* (Decisive Battles of the Second World War), ed. Hans-Adolf Jacobsen and Jürgen Rohwer, Frankfurt/M., 1960.

Kley, Stefan, *Hitler, Ribbentrop und die Entfesselung des Zweiten Weltkrieges* (Hitler, Ribbentrop and the Unleashing of the Second World War), Paderborn, 1996.

Klink, Ernst, *Das Gesetz des Handelns. Die Operation 'Zitadelle' 1943* (The Initiative to Act. Operation 'Citadel' 1943), Stuttgart, 1966.

Knipping, Franz, *Die amerikanische Rußlandpolitik in der Zeit des Hitler-Stalin-Paktes 1939–1941* (American Policy Towards Russia during the Time of the Hitler-Stalin Pact 1939–1941), Tübingen, 1974.

Koch, Hans-Adalbert, *Flak. Die Geschichte der deutschen Flakartillerie und der Einsatz der Luftwaffenhelfer* (AA. The Story of German AA Artillery and the Role of the Luftwaffe Helpers), Bad Nauheim, 2nd ed., 1965.

Korkisch, Friedrich W., *Der strategische Luftkrieg in Europa und Asien* (The Strategic Air War in Europe and Asia) in *ÖMZ* 2/3/1985.

- *Pearl Harbor. 7. Dezember 1941: Zeitenwende durch Überfall* (Pearl Harbor. 7 December 1941. Turning Point in History by Surprise Attack) in *ÖMZ* 2/3/1992.

Kosin, Rüdiger, *Die Entwicklung der deutschen Jagdflugzeuge* (The Development of German Fighter Aircraft), Koblenz, 1983.

Kotze, Hildegard (pub.), *Heeresadjutant bei Hitler 1938–1943. Aufzeichnungen des Majors Engel* (Army Adjutant to Hitler 1938–1943. Notes by Major Engel), Stuttgart, 1974.

Krancke, Theodor, *Invasionsabwehrmaßnahmen der Kriegsmarine im Kanalgebiet 1944* (Measures of Defence against Invasion by the Kriegsmarine in the Channel Area 1944) in *Marinerundschau* 3/1969.

Krausnick, Helmut and Wilhelm, Hans-Heinrich, *Die Truppe des Weltanschauungskrieges. Die Einsatzgruppen der Sicherheitspolizei und des SD 1938–1942* (The Troops of the Weltanschauungs War. The Task Forces of the Security Police and the SD 1938–1942), Stuttgart, 1981.

Krautkrämer, Elmar, *Das Ringen um die Erhaltung der französischen Souveränität in Nordafrika im Zusammenhang mit TORCH* (The Struggle for the Maintenance of French Sovereignity in North Africa in Connection with TORCH) in *Militärgeschichtliche Mitteilungen* 2/1982.

Krebs, Gerhard, *Japan und der deutsch-sowjetische Krieg 1941* (Japan and the German-Soviet War 1941) in *Zwei Wege nach Moskau* (Two Roads to Moscow), ed. Bernd Wegner, Munich, Zurich, 1991.

Krebs, Gerhard and Martin, Bernd (pub.), *Formierung und Fall der Achse Berlin-Tokyo* (Formation and Fall of the Berlin-Tokyo Axis), Munich, 1994.

Kreidel, Hellmuth, *Partisanenkampf in Mittelrußland* (Partisan Fighting in Central Russia) in *Wehrkunde* 1955.

Kriegstagebuch des Oberkommando der Wehrmacht (Wehrmachtsführungsstab) 1940–1945 (War Diary of the OKW Operations Staff – 1940-1945), pub. Percy Ernst Schramm on behalf of the Committee for Military Research, special edition in 8 volumes, Bonn, undated; original edition Frankfurt/M., 1961–79.

Krienen, Dag, *'Barbarossas' langer Bart* ('Barbarossa's' Long Beard) in *Die Achte Etappe*, Bonn, April 1992.
- *'Gewitter' oder 'Barbarossa'?* ('Thunderstorm' or 'Barbarossa'?) in *Die Neunte Etappe*, Bonn, March 1993.
Kroener, Bernhard R., *Der 'erfrorene Blitzkrieg'. Strategische Planungen der deutschen Führung gegen die Sowjetunion und die Ursache ihres Scheiterns* ('The Blitzkrieg that Froze'. Strategic Planning against the Soviet Union by the German Leadership and the Reason for its Failure) in *Zwei Wege nach Moskau* (Two Roads to Moscow), ed. Bernd Wegner, Munich, Zurich, 1991.
- *'Nun Volk steh auf...' Stalingrad und der 'totale Krieg' 1941–1943* ('Now People Arise...' Stalingrad and 'Total War' 1941–1943) in *Stalingrad*. ed. J. Förster, Munich, Zurich, 1993.
Krumpelt, Ihno, *Das Material und die Kriegführung* (Material and War), Frankfurt/M., 1968.
Kurowski, Franz, *Das Tor zur Festung Europa. Abwehr- und Rückzugskämpfe des XIV. Panzerkorps auf Sizilien, Sommer 1943* (The Gate to Fortress Europe. Battles in Defence and Retreat by XIV Panzer Corps in Sicily, Summer 1943), Neckargemünd,1966.
- *Der Luftkrieg über Deutschland* (The Air War over Germany), Düsseldorf, 1977.
- *Von der Polizeigruppe z.b.V. 'Wecke' zum Fallschirmpanzerkorps 'Hermann Göring'* (From Police Group on Special Assignment 'Wecke' to Armoured Airborne Corps 'Hermann Göring'), Osnabrück, 1994.

Lammers, Walther (pub.), *'Fahrberichte' aus der Zeit des deutsch-sowjetischen Krieges 1941* ('Reports' from the Time of the German–Soviet War, 1941), Boppard am Rhein, 1988.
Lewin, Ronald, *Entschied ULTRA den Krieg? Alliierte Funkaufklärung im 2. Weltkrieg* (Did ULTRA Decide the War? Allied Radio Intelligence during the Second World War), Koblenz, Bonn, 1981.
- *Funkaufklärung und Funktäuschung bei der alliierten Invasion in der Normandie* (Radio Intelligence and Radio Deception during the Allied Invasion of Normandy) in J. Rohwer and E. Jäckel (pub.), *Die Funkaufklärung und ihre Rolle im Zweiten Weltkrieg* (Radio Intelligence and its Role during the Second World War), Stuttgart, 1979.
Ley, Michael, *Genozid und Heilserwartung. Zum nationalsozialistischen Mord am Europäischen Judentum* (Genocide and Expectation of Salvation. On the National Socialist Murder of European Jewry), Vienna, 1993.
Lindheim, Hermann von, *Wie Hitler versuchte den Eintritt der USA in den Zweiten Weltkrieg zu verhindern* (How Hitler Tried to Prevent the USA Entering the Second World War) in *Wehrforschung* 3/1972.
Longmate, Norman, *The Bombers. The RAF Offensive against Germany 1939–1945*, London, 1983.
Löser, Jochen, *Bittere Pflicht. Kampf und Untergang der Berlin-Brandenburgischen 76. Infantriedivision* (Bitter Duty. Battle and Downfall of the Berlin-Brandenburg 76th Infantry Division), Osnabrück, 1986.
Loßberg, Bernhard von, *Im Wehrmachtsführungsstab* (Member of the Wehrmacht Operations Staff), Hamburg, 1950.

Ludewig, Joachim, *Der deutsche Rückzug aus Frankreich 1944* (The German Retreat from France, 1944), Freiburg, 1994.

Ludwig, Karl-Heinz, *Die deutschen Flakraketen im Zweiten Weltkrieg* (German AA Rockets in the Second World War) in *Militärgeschichtliche Mitteilungen* 1/1969.

Lund, Paul and Ludlam, Harry, *Die Nacht der U-Boote* (Night of the U-boats), Heyne Pocket Book No. 6137, Munich, 1983.

Magenheimer, Heinz, *Abwehrschlacht an der Weichsel. Vorbereitung, Ablauf, Erfahrungen* (Defensive Battle on the Vistula. Preparation, Course, Experiences), Freiburg, 2nd ed., 1986.

– *Der Deutsche Angriff auf Sowjetrußland 1941* (The German Attack on the Soviet Union 1941) in *ÖMZ* 3/1971.

– *Leningrad oder Moskau? Zur operativen Problematik im Ostfeldzug 1941* (Leningrad or Moscow? The Operational Problem of the Eastern Campaign, 1941) in *Wehrforschung* 1/1975.

– *Das Gesetz des Schwergewichts. Zur strategischen Lage Deutschlands im Frühjahr 1944* (The Law of Gravity. Germany's Strategic Position in Spring 1944) in *Wehrwissenschaftliche Rundschau* 1/1981.

– *Der Luftkrieg über Deutschland und die Rüstungsanstrengungen 1942–1945* (The Air War over Germany and the Arms Effort 1942–1945), in *ÖMZ* 2/1982.

– *Die Konferenz von Jalta 1945 und die 'Teilung Europas'* (The Yalta Conference 1945 and the 'Partitioning of Europe') in *ÖMZ* 3/1982.

– *Die Kriegswende im Mittelmeerraum 1942/43* (Turn of the War in the Mediterranean, 1942/43) in *Truppendienst* 3/1982.

– *Hintergründe und Wurzeln der Kriegswende 1942/43* (Background and Roots of the Turn of the War, 1942/43) in *Wehrwissenschaftliche Rundschau* 5/1982.

– *Die Sowjetunion und der Ausbruch des Zweiten Weltkrieges. Sowjetische Positionen zum Zeitabschnitt 1939–1941* (The Soviet Union and the Start of the Second World War. Soviet Positions in 1939–1941) in *ÖMZ* 5/1989.

– *Neue Erkenntnisse zum 'Unternehmen Barbarossa'* (New Insights into 'Operation Barbarossa') in *ÖMZ* 5/1991.

– *Zum deutsch-sowjetischen Krieg 1941. Neue Quellen und Erkenntnisse* (On the German–Soviet War, 1941. New Source Material and Knowledge), in *ÖMZ* 1/1994.

– *Zur Frage der Kriegswenden 1939–1945* (On the Question of the Turns of the War 1939–1945) in *ÖMZ* 4/1995.

Maier, Klaus A., *Die Luftschlacht über England* (The Air Battle over England) in *Information für die Truppe* 8/1980.

Malia, Martin, *Vollstreckter Wahn. Rußland 1917–1991* (Dementia Implemented. Russia 1917–1991, Stuttgart, 1994.

Manstein, Erich von, *Verlorene Siege* (Lost Victories), Munich, 9th ed., 1981.

Marolz, Josef, *Die Entwicklung der Verteidigung ab 1900. Zweiter Weltkrieg* (Development of Defence since 1900. Second World War) in *ÖMZ* 3/1988.

Martin, Bernd, *Deutschland und Japan im Zweiten Weltkrieg. Vom Angriff auf Pearl Harbor bis zur deutschen Kapitulation* (Germany and Japan in the

Second World War. From the Attack on Pearl Harbor to the German Surrender), Göttingen, Zurich, 1969.

– *Verhandlungen über separate Friedensschlüsse 1942–1945. Ein Beitrag zur Entstehung des Kalten Krieges* (Negotiations about Separate Peace Agreements 1942–1945. A Contribution to the Development of the Cold War) in *Militärgeschichtliche Mitteilungen* 2/1976.

– *Friedensinitiativen und Machtpolitik im Zweiten Weltkrieg 1939–1942* (Peace Initiatives and Power Politics in the Second World War 1939–1942), Düsseldorf, 2nd ed., 1976.

– *Japan und Stalingrad. Umorientierung vom Bündnis mit Deutschland auf 'Großostasien'* (Japan and Stalingrad. Realignment from the Alliance with Germany to 'Greater East Asia') in *Stalingrad*, ed. Jürgen Förster, Munich, Zurich, 1993.

– *Deutsch-sowjetische Sondierungen übereinen separaten Friedensschluß im Zwieten Weltkrieg. Berichte und Dokumente* (German–Soviet Feelers on a Separate Peace during the Second World War. Reports and Documents) in *Felder und Vorfelder russischer Gechichte* (Areas and Aspects of Russian History), ed. Inge Auerbach, Freiburg, 1985.

Maser, Werner, *Der Wortbruch. Hitler, Stalin und der Zweite Weltkrieg* (The Broken Word. Hitler, Stalin and the Second World War), Munich, 1994.

– *Der Zweite Weltkrieg – Stalins Krieg?* (The Second World War – Stalin's War?), five-part series in *Deutschland Magazin* 10/11/12/1993, 1/2/3/1994.

Masson, Phillppe, *Die deutsche Armee. Geschichte der Wehrmacht 1935–1945* (The German Army. History of the Wehrmacht 1935–1945), Munich, 1996.

Mastny, Vojtech, *Moskaus Weg zum Kalten Krieg. Von der Kriegsallianz zur sowjetischen Vormachtstellung in Osteuropa* (Moscow's Road to the Cold War. From the War Alliance to Domination in Eastern Europe), Munich, Vienna, 1980.

Matloff, Maurice, *Strategic Planning for Coalition Warfare 1933–1944*, Washington DC, 1959.

Mayer, Arno J., *Der Krieg als Kreuzzug. Das Deutsche Reich, Hitlers Wehrmacht und die 'Endlösung'* (The War as a Crusade. The German Reich, Hitler's Wehrmacht and the 'Final Solution'), Reinbeck near Hamburg, 1989.

Meier-Welcker, Hans, *Der Entschluß zum Anhalten der deutschen Panzertruppen in Flandern 1940* (The Decision to Stop the German Armoured Forces in Flanders, 1940) in the same, *Soldat und Gechichte. Aufsätze* (Soldier and History. Essays), Boppard, 1976.

– *Aufzeichnungen eines Generalstabsoffiziers 1939–1942* (Notes by an Officer of the General Staff 1939–1942), Freiburg, 1982.

Meltyukov, Mikhail, *Auch im Feidesland zerschlagen wir den Feind* (We Will Destroy the Enemy Even in Enemy Territory), in Russian in *Rodina* (Home) 5/1995.

Mennel, Rainer, *Italien 1943–1945. Ein Beitrag zur politischen Geographie eines Wehr und Kampfraumes* (Italy 1943–1945. A Contribution to the Politcal Geography of a Defence and Battle Area), dissertation, Berlin, 1971.

– *Die Schlußphase des Zweiten Weltkrieges im Westen 1944/45. Eine Studie zur politichen Geographie* (The Final Phase of the Second World War in the West, 1944/45. A Study in Political Geography), Osnabrück, 1981.

Mercalov, Andrei N., *Der 22. Juni 1941; Anmerkungen eines sowjetischen Historikers* (22 June 1941. Notes by a Soviet Historian) in *Aus Politik und Zeitgeschichte* of 7 June 1991.

Meyer, Georg (pub.), *Generalfeldmarschall Wilhelm Ritter von Leeb, Tagebuchaufzeichnungen und Lagebeurteilungen aus zwei Weltkriegen* (Field Marshal Ritter von Leeb, Diary Notes and Situation Evaluations from Two World Wars), Stuttgart, 1976.

MGFA Militärgeschichtliches Forschungsamt, *Das Deutsche Reich und der Zweite Weltkrieg* (The German Reich and the Second World War), published by the Office of Military Historic Research, six volumes, Stuttgart, 1979–90.

Michalka, Wolfgang, *Ribbentrop und die deutsche Weltpolitik 1933–1940* (Ribbentrop and German World Politics 1933–1940), Munich, 1980.

Michalka, Wolfgang (pub.), *Nationalsozialistische Außenpolitik* (National Socialist Foreign Policy), Darmstadt, 1978.

– *Der Zweite Weltkrieg. Analysen, Grunzüge, Forschungsbilanz* (The Second World War. Analyses, Fundamentals, Research Results), Piper Series No. 811, Munich, Zurich, 1989.

Middeldorf, Eike, *Das Unternehmen 'Zitadelle'* (Operation 'Citadel'), parts I and II, in *Wehrwissenschaftliche Rundschau* 10/1952, 11/1953.

– *Die Abwehrschlacht am Weichselbrückenkopf Baranow. Eine Studie über neuzeitliche Verteidigung* (The Defensive Battle in the Baranov Bridgehead on the Vistula. A Study in Modern Defence) in *Wehrwissenschaftliche Rundschau* 4/1953.

Middlebrook, Martin, *Die Nacht, in der die Bomber starben. Der Angriff auf Nürnberg und seine Folgen für den Luftkrieg* (The Night the Bombers Died. The Attack on Nuremberg and its Consequences for the Air War), Ullstein Book No. 3296, Frankfurt/M., Berlin, Vienna, 1976.

Milward, Alan S., *Der Zweite Weltkrieg* (The Second World War) in *Geschichte der Weltwirtschaft im 20. Jahrhundert* (History of World Economics in the 20th Century), vol. 5, dtv Scientific Series No. 4125, Munich, 1977.

– *Arbeitspolitik und Produktivität in der deutschen Kriegswirtschaft unter vergleichendem Aspekt* (Labour Policy and Productivity in the German War Economy as a Comparison) in *Kriegswirtschaft und Rüstung 1939–1945* (War Economy and Armament 1939–1945), ed. F. Forstmeier and H-E. Volkmann, Düsseldorf, 1977.

Moldenhauer, Harald, *Die Reorganisation der Roten Armee von den 'Großen Säuberungen' bis zum deutschen Angriff auf die UdSSR 1938–1941* (Reorganization of the Red Army from the 'Great Purges' to the German Attack on the USSR 1938–1941) in *Militärgeschichtliche Mitteilungen* 1/1996.

Molony, C. J. C. and others, *The Campaign in Sicily 1943 and the Campaign in Italy 3rd September 1943 to 31st March 1944* in *History of the Second World War, United Kingdom Military Series: The Mediterranean and the Middle East*, vol. 5, London, 1973.

Molt, Albert, *Der deutsche Festungsbau von der Memel bis zum Atlantik. Festungspioniere, Ingenieurkorps, Pioniertruppe 1900 bis 1945* (German Fortification Construction from the Memel to the Atlantic. Fortress Engineers, Engineer Corps, Construction Troops 1900 to 1945), Friedberg, 1988.

Morozow, Michael, *Die Falken im Kreml*, (The Hawks in the Kremlin), Munich, Vienna, 1982.

Mühlen, Patrick von zur, *Zwischen Hakenkreuz und Sowjetstern. Der National-ismus der sowetischen Ostvölker im Zweiten Weltkrieg* (Between Swastika and Red Star. Nationalism of the Soviet Eastern Peoples in the Second World War), Düsseldorf, 1971.

Müllenberg-Rechberg, Burkhard Freiherr von, *Schlachtschiff Bismarck – Der Bericht eines Überlebenden* (Battleship Bismarck – Report by a Survivor), Berlin, 1980.

Müller, Rolf-Dieter, *Hitlers Ostkrieg und diedeutsche Siedlungspolitik. Die Zusam-menarbeit von Wehrmacht, Wirtschaft und SS* (Hitler's Eastern War and German Settlement Policy. The Cooperation between Wehrmacht, Economy and SS), Frankfurt/M., 1991.

– *Das Tor zur Weltmacht* (The Door to World Power), Boppard, 1984.

– *Industrielle Interessenspolitik im Rahmen des 'Generalplans Ost'. Dokumente zum Einfluß von Wehrmacht, Industrie und SS auf die wirtschaftspolitische Zielsetzung für Hitlers Ostimperium* (Industrial Policies within the Frame-work of the 'General Plan East'. Documents on the Influence of Wehrmacht, Industry and SS on the Economic Objectives in Hitler's Eastern Empire) in *Militärgeschichtliche Mitteilungen* 1/1981.

Müller, Rolf-Dieter (pub.), *Die deutsche Wirtschaftspolitik in den besetzten sowetischen Gebieten 1941–1943. Der Abschlußbericht des Wirtschaftsstabes Ost und Aufzeich nungen eines Angehörigen des Wirtschaftskommandos Kiew* (German Economic Policy in the Occupied Soviet Territories 1941–1943. The Final Report by the Economic Staff East and Notes by a Member of the Economic Command Kiev), Boppard, 1991.

Müller-Hillebrand, Burkhart, *Das Heer 1933 bis 1945. Entwicklung des organ-isatorischen Aufbaus* (The Army from 1933 to 1945. Development of its Organizational Structure), vol. III, Frankfurt/M., 1969.

Münter, Otto, *Die Ostfreiwilligen. Der vergebliche Kampf der Stalin-Gegner im Zweiten Weltkrieg* (The Eastern Volunteers. The Futile Battle of Stalin's Opponents during the Second World War) in *Damals* 3/1979.

Murray, Williamson, *Reflections on the Combined Bomber Offensive* in *Militärgeschichtliche Mitteilungen* 1/1992.

Nawratil, Heinz, *Vertreibungsverbrechen an Deutschen. Tatbestand, Motive, Bewältigung* (Crimes of Expulsion against Germans. Facts, Motives, After-math), Munich, 1982.

Neulen, Hans-Werner, *An deutscher Seite. Internationale Freiwillige von Wehrmacht und Waffen-SS* (On the German Side. International Volunteers in the Wehrmacht and the Waffen-SS), Munich, 2nd ed., 1992.

– *Europa und das Dritte Reich. Einigungsbestrebungen im deutschen Machtbereich 1939–945* (Europe and the Third Reich. Tendencies towards Unification in the German Sphere of Power 1939–1945), Munich, 1987.

Neveshin, Vladimir A., *Die Stalinsche Wahl des Jahres 1941. Verteidigung oder... Die Lösung eines Angriffskrieges?* (Stalin's Choice 1941. Defence or... The Solution of a War of Aggression?) in Russian in *Otechestvennaja istorija* (Patriotic History) 3/1996.

– *The Pact with Germany and the Idea of an 'Offensive War' 1939–1941* in *The Journal of Slavic Military Studies*, December 1995.

Niepold, Gerd, *Mittlere Ostfront, Juni '44* (Central Eastern Front, June '44), Herford, Bonn, 1985.

– *Führung der Heeresgruppe Mitte von Juni bis August 1944* (Leadership of Army Group Centre from June to August 1944) in *MARS. Jahrbuch für Wehrpolitik und Militärwesen 1996*, ed. Dermot Bradley et al., Osnabrück, 1996

Nisbet, Robert, *Roosevelt und Stalin*, Ullstein Book No. 34907, Frankfurt/M., Berlin, 1992.

Nolte, Ernst, *Der Faschismus in seiner Epoche* (Fascism in its Time), Munich, 1963.

– *Der Europäische Bürgerkrieg 1917–1945* (The European Civil War 1917–1945) in the same, *Lehrstück oder Tragödie?* (Lesson or Tragedy?), Cologne, 1991.

Nolte, Hans-Heinrich (pub.), *Der Mensch gegen den Menschen. Überlegungen und Forschungen zum deutschen Überfall auf die Sowjetunion* (Man against Man. Considerations and Research on the German Attack against the Soviet Union), Hannover, 1992.

Nowarra, Heinz J., *Die deutsche Luftrüstung 1933–1945* (German Air Armament 1933–1945), vol. 3, Koblenz, 1987.

Oberländer, Erwin (pub.), *Hitler–Stalin–Pakt. Das Ende Mitteleuropas?* (Hitler–Stalin Pact. The End of Central Europe?), Fischer Pocket Books No. 4434, Frankfurt/M., 1989.

Oberländer, Theodor, *Der Osten und die Deutsche Wehrmacht. 6 Denkschriften aus den Jahren 1941–1943 gegen die NS-Kolonialthese* (The East and the Wehrmacht. Six Memoranda from 1941–1943 against the Nazi Colonial Thesis), ed. Zeitgeschichtliche Forschungsstelle, Asendorf, 1987.

Ogorreck, Ralf, *Die Einsatzgruppen und die 'Genesis der Endlösung'* (The Task Forces and the 'Genesis of the Final Solution'), Berlin, 1996.

Ose, Dieter, *Entscheidung im Westen 1944. Der Oberbefehlshaber West und die Abwehr der alliierten Invasion* (Decision in the West 1944. The C-in-C West and the Repulse of the Allied Invasion) in *Beiträge zur Militär- und Kriegsgeschichte* (Contributions to Military and War History), vol. 22, Stuttgart, 1982.

– *Vor 40 Jahren: Invasion 1944* (40 Years Ago. Invasion 1944), part I, in *Truppenpraxis* 7/1984.

Ostertag, Heiger, *Die größte Panzerschlacht der Weltgeschichte* (The Greatest Tank Battle in History) in *Truppenpraxis* 4/1993.

Overmans, Rüdiger, *55 Millionen Opfer des Zweiten Weltkrieges? Zum Stand der Forschung nach mehr als 40 Jahren* (Fifty-five Million Victims of the Second World War? On the State of Research After More than 40 Years) in *Militärgeschichtliche Mitteilungen* 2/1990.

– *Das andere Gesicht des Krieges. Leben und Sterben der 6. Armee* (The Other Face of War. Life and Death of the Sixth Army) in *Stalingrad*, ed. J. Förster, Munich, Zurich, 1993.

Paul, Wolfgang, *Die Schlacht um Moskau* (The Battle for Moscow), Heyne Book No. 5515, Munich, 1978.

Philippi, Alfred, *Das Pripjetproblem. Eine Studie über die operative Bedeutung des Pripjetgebietes für den Feldzug des Jahres 1941* (The Pripet Problem. Study on the Operational Importance of the Pripet Area for the Campaign in 1941), Darmstadt, 1956.

Philippi, Alfred and Heim, Der Feldzug gegen Sowejetrußland (The Campaign against Soviet Russia).

Picker, Henry, *Hitler's Tischgespräche im Führerhauptquartier* (Hitler's Table Talks at Führer Headquarters), revised ed. Stuttgart, 1977.

Piekalkievicz, Janusz, *Stalingrad – Anatomie einer Schlacht* (Stalingrad – Anatomy of a Battle), Munich, 1977.

– *Invasion Frankreich 1944* (Invasion of France, 1944), Munich, 1979.

– *Moskau – Die erfrorene Offensive* (Moscow – The Offensive that Froze), Bergisch-Gladbach, 1981.

– *Luftkrieg 1939–1945* (Air War 1939–1945), Heyne Book No. 6013, Munich, 1982.

– *Unternehmen Zitadelle* (Operation Citadel), Bergisch-Gladbach, 1983.

Pietrow-Ennker, Bianka, *Deutschland im Juni 1941 – ein Opfer sowjetischer Aggression?* (Germany in June 1941 – A Victim of Soviet Aggression?) in *Der Zweite Weltkrieg* (The Second World War), ed. Wolfgang Michalka, Munich, Zurich, 1989.

– *Es war kein Präventivkrieg* (It Was Not a Preventive War) in *Die Zeit* of 25 February 1995.

Post, Walter, *Pearl Harbor 1941* in *Criticon*, November–December 1991.

– *Operation Barbarossa. Deutsche und sowjetische Angriffspläne 1940/41* (Operation Barbarossa. German and Soviet Plans of Attack, 1940/41), Berlin, Hamburg, 1995.

Pötschke, Christian, *Planung und Unternehmen 'Barbarossa'* (Plan and Operation 'Barbarossa'), dissertation, Cologne, 1982.

Pron'ko, Valentin A., *Die sowjetische Strategie im Jahre 1943* (Soviet Strategy in 1943) in *Stalingrad*, ed. J Förster, Munich, Zurich, 1993.

Raack, Richard C., *Stalin's Drive to the West 1938–1941*, Stanford, Cal., 1995.

– *Stalin's Role in the Coming of The Second World War* in *Foreign Affairs*, Spring 1996.

Rahn, Werner, *Einsatzbereitschaft und Kampfkraft deutscher U-Boote* (Combat Readiness and Combat Power of German Submarines) in *Militärgeschichtliche Mitteilungen* 1/1990.

– *Wege zur historischen Wahrheit* (Roads to Historical Truth), presentation given in Munich on 28 June 1996 at the Day of the Royal Bavarian Life Infantry Regiment.

Rauh, Manfred, *Geschichte des Zweiten Weltkrieges* (History of the Second World War), part 1, *Die Voraussetzungen* (The Preconditions), Berlin, 1991; part 2, *Der europäische Krieg* (The European War), Berlin, 1995.

Reichling, Gerhard, *Die deutschen Vertriebenen in Zahlen* (Numbers of Expelled Germans), part I, *Umsiedler, Verschleppte, Vertriebene, Aussiedler 1940–1985* (Relocated, Deported, Expelled, Resettled 1940–1985), Bonn, 1995.

– *Die deutschen Vertriebenen in Zahlen* (Numbers of Expelled Germans), Kulturstiftung der deutschen Vertriebenen (Cultural Foundation of the

Expelled Germans), Bonn, 1945.

Reif, Adelbert (pub.), *Albert Speer. Kontroversen um ein deutsches Phänomen* (Albert Speer. Controversies about a German Phenomenon), Munich, 1978.

Reinhardt, Klaus, *Die Wende vor Moskau. Das Scheitern der Strategie Hitlers im Winter 1941/42* (The Turn before Moscow. Failure of Hitler's Strategy in Winter 1941/42) in *Beiträge zur Militär- und Kriegsgeschichte* (Contributions to Military and War History), vol. 13, Stuttgart, 1972.

– *Das Scheitern des deutschen Blitzkriegskonzepts vor Moskau* (Failure of the German Blitzkrieg Concept Before Moscow) in *Kriegswende Dezember 1941* (Turn of the War, December 1941), ed. Jürgen Rohwer and Eberhard Jäckel, Stuttgart, 1984.

Reuth, Ralf-Georg, *Entscheidung im Mittelmeer. Die südliche Peripherie Europas in der deutschen Strategie des Zweiten Weltkrieges 1940–1942* (Decision in the Mediterranean. Europe's Southern Perimeter in Germany's Strategy in the Second World War, 1940–1942), Koblenz, 1985.

– *Goebbels*, Munich, Zurich, 2nd ed., 1991.

Reuth, Ralf-Georg (pub.), *Joseph Goebbels. Tagebücher* (Diaries), Munich, 1992.

Rohwer, Jürgen, *Wußte Roosevelt davon? Zur Vorgeschichte des japanischen Angriffs auf Pearl Harbor* (Did Roosevelt Know? On the Background of the Japanese Attack on Pearl Harbor) in *Wehrwissenschaftliche Rundschau*, 1954.

– *Die Nachrichtentechnik und der Angriff auf Pearl Harbor. Ein Literaturbericht* (Communications Technology and the Attack on Pearl Harbor. Report on the Literature) in *Millitärgeschichtliche Mitteilungen* 2/1968.

– *Geleitzugsschlachten im März 1943. Führungsprobleme im Höhepunkt der Schlacht im Atlantik* (Convoy Battles in March 1943. Leadership Problems at the Height of the Battle of the Atlantic), Stuttgart, 1975.

– *Die alliierte Funkaufklärung und der Verlauf des Zweiten Weltkrieges* (Allied Radio Intelligence and the Course of the Second World War) in *Vierteljahreshefte für Zeitgeschichte* 3/1979.

– *Die Auswirkungen der deutschen und britischen Funkaufklärung in den Geleitzugs-Schlachten im Nordatlantik* (Effects of German and British Radio Intelligence in the Convoy Battles in the North Atlantic) in *Die Funkaufklärung und ihre Rolle im Zweiten Weltkrieg* (Radio Intelligence and its Role in the Second World War), ed. J. Rohwer and E. Jäckel, Stuttgart, 1979.

– *Die USA und die Schlacht im Atlantik 1941* (The USA and the Battle of the Atlantic, 1941) in Rohwer and Jäckel (pub.). *Kriegswende Dezember 1941* (Turn of the War, December 1941), Stuttgart, 1984.

Rohwer, Jürgen and Jäckel, Eberhard (pub.), *Die Funkaufklärung und ihre Rolle im Zweiten Weltkrieg* (Radio Intelligence and its Role in the Second World War), Stuttgart, 1979.

– *Kriegswende Dezember 1941. Referate und Diskussionsbeiträge des internationalen historischen Symposiums in Stuttgart vom 17. bis 19. September 1981* (Turn of the War, December 1941. Presentations and Discussion at the International Historical Symposium, 17–19 September 1981 in Stuttgart), Koblenz, 1984.

Rössler, Mechtild and Schleiermacher, Sabine (pub.), *Der 'Generalplan Ost'. Hauptlinien der nationalsozialistischen Planungs- und Vernichtungspolitik* (The

'General Plan East'. Principles of National Socialist Planning and Extermination Policy), Berlin, 1993.

Rückbrodt, Peter, *Die Invasion in der Normandie 1944* (The Invasion of Normandy, 1944) in *Europäische Wehrkunde* 2/1977.

– *Die Invasion in der Normandie - Überraschung und Täuschung der deutschen militärischen Führung?* (The Invasion of Normandy. Surprise and Deception of the German Military Leadership?) in *Wehrwissenschaftliche Rundschau* 6/1978.

Ruffmann, Karl-Heinz, *Schlüsseljahre im Verhältnis zwischen dem Deutschen Reich und der Sowjetunion* (Key Years in the Relationship between the German Reich and the Soviet Union) in *Aus Politik und Zeitgeschichte* of 7 June 1991.

Ruge, Friedrich, *Rommel und die Invasion* (Rommel and the Invasion), Stuttgart, 1959.

– *Rommel und die Invasion* (Rommel and the Invasion) in *Europäische Wehrkunde* 10/1979.

Rühl, Lothar, *Aufstieg und Untergang des Russischen Reiches* (Rise and Fall of the Russian Empire), Stuttgart, 1992.

Rumpf, Hans, *Das war der Bombenkrieg. Deutsche Städte im Feuersturm* (That Was the Bomb War. German Cities under the Firestorm), Oldenburg, 1961.

– *Die Verluste der westdeutschen Zivilbevölkerung im Luftkrieg* (Losses in the West German Civilian Population in the Air War) in *Wehrwissenschaftliche Rundschau* 10/1993.

Salewski, Michael, *Die deutsche Seekriegsleitung 1935-1945* (German Naval Leadership 1935-1945), 2 vol., Frankfurt/M., Munich, 1970, 1975.

Samsonov, Alexander M., *Die Schlacht vor Moskau* (The Battle of Moscow) in *Kriegswende Dezember 1941* (Turn of the War, December 1941), ed. J. Rohwer and E. Jäckel, Stuttgart, 1984.

Santoni, Alberto, *Ultra siegt im Mittelmeer. Die entscheidende Rolle der britischen Funkaufklärung 1940-1943* (Ultra Wins in the Mediterranean. The Decisive Role of British Radio Intelligence 1940-1943), Koblenz, 1985.

Schall-Riaucour, Heidermarie Gräfin, *Aufstand und Gehorsam. Offizierstum und Generalstab im Umbruch. Leben und Wirken von Generaloberst Franz Halder, Generalstabschef 1938-1942* (Revolt and Obedience. Officership and General Staff in Transition. Life and Effect of Colonel General Franz Halder, Chief of the General Staff, 1938-1942), Wiesbaden, 1972.

Scheibert, Horst, *Zwischen Don und Donez Winter 1942/43* (Between Don and Donetz Winter 1942/43), Neckargemünd, 1961.

Schellenberg, Walter, *Aufzeichnungen* (Notations), previously unpublished documents, with new comments by Gerald Flemming, Wiesbaden, Munich, 1979.

Schickel, Alfred, *Hat Deutschland den Zweiten Weltkrieg durch Verrat verloren?* (Did Germany Lose the Second World War Because of Treason?) in *Wehrwissenschaftliche Rundschau* 5/1968.

Schinzer, Dankmut, *Truppendichte und Angriffserfolg. Eine Operations-Research-Untersuchung der Ardennenoffensive* (Troop Concentration and Success in Attack. An Operations Research Study of the Ardennes Offensive) in

Wehrwissenschaftliche Rundschau 4/1982.

Schlauch, Wolfgang, *Rüstungshilfe der USA an die Verbündeten im Zweiten Weltkrieg* (US Arms Aid to the Allies in the Second World War), Darmstadt, 1967.

Schlie, Ulrich, *Kein Friede mit Deutschland. Die Geheimen Gespräche im Zweiten Weltkrieg 1939–1941* (No Peace with Germany. The Secret Talks during the Second World War 1939–1941), Munich, Berlin, 1994.

Schlögel, Karl (pub.), *Der große Exodus. Die Russische Emigration und ihre Zentren 1917–1941* (The Great Exodus. Russian Emigration and its Centres 1917–1941), Munich, 1994.

Schmidl, Erwin A (ed.), *Freund oder Feind?* (Enemy or Friend?), Frankfurt/M., Berlin, Bern, 1995.

Schmidt, Matthias, *Albert Speer: Das Ende eines Mythos. Speers wahre Rolle im Dritten Reich* (Albert Speer. The End of a Myth. Speer's True Role in the Third Reich), Bern, Munich, 1982.

Schmidt, Rainer F., *Eine verfehlte Strategie für alle Fälle. Stalins Taktik und Kalkül im Vorfeld des Unternehmens 'Barbarossa'* (A Mistaken Strategy in any Case. Stalin's Tactics and Calculations in the Context of Operation 'Barbarossa' in *Geschichte in Wissenschaft und Unterricht* 6/1994.

Schoeppner, Heinz, *Stalingrad 1942–1943*, in *MARS. Jahrbuch für Wehrpolitik und Militärwesen*, Osnabrück, 1966.

Schofield, Brian B., *Geleitzugschlachten in der Eishölle des Nordmeeres* (Convoy Battles in the Icy Hell of the North Sea), Herford, 1980.

– *Die Rolle der Trade Division der Admiralität und die Gründe für die Wende in der Schlacht im Atlantik im Frühjahr 1943* (The Role of the Admiralty Trade Division and the Reasons for the Turn in the Battle of the Atlantic in Spring 1943) in *Die Funkaufklärung und ihre Rolle im Zweiten Weltkrieg* (Radio Intelligence and its Role in the Second World War), ed. J. Rohwer and E. Jäckel, Stuttgart, 1979.

Schröder, Bernd Philipp, *Deutschland und der Mittlere Osten im Zweiten Weltkrieg* (Germany and the Middle East in the Second World War), Frankfurt/M., Zurich, 1975.

Schröder, Hans-Henning, *Die Lehren von 1941. Die Diskussion um die Neubewertung des 'Großen Vaterländischen Krieges' in der Sowjetunion* (The Lessons of 1941. The Discussion in the Soviet Union about the Reassessment of the 'Great Patriotic War') in *Der Zweite Weltkrieg* (The Second World War), ed. Wolfgang Michalka, Munich, Zurich, 1989.

– *Der 'Stalinismus' – ein totalitäres System?* ('Stalinism' – a Totalitarian System?), in *Osteuropa* 2/1996.

Schröder, Josef, *Italiens Kriegsaustritt 1943. Die deutschen Gegenmaßnahmen im italienischen Raum: Fall 'Alarich' und 'Achse'* (Italy's Exit from the War in 1943. German Counter-Measures in Italy: Cases 'Alarich' and 'Axis'), Göttingen, 1969.

– *Bestrebungen zur Eliminierung der Ostfront 1941–1943* (Attempts to Eliminate the Eastern Front 1941–1943), Göttingen, Zurich, 1985.

Schüler, Klaus, *Der Ostfeldzug als Transport und Versorgungsproblem* (The Eastern Campaign as a Problem in Transport and Supply) in *Zwei Wege nach Moskau* (Two Roads to Moscow), ed. Bernd Wegner, Munich, Zurich, 1991.

Schultz-Naumann, Joachim, *Die letzten 30 Tage. Das Kriegstagebuch des OKW April bis Mai 1945* (The Final 30 Days. The War Diary of the OKW April to May 1945), Munich, 1980.

Schustereit, Hartmut, *Vabanque. Hitlers Angriff auf die Sowjetunion 1941 als Versuch durch den Sieg im Osten den Westen zu bezwingen* (Risk. Hitler's Attack on the Soviet Union 1941 as an Attempt to Beat the West by a Victory in the East), Herford, Bonn, 1988.

Schwabe, Klaus, *Die Regierung Roosevelt und die Expansionspolitik Hitlers vor dem Zweiten Weltkrieg* (The Roosevelt Government and Hitler's Expansion Policy before the Second World War) in *Die Westmächte und das Dritte Reich 1933–1939* (The Western Powers and the Third Reich 1933–1939), pub. Karl Rohe, Paderborn, 1982.

Schwarz, Eberhard, *Die Stabilisierung der Ostfront nach Stalingrad. Mansteins Gegenschlag zwischen Donez und Dnjeper im Frühjahr 1943* (The Stabilization of the Eastern Front after Stalingrad. Manstein's Counterblow between Donetz and Dnieper in Spring 1943), Göttingen, 1985.

– *Zwischen Stalingrad und Kursk. Die Stabilisierung der Ostfront im Februar/März 1943* (Between Stalingrad and Kursk. Stabilization of the Eastern Front in February/March 1943), in *Stalingrad*, ed. J. Förster, Munich, Zurich, 1993.

Seraphim, Hans-Günther and Hillgruber, Andreas, *Hitlers Entschluß zum Angriff auf Rußland. Eine Entgegnung* (Hitler's Decision to Attack Russia. A Reply) in *Vierteljahreshefte für Zeitgeschichte 2/1954.*

Sereny, Gitta, *Albert Speer. Das Ringen um die Wahrheit und das deutsche Trauma* (Albert Speer. The Struggle for the Truth and the German Trauma), Munich, 1995.

Seydlitz, Walther von, *Stalingrad. Konflikt und Konsequenzen* (Stalingrad. Conflict and Consequences), Oldenburg, 1977.

Slutsch, Sergei, *Warum brauchte Hitler einen Nichtangriffspakt mit Stalin?* (Why did Hitler Need a Non-Aggression Pact with Stalin?) in *'Unternehmen Barbarossa'. Zum historischen Ort der deutsch-sowjetischen Beziehungen von 1933–1941* ('Operation Barbarossa'. On the Historic Position of German-Soviet Relations 1933–1941), ed. Roland Foerster, Munich 1993.

Solovyov, Boris, *Die Schlacht bei Kursk* (The Battle of Kursk), Moscow 1979, German translation: APN Publishing, Novosti Press.

– *Wendepunkt des Zweiten Weltkrieges. Die Schlacht bei Kursk* (Turn of the Second World War. The Battle of Kursk), Cologne, 1983.

Sommer, Erich F., *Das Memorandum. Wie der Sowjetunion der Krieg erklärt wurde* (The Memorandum. How War Was Declared against the Soviet Union), Munich, Berlin, 1981.

Speer, Albert, *Erinnerungen* (Memoirs), Ullstein Book No. 3026, Frankfurt/M., Berlin, Vienna, 1969.

– *Der Sklavenstaat. Meine Auseinandersetzung mit der SS* (The Slave State. My Conflict with the SS), Stuttgart, 1981.

Starkov, Oleg, *Militärischer Geheimnisverrat am Vorabend von 1941 'Barbarossa'*, (Military Treason on the Eve of 'Barbarossa', 1941), in ÖMZ 4/1991.

Stegemann, Bernhard, *Der Entschluß zum Unternehmen Barbarossa. Strategie oder Ideologie?* (The Decision for Operation Barbarossa. Strategy or Ideology?) in *Geschichte in Wissenschaft und Unterricht 33/1982.*

– *Geschichte und Politik. Zur Diskussion über den deutschen Angriff auf die Sowjetunion 1941* (History and Politics. On the Discussion about the German Attack on the Soviet Union 1941) in *Beiträge zur Konfliktforschung 1/1987*.

Streim, Alfred, *Die Behandlung sowjetischer Kriegsgefangener im 'Fall Barbarossa'* (Treatment of Soviet Prisoners of War in 'Case Barbarossa'), Heidelberg, Karlsruhe, 1981.

Stripp, Alan, *Reflections on British Wartime Codebreaking*, presentation given on 26 June 1994 in Cologne.

Ströbinger, Rudolf, *Stalin enthauptet die Rote Armee. Der Fall Tuchatschevskij* (Stalin Decapitates the Red Army. The Tukashevsky Case), Stuttgart, 1990.

Sudoplatov, Pavel and Sudoplatov, Anatoly, *Die Handlanger der Macht – Enthüllungen eines KGB-Generals* (The Henchmen of Power – Disclosures by a KGB General), Düsseldorf, Vienna, 1994.

Sun Tsu, *Traktat über die Kriegskunst* (Treatise on the Art of War), ed. J. A. Rasin, East Berlin, 1957.

Suvorov, Viktor, (pseudonym), *Der Eisbrecher. Hitler in Stalins Kalkül* (The Ice Breaker. Hitler in Stalin's Calculations), Stuttgart, 1989.

– *Der Tag* (The Day), Stuttgart, 1995.

Syring, Enrico, *Hitlers Kriegserklärung an Amerika am 11 Dezember 1941* (Hitler's Declaration of War against America on 11 December 1941) in *Zwei Wege nach Moskau* (Two Roads to Moscow), ed. Bernd Wegner, Munich, Zurich, 1991.

Tarleton, Robert E., *What Really Happened to the Stalin Line?*, part I, in *The Journal of Soviet Military Studies*, 2/1992.

Taysen, Adalbert von, *Tobruk 1941. Der Kampf um Nordafrika* (Tobruk 1941. The Battle for North Africa), Freiburg, 1976.

Tessin, Georg, *Verbände und Truppen der deutschen Wehrmacht und der Waffen-SS im Zweiten Weltkrieg 1939–1945* (Formations and Troops of the Wehrmacht and Waffen-SS during the Second World War 1939–1945), vol. 1, Osnabrück, 1977.

Thadden, Adolf von, *Zwei Angreifer. Der Angriff der deutschen Wehrmacht auf die auch zum Angriff aufmarschierte Rote Armee im Juni 1941* (Two Attackers. The Attack by the Wehrmacht against the Red Army, and the Latter's Deployment in June 1941), Essen, 1993.

Theil, Edmund, *Rommels verheizte Armee. Kampf und Ende der Heeresgruppe Afrika von El Alamein bis Tunis* (Rommel's Sacrificed Army. The Battle and Defeat of Army Group Africa from El Alamein to Tunis), Vienna, Munich, Zurich, Innsbruck, 1979.

Theobald, Robert A., *Das letzte Geheimnis von Pearl Harbor. Washingtons Anteil an dem japanischen Angriff* (The Last Secret of Pearl Harbor. Washington's Part in the Japanese Attack), New York, 1963.

Thies, Jochen, *Architekt der Weltherrschaft. Die 'Endziele' Hitlers* (Architect of World Rule, Hitler's 'Final Objectives'), Athenäum Droste Pocket Books on History No. 7235, Königstein, Düsseldorf, 1980.

Tippelskirch, Kurt von, *Geschichte des Zweiten Weltkrieges* (History of the Second World War), Bonn, 1959.

Tolstoy, Nikolai, *Die Verratenen von Jalta. Die Schuld der Alliierten vor der*

Geschichte (The Betrayed of Yalta. The Allies' Historical Guilt), Heyne Book No. 5876, Munich, 1981.

Topitsch, Ernst, *Stalins Krieg. Die sowjetische Langzeitstrategie gegen den Westen als rationale Machtpolitik* (Stalin's War. Soviet Long-term Strategy against the West as Rational Power Politics), Munich, 2nd ed., 1986 (and as a 4th ed., Herford, 1990 and 1993 entitled Stalin's War. Moscow's Grasp for World Power – Strategy and Failure).

– *'Barbarossa' – ein Präventivkrieg? Zur ideologischen Korrumpierung der Historie* ('Barbarossa' – a Preventive War? On the Ideological Corruption of History) in *Geschichte und Gegenwart*, 1/1989.

Tuider, Othmar, *Die Luftwaffe in Österreich 1938–1945* (The Luftwaffe in Austria 1938–1945) in *Militärhistorische Schriftenreihe*, vol. 54, Vienna, 1985.

Ueberschär, Gerd R., *Generaloberst Franz Halder. Generalstabschef, Gegner und Gefangener Hitler's* (Colonel General Franz Halder. Hitler's Chief of Staff, Opponent and Prisoner), Göttingen, Zurich, 1991.

– *Das Nationalkommitee 'Freies Deutschland' und der Bund Deutscher Offiziere* (The National Committee 'A Free Germany' and the League of German Officers), Frankfurt/M., 1995.

Ueberschär, Gerd R. and Wette, Wolfram (pub.), *'Unternehmen Barbarossa'. Der deutsche Überfall auf die Sowjetunion* ('Operation Barbarossa'. The German Attack on the Soviet Union), Paderborn, 1984.

– *Der deutsche Überfall auf die Sowjetunion. 'Unternehmen Barbarossa' 1941* (The German Attack on the Soviet Union. 'Operation Barbarossa' 1941), Frankfurt/M., 1991.

Umbreit, Hans, *Strukturen deutscher Besatzungspolitik in der Anfangsphase des deutsch-sowjetischen Krieges* (Structures of German Occupation Policy in the Initial Phase of the German–Soviet War) in *Zwei Wege nach Moskau* (Two Roads to Moscow), ed. Bernd Wegner, Munich, Zurich, 1991.

Verrier, Anthony, *Bombenoffensive gegen Deutschland 1939-1945* (Bombing Offensive against Germany 1939–1945), Frankfurt/M., 1970.

Vilsmaier, Joseph, *Stalingrad. Eine Armee wird geopfert* (Stalingrad. An Army Is Sacrificed), Munich, 1992.

Völker, Karl-Heinz, *Die deutsche Heimatluftverteidigung im Zweiten Weltkrieg* (German Home Air Defence in the Second World War), parts I and II, in *Wehrwissenschaftliche Rundschau* 2/3/1966.

Volkmann, Hans-Erich, *Ende des Dritten Reiches – Ende des Zweiten Weltkrieges. Eine perspectivische Rückschau* (End of the Third Reich. End of the Second World War. A Retrospective in Perspective), Piper Series vol. 2056, Munich, 1995.

– *Das Vlassov-Unternehmen zwischen Ideologie und Pragmatismus* (Operation Vlasov between Ideology and Pragmatism) in *Militärgeschichtliche Mitteilungen* 2/1992.

– *Die Legende vom Präventivkrieg* (The Legend of Preventive War) in *Die Zeit* of 13 June 1997.

Volkmann, Hans-Erich (pub.), *Das Rußlandbild im Dritten Reich* (The Image of

Russia in the Third Reich), Cologne, Weimar, Vienna, 2nd ed., 1994.

Volkmann, Udo, *Die britische Luftverteidigung und die Abwehr der deutschen Luftangriffe während der 'Luftschlacht um England' bis zum Juni 1941* (British Air Defence and the Repulse of German Air Attacks during the Battle of Britain up to June 1941), Osnabrück, 1982.

Volkogonov, Dimitri, *Stalin, Triumph und Tragödie* (Stalin. Triumph and Tragedy), Düsseldorf, 1989.

– *Stalin als Oberster Befehlshaber* (Stalin as Supreme Commander) in *Zwei Wege nach Moscow* (Two Roads to Moscow), ed. Bernd Wegner, Munich, Zurich, 1991.

Wagener, Carl, *Moskau 1941. Der Angriff auf die russische Hauptstadt* (Moscow 1941. The Attack on the Russian Capital), Bad Nauheim, 1965.

– *Der Vorstoß des XXXX. Panzerkorps von Charkov zum Kaukasus, Juni–August 1942* (The Advance by XXXX Panzer Corps from Kharkov to the Caucasus, June–August 1942) in *Wehrwissenschaftliche Rundschau* 9/1955.

– *Strittige Fragen zur Ardennenoffensive* (Controversial Questions on the Ardennes Offensive) in *Wehrwissenschaftliche Rundschau* 1/1961.

Wagenführ, Rolf, *Die deutsche Industrie im Kriege 1939–1945* (German Industry during the War 1939–1945), Berlin, 1963.

Wagner, Gerhard (pub.), *Lagevorträge des Oberbefehlshabers der Kriegsmarine vor Hitler 1939–1945* (Briefings by the Commander-in-Chief of the Kriegsmarine to Hitler, 1939–1945), Munich, 1972.

Wallach, Yehuda, *Das Dogma der Vernichtungsschlacht. Die Lehren von Clausewitz und Schlieffen und ihre Wirkung in zwei Weltkriegen* (The Dogma of the Battle of Annihilation. The Theories of Clausewitz and Schlieffen and their Effect in Two World Wars), dtv Book No. 711, Munich, 1970.

Warlimont, Walter, *Im Hauptquartier der deutschen Wehrmacht* (At Wehrmacht Headquarters), Frankfurt/M., Bonn, 1964.

– *Die Insel Malta in der Mittelmeer-Strategie des Zweiten Weltkrieges* (Malta in the Mediterranean Strategy of the Second World War) in *Wehrwissenschaftliche Rundschau* 8/1958.

Wasser, Bruno, *Himmlers Raumplanung im Osten* (Himmler's Territorial Planning in the East), Basle, Berlin, Boston, 1993.

Weber, Max, *Gesammelte Aufsätze zur Wissenschaftslehre* (Collected Essays on Scientific Theory), ed. Johannes Winckelmann, Uni Pocket Books No. 1492, Tübingen, 7th ed., 1988.

Webster, Sir Charles and Frankland, Nobel, *The Strategic Air Offensive against Germany 1939–1945*, four volumes, London, 1961.

Wegmüller, Hans, *Die Abwehr der Invasion. Die Konzeption des Oberbefehlshabers West 1940–1944* (Repulse of the Invasion. Concept of the C-in-C West 1940–1944), Freiburg i. Br., 1979.

Wegner, Bernd (pub.), *Zwei Wege nach Moskau. Vom Hitler-Stalin-Pakt zum 'Unternehmen Barbarossa'* (Two Roads to Moscow. From the Hitler–Stalin Pact to 'Operation Barbarossa'), Piper Series No. 1346, Munich, Zurich, 1991.

Weichhold, Eberhard, *Die deutsche Führung und das Mittelmeer unter dem Blickwinkel der Seestrategie* (German Leadership and the Mediterranean in View of Maritime Strategy) in *Wehrwissenschaftliche Rundschau* 3/1959.

Weinberg, Gerhard L., *'Unternehmen Overlord'* ('Operation Overlord'), preview from the book *The Second World War* in *Die Zeit* of 3 June 1994, supplement.

– *Eine Welt in Waffen. Eine globale Geschichte des Zweiten Weltkrieges* (A World in Arms. A Global History of the Second World War), Stuttgart, 1995.

Weißbecker, Manfred, *'Wenn hier Deutsche wohnten...' Beharrung und Veränderung im Rußlandbild Hitlers und der NSDAP* ('If Germans Lived Here...' Continuity and Change in Hitler's and the NSDAP's Image of Russia) in *Das Rußlandbild im Dritten Reich* (The Image of Russia in the Third Reich), ed. Hans-Erich Volkmann, Cologne, Weimar, Vienna, 2nd ed., 1994.

Wette, Wolfram and Ueberschär, Gerd R. (pub.), *Stalingrad. Mythos und Wirklichkeit einer Schlacht* (Stalingrad. Myth and Reality of a Battle), Frankfurt/M., 1992

Wiener, Friedrich, *Partisanenkampf im Balkan* (Partisan War in the Balkans), Vienna, 2nd ed., 1987.

Wilhelm, Hans-Heinrich, *Die Prognosen der Abteilung Fremde Heere Ost 1942–1945* (The Predictions of the Intelligence Department East 1942–1945) in *Zwei Legenden aus dem Dritten Reich* (Two Legends from the Third Reich), Stuttgart, 1974.

– *Rassenpolitik und Kriegführung. Sicherheitspolizei und Wehrmacht in Polen und der Sowjetunion 1939–1942* (Racial Policy and War. Security Police and Wehrmacht in Poland and the Soviet Union 1939–1942), Passau, 1991.

Wilhelm, Hans-Heinrich and Krausnick, Helmut, *Die Truppen des Weltanschauungskrieges. Die Einsatzgruppen der Sicherheitspolizei und des SD 1938–1942* (The Troops of the Weltanschauungs War. Task Forces of the Security Police and the SD 1938–1942), Stuttgart, 1981.

Wilhelmsmeyer, Helmut, *Der Krieg in Italien 1943–1945* (The War in Italy 1943–1945), Graz, Stuttgart, 1995.

Wilson, Theodore A., *The First Summit. Roosevelt and Churchill at Placentia Bay 1941*, Boston, 1969.

Winterbotham, Frederick W., *Aktion Ultra. Deutschlands Codemaschinen helfen den Alliierten siegen* (Action Ultra. Germany's Cipher Machines Help the Allies to Win), Berlin, 1976.

Wippermann, Wolfgang, *Gegen das Vergessen. Der Vernichtungskrieg gegen die Sowjetunion 1941–1945* (So Nobody Will Forget. The War of Annihilation against the Soviet Union 1941–1945), Frankfurt/M., 1992.

Wohlstetter, Roberta, *Pearl Harbor. Warning and Decision*, Stanford, Cal., 1962.

Wolf, Werner, *Luftangriffe auf die deutsche Industrie 1942–1945* (Air Attacks against German Industry 1942–1945), Munich, 1985.

Zank, Horst, *Stalingrad. Kessel und Gefangenschaft* (Stalingrad. Pocket and Captivity), Bonn, Berlin, Hamburg, 1993.

Zapantis, Andrew L., *Hitler's Balkan Campaign and the Invasion of the USSR*, Columbia University Press, New York, 1987.

Zayas, Alfred M., *Die Wehrmacht-Untersuchungsstelle. Deutsche Ermittlungen über alliierte Völkerrechtsverletzungen im Zweiten Weltkrieg* (The Wehrmacht Investigation Office. German Investigations on Allied Breaches of International Law in the Second World War), Ullstein Book No. 33080, Frankfurt/M., Berlin, 4th ed., 1987.

– *Ein Volk von willigen Henkern?* (A Nation of Willing Executioners?) in *Criticon* May/June 1996.

Zeidler, Manfred, *Kriegsende im Osten. Die Rote Armee und die Besetzung Deutschlands östlich der Oder und Neiße* (End of the War in the East. The Red Army and the Occupation of Germany East of the Oder and Neiße), Munich, 1996.

Zeitzler, Kurt, *Die ersten beiden planmäßigen großen Rückzüge des deutschen Heeres an der Ostfront im Zweiten Weltkrieg* (The First Two Planned Major Withdrawals by the German Army on the Eastern Front during the Second World War) in *Wehrkunde* 3/1960.

Zhukov, Georgi K., *Erinnerungen und Gedanken* (Memories and Thoughts), Stuttgart, 1969.

Zimmermann, R. Heinz, *Der Atlantikwall von Dünkirchen bis Cherbourg* (The Atlantic Wall from Dunkirk to Cherbourg), Munich, 1982.

Zins, Alfred, *Die Operation Zitadelle. Die militärgeschichtliche Diskussion und ihr Niederschlag im öffentlichen Bewußtsein als didaktisches Problem* (Operation Citadel. The Military-Historical Discussion and its Effect on Public Consciousness as a Didactic Problem), Frankfurt/M., 1986.

Zitelmann, Rainer, *Adolf Hitler. Eine politische Biographie* (Adolf Hitler. A Poltical Biography), Göttingen, Zurich, 2nd ed., 1989.

– *Zur Begründung des 'Lebensraum'-Motivs in Hitlers Weltanschauung* (On the Explanation of the 'Lebensraum'-Motive in Hitler's Weltanschauung) in *Der Zweite Weltkrieg* (The Second World War), ed. Wolfgang Michalka, Munich, Zurich, 1989.

INDEX